My Story
My Song

Clement James Rohee

Outskirts Press, Inc.
http://www.outskirtspress.com

Paperback ISBN: 978-1-9772-4177-1
Hardback ISBN: 978-1-9772-4201-3

PRINTED IN THE UNITED STATES OF AMERICA

Dedicated to My Wife Chamalee; My Two Daughters; Renate And Rima; My Three Grand Children; Nikhail, Amira, Mariah and in memory of Rajdai. Most of all, Cheddi and Janet Jagan.

INTRODUCTION

At an undetermined stage in every man's life he becomes more reflective about his experiences in life. It is a stage characterized by greater maturity where past experiences in life and indeed present day social and political issues are viewed from a completely different and more complex, but philosophical perspective. At a youthful age, the tendency is to be more combative, exuberant and adventurous, hardly giving any thought whatsoever to matters that would come to occupy one's attention later in life.

A colleague of mine from the Philippines once told me that there are two categories of impatient people; impatience of the young and impatience of the old. The young are impatient and even restless because they want things to happen overnight while the older ones want to clean up their act or seek forgiveness for all their wrong-doings so that by the time they arrive at the gates of Heaven they will get a free pass. I had experiences with both categories of such impatient persons during the course of my personal and political life.

Life is about experiences, observations and learning as a result of interactions with society in general and our fellow men in particular, irrespective of class, race, color or creed. Politics exposed me sometimes fully, sometimes partially to almost everything under the sun.

As a young man, just 18 years of age, growing up in the world of political activism it never dawned upon me that one day I would face the challenge to write a book of this magnitude. Several experiences influenced me to do so.

First, was the fact that I grew up in a political party with famous men and women who fought for my country's independence and who, while Guyana was still under British colonial rule, took steps to transform vital economic and social aspects of my country thus laying the basis for an independent, democratic and forward looking state with a 'Continental Destiny' but with deep roots in slavery and indentureship experienced by the peoples of the Anglo-phone Caribbean.

1

As I grew older and became more conscious of the importance of history and the role of the individual in history what I could not understand was why our great leaders, save for Cheddi Jagan, did not consider it necessary leave behind, records of their experiences and significant occurrences during their time so that future generations could make good use of them. To me, this seemed like political delinquency or a lack of appreciation for personally recorded history on their part. In the final analysis, it was a national loss for future generations that were to follow.

Secondly, having read the biographies and autobiographies of many great men and women in world history, thanks to books gifted to me by Mrs. Janet Jagan, I grew to appreciate the beauty of recorded history. My view at that time was, and still is; if men and women in other countries could record historical events of their time, why couldn't our leaders do so too?

I once asked Janet Jagan this question and suggested to her that she write leaving us some of her own experiences and perspectives. With a shrug of her shoulder, she smiled at me and said in a rather nonchalant manner, "You already have Cheddi's ' The West on Trial' don't you?" I didn't agree, but out of an abundance of respect for her I kept my disagreement to myself.

Eventually, I reasoned that perhaps our past leaders were so caught up in the whirlwind of events occurring at the that time, they probably never had the time nor saw the need to embark on what to me was important, but what to them, was not. To them it was probably viewed as self-serving or as engaging in an activity they saw as selfish or as self-adulation. These were the only conclusions I could arrive at since there was nothing available to prove otherwise. To me, it could not be self-promotion since it was almost impossible for work of this nature to be undertaken at an age of immaturity. It could only be accomplished when one would have already gone 'over the hill'. On the other hand, to keep such valuable personal knowledge and historical experience away from others, especially the younger folk would, in my view, be an act of selfishness in the true sense of the word.

Thirdly, having read Cheddi Jagan's 'The West on Trial' I was greatly impressed with the simplicity of his language and style of writing as he sought to educate readers about the history of the Guyanese people's struggles for an independent, free and democratic Guyana. And so, it was after many years of introspection and hesitation, that I settled down to begin collecting background material for this project and to actually begin drafting the manuscript.

My deep and abiding involvement in opposition party politics for fifty-two years, serving as General Secretary of the Party for four years, as a Member of Parliament for almost twenty-seven years, and as a Minister of government for twenty-three years hindered me from writing 'My Story, My Song'.

ACKNOWLEDGEMENTS

I developed the habit of keeping copious notes of meetings wherever and whenever they were held, whether at home or abroad. I learnt and developed that technique that from Dr. Jagan who made notes to either pass around with instructions or suggestions. While the minutes of official meetings proved to be extremely useful, I nevertheless made my own record of meetings since my perspective of matters under discussion were quite different from that of the official note taker. My private note books containing records of meetings in which I participated, were of great use in helping me piece together the glimpse's life and that of others I felt compelled to include in the story of my life.

It was a painstaking exercise but one filled with joy and tremendous personal satisfaction. However, without the appreciative inputs and technical support and advice received from New York-based, Devin Bissoon, Tony Andre Wesley, Dr. Tulsi Dyal Singh, Amar Awadhnarine, Joycelyn Anderson my former Senior Confidential Secretary, Ricky Hardin of the Library of the Parliament of Guyana, the United Nations Department of Information, Paul Harris, son of the cartoonist Hawley Harris, the Cheddi Jagan Research Centre in Kingston, Georgetown, Nadira Jagan-Brancier in Canada and Ramjohn Holda and the Potaro Porknockers' 'Songs of the Guiana Jungle' album, this mission would not have been successfully accomplished. I acknowledge their unreserved support and generosity.

Background information about the history of my relatives were provided thanks to the staff at the Guyana National Archives,, the General Register Office of Guyana, Records of the Bedford Methodist Church, The Parish Church of St. Paul at the Borough of Hendon, London, UK, my Aunt Ivy in California, my cousins Mervyn Nichols in Georgetown, Natalie Elder and Lancelot James in the US and Patricia Felix in the UK. I am deeply grateful to each and every one of them.

MY ROOTS…THE ROHEE'S

I was born on March 16, 1950 at lot 'N', Bent Street Wortmanville, Georgetown, Guyana. All my life I grew up in the city. My parents were simple people. I am the last of three boys. My mom was twenty-five years of age at the time of my birth. My father Robert Richard Rohee, was born on June 14, 1918 in Kingston, Georgetown. He was the son of James and Gertrude Rohee. James Rohee's parents and great grandparents were descendants of indentured laborers. Regrettably, because of the condition of the records at the National Archives, there are some gaps in the paper trail concerning the arrival of indentured laborers in the colony of British Guiana. However, in my particular case, those gaps are not so significant to change in any fundamental way the result of my research into the history of the Rohee's in Guyana.

Some 16 years after indentureship was introduced in the colony of British Guiana, a male East Indian by the name Jeebun arrived on the vessel 'Henry Moore' in 1854. His immigration certificate number was 348. Six years later, a female East Indian by the name of Rantooly arrived on board the vessel 'St. Croix.' in 1860. Her immigration certificate number was 194. Jeebun and Rantooly originated from Calcutta, India. On arrival in the colony they were 'bound' as Indentured labourers to plantation Plaisance on the East Coast of Demerara.

At the time of their arrival in the colony the East Indian population was 24,710 and the period of indentureship had been reduced from five to three years. Further, at that particular point in time, contracts for indentured laborers who had been in the colony for five years were about to expire. The immigrants had the option to return to India or to remain in the colony. Many East Indians who left their homeland on the last two ships, the SS Chenab (1915) and the SS Ganges (1917) were not from the lower castes in India, in fact a large number of them were Zamindars who were totally pauperized following the disintegration of the Zamindari system in India.

There were some among them who had supported the nationalist movement led by Subhas Chandra Bose primarily because the English East India Company, in collaboration with the local Talukdars, had seized their land. In some cases, entire villages were bought and the rules revised virtually stripping the Zamindars of their privileged status. And though they knew they were running from the British in India to the British in Guiana they nevertheless felt they would be better off in a far away landSome supporters of the Indian National Army (INA) fearing persecution somehow managed to incorporate themselves into groups of would-be indentured labourers destined for British Guiana.

Amongst the indentured labourers were individuals who, together with other like-minded labourers, had collaborated with missionaries to establish the Arya Samaj movement in the early 1900's in British Guiana. And so, it was under existing circumstances at the time, that some indentured laborers, having served out their period of indentureship began their preparations to return to India. Those who did not have the means to do so had no choice but to remain in the colony as free emigrants and wage laborers.

Jeebun and Rantooly were married. In 1872, Rantooly gave birth to a girl named Lokhi or Luckee. Her place of birth is registered as Plantation 'Plaisance'. Kudney, a female East Indian number 308 and Gokool, a male East Indian, number 110 arrived in the colony aboard the vessel 'Shaud' in 1854 and were 'bound' as indentured labourers to Plantation 'Coffee Grove', owned by S. Dobree and Sons on the Essequibo Coast.

Kudney was first married to a male East Indian named Chukun number 33 who arrived in the colony aboard the 'Ellenboro' in 1853 and was assigned to plantation 'Fear Not' owned by Thomas Daniels on the Essequibo Coast. Kudney bore a son by the name of Ramcharran for Chukun in 1857. Kudney and Chukun separated and Kudney went off to live with another male East Indian by the name of Gokool at 'Coffee Grove', the neighboring village to 'Fear Not' on the Essequibo coast. In 1872 she gave birth to another boy named Rampersad. If effect, Kudney was the mother of the half brothers, Rampersad and Ramcharran.

Kudney eventually left Gokool, her second man, and went off to live with a third man named Rohee on the Island of Wakenaam. There, she gave birth to another boy by the name of Ramlochan aka Ramlakhan. Rohee and Kudney may have met at either plantations 'Fear Not' or 'Domburg' since both plantations belonged to Thomas Daniels. Later, they went to live at plantation 'Armersfoort' owned by James Ewing on the same island of Wakenaam.

The tradition of men or women on the Essequibo Coast having relationships or marrying women or men on the island of Wakenaam in particular continues to this day. During the period mentioned earlier, the proportion of women to men in the colony was 33 to 100. In the circumstances, it should not be difficult therefore, to appreciate the challenges both men and women faced insofar as fulfillment of their sexual passions were concerned. No doubt, the desire to fulfill those ambitions resulted in all kinds of maltreatment by men to their fellow men and by men towards women as well. It was for this reason that in 1864, a law was passed protecting women from domestic violence.

But life on the sugar plantation was more than what it appeared on the surface. Cheddi Jagan in 'The West on Trial' describes it thus; 'The plantation was indeed a world of its own. Or rather, it was two worlds: the world of the exploiters and the world of the exploited; the world of whites and the world of the non-whites .One was the world of the managers and the European staff in their splendid mansions; the other, the world of the labourers in their logies in the "niggeryard" and the "bound-coolie-yard."Jagan went on to point out that indentured immigrants were subjected to severe penalties for; failure to complete five tasks per week, to answer to a daily muster roll call, and absence from work for seven consecutive days.

Rohee had arrived in the colony in 1848 aboard the ship 'North Flanders' and was 'bound' to plantation 'Domburg' owned by Thomas Daniels on the island of Wakenaam on the Essequibo River. 19 years later, he transferred to plantation 'Amersfoort' owned by James Ewing on the said island. Sometime after, Rohee and Kudney separated. And he went off to live with a woman by the name of Maholutchmee number 408 who had arrived in the vessel 'Blue Jacket' in 1857. How and where Mahalutchmee and Rohee met is not known, she however adopted the name of the man she chose to live with.

Solemnization of marriages, cohabitation, desertion, or forsaking of partners were commonplace in those days given the fact that there were so few women in proportion to men and with the women scattered far and wide across the coastland of the colony. Abandonment of plantation life by the off-springs of 'free indentured laborers' with the hope of seeking their fortunes either at the larger plantations and or in towns had become the order of the day.

It is not known what became of Ramcharran but there were now three half brothers all from one mother but three different fathers. It appears that two particular half brothers, Rampersad and Ramlochan aka Ramlakhan stuck together for reasons I cannot tell. Apparently, they left their parents and came to Georgetown to seek employment and a better life. Both settled in the Kingston area. The other half brother apparently stayed behind.

The two young men were soon to find out that being descendants of indentured laborers, and living in a Christian dominated city, a baptismal certificate with Christian names would give a tremendous boost to their search for employment.In 'The West on Trial' Cheddi Jagan makes reference to this practice; 'Another example was the practice of Indians taking Christian names although they were not Christians. In my family, the names of Derek, Doris, Patricia and Barbara eventually replaced Indian names. In my own case, in my "teens" I adopted my middle name; "Berret", for I thought it the fashionable thing to do.'

Thus, Ramlochan aka Ramlakhan adopted the baptismal name John Davidson Rohee and married Caropatti aka Lucy whose birth registration number was given as number 6071 of 1883. Rampersad for his part, adopted the baptismal name John Rohy and ended up marrying the girl named Lokhi or Luckee a Coolie native creole and the descendant of Jeebun and Rantooly of Plaisance. Both boys had adopted the same surname of their father but spelt it differently on their baptismal certificates.

It was the name Davidson, and not necessarily the spelling of the surname Rohee that was to make the fundamental difference in the lives of the two young men and their heirs in years to come. Taking his father's correctly spelt name, John eventually changed his surname from Rohy to Rohee. This put him on an equal basis, at least where the surname was concerned with his half-brother John Davidson. His full name after being baptized became John Arthur Phillip Rohee It appears that the name change from Rohy to Rohee was not appreciated by John Davidson since he had elevated himself in social standing by becoming a Marshal in the colonial civil service thus distinguishing himself from his half brother John who was a mere 'chowkidar' or watchman.

During a trip to India in January 2018, a close friend of mine who is knowledgeable about Indian immigration matters informed me that the name Rohee has its origin in Orissa now Odisha, an eastern state at the Bay of Bengal. I was further informed that though Rohee is a Hindu name, many Rohee's converted to Islam but kept their Hindu names. I can attest to this because during my travels as Foreign Minister throughout the Levant and Middle Eastern countries I came across similar names like Rohi, Roohee and Ruhi. In many of these countries the name is not necessarily a surname but a girl/ female name.

Ruhi and Rohee are surnames in India and Mauritius respectively. What is true of the name is that it has it roots in Arabic, Urdu, Hindu, Marathi and Sanskrit. Moreover, the name has a spiritual meaning viz; of spirit, or of soul. In India the name Rohee is associated with the Brahmin caste.

The Rohee's of India are to be found in law practice and government bureaucracy.

In the State of Nagpur, India I came across the name Justice Kishor Jayram Rohee. His father the late, Dadasaheb Rohee was also a judge who once practiced civil law.

My Grandparents: Gertude & James Rohee - 1912

I spoke to Justice K. J. Rohee briefly on the phone while visiting Goa in February of 2018. I wanted to let him know that there are Rohee's in Guyana. He was interested in knowing more. We agreed to maintain contact with each other. Judge Rohee was kind enough to send me a message of greetings on the occasion of my 70th birthday. This pleased me immensely.

Having attained the rank of a Marshal of the British Guiana Civil Service, John Davidson Rohee and his wife Lucy branched off on their own. Status and vanity were to be of great importance for this branch of the Rohee's. John Davidson and Lucy Rohee had six children three boys and three girls; Lilian, Janet and Phyllis and Charles, Eric and Leslie.

Charles married Winnie Drayton, Eric married Ena Luckhoo and Leslie married Marjorie Phillips. (related to Oscar Phillips of Laparkan). Lilian married Mr. Dass of Pradasco cycle store on King street, Janet married Mr. Singh and left for the USA while Phyllis remained a spinster for the rest of her life. Leslie's wife Marjorie passed away on May 30, 2019. At the time of passing she lived at Lot 33 Barrack Street, Kingston. Leslie's father John Davidson, was called 'Uncle Byah' by John Rohee's children. To them his wife Luckee, was known as 'Bhowjee.' Leslie was a public servant, he and a journalist named Gerald Phillips were friends. Phillips worked at the Argosy newspapers. Leslie and Gerald played Bridge from time to time with Leslie's uncle James Rohee. It was Gerald Phillips who introduced his sister Margorie to Leslie Rohee.

John Rohee continued working as a watchman but eventually managed to elevate himself to an interpreter. His wife Luckee bore him six children, three boys and three girls; Ellen, Beckie and Agnes called Didi, and Phillip, Duncan and James. James Rohee was born in 1888. He was to be my grandfather. At the age of 24, James Rohee stepped out side the Rohee blood line. He was bold enough to break with tradition, and on November 30, 1912 at Bedford Methodist Church at the corner of Camp street and North Road he married a Black woman by the name of Gertrude Agard. Ms Agard was eight years older that her husband. Her parents were from Barbados. Gertrude Agard worked at the Public Hospital, Georgetown while James Rohee worked as a clerk at the same institution. James and Gertrude parented 9 children, seven girls and two boys; Joseph and Robert, Enid, Gertrude, Sheila, Julie, Mabel, Ivy and Marjorie.

MY AUNTS

Aunt Enid married Wilfred Hazelton Coltress. They lived in the front house of a two-house family property at 13, North Road Bourda.Ronald Orson their only son, went off to the United States to become a US marine eventually ending up in Vietnam to fight against the Vietcong who had not so long ago defeated the French at Dien Bien Phu.Ronald returned home for a brief while following the end of the war in Vietnam. Not finding anything to do he returned to the United States as a war veteran and settled down as a married man in Kansas City, Missouri. Ronald died in the mid- 1990's in the city of Oscelo, Florida USA

Aunt Enid's and Uncle Wilfred's only daughter Diane, now occupies the said front house. Uncle Wilfred worked as an engineer with the building and engineering contracting firm, Ash and Watson. He later moved over to Taylor Woodrow construction contractors that built the Pegasus Hotel. Ash and Watson built hotels in Antigua and Barbuda. Uncle Wilfred travelled between the twin island and Georgetown several times. Whenever Uncle Wilfred was due to return home, Aunt Enid, one of her sisters and a brother- in-law would take Aunt Enid, me and my cousin Ronald to the Atkinson Airport to welcome him home. That was a trip I always looked forward to.

Gertrude married Gordon Stuart. Uncle Gordon worked as a Superintendent of Works at the Public Works Department. His job took him all over the country. He eventually ended up at headquarters at Kingston, Georgetown. After my mother's

death I was sent to live with Aunt Gertie, at 233, South Road, South Cummingsburg, Georgetown.

My Aunts Julie, Ivy & Sheila

Aunt Sheila was a nurse by profession. She married Phillip Elder. Uncle Phillip was an Anglican priest. He was posted for sometime at Suddie, on the Essequibo Coast. He later returned to Georgetown and soon after became the first Black Anglican Bishop of Stabroek.

The Elder family took up residence at the Annexe next to Alan John Knight's residence, corner of Barrack and High Streets, Kingston. On one occasion, I spent my August school holidays at Suddie with Uncle Phillip and Aunt Sheila at a big, imposing house that still stands on the manse of the Anglican Church. Huge mango trees still stand in that yard bearing delicious mangoes which I thoroughly enjoyed in those days. The Elders immigrated to the Eastern Caribbean islands then to the USA eventually settling at Maryland. Aunt Julie married Gordon Marshall. Uncle Gordon was a draughtsman at the Ministry of Public Works. He was also a weight lifter. I spent many wonderful times at Aunt Julie's house on East Street a few doors away from the Georgetown Public Hospital.

Aunt Mabel lived for a while with Ivy and Maggie in a rented upper flat on Third Street Albert town, a few doors away from where Dr. C.R. Jacobs lived. Jacobs was the PPP's Minister of Finance in the 1957 - 1964 government lived. Aunt Mabel ran off with Gordon Stuart the husband of her sister Gertrude. They eventually immigrated to the United States in the late 1960's.

Aunt Ivy married Percy King. Uncle Percy functioned for a number of years as the Chief Public Health Inspector for the Georgetown Municipality. The couple lived at Subryanville. Ivy and Percy subsequently immigrated to the United States and live now at San Francisco, California.

Percy King died in the month of November of 2019 at his home at San Mateo, in California.

Marjorie remained a spinster until her death. She lived for a number of years at the upper flat of a backhouse on Regent Street between Light and Albert Streets owned by her mother's sister. Later, she moved into the back house of the family property at 13, North Road, Bourda.

It was a very traumatic period for the Rohee sisters and for Aunt Gertie in particular when her sister Mabel ran off with her husband Gordon. At that time, I lived with Aunt Gertie but it was the first time in my life I had witnessed at first hand such a disastrous martial episode in real life. To this day, my Aunt Ivy is the sole survivor of that generation of Rohee's whose beginnings commence with John and Luckee Rohee.

As I look back on marriages of the Rohee sisters it is interesting to observe that all of them were married to Black men with the exception of Julie who married a Portuguese man and Maggie who never married. As far as I am aware, Denis and I are the only two immediate descendants of the Rohee clan that married East Indian women. As far as the two sons of James and Gertrude Rohee is concerned, Joseph married to Black woman while his brother Robert married to a Mixed-race English woman. Once during a visit to my Aunt Ivy, I asked her why this was so, her explanation was a simple and straightforward one. She told me that in those days neither race nor ethnicity mattered. What mattered was the character of the two individuals and the quality of the relationship between them.

As for the two Rohee brothers, Joseph went off as a sailor to roam the 'Seven Seas' while my dad, Robert was recruited in 1939, as a member of the British Guiana Militia Infantry Group. I have not been able to establish what became of John Rohee or John Davidson Rohee. No record of their passing was located up the time of writing.

In 1941, at the age of 23, my dad went off to serve as part of the British Army's South Caribbean Contingent during the Second World War. In England, he enlisted with the Royal Electrical and Mechanical Engineers' Corps.

ENTER KATHLEEN HOPE NEWTON

While serving in the military for four years, Dad met and eventually married Kathleen Hope Newton, a British citizen. At the time of their marriage in 1946, my Mom, Kathleen was 21 and my Dad was 28. My Mom's mother, Ellen Newton, was married to Joseph Newton who went off to serve in the army but never returned.

While living alone at 7, Sanders Cottages, Mill Hill, NW 7, London, Ellen met the 28-year-old Clement Edward Nathaniel Nichols a member of the British Guiana Militia Band. The band had travelled to England in 1924 to play at concerts as part of the British Empire Exhibition at Wembley. A relationship between Ellen Newton and Clement Nichols produced a daughter named Kathleen Hope Newton on May 8, 1925.

At the end of his mission, Nichols returned to British Guiana. He never returned to England. At home, he continued being a member of the British Guiana Police Force Military Band. He acted from time to time as conductor of the Band. To his credit, he wrote several beautiful pieces of music for the band including the famous 'Dear Demerara,' 'Good Lusignan,' 'Scotland in West Demerara,' 'Berbice on Parade' and 'Wake up Demerara.'

On one occasion, while serving as Minister of Home Affairs, I requested of Mr. Bovell, the then bandmaster, to arrange to have at least two of my grandfather's composition played for my listening pleasure. He kindly consented. Listening to my grandpa's musical compositions was indeed a joyful if not exhilarating experience for me. I enjoyed every moment of it while the band played.

THE NICHOLS

Born on June 15, 1896, Clement E. N. Nicholls was the son of William Augustus and Esther Isabella Nichols née Shepherd. William Nichols was a carpenter by profession while Mr. Shepherd was a blacksmith

Winston, Miriam (Lidda), Clement Nichols & Patricia Felix

Vat building was a big thing in those days, it brought the Nichols and Shepherds together. Their friendship resulted in the marriage of William Nicholls to Esther Shepherd, sister of Mr. Shepherd on April 30, 1834.

Twenty years later, Robert Rohee was to meet and marry Kathleen Newton, the daughter of Clement Nichols who had preceded him to the UK but on a completely different mission. Robert Rohee, unlike his future father-in-law Clement Nichols was in England not to play music but to help fight a war.

Winston Nicholls was the nephew of Clement Nicholls. He served in the South Caribbean Forces of British Army at the same time when Kathleen Newton was serving in the Women's Royal Army Corps. (WRAC).

Kathleen Newton along with her friends visited the South Caribbean or West Indian Army Club with the hope of finding one of the service men who might know of her father Clement Nichols who was in England twenty-three years ago.

It was during one of those visits she met Winston Nicholls, the nephew of her father Clement Nicholls. It was Winston who introduced Kathleen to his friend and fellow country man, Robert Rohee. This was a fascinating love story related to me by Patricia Felix née Nicholls, the sister of Winston Nicholls. Patricia left Guyana in 1959 and now resides in the UK.

Five Nicholls brothers John, William, Phillip, Andrew and Rudolph emigrated from Barbados to the then British Guiana.

Crossing the Atlantic, they came on schooners that plied the Bridgetown-Georgetown route in those days. John Nicholls married Rebecca Heyliger from the West Bank of Demerara they had a son named David aka Philip. David was married to Saint -Claire Burnham. They had five children Patricia, Winston, Rudolph, Alice and Fredrick. Patricia married was married to Aubrey Felix but they are divorced. Patricia lives in the UK with their two children Naomi and Warren Rudolph married Norma Williams both of whom lived in the UK. They have one daughter, Carol Woollery

After serving in the British army Winston returned home and married Irma Munroe. They had no children save for an adopted boy by the name of Peter Cameron. All the other Nicholls brothers and sisters left Guiana to reside permanently either in the UK, the US or Canada. William Nicholls married Isabella Shepherd. They had four children Clement, Lydda, Ivy, Edith and two adopted boys, Philip aka David and Andrew.

Sometime after his return to Guiana from the UK, Clement Nicholls married Clara Williams. It is believed that Clara and Norma Williams were related and that it was Rudolph, who hooked up his cousin Clement with Clara Williams. Clement and Clara Williams had no children as husband and wife. But Clement Nicholls had two daughters; Kathleen, my mom born in the UK and another 'outside' daughter named Barbara who was Guyanese by birth. Barbara's mother was one Clara Smith not Clara Williams. Barbara, Clement Nicholls Guyanese born daughter, enjoyed a relationship with Sonny James. From that relationship was born a daughter by the name of Claudette. Barbara registered her daughter's name as Claudette Nicholls. Claudette now lives in Georgia, USA

I was told that Clement Nicholls had another daughter with Clara Smith who was married to one Mr. Griffith and who lived on the Essequibo Coast. Hughley Griffith, the Attorney-at-law and Ivelaw Griffith, former Vice Chancellor at the University of Guyana are therefore, the descendants of Clement Nicholls and Clara Smith.

As a dashing young man belonging to the Black middle class at the time and an exceptionally brilliant and leading musician in the BG Police Force Band, Clement Nicholls found himself surrounded by many women. But he was very selective and chosen only women of lighter complexion. One such woman was Marie Beckles whom he never married but maintained his relationship with her in the same way he did with Clara Smith. Marie Beckles had separated from her husband. She was the sister-in-law of Edward Rogers a former Band Master of the same band of which Clement Nicholls was a member.

At the time of his death, Clement Edgar Nicholls lived along with his wife Clara and two sisters Lydda and Edith at 31, Gordon Street, Kitty. His daughter Barbara had invited him over to lunch on Christmas Day of 1961, but owing to an official engagement with the Police Force Band he arranged to spend New Years day with her. Clement Nicholls enjoyed a hearty meal with lots of whiskey in between. He returned home later that afternoon of news year's day and, as customary, would sit by a window in his favourite huge rocking chair.

Whilst at his favourite spot he would have at his side a jar with crushed parched nuts sprinkled a small amount of brown sugar.

He would throw small amounts of the mixture of nuts and sugar in the palm of his huge hands, then thrown it into his mouth and begin chewing to his heart's delight. That evening just around eleven o'clock he got up saying he was not feeling well. As they were walking toward his bedroom, he stopped suddenly, telling those around him that he wanted to lie down. Assisted by his wife and sisters, he was put to lie on the floor in the middle of the hall.

Whist laying there on January 2, 1962, at the age of sixty- six, Clement Edward Nicholls, my mother's dad and my beloved grandfather passed away having suffered a massive heart attack.At the time of his passing, I was twelve years old and was living with my aunt since my Mom's death three years ago. I cannot say if my Dad attended his funeral nor do I recall being told anything by my aunts. Edith, Clement's sister was married to one Mr. Martin. They had two daughters, Lorna and Stella and a son by the name of Rudolph. They all migrated to Canada. Lydda, Clement's sister married Charles Hamin they have three children; Maxine, Jacquelyn and Mervin Maxine and Jacquelyn live in America. Mervin resides in Guyana. I consider them my first cousins.

During my visit to 7 Sanders Lane, I was shown an abandoned 1945 military base just a stone's throw away the village. The close proximity of the village and the base, made me draw the conclusion that soldiers stationed at that base must have frequented the South Caribbean or West Indian Army Men's Club also located near the village. And, as fate would have it, it was at the servicemen's club my father was introduced to the girl who was to be his future wife. Robert Rohee and Kathleen Hope Newton were married on 27, July 1946 at the Parish Church of St. Paul, Mill Hill, at the Borough of Hendon, London.

While my Dad was soldiering in England his mother and father passed away. James Rohee, son of John Rohee died on April 12, 1944 from high blood pressure while his wife Gertrude died on May 24, 1946 from cholecystic, an inflammation of the gall bladder. Robert and Kathleen Rohee returned to British Guiana on April 7, 1948

LIFE AT WORTMANVILLE

On their return from England my Dad and Mom lived at 'N' Bent street Wortmanville, Georgetown. Six of her seven children were born while residing at Wortmanville. In those days, delivery of babies at home by a registered midwife was a normal practice

My Parents Robert & Kathleen Rohee - 1946

THREE BOYS AND THREE GIRLS

Robert and Kathleen Rohee were the parents of six children; Sandra, Clement, Margaret, Clifford, Alexander & Carol.

My Siblings L-R; Sandra, Clement, Clifford, Alex, Carol and Margaret - 1959

Carol had a twin brother named, Carl Anthony. He died just a few months after he was in born on August 16, 1952 just after we moved to North Road. My parents named me Clement. The first name of my grandfather on my mother's side and James, the first name of my grandfather on my father's side.

Wortmanville is one of the several Wards of Georgetown and Bent Street at the time was a kind of homely street where neighbors specifically and people in general mixed and mingled quite easily with each other. This was quite typical of life in the colony. My mother sent us to Sunday School held on Sunday mornings at the building housing the Tutorial High School a few houses down to the western end of Bent street just before Louisa Row.

There were bakeries at the eastern end of Bent and Hardina street and at the western end, at the corner of Bent street into Louisa Row. The delightful smell of freshly baked bread early in the mornings was something to savor.

And if it was not running early in the morning to buy the 'penny loaves' of bread at either of the two baker shops, it was the anxiety of listening out for the shout of Mr. Bedford the 'bread man' shouting 'Bread! Bread! while on his carrier bike with his bread basket containing the crusty loaves covered with a lily-white cloth, from whom we would purchase our daily bread.

A tall 'red-skinned' lady who rode a 'preggy' bicycle had a 'bottom house' kindergarten school on Bent street not far from where we lived. My mom sent me and my two brothers there to learn to read and write.

Our home always had visitors. If it wasn't Guianese ex-soldiers who had returned home from the war with their English born wives and who my Dad met while serving in England, it was her Guyanese born sister, Aunt Barbara or Aunt Patricia or local womenfolk who came to visit and would chat for long hours with my mother, the 'White lady.' Aunt Barbara was special to my mom primarily because they were of the same father. She was just as beautiful as my mother with a lively personality. It was always fun when she was around. She made my mother happy. Winston Nicholls, cousin of Aunt Barbara and my dad were very good friends since their days serving in the military. He would visit our home from time to time. And, whenever my dad visited his friend's home at Alberttown, he would take me along with him. Sometimes my mom would take me on her visits to the home of Aunt Patsy and Uncle Winston, cousins of her sister Barbara, another of the Nicholls family, at their home at Forshaw street, Queenstown. Visits were paid also to my grandfather's home. He lived in a big house on Laluni street in Queenstown with his wife, sisters and their children. It was as a result of these back and forth visits, that my Mom learnt to prepare Guyanese dishes and to know the ways and means of the city and its inhabitants.

It must have been difficult for my mother to make the mental and psychological transition from London to Georgetown, but from what I can recall, she certainly did, notwithstanding the many socio-economic challenges prevailing at the time in the colony and with six children to care for. Perhaps it was because of the Guyanese blood in her veins and the many helping hands that came to her assistance that helped through the many challenges.

In retrospect, I believe that it was because of both of my parents' strong African-Guyanese parenthood and family relationships, that I grew up and continued to shun any prejudices against people of African or Indian descent. In fact, it was the death of my mother that brought about a dramatic turn in the family relationships I had grown up in for nine years. With my mother's death, my life began to transition from her English-African ancestry, to my father's African- Indian ancestry. Just as the African influence was the most dominant in my life while my mother was alive, the Indian influence became more dominant when I went to live with my father's relatives following my mom's passing. In the end, I found myself saddled with the psychological task of managing a balance in my perspectives of life and living.

In Guyanese politics, it is always an internal struggle for the Party faithful to maintain a balance between the subjective and objective factors in one's analysis of domestic and international political developments. That balance and objectivity can be turned upside down, when political analysis is required and more so, when Party politics becomes the dominant factor in the totality of things and particularly, in a society where politics and elections are deeply polarized along racial and ethnic lines. These imposing psycho-sociological factors makes objective analysis even more challenging. Worse yet, the challenge can be further compounded when political opportunism seeps in and colours the entire analysis.

Membership in the PPP is perceived by those opposed to the politics of the Party as being politically biased in favour of the Indo-Guyanese population. The class and ideological considerations are either grossly underestimated, or, completely ignored, probably through no fault of theirs, but because the Party failed to do more political and ideological work among Afro-Guyanese in particular.

Little did I know at that time, that in years to come, I would find myself being both a beneficiary and victim of that very problematic. And even though I consider myself quite capable of managing the phenomenon, the point is that balancing the complex dimensions of my political/ideological orientation against the socio-psychological implications can prove difficult in an evolving political and social environment.

My mom made the best Guyanese 'cook-up rice' in the world. The funny thing is she never cooked on a rainy day. Instead, she would serve us fruit and a piece of cake she would have baked in a small oven mounted atop a 'coal pot'. My mom never sent us to school when it rained 'cats and dogs' though she made it clear to

21

us that not going to school did not mean we were not to 'pick up our books' while at home.My Mom always had in store a variety of local fruits which would be served for lunch. If it wasn't fruits, it would be baked beans with bread or 'sweet biscuits' with Quaker Oats. The love for fruits has stayed with me to this day. Sometimes when mom was not working, and Dad's month salary did not arrive in time it would be hot 'sugar water' with biscuits and 'salt butter'. On Sundays, mom would send us to pick daisies from the roadside parapets or 'sweet broom' plants to be brewed for tea.

Soldier Rohee was not fond of fruit nor cake. He would simply ignore his share covered at the head of the dining table. He would leave the house, taking me with him. We would return with food purchased from a Chinese restaurant on Regent Street. On our return home, he would call everyone out, including his wife to sit around the dining table and ask Mom to share established portions to each of us.

My Dad went to work as a fitter/mechanic at the central workshop of the Transport and Harbours Department located at Water Street, Kingston, at the northern end of the city He always wore khakis and a dark brown beret over his already bald head. He would ride to and from work on a second hand 'gents' bicycle he had bought.

LIFE AT 13, NORTH ROAD BOURDA

Some time in the early 1950's we moved from Bent Street to 13, North Road, Bourda, a Rohee family property with two small houses on the land. We lived in the house just behind the front house where Aunt Enid, her husband Wilfred and their son Ronald lived.

A daughter named Diane was to come later.

The front house was partly shaded by a golden apple fruit tree. When in season, the fruit was in abundance, but because the tree harbored many 'hairy worms' we were warned not to climb it to pick the fruit. To accomplish the task of harvesting, Uncle Wilfred fashioned long stick with a hook at the end. Aunt Enid's house faced a canal sandwiched between Church Street and North Road. The canal ran from East to West beginning from the Lamaha canal in the east, neighboring the Botanic

Gardens up to Camp Street where the old 'Water Works' once stood directly opposite the St. Roses High School and the Ursuline Convent on Church Street.

Years later, the canal between Albert and Light Streets was filled with truck loads of earth creating what later became known as Merriman's Mall. Two smaller canals or trenches, parallel to each other but running the length of North road and Church Street were dug to prevent flooding on the Northern and Southern sides of North Road and Church Street Further down Church Street at East Street, another canal was completely filled. That canal ran from North to South on East Street, beginning from Church Street up to a canal on the Northern side of Lamaha Street.

On the eastern side of our house on North Road was a three 'story' house occupied by the Ally's, then by the Hills and much later by former President Hoyte, his wife Joyce and two daughters, Maxine and Amanda. Both daughters were killed in a car crash on the Linden-Soesdyke highway while returning from the bauxite mining town of Linden where they had accompanied their dad to an official function.

Separating our house from the Coltress' front house, was a huge sapodilla tree. When the fruits were ripe, they would fall to the ground mainly because bats loved the fruit. Climbing the tree was always fun, on the way up I could peer into my Aunt's kitchen and siting on one of the sturdier branches further up, I could see over the tall fence into the lawns of the Hills. On the western side of our house were the Cartos; Billy, his wife and three children Andy, Cathy and another sister whose name I cannot recall.

Then there was Magistrate Morris who drove a sleek looking De Soto or Pontiac motor car. His wife and two children Lyn and Lee lived in the front house opposite the Coltresses.

Facebook, it is said, brings people together, and that is so true because after many, many years I found Lyn Morris on Facebook. Lyn broke the sad news to me of her bother Lee's death. I have kept in touch with Lyn from time to time.

Directly behind our house was an alley way. On the southern side of the alley way lived the Cumberbatches who's three 'story' houses were actually on Robb Street which ran parallel to the south of North Road. Whenever Dad was at home he would invite over his friends for drinks and to reminisce about their days in the army during the war and about work-related matters. I would be the one that was called to 'run around corner' to the Polar Beer rum shop at the corner of Regent Street and Light Street to purchase either 'halves' or quarters' of the Polar Beer rum for consumption by his 'old soldier crew.' Running errands for my mum and to purchase cigarettes for my Dad was common place. Cleaning and polishing his shoes and preparing his shaving accoutrement was a daily routine for me.

My dad took me wherever he went to visit his close friends including, Mr. Curtis on Saffon Street, the De Groots at Durban Street, Lodge, the Skeetes on East Street or just around the corner at Mr. Barker, a strange looking man of European decent. He had a long grey beard and whitish looking hair and spoke with a deep English accent. Mr. Barker lived with a woman of African decent in a rickety cottage that looked as if it was about to fall apart at the corner of Robb and Light streets. My Dad was transferred from the Transport and Harbours Department, (T&HD) Central workshop, Kingston, Georgetown to its East Berbice Branch as part of a team to build the three and five gate iron sluices or kokers at the Torani Canal which lies between the Berbice and Canje Rivers.

Mom secured a job as a sales clerk at W.M. Fogarty's department store, on Water street. I guess she decided to find a job because she was not the 'stay at home' type of person and in addition, she had to 'make ends meet' since, there were times when Dad's money grams did not arrive in time. In those circumstances, she was forced to borrow cash from her in-laws or to 'trust' goods from the grocery around the corner. It so happened that in both cases, I was the one who was usually called upon to 'run' to the grocery with a shopping list or to go to the in-law to pick up the cash.

My Mom would walk to and from work every morning. Sometime after, she left the job at Fogarty's and went to work at Abdool Majeed and Sons Ltd. on Water Street. While there, she managed to save enough money to purchase a Humber lady's bicycle and would ride to and from work. My Mom had a terrible sweet tooth, every Friday after work, if she didn't bring home a box of imported Walls tri-flavored ice cream, she would take us in the evening to Nifty's Soda Fountain on North Road or Camp Street for milkshakes.

On some occasions like Boxing Day during the Christmas holidays or Easter Monday, me and my two brothers would be called by mom and told to 'go get dressed, you boys are going to the cinema'. We would receive our 'matinee bill' as it was called in those days. I in particular, was overjoyed on those occasions. The first movie we saw was 'The Ten Commandments' at the Astor cinema. Months later, we would go to see 'Ben Hur.'

From time to time we went to the Metropole cinema to see cowboy movies starring Audi Murphy in 'Last Train from Gun Hill,' 'Blood at Sundown,' and 'North to Alaska' with John Wayne. Cinema going was restricted to holiday weekends but not all holiday weekends. Preparations for the Christmas holidays would see my mom work herself up to a frenzy. Old wall paper would come down and be replaced by 'better looking ones', linoleum would be replaced, new curtains for the doors and the windows would go up and the front and back steps would be scrubbed clean with a 'scraper.' I guess it was all the excitement of Christmas preparations that influenced me through the years to appreciate and enjoy the Christmas Season more than any other holiday of the year.

When Dad came home for Christmas the house was already 'spic and span' and with Christmas decorations and a Christmas tree. Sometimes, while he worked in Georgetown, Dad would come home with his heavy tool kit painted in red. And though he never told me, I assumed he brought it with him on his return from England. I used to like to fetch the kit for him on his arrival at the gate to our yard. I would carry it from the gate to the bottom of our house where it was stored in a wooden cupboard a friend had built for him. But the kit was so heavy, I could only fetch it a short distance. If it was not his tool kit, it would be his bicycle I would take from him and wheel it into the yard to be parked and locked under our house.

TRAMPING' BEHIND THE STEEL BAND

When Dad was away from home, my mom reluctantly allowed her three boys to go 'Tramping' behind one of the steel bands that would take to the city streets on the evenings at Christmas time. We had to return home by nine o'clock. As typical city boys we would 'tramp' behind one of the more popular and larger bands which was either the 'Quo Vadis' or the 'Invaders.' There were about two or three other city-based steel bands. The band that practiced in a tenement yard on Robb Street, few doors east of Bourda Market and around the corner from where we lived on

North Road was the band of our choice. It was real fun to go tramping behind a steel band.

Steel pan music is fascinating. This unique musical instrument, is made from steel barrels used in those days to import fuel. Experts say, it is the only hybrid percussion instrument in existence today, with three basic types of pans, tenor, rhythm and bass. The skill of the pan men with their rubber-tipped sticks in their nimble hands, striking against the surface of the pan that had been beaten to make such melodious 'jump up tunes' was what enticed scores of ordinary Guyanese to follow the band of their choice.

I always felt a deep love and affection for my Mom for allowing us, on some occasions, to do as we wanted. Though she was not born in the colony of British Guiana, nevertheless, she understood the need for her boys to go out and enjoy the fullness of city life. As boys growing up in her presence, we never saw her as different from other Guyanese women even though her accent and complexion were different compared to the typical native Guyanese woman. Maybe because it was from her, we were born and made to live in our world, that we saw no difference between her and other women. The fact that she was our own, and we, her own, made us blind to colour.

MOM AS A VOLUNTEER

Mom was a volunteer with the Saint John's Ambulance Brigade. Her volunteer work entailed delivering hot meals to 'shut-ins' and senior citizens in Georgetown. She would sell poppies in the month of October and participate along with Dad at Remembrance Day observances at the Cenotaph in the heart of the city. Remembrance Day was a very busy day for both of them. Mom would rise early and prepare something for herself, husband and her six children before leaving home to return just after lunch. I saw the joy in her face and the excitement in her body language as she readied herself to accompany her soldier to the Cenotaph every Remembrance Day.

TORANI

My Dad was stationed at the Torani Land Development and Irrigation Scheme for several years but he came home dutifully at the end of every month to visit his family and to provide for his wife financially.

The Torani Land Development and Irrigation Scheme was a British-funded project aimed at addressing flood control, drainage and irrigation and agricultural development of the colony's coastal areas. The construction of the Torani sluices was part of a comprehensive development plan comprising of schemes such as the Black Bush Polder, Brandwagt Sari, Mara, Capoey, Boerasirie, Tapakuma and Canals Polder under the then PPP Government. Twice while dad was away from home, Mom fell ill and had to be hospitalized.

MOM IN HOSPITAL

On the last occasion in late April, 1959 when Mom was admitted to the Public Hospital in Georgetown she never returned home, she died on May 2, 1959 at the age thirty-five. The cause of death was reported as rheumatic heart condition. Dad came home a broken man. He never recovered from the loss of the woman he loved and who cared for him. It took many years for him to realize that she was no longer there. I have never forgotten that afternoon when I last saw my Mom as she lay in bed with that beautiful smile on her round face still with slightly pinkish cheeks. Her beautiful brownish hair still looked fresh as if she had just arrived from her country of birth.

Every afternoon after school I would go visit her. Long before the official visiting hours, I would hang around the entrance to hospital compound awaiting its opening to visitors. Being late meant shortening the time I could spend attending to her needs. I exerted every effort to avoid that by going straight from school to the hospital. Her favorite treat during visiting hours was a quarter pint of 'Brown Betty' ice cream. She would direct me to a cupboard at the side of her bed where she kept her favorite blue and white hand bag, telling me how much money I should take.

Then off I would run to a nearby shop to buy her favourite vanilla flavored ice cream. Her eyes would light up on seeing me return with the brown paper bag in my hand. Sitting up in bed, she would thoroughly enjoy her ice cream, taking her time to savor the flavor but she would always leave two or three tiny scoops for me. On finishing her ice cream, she would look happy and contented and, while lying on her bed and I sitting on a wooden chair at the side of her bed, we would chat about all kinds of things most of which I can't remember at all.

One afternoon, a number of friends came to visit her, after they had sung a few get-well hymns in their low voices she looked at them and, to pointing to me, said with her English accent; 'He will be the luckiest of all my children.' My mom always turned to me to run her errands, to do her purchases at either Bourda Market or around the corner at a grocery at the corner of Light and Robb streets. In retrospect, it seems that both mom and dad looked to me as the steady hand among their children. The girls were too young to be sent on errands and in any event, in those days, a 'girls' place' was at home.

DEATH OF MOM

Our fun days ended with the hospitalization of my mother.

One evening after visiting hours, I found to my surprise, that they moved my Mom from the female open ward to the Seaman's Ward. I heard people say she was moved there because she was a Volunteer with the St. John's Ambulance Brigade and because my Dad was a member of the British Guiana Legionnaires.

One morning before going to school, I went to see Mom. To escape the watchful eyes of the hospital guards I 'bored' through a hole in the chain linked fence on Lamaha Street and sneaked up the stairs leading to the room she occupied. I peeped into the room but the bed was empty and the mattress was rolled up. I approached a nurse and enquired about my mother. The nurse asked about my relationship, I told her I was the patient's son, with that she broke the sad news to me. I was shocked. I immediately ran crying all the way home at North Road where we lived. I couldn't imagine life without our mother. I broke the news first to my brothers and sisters and to Aunt Lorna, a relative of the Nicholls and my mom's good friend who was a cook at the HQ of the Guyana Police Force who my mom had asked to come live in and to take care of us.

28

I went to the front house where Aunt Enid lived and gave her the sad news. The next thing I knew my Dad was in town. It was a devastating blow to him but he was a strong man. I didn't see him cry, if he did, he made sure he didn't do so in our presence.

The night before her burial Dad called me to sit and chat with him on the front stairs of Mrs. Wharton's home at 28, Third street, Alberttown. He told me of his plans and how he would have to split us up and send us to live with close friends and relatives.

Mrs. Wharton was the wife of a soldier friend of Dad. Mr. Wharton had returned to British Guiana after the war but left soon after to be a seaman. We had all gathered at the Wharton's in preparation for mom's funeral and burial. Of all his children, my Dad always took me into his confidence. He never told me why and I dared not ask. My Mom died six days before her 35th birthday after living just 8 years with her husband and six children in British Guiana.

If there was one thing that pleased me as I grew with my Mom, it was though she knew that her boys suffered from the brutal class distinctions between her boys in particular, and those who belonged to the middle and upper classes in British Guiana at that time. Mom never made us feel inferior to the 'well-to-do boys' in the neighborhood, because according to her; "The things we could do and the places we could go those boys couldn't, so we couldn't be like them and that was quite alright". "Boys will be boys" she would a say.

ESCAPADES WITH MY BROTHER, CLIFFORD

Clifford Michael Rohee, my eldest brother, was born on May 12, 1947. My mother was just 22 years of age at the time of his birth.

Clifford had become difficult for my parents to control, no amount of advice and guidance by mom nor flogging by dad helped. He became wayward always following bad company. He took advantage of my dad's absence from home.

My eldest brother Clifford

They say the 'devil is a busy man' and that he 'finds work for idle hands to do' Older folks say we must never speak ill of the dead, but sad to say, it seemed as though the 'devil' had taken hold of Clifford for a while.

On one occasion, Clifford encouraged me to 'skulk' from my school's afternoon session. He took me for a swim with some friends at the old waterworks site between Alexander and Camp streets. The site was divided into sections by walls of brick. Rain water had settled in each section which was about 4 to 6 feet deep.

When I refused to undress and to be naked in public, he pulled from his pocket a beret with two slits and encouraged me to put in on as a make-do 'bukta.' With nothing else available and since my skinny legs allowed the 'bukta' to fit, I did as I was told and jumped into the water waist deep. I felt a sudden burning pain under my left foot. I came out of the pool immediately only to find a huge gaping wound under my left foot. Blood was flowing freely. An old broken bottle under the water did the damage.

I was rushed to the Public Hospital to have the wound stitched and taken home. I confessed the entire occurrence to my mother. As far as she was concerned, though Clifford was to be blamed, "I should have known better." Skulking from school was never repeated ever again.

On another occasion, this time a Saturday morning, Clifford and I, along with some friends, set out for the groyne at Kingston behind the recently built Marriot Hotel. Groynes were built of stone by the Dutch colonizers as means of sea defence. They would break the impact of strong waves during spring or high tides from the Atlantic Ocean.

Historically, the Kingston area, located at the mouth of the Demerara River and the Atlantic Ocean, has always been prone to flooding since it faced the ocean directly. What made matters worse, was that since Guyana's coastland was below sea level, as far as the capital city was concerned, Kingston was the first point of contact for huge amounts of water rushing over the sea wall. Compounded with heavy rainfall, flooding was a nightmare for residents of Kingston. Before setting out for the groyne, each of us were armed with pieces of wood about two feet long and an inch and half wide to which we attached hooks made of wire. This was to be used to catch a specie of fish called the 'Paku.' The Paku is an unscaled, ugly looking unscaled fish with a big mouth. It secludes itself between the huge boulders used to fortify the groyne. To catch the 'Paku' we had to dive under water, and push the hooked instrument as a kind of 'jukker' between the boulders hoping that the hook would pierce the unscaled soft skin of the Paku. When hooked and while pulling the Paku wedged between the rocks, it would emit a groaning sound.

But it was not so much the groaning of the hooked Paku that was somewhat frightening, it was more the treacherous nature of the waters at the location that posed the greatest danger.

The groyne is located at the confluence of the Demerara river and the Atlantic Ocean where the underwater currents were strong enough to pull the inexperienced swimmer out to sea. Many had gone swimming at that location and had drowned. Days after, their lifeless bodies washed up either on the Kingston or Vreed-en-hoop foreshores. Since I was not an experienced swimmer, I ventured into a section of the groyne where I felt safe enough to hold on to a boulder in case I had to scramble ashore for safety. Up to this day, I cannot understand why, not knowing how to swim in such treacherous waters, I took the risk of going underwater while holding on to a slimy rock to catch a fish. What a 'Paku' I would have been branded had I been swept away to my death by drowning because of the strong underwater currents in that area. But there is yet another adventurous event inspired by my brother Clifford.

One day, during school holidays, a group of boys from our 'hood' decided we would go scouting aback the Botanical Gardens.

THE BOTANICAL GARDENS AND BEYOND

The Botanical Gardens is largest of the two gardens in the city of Georgetown, the smaller one being the Promenade Gardens located at the Northern end of the city opposite the Parade Ground to the South and State House to the West.

Both gardens are beautiful and famous for the wide array of flora and fauna to be found there. Like nature parks, with spacious lawns of grass and huge palm trees, families, tourists, young lovers and senior citizens would frequent both gardens to listen to renditions from the Guyana Police Force Band, for a rendezvous or simply for relaxation. Located at the Botanical Gardens are the iron-made 'Kissing Bridge,' the manatee pond and the Zoological Park.

The 'Kissing Bridge' which spans the manatee pond, provides an enchanting backdrop for photographs for newlyweds, engaged couples and tourists. The construction of the curved iron bridge was completed in1885

My mom took us frequently to the Botanical Gardens. She liked it there. It was spacious, had well kept lawns, beautiful trees of various species and the air was clean and smelt fresh. Some Sundays she would pack a basket with food, snacks and a homemade drink and walk with us down to the gardens. There she would spread a blanket on the grass at a nice shady area where we would sit, run around, eat, and listen to stories she would tell us.

It was during one of those family picnics that Clifford mentioned quietly to me that he wanted to know what is at the Eastern end, aback the Botanical Gardens. The opportunity presented itself during what is known as the 'August school holidays.' Clifford managed to influence a group from the 'Hood' to go explore the back of the gardens.

Passing through the Botanical Garden, we reached the 'Lamaha Canal.' Walking on its left bank, we followed the canal, until we arrived at a point where we could see sugar cane fields on the opposite side of the canal. The group decided to cross over from where we were to the opposite side where the cane fields were. Clifford and his crew plunged into the 'black water' and reached the other side. I stayed behind to be the 'lookout' and watch over their clothes.

Suddenly, shots rang out, POW! POW!' two men who we later understood to be rangers were in the vicinity and had spotted the intruders from a distance. Clifford and the others beat a hasty retreat, they jumped back into the water with sugar canes in their mouths and swam to safety. Back on the other side of the canal in record time they ran naked with clothes and sugar canes in hand to what we considered a safer location. We caught some 'ground doves' roasted them on a small fire, eat them and then 'chased it' with the juice from the sugar cane. Being with Clifford was fun, but he was also dangerous person to be with. He was capable of pushing us beyond the limits into very risky circumstances. Under such conditions, I was not prepared to go along at all times.

My mom was pregnant with Clifford when she arrived in British Guiana. Being her first child, Mom had some affection for him, his wayward ways notwithstanding.

Clifford slept away from home many a night, and when he came home the next day, he would terrify mom to such an extent, that in the end, she would oblige and hand him whatever 'small change' she had in a small purse she kept in her bosom. Clifford would say thank you and run away never to return until her death.

MY BROTHER ALEXANDER

Alexander Bernard Rohee, my second eldest brother, was the easy-going kind. He was born on December 17, 1948. He had straight hair and all the features of an East Indian boy, no doubt the hereditary strain of Charles Rohee, my grandfather.

My Brother Alexander

Alex did whatever he was called upon to do but was always playful and was not looked upon as reliable nor willing. Not that he would ever refuse to do what he was called upon to do, it was just that he wasn't the 'kinda guy' to run errands and return quickly. We all accepted him for what he was, the 'cool one' after all, he was one of us.

SPLITTING UP

The separation of her six children following her passing was unavoidable, since our Dad worked in the interior of the country at the time.

Following the burial of Mom, we returned home, packed our individual belongings and left our home at North Road, heading in different directions never to return to live there again. It was not after many years that I did return to my old home to visit my Aunt Maggie who had taken up residence and lived there until she died. While she was still alive, she made it her duty to come visit me either at my office at the Ministry of Home Affairs or at home with my family in Queenstown.

My three sisters, Sandra, Carol and Margaret, stayed for a while with the Whartons, at Third Street Alberttown, while my two brothers went to live with the DeGroots, another family friend at D'urban Street, Lodge, Georgetown. Mr. DeGroot was a disciplinarian, I surmised that that character came from his soldiering days. With my Dad it was the same. Both of them served in the army in England during the war.

It always puzzled me why I was singled out and separated from my brothers and sisters to go live elsewhere.

LIFE WITH AUNT GERTRUDE

At age 9, I went to live at 233, South Road, between Cummings and Light Streets Bourda with Mrs. Gertrude Stuart my father's sister.South Road runs from East to West in the city of Georgetown. It is on the Northen side of a parallel canal that separates South Road from Croal Street located on the Southern side of the canal. Aunt Gertrude lived on the upper flat of a two story apart building on South Road.

I learnt a lot living with my aunt. She was a health visitor and midwife by profession. She was strict, and a disciplinarian. My aunt taught me to read the newspapers, and to improve on my English grammar and arithmetic. She made sure I went to school and did my homework every evening. Every Sunday, she sent me to 'Sunday School' at the Elim Missionary Church on Albert Street just around the corner to the south of Regent street.

From my aunt, I learnt how to shop for bargains at Bourda market and to compare prices for items on sale at the Chinese supermarkets. Aunt Gertrude taught me to make garlic pork, pepper pot, how to stuff a chicken, stitch it up and to bake it in the oven. I was also taught to make home made drinks such as fly, mauby, ginger beer and sorrel.

Preparing for the Christmas season with Aunt Gertie meant lots of work. Vacuuming the carpets, removing cobwebs from the roof with a pointer broom attached on a long stick; polishing and shining the floor and stairs; dusting the furniture; polishing and shining the silver and bronze ornaments and wares; pounding mace, the flower of the nutmeg in a mortar to make Fly; grinding fresh peppers to make pepper sauce and helping with the cake mix for the traditional 'Black Cake' and fruit cake.

Aunt Enid & Aunt Gertude

I would be rewarded either with a matinee bill or a ride in the Yellow City Bus that traversed the route that took me from where we lived on South Road to Subryanville and back. When the long August school holidays came, I was sent to spend time with either relatives from my father's side as well as at family friends of my aunt. There were the Jacob sisters, Lily and Ivy of Buxton village. They were the daughters of my grandmother's sister, Johanna Agard. Lily was married to George O'Jon a missionary priest who traveled around the country establishing branches of his church. Her sister Ivy remained a spinster. The O'Jon's owned properties at Buxton village, Wismar/McKenzie and on Regent Street, Georgetown. Their house at Buxton village was on the street that led to the sea wall. Both Lily and Ivy were teachers, so were the three daughters of Lily; Joy, Irene and Gertrude. Joy O'Jon was at one time headmistress at Bishop's High School. Me and Lancelot James, the son of Shirley James née Pilgrim, a first cousin of the Jacobs, spent some happy days at the home of the O'Jon's at Buxton Village. We spent days exploring the village walking along a canal that ran from North to

South. We would hang around the train station awaiting the arrival and departure of the trains and to witness the hustle and bustle of the passengers and others standing by. Holidays were also spent at the homes of Henry and Sheila Dolphin and their son Junior at Suddie on the Essequibo coast. As well as at my Aunt Sheila and her family who lived at Suddie too.

I liked spending time at Aunt Enid's. Her home was the venue for Rohee family gatherings where politics, current affairs, family matters and almost everything of interest to the Rohee Clan was discussed. My 'place' was to sit and listen, eat and drink whenever a light snack was served. During school days I would have lunch at Aunt Enid's. It was my responsibility to take her daughter Diane from school on my way to and from her home. Uncle Wilfred was fun, he would always have a riddle 'up his sleeve' to throw at me to test how smart I was.

One of his favourite riddles was, 'House full kitchen, kitchen full can't catch a thimble full' what is it? He would ask. After several failed attempts, I later learnt the answer was 'smoke!' Whenever uncle Wilfred let out one of is traditional loud farts in my presence, he would suddenly turn to me and ask, 'Did you see that rat that just ran across the sitting room?' As if to distract my attention from what he did. I knew this trick so well that whenever Uncle Wilfred asked me the question I would reply saying 'yeah! it just ran under your rocking chair.'

HOLIDAYING AT TORANI

Torani is one of the most beautiful and serene part of Guyana where the brown water of the Berbice River and the 'black' water of the Torani Creek meet. Me and my two brothers had gone there in 1959 to spend the August school holidays with my Dad following our Mom's passing. On that occasion, we spent the time exploring the forested areas and traveling by canoe visiting nearby villages. We trekked through the thick rainforest where footpaths existed. The chatter of monkeys, mingled with howling baboon monkeys and the cries of macaws and parrots would be heard. As we walked deeper into the forest, we would spot a monkey or two, slinging from tree to tree or a sloth clinging to a tree with its long nails. The incessant whistling or warbling of a variety of birds was as amazing as it was joyful to hear.

On Saturdays, Mr. Harris, a Portuguese co-worker of my Dad would take us by canoe to a Seventh Day Adventist Church where we would spend almost the entire day. For us, Church going was an outing we looked forward to. It provided an opportunity for families from the isolated villages along the Canje creek to meet and greet each other. It was at Torani I saw for the first time and learnt about the dangers of the tarantula spider that lived under the fallen leaves of the cocoa trees cultivated by farmers at nearby villages.

We were warned to look out for the labaria and bushmaster snakes when walking about the Scheme as well as the piranha whenever we were near the creek. That explained why no one ever swam in that creek. We ate lots labba, (Cuniculuspaca) sweet water fishes, and iguanas including the eggs of the iguana. Ground provisions, corn (boiled or roasted) and fruits were in abundance. I loved observing the tugs pushing the pontoons loaded with the raw bauxite ore coming down the Berbice river from Kwakwani. It was fun to watch the captain, who after sounding his horn to warn any oncoming vessel, would skillfully navigate a sharp turn in the Berbice River and then head out to where the Canadian Saguenay line ships would be waiting to be loaded with the precious mineral that would be smelted into alumina and then aluminum for the aviation and boat building industries.

The amazingly thick mist resting on the water that greeted us each morning always fascinated me. Toucans and woodpeckers were in abundance in the area and they were loud in making their presence felt.

The interior of my country is not only fascinating, it brings joy to the eyes and ears. The forests, the grass, the water, the animals, fish and the mists combined creates a mystical atmosphere and a scent in the air that tells you, you are at a place where you are at one with the inspirational, beauty, strong and nurturing spirit of Mother Nature.

CLIFFORD'S DEATH

It was during my sojourn as a bachelor' in residence' at Freedom House that Clifford, I learnt my eldest brother was murdered on November 10, 1968 on an American-owned fishing trawler while at sea. I was invited to the Brickdam Police Station to identify his personal belongings and later, to the mortuary to identify his body. This was the second loss for my family nine years after my mom had passed away. Why I was asked to fulfill these responsibilities I cannot recall, nor can I say, save that the police knew I was employed at Freedom House. The Party, through Mrs. Janet Jagan was kind enough to help me with the funeral arrangements and expenses well as with the necessary paper work. My father came to town for the funeral after which Clifford, my dad's first child was interred at the La Repentir Cemetery.

Clifford was a passionate young man with a temper that was at times uncontrollable. A sketchy report to the police from the captain of the vessel informed that there was a heated argument between my brother and another crew member. The argument ended up in a fight during which my brother was stabbed in the lungs. He died soon after. No one was charged for murder or manslaughter since it was alleged that the incident took place on international waters. The police never pursued the matter further. Clifford never married nor did he ever have a permanent relationship with a woman. As far as I am aware, he had no children.

ALEXANDER PASSES

Alexander my second brother was born on December 17,1948. He married Tennegee but later he divorced her and lived with two different women at different times until he left his job at the Guyana Prison Service. He died of a heart attack at his home on May 20,1998. Alex as we called him, was a heavy drinker and smoker. And though he could be serious at times, he lived a carefree life even though he had a wife and three small children. The bulk of his salary was spent on his friends and work mates drinking beers and consuming lavish meals at Chinese restaurants.

One night on arrival at his home on the East Bank, following one of his late-night drinking sprees, he found his belongings on the front doorsteps of his house. The doors and windows were shut tight. No one answered to his calls and he never gained admission to the home again.

Alex was a handsome young man with a pleasant personality. He had thick black wavy hair that was always neatly combed. Because he looked East Indian, he stood out from me and Clifford. Alex was lucky with the girls and always managed to find one that was considerate and affectionate. At the time of his passing, Alex had five children.

Carol, the second of my three sisters was born on August 16, 1952. She was an epileptic. And though she did not go far at school, though she was smart and efficient at whatever she did at home. She never married but had a son. Carol died at the bauxite mining town of Linden on July 20, 2000 Sandra was the first of my three sisters she was born on September 15, 1951. Sandra worked as a technician at the Milk Pasteurization Plant at Kingston, Georgetown. She subsequently got a job at State House to attend, along with others, to the household needs of President Jagdeo and the then First Lady, Varshnie. Sandra was very close to my family and was a regular visitor to our home with her three children. She had a jovial personality and was a stern mother. She assumed the role of 'Keeper of the Rohee family history'. Sandra was a diabetic, regrettably, she did not take care of herself health-wise, as a result she lost one of her feet. She eventually passed away on October 5, 2007. Margaret, the youngest of my three sisters, was born on December 24, 1954. After leaving school, she joined the Signals Branch of the Guyana Defense Force (GDF). On retirement, she joined a private security company. She never married and survives to this day.

SCHOOL DAYS

I attended Our Lady of Fatima Roman Catholic School later renamed Bourda RC School following the conversion of all schools to government-controlled schools.

My Aunt arranged to have me transferred to Bedford Methodist School, located at that time west of Bourda Market. After spending some time at that school, and finding I was not making progress, my aunt transferred me back to Bourda RC where I sat the College of Preceptors exams in 1964 and thereafter, I finished attending public school. I received my formal education up to an examination called College of Preceptors while the PPP was in office. That was in 1964. At that time, I was a pupil at Our Lady of Fatima Roman Catholic school at 112 Regent street between Light and Albert streets.

It was during this period that I lived at 13, North a Road, Bourda with my parents and brothers and sisters. I thoroughly enjoyed my days at school. I had a group of schoolmates who had fun and frolic together. I became friends with a few of them after a few scuffles and an exchange of punches outside the school yard. I was not good at street corner fist fighting and preferred to avoid making enemies with my class mates. What I liked about my class in particular and the school in general was the multi-ethnic composition of the pupils as well as its teachers

My closest friends were David Fernandes the son of the flamboyant insurance agent popularly called 'Duck eggs.' Errol Parris, son of the tailor who had his tailor shop a few doors just over Albert street, Aubrey Smith, son of the seamstress who lived on Oronoque street, the two sets of Persaud brothers, one set whose father made dentures at his lab on Charlotte street, while the other set of Persaud's lived on Wellington street where their parents ran a guest house.

My Friend David

Then there were the two Lall brothers whose father was a joiner and owned a workshop on Charlotte street. There was 'Monty' Smith whose father was the

41

'important looking man with the pipe' who lived on Regent street just up the road from the school.

There were a few girls in our class who attracted my attention. Among them were; Yvonne Persaud, Marlyn Whyte, Emelda VanSluytman, Maude Hamilton, Jacquline Hayde, Desiree Fernandes, Marlene Moonsammy and Desiree Hoenkirk.

The girls were the brightest in the class, always excelling at the end of term exams. We enjoyed teasing the girls and so did the they. We had a wonderful bunch of teachers who made learning fun at school.

Mr. Van Cooten, was a heavy smoker his favorite subjects were geography and current affairs. Mr. Nigg was from the Corentyne, his favourite subjects were mental arithmetic and arithmetic. Ms. Jonas, the lady who rode the Honda motorcycle, was very good at mathematics and algebra, Mr. Yaw, the smooth talker was the best at the English language.

These were all great fourth and fifth standard teachers who had a passion for teaching and made it their duty to ensure that we learnt our lessons if not by persuasion at least by the cane.

But there were fabulous teachers in our earlier classes. They were all female teachers. Amongst them were Teachers Rockliffe, Van Rossum, Lee Yung, Elcock, Forde and Best. They dominated the lower flat of the school building while the upper flat was a mixture of male and female teachers.

Our head masters were Mr. Luke followed by Mr. Lucas. Mr Luke was an affable and approachable. individual. He took his job seriously and taught English and Arithmetic as if he was at QC. His replacement, Mr. Lucas was more of the standoffish type and had little to do with the pupils. He had a preference to address matters through the teachers only.

Mr. Luke had a nephew who attended the school and was in our class. He came from a family of teachers and was inclined to be the bookish type. Amazingly though, when his uncle was not around, he would 'free up' in such a jovial and happy manner that those of us around him would embrace him in a spirit of youthful solidarity and shared happiness. However, whenever his uncle the headmaster appeared under such circumstances, he would transform into that sombre and sad looking pupil.

One midday during our lunch break, just before the school bell rang for assembly, Mr. Luke's nephew, not recognizing the time, bought what was known then as a 'flutee' usually sold at the entrance to the school. A 'flutee' is a small block of frozen water measuring 2"X 2". It is composed of a mixture of sugar, artificial flavoring and would come in different artificial colorings but mostly in red or orange. It is consumed by constantly sucking on it until it eventually melted away either in your hand or mouth. It has since been replaced by the 'Icicle' another iced cooler packaged cylindrically in plastic.

The young man chose a red flutee but no sooner had he bought it he spotted his uncle approaching. The young man panicked! In fright he slipped the flutee into the pocket of his kakhi pants and hurriedly joined the line of the pupils preparing to march up the stairs into the school and to their respective class rooms.

Mr Luke stood at the top of the stairs supervising the pupils as they walked past him. As his nephew approached, Mr Luke, peering under his glasses, spotted a red stain around the crutch on his nephew's kakhi trousers, he stopped the frightened boy in his tracks and enquired whether he was feeling well.

After discovering what was the cause for the red colour at the crutch of the boy's pants, he immediately sent him home for the remainder of the day since he lived some distance away from school.

1962 -1964

While at school, the political situation in the country had reached a boiling point. A general strike had been called by the political opposition in cahoots with the trade unions opposed to the Jagan government. People with placards in hands could be seen marching up and down the streets of Georgetown shouting "Axe the Tax" and "Hit the Road Jack" They were protesting the tax on banks beer, produced by Peter D'Aguiar's brewery, alcoholic beverages, cigarettes and other non-essential items proposed in the so- called 'Kaldor budget'. The 'Jack' they were referring to was Jack Kelshall a National of Trinidad and Tobago, an advisor to Cheddi Jagan who was the Premier at the time.

Outside the General Post Office large numbers of women could be seen squatting almost on a daily basis in from the main entrance facing the National museum singing protest songs. It was predominantly men who blocked the eastern and western entrances to Parliament buildings. Gasoline and kerosene were in short supply and long lines of cars, vans and trucks formed winding lines outside gas stations. Men and women including children including me with containers in had formed long queues waiting to purchase limited amounts of kerosene. Gangs armed with sticks and bicycle chains roamed the city on bicycles. Whenever they spotted an East Indian man or woman they would stop, rob and then beat them mercilessly. I saw this with my own eyes.

A criminal enterprise known as 'choke and rob' became widespread at that time. Soldiers and riot squad ranks armed with guns and bayonets could be seen patrolling the streets in open-back land rovers and trucks. Stores and shops owned by East Indian and naturalized Chinese were invaded by armed gangs who chased customers and the proprietors out of their own business places then engaged in rampant looting. The 'Riot Squad' of the British Guiana Volunteer Force along with the 'Black Moriah' drove fear in the ordinary citizenry when ever they appeared but the marauding gangs couldn't careless about the patrols of the law enforcement units, they simply carried on with their thuggery and looting. This conveyed the impression of complicity between those who controlled the gangs and law enforcement.

I lived on Regent Street next door to our school at that time.

I sat the College of Preceptors examination in the month of July 1963. Just after we had finished the final exam paper, we heard a very loud explosion. We rushed out of the school building onto Regent street and looked in the westerly direction. People were rushing up the street. A group of us decided to venture in the same direction. When we reached Camp and Robb street opposite AH&L Kissoon furniture store we saw people looting. We proceeded further west down Robb street until we reached Wellington street.

From where we stood at the eastern side of the of corner of Robb and Wellington streets, we could see a building had collapsed near another building that had written on it, in bold red capital letters FREEDOM HOUSE and in smaller capital letters, 'Headquarters of the PPP.'

Bombing of Freedom House in Georgetown

The front of the eastern half of that building was partially destroyed.

A huge crowd had gathered and riot squad police had cordoned off the area. A few of us managed to cross over to the western side of Wellington street just on the edge of the pavement leading to the Metropole cinema.

Broken glass was all around and what looked like charred body parts could be seen here and there. Suddenly we head the sound of shots. Tear gas was being fired. A police man was atop a land rover was calling over a loud hailer on everyone to disperse and to go home.

We quickly ran into an open 'range yard' on the eastern side of Wellington street not far from North road. We were looking for a standpipe with water available to soak our faces and to protect our eyes from the burning effect of the teargas. We moved out of the danger area. We walked all the way in an easterly direction on North Road. At Light street we branched off and went our separate ways. As we walked and talked, we saw looters hurrying past us with their ill-gotten gains. We saw a man fetching a refrigerator on his back. It was a day I would always remember.

Little did I know at that time, that four years later, I would spend the larger part of my adult life, as a member of the party that was housed in the same building that was bombed on that eventful day. During that period whenever my aunts and uncles met, there would engage in lively political discussion among themselves. The majority voiced their support for the Jagan government. Some were neutral while others were inclined to support Peter D'Aguiar's United Force.

As a thirteen to fourteen-year old youngster at the time, I was exposed to a host of political views since the Rohee's appeared to be a highly politically conscious family.

It was through those family debates that I became acquainted with the Evening Post, the Argosy, Chronicle and the Graphic newspapers since the Rohee family members, in the course of their friendly back and forth arguments would make constant references to the newspapers all of which were viciously opposed to the Jagan administration and was carrying in their pages on a daily basis, heavy doses of anti-communist propaganda.

I never knew nor heard my father's political views because he was far away at the Torani scheme, in the Berbice river. And even when he was around local politics was not one of his favourite subjects. He preferred to talk about his experiences during the Second World War and the intricacies of a fitter/ mechanic's job.

The Bourda RC school building has since been demolished and a new commercial structure now stands in its place.

After living with my aunt for about five years, I finished public school in 1964 just two years before my country's independence on May 26, 1966.

MOVING FROM PLACE TO PLACE

After Aunt Gertie's husband had ran off with her sister Mabel, we moved from 233 South Road to 112 Regent Street Bourda, then to Fifth Street Albert town, then to Forshaw and New Garden Streets Queenstown, ending up at 350 East Street in South Cummingsburg.

At South Road, our neighbor to the East were the Jaigobins, a huge Indo-Guyanese family with about fourteen children. Mr. Jaigobin, was a slim, brown-skinned, Indo-Guyanese man. He wore round rimmed spectacles and a Panama hat. He started out as a small businessman with a stall at the Stabroek Market but he later moved out of the market and bought two properties obliquely opposite each other at the corner of Regent and Wellington streets. Me and Mr. Jaigobin's three younger sons attended school together. To the western side of our South Road flat lived a devout Catholic Portuguese family who loved singing hymns and would go to Church every Sunday morning. Behind us lived a man who made dentures and an insurance agent.

On Regent Street, the Yankana's lived directly opposite us. Our Lady of Fatima school was to the west and a Portuguese family on the Eastern side of our rented house. There was a soda factory at the Eastern corner and a huge house opposite the factory where the Samuels lived.

Exploring the neighborhood early one morning, I discovered that a German National by the name of Mr. Winfred Fries had started manufacturing furniture below the huge house owned by the Samuels. It turned out that Mr. Fries was married to one of the Samuels girls, but he later divorced her and married Barbara Jagan, one of Cheddi Jagan's sisters.

THE KILKENNY'S

Living at Forshaw and New Garden streets was fun. At the Eastern half of New Garden Street, exactly opposite the building where we lived, stood a quaint, rickety looking wooden house whose exterior walls were covered with unpainted shingles from the Wallaba tree. Shingles contain high gum oxudates and oil resin that makes them highly resistant to decay and dry wood termites. Shingles are used for roofing and outer walls to protect houses from water damage whenever rain fell. Some windows at the front of the house looked as though they were about to fall off their hinges. In the yard was a huge genip or Spanish Lime tree that bore very sweet genips, a tropical fruitGenips contain amino acids that help to lower blood sugar and cholesterol levels and boost the immune system.

When the fruit was in abundance, an old lady who lived there would set up a wooden tray full of genips atop some old 'drinks' boxes just outside the gate of her house. She would then mount a small sign written on cardboard between the genips marked 'For sale!' The old lady had a flock of geese numbering about forty. In the early morning hours, she would release the geese from their pens. With their loud honking noise, the geese would make their way into the huge yard where an improvised pond filled with water at the eastern had been dug at the far eastern end of the yard. At evening time, the geese could be seen walking, one behind the other, back to their pen on their own.

According to neighbours, the old lady was a 'See Far' Dutch woman or what is now called a 'Psychic,' who came from Suriname. In fact, when certain visitors came, she could be heard speaking in a strange tongue which no one understood. And as though to validate what was said, it was not unusual to see some highfalutin looking individuals or couples drive up in their fancy-looking motor cars, enter the old lady's yard only to emerge a few hours later talking in low tones almost whispering to each other.

Our neighbors to the West of our apartment were the Paris,' they lived in the front house of the yard next door while the Killenny's lived at the back. The Kilkenny family included Alfred, Ruby and their three children, Louis, Ivy and Orin. We became very good friends. I have kept up our relationship to this day.

I enjoyed every moment I spent with the Kilkenny's. Mrs.Killenny was a nurse/ midwife. Her husband Alfred, was a clerk. They both worked long hours during week days and would be at home together on weekends.

Mrs. Kilkenny was a fantastic homemaker, cook and baker. Her homemade shepherd's pie, bread, buns and refreshments made from local fruit were the best! She loved bougainvillea plants that bore flowers of various colours but most of all, she adored the anthurium lily, many of which adorned the front of her yard much to the admiration of visitors and friends.

The Killenny's belonged to the Moravian Church, one of the oldest Missionary churches in Guyana whose establishment dates back to 1902. Every old years' night the entire family would take me along with them to the midnight church service held at the Queenstown Moravian Church at the corner of New Garden and Anira Streets. After the Church service we would return to their home and have a light snack.

Louis and Ivy were students at Queen's College and Bishop's High School respectively while Orin attended the Queenstown Comenius Moravian primary school. Orin was just about my age which allowed us to bond closer together more than with his elder brother and sister.

With Louis, Ivy & Orin

Grandfather Philip Calder, Mrs. Kilkenny's Dad, used to like test Orin over and over again with the same question. His question to Orin was about the names of the five Great Lakes of Canada. He would ask the same question over and over merely out of fun even though he knew that Orin, having committed the names of the five lakes to memory, could repeat by rote answer to his question. But the old man just like hearing the answer from his grandson, so suddenly out of the blue he would put the question to Orin. The correct answer gave the old man a sense of pride and satisfaction that he had taught Orin a thing or two. He would sit back in his favorite rocking chair smiling to himself.

The Killenny's were a wonderful family to spend time with. They embraced and treated me as one of their own. Like so many Guyanese the Killenny's migrated to the United States in 1965 at a time when our country was experiencing political and economic turmoil of the worst kind.

It was only after a change of government in 1992, during my frequent travels to the US as Minister of Foreign Affairs that I managed to establish contact with the Killenny's once again. Mr. and Mrs. Kilkenny took me to their home in Brooklyn for the traditional Kilkenny snack. Both Alfred and Ruby Kilkenny have since passed on, but I am still in contact with my childhood friends Louis, Ivy and Orin.

MY FIRST JOB

My first job was at William Fogarty's Ltd. on Water street. I worked as a 'Cash Boy' during the 1965 Christmas season at Fogarty's Department Store, one of the oldest, and the second largest store of its kind in downtown Georgetown. I managed to get the job through Mr. John O'Dowd, an Irishman who lived not far from an apartment my aunt had rented at 260, Forshaw and New Garden streets in Queenstown. The job was not meant to be a permanent one because I was still at school. In those days, such a job was known as a 'Christmas Hand.

TRYING WITH A TRADE

When I finished school, my aunt sent me to the National Evening College on East Street to get a higher education. I enrolled to do the courses in English along with West Indian History and literature, fully aware of my lack of interest in my maths.

My aunt had tried unsuccessfully to get me enrolled at the Government Technical Institute (GTI) where Mr. Alan Munroe was the principal. Mr. Munroe was a relative of Mrs. Lucille Romeo, a colleague midwife of my aunt Gertrude. They worked together as Health Visitors during a public health visitors' programme initiated by Mrs. Janet Jagan, the then Minister of Health.

Ante-natal clinics were opened throughout the country using Community and health Centres. Visits were made by the Health Visitors to rivers-in areas by 'launches' or medium sized passenger boats. Clinics were established on the East Bank of Demerara from Houston to Timehri and visits made to rivers-in areas as well as to the islands on the Demerara river.

During the August or summer school holidays my aunt would take me along with her on some of their visits. Through Mrs. Romeo, Mr. Munroe arranged for me to join the next batch of applicants selected to sit the entrance exam for a place at the GTI. I did sit the exam but I later learnt that the exam I sat for placement as a draughtsman was oversubscribed. I was told I would have to await the next entrance exam which would have been the following year. I lost interest in the matter.

My aunt probably felt that because I attended and did well at the Kingston Handicraft Centre which fell under the Ministry of Education, that I should go a step further to advance my knowledge in either joinery, draughtsmanship, or mechanical and electrical engineering.

Little did she know that among the reasons why I liked attending the handicraft centre at Kingston was because the milk plant was next door and it from that plant, we got our supply of pasteurized or chocolate milk which I thoroughly enjoyed.

Also nearby was the molasses bulk storage facility which was just across the road from the centre. It was there me and my friends with the help of the guards, would collect some molasses which we held in our hands and ate while on our way home. There was the fishermen's make shift wharf near the Kingston koker where we would go during lunch breaks to chat with fishermen who were either mending their nets, repairing their boats or packing the hold with ice in preparation to go out to sea.

The fishermen would tell us fantastic stories, some of it embellished, about fishing out in the open Atlantic Ocean.

These stories conjured up images of excitement and adventure in our thoughts so much so that some of my friends were bold enough to ask to be taken on a trip out to sea to which the fishermen would say; "Go ask your parents first."

None of us dared ask our parents.

ERNEST BOYER & SONS

After leaving school, my aunt Gertie with whom I was living, got me my Second job through Ms. Pariaug, a colleague nurse of hers. The job was at an establishment called 'Boyer's Furniture Store.' on Robb street between Alexander and Camp streets. The proprietor was Ernest Deygoo or Boyer. He was an elderly man of East Indian decent.

Mr. Boyer came from a generation of Indo-Guyanese businessmen who emerged in the late 1940's in Georgetown and prospered. Among them were; the Raymans, the Ali Shahs, the Sankars, Bhaichandeens, Y. Bagh Khan, Gafoors, Muneshwar's and AH&L Kissoon.

Later came the Indian Nationals; Mr. S.K. Puri, D.A. Thani, Kirpalani Bros. Bhojwani, Mohan's and many others. The enterprising SK Puri ventured into the paint business while his countrymen restricted themselves to the clothing, raw cloth, suiting's, lingerie, sarees and the footwear business.

The Indo-Guyanese businessmen had opened hardware and haberdashery stores in competition with the Portuguese and Lebanese businessmen like the Gomes, Abdelnours and Psaila Bros. who had long been in the same business of importing and selling hardware goods. Some Portuguese owned and operated grocery shops as well.

The Chinese at that time had restricted themselves to restaurants, laundries, bakeries and corner-shop grocery stores.

Mr. Boyer belonged to the Salvation Army and gave generously to the organization. The Salvation Army is well respected for their social work in Guyana since colonial times. They have succeeded in maintaining that image in these challenging times especially in the area of drug rehabilitation at a rehab centre established at its Kingston centre. Mr. Boyer's three sons, John, Tyrone and Edward lived in the UK. He invited them to join him at the business with a view to them eventually taking over the management and administration of the business

Mr. Boyer wanted to retire since the work- load was taking a toll on his health as a diabetic.

First to arrive was John, but he left about a year after. It was too much for him. Then Tyrone came, but he left in a matter of months. Managing a hardware store was certainly not his piece of cake. Then Edward or 'Eddie' came.

Eddie appeared to be in his mid-twenties but amazingly, he took over his father's small business with such zeal and confidence that in a relatively short period of time he transformed his father's small business into one of the largest whole sale and retail hardware and general stores in Guyana. He rebranded it 'National Hardware and General Store.'

While the business was yet a furniture store, Eddie and I delivered furniture to the homes of customers.

Eddie and I would load furniture into a blue Volkswagen delivery van until it proved useless. Sales increased especially at Christmas time. A small truck was bought to replace the Volkswagen.

We would fetch furniture up the long or short stairs of the homes of customers.

After a day of hard work Eddie would invite me to his home at 213, Camp Street where we would listen to music and have light non-alcoholic refreshments. We would chat about life in London and his plans for his father's business. He was a young man with big ambitions and a vision.

While Eddie moved on to become a big business magnate in Guyana, I moved on to politics to serve the working people, a not for profit vocation.

I worked with Eddie's dad till I left the job sometime in 1968 to become a full-time party activist with the People's Progressive Party.

MORE EDUCATION

While I lived with my aunt, we moved from Queenstown to a rented property at East Street, North Cummingsburg. East Street runs from north to south. There was once a canal that separated the eastern from western half of the street. The house in which we lived had two bedrooms, a master room which my aunt occupied and a smaller room that was allocated to me. The National Evening College was just next door to the North of our house. From my bedroom window I could see a section of the class taught by Mr David Chanderbally. I could also hear everything that was being taught. I decided to arm myself with a notebook and pen and from my window, be part of the lessons that were being taught free cost.

I eventually ended up attending formal classes at the bottom house evening College.

The college was established by Bhalla Kant brother of Shurti Kant, two Indian Nationals who had taken up permanent residence in Guyana and had invested in the establishment of the two educational institutions; The Guyana Oriental College on Thomas Street and the National Evening College on East street.

The classes were usually packed to capacity. It was amazing to see the large number of young people representing all the city's ethnicities who, after work, would attend the classes seeking a higher education.

Noticing my interest in the classes and having nothing to do in the afternoons my aunt enrolled me at the Bottom House College to sit three subjects, maths, English language and literature.

I did poorly in maths, but the grades in English language and English Literature were pretty good.

My friends in the class got passes in the subjects they sat. We used the occasion as an opportunity to celebrate at a quiet liquor restaurant and bar on Water Street. Smirnoff vodka and Trout Hall orange juice were our choice for celebrating.

I was able to do this only because my aunt had left for the United States with the aim of 'killing two birds with one stone'. One, was visit old acquaintances while on vacation and secondly, to find a job as a nurse in New York. She succeeded in both, and eventually migrated to the United States. Soon after her return, and unknown to her I left our home and headed for Torani to stay awhile with my father.

On my return to Georgetown, I resumed duties at Boyer's Furniture Store and booked a room at a boarding house owned by a school friend's father.

ON THE MOVE WITH AUNT GERTIE

Constant moving from one rented house to another was occasioned by race riots and political and ethnic violence and disturbances in the country, but more particularly manifested in the city of Georgetown in the 1962 to 1964 period.

While living at that time at both Fifth Street Albert town and Forshaw and New Garden Streets Queenstown, I witnessed from the windows of our house the ambushing and senseless beating of Indo- Guyanese by African Guyanese on city streets. It was until Guyana was granted independence with the People's National Congress; the Party led by Forbes Burnham in office that the casus belli came to an end.

The then British Government, in collaboration with the then US administration had conspired with Burnham to foment the disturbances in the colony. Neither did the police nor the armed forces give full and firm support to the then Jagan government to quell the disturbances. The joint effort to remove Jagan from office was reflected in advice from Arthur Schlesinger Jr. a former adviser, to President Kennedy. As he put it; 'An independent British Guiana would under Burnham would cause us many fewer problems than an independent British Guiana under Jagan.'

DENIS AND LEILA

Another factor that influenced our moving from place to place was the fact that on November 23, 1963, at St. George's Cathedral, my aunt's only son Denis married the vivacious Leila Shamyn Alli-Shaw. The fashionable wedding ceremony took place at the St. George's Cathedral while the reception was held at the Park Hotel on Main Street. Amazingly, the wedding took place during the height of the disturbances in the country. Denis was 24 while Leila was 21 years of age at the time of their marriage. Consequently, more room had become necessary since the newly wedded couple came to live with us.

Leila was one of four daughters and one son of Dr. and Mrs. Meer Shafdar Ali-Shaw who came from the island of Wakenaam. Her father was a well known and highly respected medical doctor. He was successful in establishing one of the first, modern private hospitals, located at the corner of Croal and Brummell Place in Georgetown.

Dr. Ali-Shaw established the fabulous 'Golden Lotus' night club, on the northern half of Robb street, between Wellington and Camp streets. His restaurant was one of the better restaurants and night clubs in the city. He later established the 'Half-Way Inn Restaurant and Bar' at Farm village on the East Bank of Demerara. Behind the 'Halfway Inn' was a fruit and vegetable farm as well as a poultry farm branded 'Farm Fresh.' Some products from the farm were used as supplies for his restaurants. Other products were bought by vendors to be sold on the local market Denis and Leila Stuart moved from Queenstown to live at their new home at Farm with their two kids. First came Gregory and later, Denise. Some years later, the entire family migrated to the United States. Denis and Leila have since separated but like Gregory and Denise, they all live in America.

ASSERTING MYSELF: OFF TO TORANI

I had lived with my aunt for almost nine years, but I was growing older and becoming more and more assertive. I wanted to branch out on my own.

One day while my aunt was away at work, I packed my belongings and with help from my Dad's friends I travelled alone all the way to the Torani Scheme, to spend sometime with my Dad. I left a note for my Aunt thanking her for all she had done and wrote that I was leaving for my father at Torani.

I sent a message to Mr. Boyer with my co-worker Samuel Williams or 'Sammy' as we called him, advising our boss that I would be away visiting my father. To get to Torani I had the option of traveling by train from the Central train station located on Lamaha Street facing Carmichael Street or by bus at the terminal located at the eastern front of Stabroek Market.

I chose to travel by bus. It was much cheaper compared to traveling by train. In addition, I could see much more of the countryside. The journey on the 'red' dusty East Coast road always amazed me as I gazed at the beautiful green and lush rice fields, the trenches and swamps filled with brown or clear rain water. The added attraction was the scores of white egrets or 'Gaulins' as they were popularly called by Guyanese.

'Chicken hawks,' one of the three species in the Accipitridae family could be seen perched on the branches of trees hanging over the canals patiently waiting to swoop down with amazing speed and accuracy after spotting with their sharp eyes either a snail or 'creketeh' or the small Kakabelly fish.

On the way to Rosignol, there are some lengthy stretches of road where not a single house could be seen save for the villages whose residents had built their homes on the northern and southern sides of the long, winding, bumpy and dusty public road.

After several stops near train stations at the more densely populated villages, the conductor of the bus built of wood would climb atop the bus laden with baskets, crates and jute bags with all kinds of items brought from the city.

Together, with the owner of the cargo, he would load the items onto waiting 'donkey carts' or 'push carts' or simply leave them on the parapet with their owners who appeared to be waiting on their own means of transportation or engaged in negotiating a good price before moving with what remained to the villages.

While the bus was loading and unloading cargo, two or three local buxom Black women would walk on the left- and right-hand sides of the buses shouting out aloud "get yuh lovely fish and bread! "Yes, get yuh hot and spicy fish and homemade bread!" Only those who could afford would buy, but others like myself who could not afford would watch on and enjoy the scent of the fish and bread being sold from a wooden tray seated on the heads of the women and covered with a lily white piece of cloth held down with clothes pins or the fingers of the women.

While passengers ate their fish and bread, I would observe the goings and comings of people from my window to avoid any stomach driven embarrassment.

The bus rumbled on until we reached the village of Rosignol its final destination. All passengers disembarked after paying their "passage" and headed for the 'Torani,' the ferry that shuttles on the Berbice River between Rosignol and New Amsterdam. The MV Torani was built during the colonial period at Sprostons on Lombard street. It is one of a family of two other ferries, the Makouria and the Malali

The MV Makouria traversed the Demerara River between Georgetown and Vreed-en-Hoop while the MV Malali ploughed the Essequibo River from the village of Parika on the east bank of the river to Adventure village on the Essequibo coast. The ferry had scheduled stops at the island of Wakenaam. Crossing the Berbice River with the MV Torani was a joy to behold with trucks and other vehicles, motor cycles and bicycles on the lower deck with passengers mingling in between. The upper level of the ferry was populated with scores of passengers who preferred to be seated amongst them were many school children.

On arrival at New Amsterdam all passengers disembarked at the stelling. The steamer for Torani would depart just before midnight and arrive at its destination around 5 or 6 am the following morning because of the distance and the stops it made along the way. The family of a friend of my dad gave me food and shelter while in transit from New Amsterdam to Torani.

THE GOING GETS TOUGH

At age 18, I returned to my job in Georgetown after spending about two weeks with my Dad. Mr. Boyer was reluctant to re-hire me but thanks to the intervention of my aunt's friend he conceded. Instead of returning to live with my Aunt, I rented a small room at the Indra mahal Guest House on Wellington Street between Regent and Robb Streets. I lived there until I took up 'residence' at Freedom House, headquarters of the People's Progressive Party (PPP) on Robb street.

The Indra mahal Guest House was part of a three-story building with a bakery on the ground floor.

On the second floor lived the Persaud family. I had attended Our Lady of Fatima Roman Catholic school on Regent Street with the three sons and one daughter.

The Persaud's were very hospitable and respectable family. The boys and I struck up a healthy relationship. I was attracted to their sister Yvonne who was one of brightest girls in our class but who shunned anyone who made a pass at her for fear that her parents would chastise her if it had come to their attention that she encouraged such 'unacceptable' behavior.

I took note of the strong cultural and religious traditions of a typical Guyanese family of East Indian descent. I kept my distance and restrained myself from pushing any amorous ambitions with anyone in the Persaud family.

While I lived at the Persaud's Guest House, I continued working at Boyer's furniture store. From my weekly wages I paid the rent for my room and ate regularly at various snackets and Chinese restaurants. After work I would end up at the PPP's Progressive Library or to watch a film show on the war in Vietnam, or the Civil Rights struggle in the United States using a Russian manufactured 16mm projector.

I wanted to change my job, so I wrote to the Guyana Police Force applying for a job as a member of Special Branch or as a detective with the Criminal Investigation Department.

It was a joy to receive an acknowledgment of my application and the invitation to write the entrance examination. I wrote the exam along with several other applicants at a building on Camp street belonging to Booker Group of Companies. I never heard from the Force again. I left my job at the furniture store hoping that before I exhausted by meager savings, I would have found another job. I never did.

I wrote several applications, visited many offices and stores enquiring about vacancies but without success. On returning one day at the guest house to my astonishment I found that my room was burgled. My savings were all gone. I was devastated. I had stashed away sufficient money to pay for another two weeks rent and some extra cash for meals but now I was pennilessness.

In the wake of such dire circumstances, I immediately went to party headquarters and explained the situation to Comrade George Lee who had become a close friend. After George had consulted with his senior party comrades, I was allowed to sleep at nights at Freedom House.

I sold all the household items I had accumulated including my bicycle to CJ's a small store on Wellington street that bought and sold second hand items, in that way I managed to accumulate some badly needed cash.

In the midst of all these happenings I learnt that my Aunt Gertie had migrated to the United States. She never returned to Guyana.

JOB HUNTING

At Freedom House I slept on an old abandoned desk on the upper floor of the building. A stack of old magazines was used as a pillow. My clothes were stored in a covered wooden box hidden at the back of the building. An outhouse made of corrugated sheets was at my disposal. Baths were done in the open from a standpipe aback the building.

I was advised that all my personal activities must cease by 7 am each morning and that I must be out of the building by 7:30am, half an hour before the offices were open for business.

During the day I would go job hunting but with little or no success.

The only qualifications I had were those of the College of Preceptors examination and the one subject in English having succeeded at the General Certificate of Education (GCE) exam.

I finally managed to get a part- time job at the 'Le Ponsietta' a private club and restaurant on Church street, a few doors away from the Public Free Library. The proprietor of the club was a French immigrant resident in Guyana. My job was to tidy up the interior of the club each morning and to remain there until about three in the afternoon until the Frenchman returned. My services were not needed during the club's business hours. The wages I received was enough to keep me going on food and to purchase personal necessities.

'Johno's' at the corner of Robb and Wellington streets was my favourite shop for midday meals. His dhall puri, boiled channa and potatoe (alloo) balls were affordable and filling. My favourite soft drink was the 'Icee orange' manufactured by Banks DIH.

While at Freedom House, I read anything and everything I could put my hands on, magazines, periodicals, newspapers, books and booklets even pamphlets. I joined the party's 'Progressive Library' and frequented the Michael Forde Bookshop. With nothing much to do during the day, reading and listening to political and ideological lectures and panel discussions, blended with the street sense I had acquired over the years, gave me a perspective that was to be with me throughout my political career. When I discovered that the 'Progressive Library' lacked certain books that I wanted to read, I joined the Public Free Library in downtown Georgetown only to discover that Mrs. Jagan was a long-standing member of that library. She would walk all the way from Freedom House to the library and back. On some occasions we would do so together if the dates for returning the books coincided.

One evening, while reading a publication from a West German NGO, I came across a small article in 'fine print' revealing that the German Ambassador to Guyana was a former nazi.

At that time a full-fledged German Embassy was to located on North Road and Company Path obliquely opposite Saint George's Cathedral.

I was intrigued at unearthing this interesting piece of information. I handed it to Mrs. Jagan on her arrival at the office the following day.

The expose was published in the MIRROR newspaper and with the blink of an eye the Nazi ambassador abandoned his post and slipped out of the country.

GETTING POLITICALLY INVOLVED

Encouraged by Cheddi Jagan who I met while he was doing some purchases at Boyer's furniture store for a house, he was building at plantation Bel Air, I joined the Progressive Youth Organization (PYO) and the People's Progressive Party (PPP) in 1968. Dr. Jagan and his family lived at the time in a house rented from Mr. Ernest Boyer at 213, Camp street a few houses just before Lamaha Street in Georgetown.

At the end of every month, Mr. Boyer sent me to Freedom House to collect the rent from Mrs. Jagan. That's how I got to know her.

During that same year I worked on a part-time basis for the Party in the run up to local government elections under the guidance of EMG 'coco' Wilson, one the greatest and humane Black leaders of the PPP, a teacher, mentor and above all, a disciplinarian and master organiser.

POLITICAL EDUCATION

In 1970, I attended a three-week live -in course at Accabre College of Social Sciences- the ideological School of the PPP. The college was located at Land of Canaan, a small village on the East Bank of Demerara.

Attending Accabre was a once-in-a life-time experience for me. Whilst there, I received great educational lectures in politics, ideology and philosophy all delivered by foremost leaders of the Party at the time.

Accabre College was launched in the mid-1960's. At that time, the college was located at the village of Success on the East Coast of Demerara. The college was named after Accabre, one of the more disciplined and military conscious leaders of the Berbice slave rebellion of February,1763. It was at this institution that the Party prepared its cadres politically and ideologically.

On completing the course at Accabre, I was temporarily employed at the Michael Forde Bookshop located on the ground floor of Freedom House. The Bookshop was popular at the time because it was the only one of its kind in the country that sold Marxist classics, progressive literature, magazines and newspapers from Cuba, China, Russia, Africa, Latin America and the Middle East. What made the bookstore even more popular was the wide range of school books that were readily available.

Just before the end of the August holidays parents and guardians would rush to the bookshop in large numbers to purchase school books. This was the most exciting period for us at the bookshop. Extra hands had to be hired to assist and we would spend long hours after the shop was closed to replace books that were sold.

In an effort to expand sales, branches of the bookshop were opened on the Corentyne and Essequibo Coast and at the North West District. The bottom flats of the homes of party comrades were used for this purpose.

But the bookshop soon felt the pangs of corruption and theft when the manager Robert Jagnandan and his assistant Kishore were found guilty of theft of huge sums of money belonging to the bookshop. The two men soon disappeared. According to reliable sources they both left the country.

MY POLITICAL UPBRINGING

As a member of the Party's youth organization, selling party literature in the towns and villages, joining in picketing exercises, going on house to house membership and literature sales campaigns was both fun and educational for me and other PYO members of my time. Fun because as teams we enjoyed working, sharing experiences and participating in many other sharing activities together.

As youngsters we were led by one or two senior party leaders who guided us along the way teaching us how to approach prospective members or supporters in African or Indian dominated or mixed communities. We were taught how to answer questions posed by enquiring persons from all walks of life. Complicated questions and answers were left to the seniors but we stood by to listen and learn. In effect, this was the real political upbringing that created a generation of party cadres who emerged from the end of 1960's up to the end of the 80's within the ranks of the Party.

It took almost twenty years for the party to create a solid generation of cadres who would be the reservoir from where the party would draw its future leaders. I was fortunate and indeed proud to be among that generation of party cadres.

It was in the course of the many aspects of party work that I came to realize how painstaking and methodical political work is required to build and sustain an organizational structure that would endure for years to come.

But what is equally important is that the leadership of the organization must be prepared to service that structure and above all, support the foot soldiers on the ground who work so hard, day and night to keep the organizational machinery intact and ready at all times to respond to any eventuality.

This appreciation of what is required of party organization put me in good stead later in my political life as I was called upon to go out to do political work as an activist this time, with my own team of younger comrades.

During my days as member of the PYO I grew to appreciate what was politically practical but also the theoretical aspects that must go hand in hand with practice.

I joined the PYO in 1968 at a time when the party had decided to resuscitate its youth arm after the latter had become dormant with the removal of the PPP from office in 1964 and a split in the PYO in 1965 following the expulsion of Moses Bhagwan, Chairman of the organization. Bhagwan's expulsion had repercussions. Some of the top leaders of the PYO including; Neville Anibourne, George David, Desmond Shepherd and Leslie Premdass, left the organization.

Annibourne went over to the PNC while Bhagwan went to study law.

Other PYO members including Ramon Gaskin, Alfred Jadunauth, 'Boyo' Ramsaroop, Narbada Persaud, Rajkumarie Mudas, Bryan Rodway, Johnny

Kowlessar, Raymon Mandal and Joseph O'Lall among others proceeded on scholarships to study various disciplines in Eastern European socialist countries. On their return, some fell under the influence of anti-PPP, ultra-left influences, while others remained faithful to the PPP. Narbada Persaud, 'Boyo' Ramsaroop and Joseph O'Lall were among such persons.

I knew many of these individuals personally notwithstanding the fact that I had joined the PYO in 1968, a mere three years after the internal turbulences that had crippled the organization. By that time, many of the comrades who had been trained abroad began returning to their homeland. Others returned much later.

STARTING MY POLITICAL ACTIVISM

Many staunch young members, who had stuck with the party notwithstanding it being cheated out of office were mobilized to take up the challenge to put the PYO back on its feet.

Already active in politics – 1970s

Amongst them were; Sheik Feroze Mohammed, Inderjeet Singh, Narbada Persaud, Rudolph Persaud, George Lee, Harold Snagg, Dutchin, Meethulall Mangal, Ally Baksh, Ricabdeo Chowbay, Naseeb Gafar, Komal Chand, Albert Bodhoo, Harrynarine Nawbatt, Roy Bishamber, Moses Nagamootoo, Halim Majeed, Aria Thantony, Ruth Sukwah, and many others.

The first congress of the PYO was held in 1968 at Accabre College, the party school at a village called Land of Canaan on the East Bank, Demerara. I could not attend that congress because I did not qualify to do so, since I had just joined both the party and the PYO in that very year. I was however at Freedom House when some of the delegates and observers returned and spoke about the success of the congress and announced that that Sheik Feroze Mohammed had received the highest number of votes at the Congress.

At the first meeting of the newly elected Central Committee of the PYO Feroze was elected First Secretary of the organization. The PYO under the leadership of Feroze, once again, became a vibrant and militant youth organization in Guyana. Its only rival was the Young Socialist Movement (YSM) youth arm of the PNC.

There was another government-sponsored youth organization called the Guyana Assembly of Youth (GAY) but it was basically a talk shop and debating club of Black middle-class youths who looked to the government of the day for jobs, recognition and sponsorship for their outreach activities. The PYO had groups in almost every village of Guyana. Its organised membership campaigns, picketing demonstrations and public meetings. It held seminars and lectures and sent its members to Accabre College. I recall three of the many picketing exercises as I participated in that were to influence my political upbringing in years to come. First was a counter picketing exercise on Robb street in front of Freedom House that was mounted by the party.

The United Force and other fringe elements had mounted a picketing exercise in front of Freedom House calling for the withdrawal of Soviet and other Warsaw Pact troops from Czechoslovakia.

Twenty-three years later, following the end of the Second World War, a socialist bloc country comprising Albania, Bulgaria, Czechoslovakia, The German Democratic Republic, Hungary, Mongolia, Poland, Romania and the USSR and Yugoslavia had emerged.

To consolidate themselves economically, these countries except Albania and Yugoslavia established the Council for Mutual Economic Assistance (CMEA or COMECON) in 1949. The CMEA was in response to the establishment of the Committee for European Economic Cooperation which later became the European Economic Community (EEC)

Later, in 1955 seven of the Eastern European socialist countries signed onto the Warsaw Pact in response to the establishment of the North Atlantic Treaty Organization (NATO) the military alliance between the United States and the countries of Western Europe who had benefited greatly from the Marshall Plan. By the mid- 1960's the socialist bloc countries particularly Czechoslovakia began experiencing economic and financial difficulties.

Under tremendous pressure from the Czech people, the government of Alexander Dubcek decided to implement a number of reforms that would bring it closer to the economies of the Western European countries. This was opposed by the other Warsaw Pact countries for fear that it would result in other countries in the bloc following suit. Thus, under the pretext of protecting socialism and its economic and military gains Warsaw Pact troops entered Prague. At the political level, changes were affected in the leadership of the ruling communist party and government.

It was this development in the socialist bloc in Europe and the fact that the PPP was already inclined ideologically and politically to support the foreign policy of the Communist Party of the Soviet Union that parties like the PPP was motivated to react in the way it did to the UF's picket opposing the invasion of Czechoslovakia. I remember vividly that mid-morning, as I stood witnessing the UF's supporters quietly flaunting their placards on the street, inside Freedom House Mrs. Jagan called out to the employees at the time in the office and handed to them cardboard mounts and markers and told them to copy on them slogans which she herself had written.

Placards were them handed out to everyone present including me and we marched down the stairs onto the streets with Dr. and Mrs. Jagan leading the way. No sooner had we taken to the street, about half hour after, the UF protesters folded their placards, piled into a waiting Volkswagen and drove away.

A few days after the Party organised a public lecture at Freedom House's auditorium. Dr. Jagan delivered the lecture on the subject to a packed audience from who extended general support for the party's position on the matter.

My second experience had to do with a visit to Guyana by the American business tycoon and Vice President Nelson Rockefeller who was touring Latin America and the Caribbean to drum up support for the US foreign policy in general and its war in Vietnam in particular. In preparation for his visit in August 1974, me and a number of PYO members, including me, were mobilized a few days before and briefed on the course of action to be taken to protest the visit.

Unlike other protest actions there was some secrecy involved in this one. On the front of the T shirts we were handed was printed 'ROCKY GO HOME ' while at the back the initials PYO with its symbol could be seen. We were instructed to wear these under a shirt or jersey. Nelson Rockefeller had arrived in the country and was scheduled to address the National Assembly. This was to be the venue of our protest action.

We arrived intermittently in pairs at the appointed day and time and took up our positions on the pavement opposite the parliament building. Rockefeller arrived at approximately 2:45 pm. In a matter of seconds just before the vehicle transporting the Vice President drove directly in front of us, we all took off our shirts and shouted; "Rocky go home!!" "Rocky go home!!"

Almost immediately about dozen plain clothes policemen surrounded and arrested us and carted us off to the Brickdam police station where we were held until Rockefeller headed for the airport following his address to members of the National Assembly.

We were subsequently released without any charges being laid.

Finally, worthy of mention were protest demonstrations in front the still standing old US embassy building to the northern side of the New Thriving Chinese Restaurant on Main Street. There we mounted numerous protests against the war in Vietnam. On one occasion we burnt the US flag and an effigy of the then US President, Richard Nixon

Then there was the protest in 1974 against the military dictatorship in Brazil. This was held outside the Cathedral of the Immaculate Conception or Brickdam Cathedral where I presented a letter of protest to the then Brazilian Ambassador;

A memorable protest was a demonstration in 1986 against the use of the thallium chemical imported by the Guyana Sugar Corporation to kill off a rat infestation in the sugarcane fields. This practice resulted in death by poisoning of several sugar workers. Diamond and LBI sugar estates were closed as a result of reports that a number of sugar workers were affected by the chemical substance.

I was called upon by Mrs. Janet Jagan to organize a protest action on the matter and to do so in a manner to capture the public's attention. I called upon Comrade Kellawan Lall to assist me. 'Peck' as he was popularly called, had returned from studies at the Patrice Lumumba Friendship University in Moscow. He was a talented Comrade with some creative artistic skills. I suggested to Peck that we outfit the protestors with black 'ponchos' and paint their faces in a death-like white color. He agreed.

A few bolts of black cotton donated by friends of the Party were cut into ponchos. Placards were written on old pieces of discarded cardboard.

I visited the popular Lee's funeral parlor at Lamaha and Camp streets. I knew the manageress there. My request to her was to loan me an old wooden coffin for use in the protest. The kind lady willingly obliged pro bono. We applied and got permission from the police for permission to have a procession through the downtown area Georgetown. Just before the activity started, I was summoned to Dr Jagan's office. He enquired whether it was true that I had requested money to pay for a coffin. My answer was in the negative. He said 'ok' and wished me well for the protest action. Dr. Jagan eventually joined the protest.

With just about twelve of us, and with Dr. Jagan leading the march through the city streets, the protest action was a tremendous success. Its creative but sombre message attracted the attention large groupings of people as we proceeded in kind of slow march pulling the coffin on an oblong wooden platform with wheels through the streets of downtown Georgetown as if in a funeral procession. The press was also present and carried a full story on the protest with photos in the next days' newspapers. Guysuco was forced to halt the use of the chemical in the sugarcane fields.

The PPP was known for its militancy in and out of parliament. Dr Jagan always emphasized the need to combine the parliamentary with extra- parliamentary struggle. There was hardly an international issue that had to do with the struggles of the oppressed people in Africa, the Middle East, Asia or Latin America against military or pro- fascist dictatorships that the party did not take up at one level or another.

From its beginnings the Party was moulded in the spirit of internationalism. Janet Jagan is on record in her prolific writings about the internationalist spirit of the party giving examples too many to mention.

I grew up in the party with that very spirit flowing in my veins. Thousands if not a few millions of dollars were invested in me by the party to ensure that, on the one hand, I had a fairly good grasp of international affairs even though I never had a college or university education on the subject.

On the other hand, I suppose the party did this investment because it wanted to ensure continuation and representation of its internationalist outlook whenever I was sent abroad to represent it at conferences or congresses of fraternal parties and movements around the world. In retrospect, it would seem that my journey into the international area started in 1972 when I travelled to Cuba as the representative of the PYO. Then in 1973, I travelled to East Berlin, capital of the then German Democratic Republic to participate in the 10th World Festival of youth and students. But while facilitating my travels abroad, the party made sure that my political work was well balanced and not restricted to overseas travel. During this period and up to the time when I became the Party's General Secretary no one ever told me that they had to fetch me on their backs.

In December, 1978 I represented the PYO at a youth and student seminar in Nicosia, Cyprus from there I travelled to Beirut, Lebanon to join in the anniversary celebrations of the founding of the Palestinian Liberation Organization (PLO). Interestingly, on returning home via Port of Spain, Trinidad and Tobago, I was detained at Piarco International Airport by that country's Immigration authorities accompanied by Special Branch of the T&T Police Force who interrogated me for a few hours about my visit to Lebanon.

This experience taught me how the intelligence services of some countries collaborated with each other in respect to the movements of persons of interest to them.

At home I was deeply involved in the July 16, 1973 elections. Interestingly, soon after those elections, in September of that same year Fidel Castro visited Guyana. The PPP was not pleased with the timing of the visit, it seemed as if the Cubans were legitimizing a regime that had just rigged an election with the help of the military. To show its displeasure and to the surprise of many, the PPP mounted a picketing exercise protesting the visit by Castro.

ITABO

I met many of these self-made intellectuals, their friends and PYO supporters at a place called 'ITABO,' their afternoon 'hang out' on Murray Street now Quamina street, in Georgetown. Itabo was known for the robust political and ideological debates that took place amongst the youthful and exuberant regulars over coffee and cigarettes. There they exchanged views on several topics such as the various forms of struggle necessary for a socialist Guyana and about the direction the PPP should take to achieve that goal. At age 18 I became a regular visitor at that 'hang out.' It was at 'ITABO' that I learnt about the differences on strategy a tactics that broken out between the Communist Party of China and the Communist Party of the Soviet Union. The discussants soon found themselves in groupings branded as 'Stalinists' or 'Maoists' or 'Leninists.'

BRINDLEY HORATIO BENN

Brindley Horatio of a Benn, a former Minister of Agriculture in the 1957 to 1964 PPP

Government had by that time broken with Dr. Jagan over ideological issues and had established the Working People's Vanguard Party (WPVP) a pro-Maoist party.

He had a small office at 69, Main Street in Georgetown which became the centre for the distribution of literature published by the Communist Party of China and Mao Tse Tung's 'Little Red Book'

What amazed me was that even though Cheddi and Brindley had parted ways on ideological grounds they still maintained contact with each other by exchanging literature.

From time to time I was tasked with the responsibility of taking correspondence either from Dr. or Mrs. Jagan to Brindley's Main Street office and was able to see at first hand the cramped conditions under which he worked and published a pamphlet titled at one time 'The Vanguard', another time 'The Patriot' and yet another time ' Dayclean'. For some reason the publishers of the pamphlet kept changing its name maybe to avoid legal penalties. Benn was assisted by two of his loyal colleagues; Thelma Reis and Victor Downer.

I continued to be a keen listener to the heated ideological discussions at 'ITABO' for about one year but it was the cultural evenings, when there would be readings of Martin Carter's and other poems that I enjoyed even more.

As time went by, I became disillusioned with 'ITABO' since the exchanges there became sterile. The truth is the debates were never ending and as such no action followed. I left the ITABO never to return again. Freedom House on Robb street became my Mecca.

The next opportunity I had to be involved in an ITABO- type organization was during the 1969 to 1971 period A long standing PYO activist by the name of Clement David who worked as a security detail at Freedom House and who had introduced me to 'ITABO' soon recognized that I no longer frequented the 'hang out' and enquired as to the reason, I simply told him "nothing."

I remember well that grin on his face while he stroked his beard and said to me; "well, you're at the right place now."

1968 and 1969 were tumultuous years for me in my personal life. I became so involved in the politics of the PPP and its youth arm that I did not realize how far out from the shore I had swam before the tides of politics would sweep me away forever from the mundane and placid every day life of a 19 year old boy growing up in a newly independent Guyana.

An Independent Guyana with Dr. Jagan out of office was bewildering to me as it was for thousands of Guyanese who saw Dr. Jagan as the true fighter for our country's independence.

THE MOVEMENT AGAINST OPPRESSION (MAO)

Sometime in 1971, a police patrol in Georgetown shot and killed a young Black youth who, according to the police was a 'wanted criminal.' The execution-style action by the police drew condemnation from sections of the city's population and as a result, a protest march through the streets of Georgetown was organized. The march saw the participation of a wide cross-section of city folk including university academics. The PPP took part in the march, it's Representatives were Cheddi Jagan, Harold Snagg and Clement Rohee.

Soon after the march, with a sense of urgency and determination, the organizers of the march went a step further, they formed themselves into an Organisation they named '' Movement Against Oppression (MAO). MAO was headquartered in the bottom flat of a building at New Market street in the 'Tiger Bay' area. The building was the property of Hubert Urling a/ka 'German'

The 'Tiger Bay' area had a reputation for being 'off limits' since the perception was that it was infested with criminals, rogues and vagabonds. The police patrolled the area to the extent that the residents felt that they were being unnecessarily targeted and harassed and bad for the small shops that populated the community.

The membership of MAO, the majority of whom were middle class academics, university intellectuals, German and some of his key men, grass roots youngsters like me and Harold Snagg who represented the PPP, as well as some lumpen elements who had gravitated to the organization. We would gather mainly on Sunday mornings or Saturdays after lunch, to discuss the political and economic situation in the country and its impact on the poor and dispossessed.

Persons like Andaye, Bonita Bourne, Dr.Joshua Ramsammy, Prof.Clive Thomas, Brian Rodway, Alfred Jadunath, Errol and Mrs. Fraser, Dr. Omawale, Marc Mathews, Eusi Kwayana, Diane Mathews and Dr. Maurice Odle, would engage in lengthy intellectual exchanges spattered with some elements of Marxism, Maoism, Fanonism, anti-imperialism, Black nationalism but fundamentally anti-establishment in character.

These were left-wing radicals but brilliant sons and daughters of Guyana probably the best of the crop at that time, but amazingly due to their petit-bourgeois class and academic orientation, situating the working people's problems in the context of their academic analysis is what was woefully lacking.

Sometimes I could not figure out 'head from tail' what they were talking about.

To my mind had it not been for Eusi Kwayana, Andaye, Brian Rodway, German and his crew, who had their feet on the ground, the grouping would have lost its way wrangling intellectually over matters that were rather esoterica making it almost impossible for initiatives to be taken representing residents in depressed communities.

MAO served the purpose for its existence. It raised its public profile by effective representation on social and economic problems affecting communities where the poor and downtrodden lived.

German with some members of MAO - 1971

But the political situation was evolving rapidly. A number of individuals in MAO advanced a case for the organization to be transformed into a 'Third (political) Force' since according to them, 'the plague was on both houses' meaning it was the PPP and the PNC that was responsible for the suffering and economic marginalization of the working people.

Others members were unsupportive. They preferred MAO to remain neutral politically but to continue making representation for poor people wherever and

75

whenever needs be. Eventually, the curtains were drawn finally for MAO. Some say that MAO was infiltrated by agents of the Special Branch of the Guyana Force Police and that this contributed to the dissenting views within the organization.

Not surprisingly, those members who belonged to the University of Guyana- based Ratoon Group and, who had pushed for a political formation, entered into an alliance with the Working People's Vanguard Party (WPVP), the Indian People's Revolutionary Associates (IPRA) and the African Society for Cultural Relations with Independent Africa (ASCRIA) and launched the Working People's Alliance (WPA) in 1974.

MY FIRST TRIP ABROAD

In 1972, I was nominated to travel to Cuba to join the Julio António Mella international volunteer brigade. This opportunity marked a big turning point in my youthful political life.

To travel to Cuba in those days was problematic. Cuba was in the throes of a severe economic blockade. It was not easy to get there.

I had two options; to travel through several countries in Latin America or to travel to London, then to Moscow and from Moscow to Havana. I chose the Latin American itinerary.

On the morning before leaving for the airport Mrs. Janet Jagan presented me with a small blue green hand bag marked BOAC the initials for British Overseas Airways Corporation, the forerunner of British Airways

In the bag was a Collins English- Spanish pocket dictionary, a pen, a scratch pad and some US dollars.

I departed Guyana in February 1972.

The first leg of my journey was Georgetown to Port of Spain, Trinidad and Tobago.

From Port-of- Spain I travelled to Caracas, Venezuela where I spent one night.

On exiting the Maiquetia International Airport at Caracas, I was amazed to find that the airport taxis were either a Cadillac, a De Soto or a Pontiac motor car.

Thinking it might be too expensive to hop into one of the exquisite and sleek looking vehicles to take me to my hotel located about forty-five minutes from the airport, I looked around for an Austin Cambridge or a Morris Oxford motor car, the type of vehicle available at home that time, but I could not find any.

Realizing that Venezuela was more oriented to the United States unlike Guyana, a former British colony, it subsequently dawned upon me that I had no alternative but to enjoy the pleasure of riding in one of the imposing and fashionable American made cars.

This was my first lesson in practical politics that appeared to be contradictory to the revolutionary pro-poor lessons I was taught at the Party school.

Considering myself a 22-year-old recently minted youthful enthusiast, here I was in Caracas, Venezuela's booming capital city, to the west of Guyana and riding in a Pontiac to the Hilton, one of the iconic international hotels, symbolic of a thriving free market economy.

From Caracas I traveled to Bogota, Colombia and then to Santiago, Chile. My itinerary envisaged me spending a few days in Santiago. From there I was scheduled to fly direct to Havana, Cuba. The travel agency in Guyana had advised us that two airlines, Cubana de Aviacion and LanChile were available to travel from Santiago to Havana. I had a confirmed reservation to travel to Havana with Cubana de Aviacion

ALLENDE'S CHILE

Having ensconced myself at the Hotel Conquistador located in Santiago, the capital city, I made contact with the comrades whose names were given to me before I left Guyana.

At the time of my stay in Chile, the country was experiencing tremendous political and social upheaval.

Opposition street protests against the pro-socialist policies of the Popular Unity government of Salvador Allende were an every-day occurrence in the city.

Not far from my hotel, I encountered street protests with scores of women banging pots and pans, while gangs known as 'Los Momios' roamed the city streets targeting persons perceived to be supporters of Allende's Unidad Popular government.

Salvador Allende had been elected in 1970 as President of the Republic. Allende headed a coalition known as the Unidad Popular Government. Allende was one of the founders of the Partido Socialista de Chile. As President of Chile, Allende's Government initiated a much-needed agrarian reform and nationalized Chile's copper industry. His government brought many large-scale industries under state control. Reforms were implemented in Chile's education and health care systems as well as in public administration.

While in Santiago, I had the opportunity to visit La Moneda palace, the seat of the Chilean government where Allende's Official office was located. My visit to the Palace was to make contact, and to meet separately with the Prensa Latina representative and the Chilean youth and student movement associated with Allende's Popular Unity Government. The media together with Chile's latifundistas and the industrial bourgeoisie, with help from the CIA fomented destabilizing activities through out the country including strikes by truck drivers and employees in the state sector as well as the small and medium sized businesses. The plan was to cripple the economy.

The nationalization of the copper industry was the main bone of contention between the Chilean Government and the transnational corporations opposed to government take over.

I was in Chile just two years into Allende's government and it was evident to me that opposition forces, working with external influences had become a powerful political force in the country.

My Chilean friends tried in vain to secure a seat for me on either of two flights destined to Havana, Lan Chile or Cubana de Aviacion. Eventually, we had no other option but to adjust at no cost, my itinerary to travel Cuba via Mexico. Having obtained my Mexican visa, I departed Chile for Mexico City. I spent one night at a hotel near the international airport in Mexico City.

The following morning, after a hearty breakfast free of cost, I departed for the airport and thence to Cuba.

FINALLY, CUBA

My arrival at the Aeropuerto Internacional Jose Marti at Havana in early March 1972, found me feeling unwell. During the flight on Cuban airline, I was offered a Cuban cigar, un cafecito and a schnapp of Cuban rum. My exuberant indulgence in the alcoholic beverage and tobacco turned out to be a physical disaster.

While awaiting transportation from the airport to el campamento where I was to be accommodated for the rest of my stay in Cuba, I had a spell of vomiting and diarrhea. It took a heavy toll on my physical well-being so much so that I had to rest for about an hour before I was able to board the bus and head out to my destination.

LA BRIGADA INTERNACIONAL, 'JULIO ANTONIO MELLA'

I spent eight months in Cuba during which time I joined with volunteers from other countries to help construct a basic secondary school in the countryside. We formed the Brigada International: Julio Antonio Mella. Mella was the founder of the

Federation of University Students (FEU) of Cuba and the Cuban Communist Party (PCC).

On completion, the school was inaugurated by Fidel Castro who named it after the great Bulgarian anti-fascist fighter and patriot, Georgie Dimitrov. I worked at the carpentry section made up mainly of Cubans along with an Italian, an Argentinian and a Costa Rican. While in Cuba with help of the Costa Rican comrade and others I learnt the Spanish language, which helped me communicate with the Cuban people and to understand what the socialist project on the island was all about.

One day while at work, an announcement was made that delegates attending the congress of the Communist Party of Cuba, and who had volunteers working at the site would pay a visit to the location. The day the delegates arrived, I was pleasantly surprised to see Comrade Shreechand and Clinton Collymore. They were representing the Party at the congress.

After a long chat, I took them on a tour around the worksite and the campamento which was not too far away. The joy of meeting with my own comrades after being away from home for such a long time was tremendous. When Shreechand and Collymore boarded the bus to leave I felt satisfied that at least comrades from the party had visited and witnessed the contribution the party's youth organization was making in fulfillment of its commitment to international solidarity.

After the school was commissioned, all the volunteers were taken on a tour of all the provinces of Cuba. For me this was really an educational exercise.

The tour was by an old greyhound bus. It lasted for about one month because we spent about two days visiting places of interest and meeting with local organizations at each province.

The tour helped us gain a better appreciation of Cuba's history but above, all we were given the opportunity to witness at first hand, the challenges facing the Cuban people, as well as their resolve to defend their achievements.

Life for the Cuban people was difficult in those days. Rationing of basic food items was introduced and public transportation was insufficient to facilitate the millions in Havana.

How they manage, it's hard to say, but I have to concede that the resilience and fortitude of the Cuban people in the face of these tremendous hardships was something to be admired and respected.

The US imposed blockade continues to have a tremendous impact on the economic and social life of the Cuban people. It was tough, real tough at that time. But the Cubans are a tough and resilient people. Indeed, it was enlightening to witness and to read about the tremendous sacrifices they made to bring their country to what it is today:

Cuba is a country with a booming tourism industry, a vibrant manufacturing industry especially in pharmaceuticals and agri-food processing, and a world class public health and educational system - deemed by PAHO/WHO and UNICEF to be the most advanced in Latin America. Cubans are now free to travel internationally. Thousands travel to Guyana on a daily basis to purchase, and take back with them huge amounts of clothing, footwear and electronic equipment. Back in Cuba, such items are sold freely on the local market. That market is gradually being freed up due to the new economic policies adopted by the Cuban government.

These new economic and social policies are enshrined in a new constitution adopted by the Cuban National Assembly in 2019. On my return to Guyana in October 1972 I threw myself fully into the vibrant political life of the Party, it's youth arm and politics of the country as a whole.

With the approval of the Editor of the MIRROR newspaper, I settled down to writing a series of articles for the newspaper about my stay in Cuba these included;
'

'La Brigada Internacional' The Brigade's origin,' (14/1 / '72) The Inauguration...and the honour of Meeting Fidel,' (21/11/ '72) Touring the land of liberty', 28/11/ '72) and later 'Remember the Bay of Pigs,' (14/4/ '73).

THE GUYANA CUBA FRIENDSHIP SOCIETY

With the presence in Guyana of a large number of individuals who had either studied in or visited Cuba during the 1960's as well as the fact that there were

81

many other supporters of the Revolution who were either party members or persons who were privately employed, there was a general consensus among us that there was a need to establish a Guyana Cuba Friendship Society. The PPP supported the initiative.

The Society was launched on July 7, 1974 at the Georgetown Reading Rooms situated at the time in the building housing the National Museum that once housed the Royal Agricultural and Cultural Society (RACS) facing Guyana stores. Dr. Cheddi Jagan was the guest speaker at the launch of the Society.

The Friendship Society had its own constitution, membership cards and calendar of activities based on historical and contemporary aspects of the evolution of Cuban society and the 1959 revolution. The Friendship Society's membership grew exponentially. A general membership meeting was held at which the constitution was adopted and an Executive Committee elected that included: Lallbachan Lallbahadur (President), Dr. Moti Lall (Vice President) and Clement Rohee (Secretary). Members of the committee included, Charles Cassatto, Cecil Ramsingh, Maurice Herbert and Louis Mitchell. The Society held lectures, symposia, photographic exhibitions, and fund-raising activities in various parts of the country. The Cuban Embassy in Guyana supported the activities by sending its Ambassador to speak at functions hosted by the organization.

Later, after Lallbachan Lallbahadur had defected to the PNC, Dr. Moti Lall, a specialist in lung diseases who had returned home after graduating in the German Democratic Republic (GDR) was elected President of the Society So influential and broad-based had the Society become that the ruling PNC, by way of a political agreement, sought to have representatives sit on the Executive Committee of the organization without being duly elected at an Annual General Meeting of the Society's membership to do so

After much discussion, it became clear that the real motive of the PNC was to seize control of the organization. The matter was brought to the attention of the general membership of the society who rejected the government's overtures and resolved to maintain the independence of the Society.

GUYANA CUBA RELATIONS

The PPP's relations with Cuba had its ups and downs. In the early 1960's the PPP Government of the 1957-1964 period extended support and solidarity to the young Cuban Revolution. That support went against the blockade imposed by the then US administration. Premier Jagan's support and solidarity with Cuba was driven principally by ideological convictions as well as the exigencies of the difficult economic and social conditions that obtained in Guyana at the time due to the actions of internal reactionary political forces to destabilize the Jagan administration because of its left leaning, pro-socialist and pro-poor policies.

The Jagan government broke the US-imposed blockade of Cuba by opening trade relations and promoting cultural cooperation with the island. Shipments of timber and rice from Guyana in exchange for petroleum, steel, generators and cement from Cuba were very prominent during that period and the exchange of cultural groups was actively pursued notwithstanding efforts to sabotage the boats bringing cargoes to Port Georgetown. In the pipeline, was a loan of US$5 million towards the cost of constructing a $32 million hydro-electric power plant at the Malali Falls on the left bank of the Demerara River and a further loan for the establishment of a wood pulp plant.

With the change of Government in 1964, the PNC/UF coalition government, under pressure from the Kennedy administration, shelved all the PPP's development cooperation programmes with Cuba. However, years after, when Burnham's relations with the US went sour, he opportunistically embraced Cuba, pretending to be anti-imperialist and non-aligned, Cuba reciprocated and went so far as to grant its highest, Jose Marti National Award to Burnham totally oblivious to Burnham's predisposition to rig national elections to stay in power.

The PPP protested the granting of the award to Burnham on the ground that he was undeserving as a dictator who rigged national elections in a country where the constitutional rights of the Guyanese people were trampled upon and where democracy and the rule of law were non-existent. Throughout this period, and while in opposition for twenty eighty years the PPP maintained Party to Party relations with the Communist Party of Cuba, (PCC) but the relationship had its high and low points from time to time.

 While PPP watchers would have expected its relationship with the PCC to be fraternal and unshakeable in the true sense of the words, ironically, it was during the 1974 to 1985 period that the PPP's relations with Cuba were strained and was known publicly. It was only years after, during the Bharat Jagdeo administration that relations with Cuba at the government to government level improved significantly but at the Party to Party level the relations remained luke-warm to say the least.

It is apposite to recall that, following the removal of the PPP from office in1964, that there were some in the leadership of the PPP who argued that the Party and government should not have flirted with the Soviet Union nor embraced the Cuban Revolution knowing the US policy towards Cuba and its imposition of the blockade. Those individuals were of the view that it was adventurous and fool hardy to have embarked on such a policy. But what those individuals failed to recognize were the statesman-like efforts by Jagan himself to engage directly with the Kennedy administration particularly with a view to convincing them that there was nothing to fear ideologically nor strategically insofar as the PPP's and Jagan personal objectives were concerned. Dr. Jagan had gone as far as to propose entering into discussion with the US administration towards a treaty settlement which would reassure the United States Government, on issues of hemispheric security.

SOLIDARITY WITH CHILE

Back home I received the news on September 11, (1973) about the overthrow of Allende's government by a military coup and the bloodbath that followed. My heart full of pain and sorrow, went out to my Chilean friends and comrades who had demonstrated firmness in their friendship and solidarity with us in the Party and youth organization.

Following a suggestion by Janet Jagan a few of us in the Party and its youth arm set up a Committee for Solidarity with the People of Chile.

On September 23, 1973, at Good Hope on the East Coast of Demerara, the Solidarity Committee and the Party held a mass solidarity rally with the people of Chile where it denounced the military overthrow of Salvador Allende. I had the honour of chairing the event at which Dr. Jagan was the main speaker. Thousands came out in support of the event. It was a massive demonstration of solidarity with the people of Chile, another manifestation of the internationalist spirit of the PPP and its supporters.

One year later, on September 4, 1974, the Burnham dictatorship refused to allow a group of us to lay wreaths in honour of Salvador Allende at the monument dedicated to the founders of the Non-Aligned Movement located at Company Path. Dr Jagan spoke at the event in the presence of over one hundred persons. And Martin Carter paid a moving tribute to the famous Chilean poet Pablo Neruda killed by the military junta.

Forty-seven years after, I have lived to see the spirit of Salvador Allende, Pablo Neruda and Victor Jara alive and well in Chile as the working people, the youths and students take to the streets in the thousands demanding a better life and a change of government.

ELECTIONS 1973

By 1973, I became a full-time employee of the party. I was requested to concentrate my efforts in the city of Georgetown during campaign for the infamous July 1973 general elections. Dr. S.A. Ramjohn, a senior Party leader was responsible for elections work in the Kingston/Queenstown/Alberttown/ North Cummingsburg area. He lived on Lamaha street about two or three doors east of Camp street.

Unknown to the Party's leadership Ramjohn abandoned his post and medical practice and secretly left the country without informing the Party's leadership. I was called upon to fill the gap. The organizational and communication skills I had learnt from EMG Wilson came in handy.

Fortunately for me, the party groups in Georgetown were well organized, active and had a large number of experienced comrades who were seasoned campaigners. The majority of the Comrades were Afro- Guyanese. We worked well as a team.

Those elections were shamelessly rigged with help of the military who intervened in the elections and took effective control of the ballot boxes and handed them over to elements of the so-called 'deep state'

The Army seize ballot boxes - 1973

It was PNC elections machinery operatives who opened the ballot boxes, switched ballots favoring the PPP, replacing them with votes favoring the ruling PNC.

ELECTIONS 1973, THE ARMY INTERVENES

General elections in 1973 was a watershed in Guyana'a chequered history of electoral politics.

That election cost the lives of two young members of the Progressive Youth Organization (PYO)at the Number 64 village, Corentyne, Berbice. In their efforts to protect the ballot boxes, seventeen-year old Jagan Ramessar and forty-three, year old Jack Bhola Nauth (Parmanand) were shot dead by ranks of joint services.

David Granger, former President (2015-2020) who was at that time commander of the Joint Services denied any role in the horrendous military operation. It was the first time in our country's electoral history that the military had intervened in the electoral process by taking control of the ballot boxes at the close of poll on July 16, 1973. David Granger, is on record praising the military for playing an "exemplary role in protecting the ballot boxes!" on the day in question.

A Commission of Inquiry established to investigate the circumstances leading to the death of the two Comrades exonerated the Joint Services of any responsibility for the killings, however, the army's involvement at the time, remain etched in the memories of members and supporters of the PPP who, on an annual basis, would journey to the burial place of those killed to commemorate the sacrifice they made for free and fair elections.

For the 1973 elections, I was appointed a party polling agent in Georgetown. I was 23 years old at the time. I was assigned to one of the four polling stations at the Saint Gabriel's Primary School at the corner of Oronoque and Almond Streets, Queenstown.

During the day all went well at the polling station. I made copious notes of everything that occurred, however between 1600hrs and 1800hrs strange occurrences began whereby an unusual number of young African Guyanese males and females turned up at the polling station and in a rowdy manner demanded that they be allowed to vote. They had no form of identification. The names of the trouble-makers were not on the voters list.

They were transported to the polling station in open back vehicles belonging to different government ministries and were accompanied by some bulky looking thugs who made sure that they were not prevented from accomplishing what they were brought to the polling station to do.

At first, the elections officials put up a show appearing as though they were opposed to the demand by the 'new voters' but from all indications, it was clear that they were expecting the 'new voters' around that time of the day. Clearly, the polling station officials had advance notice about the mission of the 'new voters.'

Subsequently, after appearing to be bullied, the Presiding Officer instructed the Poll Clerk to hand more than one ballot paper to each of the 'new voters' allowing them to vote several times. The ballot boxes were stuffed with fraudulent votes several times over the number of voters registered to vote at that polling station.

All polling agents save the one representing the PNC objected loudly to what took place but to no avail. We were ignored, even threatened, bullied and told to 'watch yuhself' while the electoral process was raped blatantly and indiscriminately before our very eyes. A police constable who stood outside the polling station paid no attention whatsoever.

Having accomplished their fraudulent deeds the 'new voters' were escorted back to the vehicles that brought them to the polling station. From reports later received, bands of 'new voters' were shuttled from one polling station to another in town and country to thwart the democratic will of the electorate. In those days, there was no law nor practice in place to count votes at the place of poll.

There was however, a practice allowing for polling agents to accompany the ballot boxes to the place of count. However, on that occasion, I was not allowed to follow the ballot boxes to Queens College, the designated central counting station where ballot papers from all over the country were to be counted. I immediately proceeded to party headquarters to report on what took place at my polling station.

While at Freedom House I noticed a steady trickle of fellow polling agents from a number of polling stations across the city. There was one common occurrence in all their reports; every one of them had witnessed ballot box stuffing at the polling stations where they worked.

From those, and subsequent reports, it was clear that a well-organized rigging machine had swung into full gear across the country. The GDF, in cahoots with the PNC was in complete control of that machine.

Chaired at the time by Sir Donald Jackson, a known supporter and admirer of Burnham the dictator, the Elections Commission had long become what was to be later described as a 'toothless poodle.'

Sir Lionel Luckhoo, the serving PNC member on the Commission at the time was quoted saying: " I was horrified to find that the Commission had no power, no executive authority. All we can do is to make representations. The Commission has been denuded of any power." Later, that evening I was despatched to Queens College (QC) to observe the assorting and counting of the ballots.

It was just after eight o'clock that night when I walked from Freedom House, all the way to QC. I presented my credential as a counting agent of the PPP and was allowed to cross the barricade into the compound of the college where GDF ranks, armed to the teeth stood guard. The ballot boxes arrived sometime after 11pm after a long, long wait. In the meanwhile, Janet Jagan, the PPP representative on an 'Elections Watch' radio program kept asking about the whereabouts of the ballot boxes. Not even the Chairman of the Elections Commission could provide an answer. Except for the PNC, the PPP had lost track of the boxes between the time they were retrieved by GDF ranks from the polling stations across the country to the time of their arrival at QC.

It soon became obvious that mischief was afoot during that interregnum.

The boxes arrived at QC in army trucks and were fetched up the stairs by soldiers in uniform to a large auditorium on the Northern side of the building where huge tables resembling those used for table tennis had been joined together. The ballots were all dumped on the tables arranged according to electoral districts.

I objected to the way ballot boxes were opened without any prior examination to determine whether they had been sealed in accordance with the rules. As more and more boxes arrived and their contents dumped on the tables it became obvious that the boxes were tampered with. Padlocks were broken and the Party seals on the boxes were either badly damaged or not there. When the boxes were opened and the ballots dumped on the tables bundles of ballot papers wrapped in rubber bands were seen among the loose ones.

When I drew this highly unusual occurrence to the attention of the counting officer, a huge, well built tall man in short sleeves stepped forward and shouted at me telling me get out. I recognized the man to be Claude Merriman the proprietor of Merriman's Funeral Parlour and a PNC member of the Georgetown City Council. He was at one time a Minister Labour and Social Security in the Burnham administration. He later became Deputy Mayor and then Mayor of the capital city.

Merriman assumed the attitude of a bully conveying the impression to all present with his booming voice that he was in charge of the entire counting operation. I stood my ground protesting, knowing full well that Merriman could do me no physical harm with so many people around. This infuriated him but knowing he could do nothing, he eventually moved away from within my sight even though I could still see him looking threateningly in my direction.

What gave me great strength and courage at that time was my knowledge of the fact that party leaders were at the same time, raising embarrassing observations and vehement objections on radio thus sensitizing the populace about the widespread rigging that was taking place.

As was anticipated, tampering with the ballot boxes by PNC activists with the help of the military gave the PNC a whopping but fraudulent 71% of the "votes." cast. The July 16, 1973 elections went down in history as the 'Fairy Tale Elections.'

I remember well those events because they were my second real life experience where I was able to witness at first hand how rigging can be perpetuated to allow a despot to hold on to political power by fraudulent means, this time with the help of the military.

What was significant in these elections was the realization once again of the enduring belief of Cheddi Jagan in alliances. And that even in the face of tremendous odds he recognized the need for the PPP to work together with other political parties. In the 1973 elections the PPP entered into a loose opposition alliance with the Liberator Party led by Dr. Gunraj Kumar and the People's Democratic Movement led by Llewelyn John.

Following the massively rigged elections in 1973, and the shooting to death of its three activists, the PPP initiated a process of internal discussions and consultations with its membership. Arising from a rather lengthy consultative process, the PPP boycotted the parliament from 1973 to 1976.

Janet Jagan documented the entire episode in great detail in her booklet; 'Army Intervention in The Elections in Guyana'

ELECTIONS EXPERIENCE

My previous experience with general elections was in 1968. That election put me in good stead for the elections held five years later. The 1968 elections were blatantly rigged just as those held in 1973. In the run up to the elections of 1973, I was actively involved in house-to-house campaigns in the city of Georgetown.

EMG Wilson was put in charge of the entire elections campaign. 'Willo' or 'Coco Wilson' as he was popularly called put me to work in Lodge Village and housing scheme as it was called at the time.

During the 1957 to 1964 government of the PPP, Comrade Wilson was Minister of Transportation and Communications. It was during his tenure that the MV Malali, Torani and the Makouria were commissioned with coconut water thus the name 'Coco Wilson.' The General Post Office and the telecommunications building now housing GT&T were all Commissioned during EMG Wilson's tenure as a minister of government. One of his main challenges came during the 1962 to 1964 period when he took on the responsibility to keep the wharves and stellings operational and protected and to ensure that all imports and exports did not suffer let or hindrance by political activists associated with the PNC.

I liked working with Comrade Wilson mainly because of his wide and deep grass roots connections and experience with the local authorities and his results-oriented approach to party work. EMG was a no- nonsense supervisor and chief party organizer. Later, he became the Party Secretary for mass organizations EMG Wilson was the chairman of the basic party organization in Georgetown for years. I was the Secretary of the group for years too, and it was in that capacity that I learnt how to prepare and send out invitations for meetings, how to write up the minutes of a meeting, how to follow up on decisions to ensure implementation and how to conduct elections for office bearers. Learning these things put me in good stead for my future as a professional politician.

Looking back, I am convinced that his results-oriented and disciplined approach to work had a tremendous and lasting impact on my upbringing as a political activist, but that style of work had its advantages and disadvantages. In retrospect, that style of work did not work in my favour when I became the party's Executive Secretary and much later, General Secretary.

The slackers and loafers at various levels of the Party structure did not want to be pushed, criticized nor held accountable for their laise d'afaire attitude towards party work. They nevertheless looked forward to being promoted or elected to leading party bodies.

In the case of paid functionaries, they looked forward to receiving their salaries at the end of the month regardless of the poor quality of their work. I had serious difficulties with this attitude displayed by some members. I suppose they had difficulties with my style as well.

This shortcoming on my part was exploited by some to undermine my authority and influence as General Secretary and as a long-standing party leader. Whisper campaigns about my style of work were a regular occurrence. And initiatives I took to advance the interests of the party were either criticized or shunned.

IN THE VINEYARDS

My immediate supervisor during the 1973 elections campaign was Cyril Belgrade, a tough but considerate Comrade. Cyril was a waterfront worker like Victor James, the Party organizer for Georgetown, they both knew the city 'like the back of their hands.'

Lodge Village, as it was then known, was a very difficult place to do political field work. It was, and still is predominantly Afro-Guyanese populated with a spattering of either mixed or East Indian dominated enclaves.

The party had many stalwarts living in Lodge at the time. They included, Stella Singh and her children especially Vashti who was the more politically motivated and engaging with those she found either supportive or opposed to the PPP. Vashti was a down-to-earth person and a hard worker.

Lucille Logan had migrated from Wismar/ McKenzie to Lodge village following a period of ethnic cleansing during the 1962 to 1964 disturbances which resulted in most Indo-Guyanese being forced to flee the Wismar/McKenzie area for safety of their lives. Many were forced to leave their moveable and immovable property behind.

The Herberts lived in Lodge too. They were strong Party supporters owing to the fact that Charles Herbert, a stevedore, had worked for years at Sprostons (Curtis Campbell) No. 2 wharf, at La Penitence.

During the 1962 to 1964 disturbances Herbert, worked along with a number of Black Stevedores who had refused to take strike action against the Jagan Government.

Charles Herbert was a brave man. He did not to join the general strike that was called by his Union, the General Workers' Union in support of the Burnham/D'Aguiar alliance who had launched an all-out campaign to destabilize the Jagan government.

Shirley Edwards, her mother, two sons and three daughters lived at Princess Street Lodge, she was a known PPP activist and faced physical threats several times because of her affiliation to the Party. Out of fear for her safety, the party did not assign Comrade Shirley to work along with our team in Lodge.

It was generally felt that Shirley's presence might attract attacks that would bring physical harm to her and family. Shirley was therefore assigned to work in another area outside of lodge in Georgetown.

In light of the experience I gained while working in Lodge and other Afro-Guyanese dominated communities across the country, especially in Georgetown, I became conscious of the fact that PPP members of African descent were prime targets of vicious personal and racist attacks by the PNC who just could not stomach Black people supporting the 'Indian PPP.' To them it was a betrayal of their ethnicity.

Interestingly, the converse took place when an erstwhile member of the PPP crossed over to the PNC. They too became the target of vicious attacks this time from the PPP who branded them 'Namakarams' and 'Harkatees' meaning traitors and ungrateful. This socio-psychological phenomenon was the reflection of a syndrome that permeated both the body politic and the political culture of Guyanese society.

So great was the hostility towards our team of Party workers in Lodge that on one occasion, after identifying ourselves to a household in a yard, a potty filled with urine was thrown at us from a window on the upper flat of a wooden house. No doubt the 'blessings from above' was from PNC supporters. In the circumstances, a bath, and clean clothes, was the next thing I urgently needed. We suspended our campaign for the remainder of that day in that particular yard at Lodge. Much to the consternation and disgust of some villagers, who felt the PPP had no place at Lodge, we returned the following day to continue working in the same area but not in the same yard.

The night before at our usual caucus meeting held to assess our work in Lodge, we agreed that we should not abandon our work in the village lest our action be perceived as an act of cowardice after being chased out by the villagers. That would have been viewed as politically damaging for our party. In the course of our deliberations, I drew to my Comrades attention, an observation I thought might be of interest to them. I told them I had discerned a sense of respect on the part of some villagers when they saw us return to campaign in their community notwithstanding the harsh treatment some of their "mattee" villagers" had meted out to us the day before.

That experience and observation taught me an important lesson as regards my political upbringing, particularly in respect to political work at the grass roots level in non-traditional areas where the party lacked political support.

Debates among my Afro-Guyanese comrades on this important aspect of party work helped bring me up to speed on the ways and means of working in those areas where ethnic insecurity and political prejudice against the PPP but favorable to the PNC was a dominant factor.

Grounding with my Afro-Guyanese party comrades was for me an everyday occurrence primarily because they dominated the party structures in Georgetown and because I resided and worked in the city. As I grew in the party, I became increasingly appreciative of the immense value of Black Comrades in the party.

I noticed how Dr. and Mrs. Jagan would often invite these comrades, as well as those in the countryside, to Freedom House to consult with them on matters of concern to both of them. These comrades were fearless and never backed away from tasks assigned to them.

I recall one example when, during the 1973 elections campaign, me, Cyril Belgrave, Gladwin Levius and George Lee were out in an old Land Rover late one night painting VOTE PPP! on the streets of Georgetown, a van loaded with PNC thugs crept up on us with sticks in hand, Belgrave and Levius told me to run back to our vehicle, they stayed behind and fought off the thugs with paint buckets, paint was thrown in the faces of the thugs who, blinded by the paint quickly withdrew and drove away.

It was these Black party stalwarts who stood guard at Freedom House in times of tension, they helped protect speakers at party public meetings and they mobilized polling agents to work at polling stations for elections day.

Michael Forde's death while protecting Freedom House is a good example that show of how these comrades were prepared to pay the ultimate sacrifice because of their commitment and dedication to the cause.

RIGGED ELECTIONS IN GUYANA

From 1973 onwards, elections have been rigged in my country. Many, many Party Comrades were imprisoned, beaten by the police and PNC goons at the thousands of PPP public meetings and picketing exercises calling for free and fair elections.

Many had their homes searched and yards dug up. They suffered harassment, racial and political discrimination and intimidation. Hundreds who were forced out of their jobs, left the country to seek their fortunes in other lands. The demand for free and fair elections and a return to democracy became the rallying call of the party.

During the period 1968 and I985, the PPP was the bulwark of the struggle for free and fair elections. It took the brunt of the attacks from the Burnham dictatorship. For years it was alone in this battle. A general fear prevailed throughout the country that, to challenge Burnham meant death or imprisonment or seizure of one's private property or physical disappearance

It was for these and other striking socio- economic similarities that Guyanese drew comparisons with Haiti at the time.

OVERSEAS ONCE AGAIN

Just three weeks after the infamous July 16 elections, our youth organization was invited by the World Federation of Democratic Youth (WFDY) to send an eleven member delegation to the 10th World Festival of Youth and Students scheduled to be held from 28 July to 5 August 1973 in Berlin, capital of then German Democratic Republic (East Germany). Moses Nagamootoo was selected to head the delegation with me as the deputy head.

The Party and youth arm settled on the other members of the delegation which included a Trinidadian and a Vincentian. They were included in Guyana's delegation following representation made by Dr. Jagan, a strong internationalist who recognized that young people from other Caribbean countries who could not be present at the festival, could do so as part of the Guyana delegation.

Our participation in the festival was a great success. We shared our experiences in political struggle with youth and students from around the world. The festival exposed us to the political and cultural peculiarities of many countries with whom we interacted. Thirty thousand youth and students from 140 countries participated in the Festival. Three well educated and polite German guides were assigned to our delegation one of whose name was Renate.

RENATE, MY FIRST DAUGHTER

When our first daughter was born on July 24, 1974, I had the option of providing her first name and my wife the second. I chose Renate while my wife chose Vidya. Up to the time of Renate's birth, we lived in a rented room at Stella Dac Bang's home on Robb street.

MARRIAGE LIFE

On Wednesday, September 19, 1974, before leaving for the festival in the GDR, I married Gangadai aka Rajdai (Singh) Renate's mother Rajdai, came from a very poor family of eight who lived at La Bagatelle, a prosperous rice farming village on the island of Leguan on the Essequibo River.

My first wife Rajdai & daughter Renate: 1976

Rajdai's mother, Parbattie, belonged to the third generation Indo-Guyanese. Her father, had passed away some years before. She had four sisters; Data, Chan, Tulsie and Ramo. Also, there were three brothers; Paso, Bhai and Kumar.

Data was the eldest. All the sisters eventually left Leguan and came to live with Data at Kingston, Georgetown. By some strange coincidence, Data's one bedroom, bottom house apartment was located on Barrack street exactly opposite the old Kingston-wooden style house in which Mrs. Bacchus or Aunt Didi lived.

Aunt Didi was the sister of James Rohee, my grandfather on my father's side.

Quite often during visits to my intended wife, I would hear a voice calling out to me from that very house; it would be my dad who paid frequent visits to his Aunt Didi.

It became obvious to my Dad and great aunt that I was courting a young lady in the neighborhood. It took me awhile before I could muster the courage to take Rajdai over to my relatives to introduce her to them as a matter of respect, if not courtesy.

I met Rajdai while she worked as a volunteer at Freedom House during the 1973 elections campaign. She was the typical Indo-Guyanese peasant girl; easygoing, kind and generous but eager for a family and home of her own. She became pregnant before we got married.

We were married on Thursday, September 19th, 1974 at the General Registers' Office at the General Post Office in Georgetown. Fortunately for me, her mother, sisters and brothers were supportive of our relationship and marriage.

Rajdai's eldest sister 'Dats' and her husband, as well as two of my close Comrades, Feroze Mohammed and Balchand Persaud attended our simple civic marriage ceremony as witnesses.

Afterwards, we celebrated over a small lunch at the Golden Lotus Chinese restaurant, on Robb street, five doors East of our Party headquarters. Feroze Mohammed, Rudolph Persaud, Vincent Teekah and Balchand Persaud, all Party leaders were present.

To this day, I have no idea why my Dad was not invited to either of the two events.

COMRADE NGUYEN DAC BANG

We sub-letted one of three bedrooms at the home of Stella Dac Bang, a party activist who lived on Robb street about six doors west of Freedom House. Stella was married to Nguen Dac Bang a Vietnamese freedom fighter who fought against the French occupationists. He was captured and exiled to Devil's Island in French Guiana.

Some years later, he escaped to British Guiana.

After settling in Guyana, the diminutive but enterprising Vietnamese opened a small restaurant which he named 'The Fraternity Restaurant.' The restaurant was situated on the ground floor of a wooden two-story building on Robb Street between King and Wellington Streets. Robb Street at that time was famous for restaurants ranging from Chinese, American, Indian and creole.

Above his modest restaurant Dac Bang established guest house with about a dozen rooms, and a common washroom.

KOREAN VISITORS

I recall when Mrs. Jagan received news that the first ever delegation from the Workers' Party of the Democratic People's Republic of Korea (DPRK), with whom our Party had fraternal relations, was en route to Guyana, I was called upon to make transportation and accommodation arrangements for the delegation. However, we were not informed about the size of the delegation nor of the length of their stay in Guyana. I met the delegation on arrival at the airport, it turned out that it was an all male delegation of about twenty-five persons. Additional taxis were hired and the delegation was transported to Georgetown.

Arrangements were made for the delegation to be accommodated at Dac Bang's Guest House which proved inadequate owing to the size of the delegation. At their request, they eventually moved to the Hotel Tower on Main Street. The Party had arranged a programme for its guests but on completion of their programme with the PPP the entire North Korean delegation suddenly became the guests of the then PNC government!

We were just as disappointed as Dac Bang was!

Dac Bang expanded his business opening another restaurant on Holmes Street in the 'Tiger Bay' Area. He never returned to Vietnam but gave unstinted support to the PPP until he migrated with his entire family to Canada many years later.

LIFE ON ROBB STREET

While living in our one-bedroom apartment with Stella Dac Bang our earthly possessions comprised of a metal frame coil spring bed and a foam mattress on which me, my wife and our daughter slept.

My colleague Balchand Persaud, the party's chief organizer at the time invited me to accompany him to AH&L Kissoon & Sons at Camp and Robb streets. Whilst there, he surprised me when he told me that the bed and mattress were his wedding gifts to me and my wife. Under the bed were three 'carnation' milk carton boxes containing separately my wife's, our daughter's and my own clothes.

A one burner 'Made in China' kerosene oil stove, borrowed from Freedom House, was used to cook our meals. Later, a small wooden safe was bought to store our ration.

Life on Robb Street at that time was an exciting place to be. Apart from Regent Street, Water Street, Camp street, and the Bourda and Stabroek market areas, Robb Street was known for Chinese and the most prestigious restaurants, watch and clock repair stores, bookshops, rum shops, bakeries, groceries, record bars, low-cost guest houses and hotels, drug stores and the popular the Metropole Cinema. It was therefore not unusual to find on a daily basis, throngs of shoppers, eaters, cinema-goers, hotel guests and window-shoppers on Robb Street.

Moreover, because Freedom House, headquarters of the PPP was located on Robb Street, party leaders and political activists were to be found from time to time congregating outside Freedom House or huddled in hushed political discussions or simply executing security duties. The Mirror newspaper was sold every afternoon by Mr. Britton the vendor outside Freedom House.

To the East of Freedom House was an empty lot, a kind of memorial to the bombing of Party headquarters. To the West was a Chinese restaurant. To the North aback Freedom House is an alleyway and residential quarters and directly in front the party's headquarters, was another Chinese restaurant and a store that sold motor cycles and parts. Obliquely opposite Freedom House stood the Metropole cinema. Robb street therefore, was a hive for activities, night and day.

SHEIK FEROZE MOHAMMED

From 1968 to 1974 I lived at Freedom House. Sheik Feroze Mohammed had arrived from Adelphi, Canje, Berbice to occupy and administer the affairs of the Progressive Youth Organization (PYO) from its central office located at Party headquarters in Georgetown.

Feroze was also resident at Party HQ for a while. He took up residence in a small cottage aback Freedom House until he married his beautiful fiancé, Kamla and went off to live at Prashad Nagar with his vivacious bride.

Feroze was excellent at inspiring and encouraging young cadres like myself to go the extra mile. He was a great organizer for the youth organization at the central level. He encouraged political debates and discussions at all levels of the organization.

Feroze was ideologically and theoretically prepared from a Marxist-perspective. He helped set up the Student section of the PYO and the UG-based PYO Group.

Feroze was instrumental in securing the affiliation of the PYO and its student arm to the World Federation of Democratic Youth (WFDY) and the International Union of Students (IUS) Under his leadership, relations with a number of youth and student organizations around the world were established.

Two publications, 'The Flame' and 'Youth Advance' reflecting the views of the student and youth organizations respectively were published for the first time during his tenure.

Before traveling abroad to attend international events, Feroze insisted that delegates prepare their speeches before leaving, and take party and PYO publications for distribution at the event. Feroze would offer advice as to which foreign delegations our delegates should have bilateral meetings with while at an international gathering. As far as Feroze was concerned, advance preparations or forward planning were sine-qua-non before participating in any meeting at home or abroad.

Feroze was one of the best elections managers we ever had. He was great at putting the various teams together to take care of the complex aspects of an elections campaign. He himself took charge of the party's elections machinery to shadow that of the Guyana Elections Commission. As campaign manager, Feroze successfully delivered electoral victories for the party in 1992, 1997,2001 and 2006.

On the Party's assumption to government and while in opposition, some of Feroze's colleagues in the leadership of the PYO succumbed to political opportunism and abandoned what they once professed to be committed to. Feroze's modesty would prove to be his Achilles heels in years to come. He passed away on May 1st, of 2020

SAILING WAS NOT FOR ME

In 1968, with the help of Janet Jagan, I was offered a job at Mazarally sawmills. The job entailed working on one of their schooners used to ship lumber from Guyana to the Caribbean islands.

I took the job but soon after the boat arrived at Supenaam, on the Essequibo coast to be loaded with cargo I fell ill. The boat captain who was a national of St. Vincent and the Grenadines recommended that I be sent back to Georgetown.

On my return to the city, I visited Mrs. Jagan at her office and reported to her what had transpired. She advised that I put it down as experience.

THE MIRROR NEWSPAPER

In 1969, I was offered a job at the New Guyana Company Ltd, printers and publishers of the Mirror newspaper.

The company was established in 1962 and in the same year the newspaper appeared for the first time in the urban and rural areas of Guyana.

The Mirror was born at a time when the country was in the throes of its worst ever political crisis characterized by racial conflict engineered by the opposition People's National Congress (PNC).

A daily working-class news paper was badly needed in the colony to counter the hostile press which included the Evening Post, the Sunday Argosy, the Chronicle and the Guiana Graphic. They all launched persistent attacks against the PPP with the aim of destabilizing its tenure in government during the 1957 to 1964 period.

The Mirror was born as a fighting newspaper.

On assuming duty at the New Guyana Company at Ruimveldt, I was placed in the binding section of the job printing department. About a year later, I was transferred to the Linotype department.

I would walk every morning all the way from Robb street to the Ruimveldt, but after work, I would catch the popular yellow bus on the West Ruimveldt 'backroad ' which took me all the way to Regent and Wellington Streets with Freedom House just around the corner.

Working at the Linotype machines opened up my understanding and appreciation for progressive journalism, movies, as well as national and international politics.

Another reason why I enjoyed working at the Mirror was because some Friday afternoons when certain Linotype operators and other staff members were free, we would meet at a popular rum shop in Alexander Village to imbibe in at least two or three bottles of Bardinet Brandy 'chased' with Seven Up or plain water.

'Cutters' would be fried shark with hot fried plantain chips. We ate the 'cutters' with hot pepper sauce mixed with ketchup. "

I was not a heavy drinker like the others especially MZ Ali, Mr. McDonald, Kelvin Andrews and George Teekah but I accompanied them mainly because I liked the fried shark and plantain chips and took my one or two 'tups' in between. As a youngster, I wanted to learn the ways of big men' with wine, work, women and song.

The New Guyana Company was divided up into several departments; management, accounts, circulation and advertising, binding, editorial, linotype, proof reading, composition and printing.

The staff at New Guyana was a mix of highly skilled and semi-skilled men and women in each department. The staff was multi-ethnic. It was interesting to observe how well they worked together.

Mrs. Jagan succeeded Herman Singh as Editor of the Mirror. Later, Henry Skerret was employed as sub-editor and much later MZ Ali as sub-Editor.

Mrs. Jagan was supported by a competent and versatile team of journalists comprising of Clinton Collymore, Iris Persaud, Moses Nagamootoo and Kellawan Lall aka 'Peck'. Bill Carr, a UG lecturer would contribute with articles from time to time. Cheddi Jagan wrote a weekly article entitled 'Straight Talk.'

Skerret eventually left to join the New Nation, the official organ of the ruling party, and MZ Ali migrated to Suriname with his 'child mother' who worked in the binding section of the company. Robert Persaud joined the team much later.

A popular section of the newspaper was the section that offered horse racing tips. Many punters were handsomely rewarded by placing bets based on those tips.

For many years Hawley Harris worked as the cartoonist for the newspaper. His cartoons angered the ruling PNC so much so that he was invited by the leader of that party to produce cartoons He for a better price for the New Nation. Hawley turned down the offer. So, I was told.

Nagamootoo went off in the mid- 1980's to work at the Novosti/ Tass News Agency office in Bel Air Georgetown. He was after a better salary.

PRACTICING JOURNALISM

It was around this period that the Union of Guyanese Journalists (UGJ) was established with Janet Jagan as president.

The Union applied for membership in the International Organisation of Journalists (IOJ) based in Prague, Czechoslovakia. Its application was accepted.

As a member of the UGJ, I represented the Organisation at one of the IOJ's assemblies in Harare, Zimbabwe.

Ricky Singh, an outstanding Guyanese and Caribbean journalist and Earl Bosquet of St. Lucia participated in the assembly. We collaborated as a Caribbean team in the various sessions of the assembly.

That was my first trip to Africa. Zimbabwe was in the news because of the internecine tribal conflict between the Shona led by Robert Mugabe and the Ndebele led by Joshua Nkomo; Mugabe had outmaneuvered Nkomo becoming the President of Zimbabwe and soon after had launched a vengeful campaign against the White land owners who owned and controlled the country's vibrant and productive agricultural sector. It was a move that contributed decisively to the collapse of Zimbabwe's once prosperous economy.

It was during my stint at the Mirror that Mrs. Janet Jagan encouraged me to write articles for the newspaper's 'Youth Page' - a skill I lacked and a vocation I had little or no knowledge of.

I wrote under the pen-name 'Borretto' the first name of an Amerindian student by the name of Borretto Mausir who had come to Georgetown to attend St. Stanislaus College on a government scholarship and whom I had come to know while living with my aunt in Queenstown.

Later, between 1974 and 1989 I began writing in my own name. Among the numerous articles I wrote were; 'Kenya -still fighting for UHURU,' 'That Scoon visit,' 'Guyanese must oppose military invasions,' 'Death warrant served on Apartheid,' 'Socialism and local business,' 'The battle is on,' 'Bolivia, Guyana and SIMAP,' 'From Belgrade to Kuala Lumpur,' 'Time for change,' 'Foreign policy compromises,' 'Food and changing moods,' 'Elections Commission remains toothless,' 'Songs and politics,' and ' Liberation and Christianity' just to mention a few.

I was also assigned by Mrs. Jagan to cover press conferences and to write film and book reviews for the newspaper.

The first movie I was assigned to review was playing at the Astor cinema. It was 'They Shoot Horses Don't They' with Jane Fonda. Mrs. Jagan, I believe, had her reasons for sending me to review that particular movie. The movie was highly political. It is based on life in the United States during the period of the Great Depression. 'Marathon dances' were organized by syndicates as a money-making form of entertainment.

Young men and women were 'employed' and provided with boarding and lodging but ended up being prisoners of the syndicates who would intimidate and threaten them if they demanded payment and expressed a wish to leave. They were told that they owed a ton of money to the syndicate for boarding and lodging and had to continue dancing in order to pay off their 'debt.' Theirs were a 'debt' that could never be re-paid and so they danced until they dropped, and in many instances died.

In Cheddi Jagan's 'The West on Trial,' I found an interesting description of the impact of the Great Depression on British Guiana's economy;

'The Great Depression of the 1930's and falling sugar prices on the world market had left their mark. The price of sugar had fallen to an all-time low level of eight Pounds, ten Pence per ton in 1936. Protective duties had to be imposed and other forms of assistance given to save the sugar industry, the sheet anchor of the Caribbean, from ruin. Living standards had deteriorate.'I wrote and re-wrote my review three times before Mrs. Jagan accepted it. Again, she had her reasons. I never asked why.

What I do know is that in retrospect, sending me to review that movie was educational for me and part of my political upbringing.

On another occasion, I was assigned go to the Astor cinema, to see and to write a review of the movie: 'Z', an Algerian-French politically fictionalized thriller, depicting the accounts surrounding the assassination in 1963, of Grigoris Lambrakis, a popular and progressive Greek politician. The film showed the ugly and conspiratorial side of Greek politics at that time, involving the military, big business, the mafia and corrupt politicians who, acting in consort, resorted to terror and assassinations to get rid of progressive, democratic political party and student leaders during the rule of the military dictatorship in Greece during the 1967 to 1974 period.

After writing a review of the movie 'They Shoot Horses Don't They' I had little difficulty writing a review of 'Z' maybe because it was thriller movie and a totally different genre from 'They Shoot Horses Don't They.'

On another occasion, I was assigned to cover a press conference hosted by Mr. Roderick Rainford the then Secretary General of the Caribbean Community (CARICOM).

Mrs. Jagan subscribed to the National Geographic magazine. When she was finished with them, with a pleasant smile, she would hand them to me encouraging me to read the contents. I had a copy with me at the press conference she had assigned me to cover at the Bank of Guyana Building where the CARICOM secretariat was housed at that time.

While awaiting the commencement of the press conference, an elderly man entered the room and sat next to me. He enquired which newspaper I was representing, I told him I was representing the Mirror newspaper. On seeing hearing that he exclaimed; 'Oh, that communist paper?"

I did not respond.

Noticing I was browsing through a magazine, he again asked, what was it I reading, I showed him the cover of the National Geographic magazine. His response was 'Oh! I didn't know communists read that." That experience stayed with me throughout my entire life. It taught me how some people misjudge others ideologically.

For my first book review, Mrs. Jagan lent me her copy of Herman Melville's 'Moby Dick' with a request that I read it and try my hand at a review. After plodding through the first two chapters I found going further difficult, if not somewhat tedious but I persevered.

I returned the book to Mrs. Jagan with a note explaining what I had accomplished in terms of the review she had requested. She never replied but invited me to her office to sit and talk about the book. In the course of our discussion she asked a simple question; what did I find noteworthy while reading the book? I offered a number of conclusions but she just nodded her head with a few "hmmns" in between. Then she asked, "Have you ever heard about concepts?" She elaborated on the subject and suggested that I go over the book once again and be on the look out for concepts. I quietly groaned as I left her office. "Why is she doing this to me?" I asked myself?

I shelved Moby Dick for a while, but knowing that Mrs. Jagan would one day approach me again on the subject, I did as she had suggested. She was correct. But strangely, she never broached the subject with me again. Did Mrs. Jagan know I did as she had suggested? Who knows? I never told her I did. Little did I know that in this way, the Party through Janet Jagan was building in me capacities that would put me in good stead in years to come.

Mrs. Jagan later introduced me to the works of classical French writers such as Honore de Balzac, Víctor Hugo and Emile Zola.

Victor Hugo's 'les miserables,' Zola's 'Germinal' and Balzac's works impressed me most of all. Reading books written by these classic literary giants as well the writings of Chekov, Dostoyevsky opened up fresh perspectives in my cultural, political and ideological upbringing.

Later, I grew to appreciate the works of Martin Carter, Derek Walcott, V.S. Naipaul and other Caribbean poets and writers.

PROBLEMS AT THE MIRROR

At the New Guyana Company, printers and publishers of the MIRROR, the Board of Directors was plagued with many problems including theft of materials, internal corruption, misappropriation of funds, cover-ups and mismanagement.

Participants at a shareholders' Annual General Meeting called for radical action to correct hemorrhaging of the company's assets.

A new Board of Directors was installed and Mr. Ivan Remington, a PPP Member of Parliament from Agricola replaced Mr. Mohammed Yassin as Chairman of the Board.

It was during this upheaval I was appointed a member of a new Board of Directors of the company.

Michael Shreechand was re-assigned from his trade union, desk at the Guyana Agricultural and General Workers' Union (GAWU) to the New Guyana Company as its financial controller and Secretary of the Board. He was assigned manager of the Company.

Shreechand fulfilled his responsibilities admirably. He was an efficient and effective task-master.

When the PPP assumed office in 1992, he was assigned the portfolio of Minister of Trade, Industry and Tourism - a position he held until his death in January 2000, from brain cancer.

Shreechand along with Dr. Roger Luncheon and Dr. Bheri Ramsarran served as the interlocutor for the PPP in the Inter-Party Dialogue Process, within the meaning of the Herdsmanston Accord and the St. Lucia Statement during the Janet Jagan Presidency. His service was recognized and honored by the party and government.

While Shree Chand worked overtime to bring the company's finances in order and to rid management of 'deadwood,' I was called upon to affect some internal and external infrastructural changes to the building which had deteriorated due to neglect by the previous management. To do so, I was allocated a small budget.

Enhancement of the security of the property was also in the cards.

By contracting carpenters who were party supporters, the project was completed within one month to the satisfaction of the Board. During that period, Dr. Jagan, was mandated by the Company's Board of Directors to begin a search, with a view to purchasing a new printing press for the Company.

Within weeks Dr. Jagan reported to the Board that contact was made with manufacturers in India, China, the US, the German Democratic Republic and the Soviet Union. From time to time Dr. Jagan would bring quotations to the Party Secretariat and thence to the Board for consideration.

There were agreements and disagreements amongst members of the Secretariat about the company from which a printing press should be sourced. The discussions would go on and on for hours on prices and specifications of each printing press. And although Dr. Jagan had a fantastic grasp of economics and financial matters he never sought to dictate or impose his preference on his Comrades at meetings of the Board or the Secretariat. He was a consensus builder.

Eventually, after months of discussion the Board finally agreed to purchase a Goss printing press from a company based in the United States.

The deal breakers were price, features, shipping costs, availability of spares, technical assistance to assemble the press and an offer to train press men locally. All agreed that it was a good deal. The press was purchased and installed.

Dr. and Mrs. Jagan had differences of views regarding recruitment and training of journalists for the Mirror newspaper.

Dr. Jagan's view was that the Party should recruit potential journalists from within its ranks since the Mirror is a political newspaper. He argued that on recruitment, the journalists should be sent abroad for training and on their return, they need not be at the Mirror on a full-time basis.

He argued that journalists should be allowed to work from their homes with the help of desk top computers and with internet connectivity using a wide area network (WAN) which was already in use many other countries and which had just been introduced in Guyana.

Mrs. Jagan was of a different view. While she agreed that potential journalists should be recruited from the within the Party's membership and from amongst its supporters, she was not convinced that they should work from home nor was it necessary to take up offers for their immediate overseas training.

Mrs. Jagan was a staunch advocate of on-the- job, in-house training in the editorial room of the newspaper. She insisted on assigning new recruits to the practical side of reporting, that is, to cover meetings of the City Council, sessions of the National Assembly, the Courts and public events organized by political parties such as street corner public meetings and rallies.

Mrs. Jagan advanced the view that participation in international workshops and seminars organized for journalists was necessary for journalists provided it would bring long- term benefits to the journalist and the newspaper. She further insisted that the newspaper cannot afford to train journalists overseas only to eventually lose them to another newspaper for a better salary.

She suggested that these matters could be settled by senior staff at the editorial room. Dr. Jagan conceded to the more realistic and practical approach advanced by Mrs. Jagan.

The Mirror faced another serious challenge which threatened the cessation of the newspaper. Forbes Burnham, the then Prime Minister of Guyana imposed a prohibition on the importation of newsprint for the MIRROR newspaper. His excuse was that the country was suffering from a severe shortage of foreign exchange. The entire country knew his action was politically motivated and vindictive. The MIRROR as an opposition newspaper had become too hot to handle. Donations of newsprint from sympathetic printing and publishing houses in the Caribbean were refused entry. The matter was taken to the court and the judge ruled that Burnham's actions were unconstitutional since it violated freedom of expression and access to information. After several years at the Mirror, I left to pursue studies in political science in the Soviet Union.

LIFE AT MIDDLE ROAD LA PENITENCE

On my return from the USSR, I began working full time at Freedom House. With my salary and additional financial help from Mrs. Jagan personally, I was able to rent a small, one-bedroom apartment for me and my family at Middle Road La Penitence.

George Lee, the Party's photographer and technician had found the apartment for me through a sister of his who lived nearby in North East La Penitence. It was a happy day for me and my wife. Finally, we were to have privacy in our own apartment.

The apartment had one bedroom, a small kitchen, toilet and bath and a small sitting room in which a wooden dining table with four wooden chairs was placed making it serve at the same time, our dining room.

Bit by bit, following the Guyanese proverb; 'wan, wan dutty does build dam' we were able to furnish the apartment with a three-piece suite, a vanity case, a cabinet and a safe all of which I bought on hire purchase from Mr. Kellman of Kellman's Furniture Store on Regent Street next door to GIMPEX.

I was introduced to Mr. Kellman by Comrades Belgrave and Herbert two party stalwarts.

Mr. Kellman was extremely considerate with his prices after he heard how I was struggling to establish the first home for my family.

Not long after me and my family had settled down in our small apartments Middle Road, La Penitence, we began receiving threats through written scrawled notes slipped under our door.

The neighborhood was not a very friendly one though I could discern some quiet support for the PPP among some residents. I was advised by Comrades at party headquarters who were knowledgeable about such matters to ignore the death threats and calls to move out of the neighborhood. I was advised to act normally as though I never received any such threats. I did as I was advised and, as predicted nothing ever happened.

Later, the Party bought a bicycle for me from GIMPEX to facilitate my political work in Georgetown and for my personal use as well. The bicycle was used on a daily basis as a means to transport my wife to and from work and my daughter to and from play school.

GIMPEX

Guyana Import Export (GIMPEX), was the agents for Chinese bicycles, MZ motor cycles and Fiat, Lada, Simca and Contessa motor cars. The store had a modern servicing/repairs workshop and a huge, well stocked spare-parts department.

The staff at GIMPEX was made up of many seasoned Party stalwarts like Charlie and Beatrice Casatto, Maurice Herbert, Yusuf Mohammed, Mohammed Yassin, Mrs. Ally, Mr. Gomez, Carl Rodgers, Ms. Joan Dutchin and Eric Gilbert among others.

GIMPEX was established as a public shareholders' company during the 1957 to 1964 PPP government. It was subjected to harassment and bombings by terrorists organized and financed by the PNC during its 1962 to 1964 campaign to destabilize the PPP government.

At that time, the GIMPEX building was located at Brickdam, Georgetown.

Listening to the experiences of these Comrades in respect to the disturbances in the 1962 to 1964 period was of great interest to me and lent to my political awakening.

GIMPEX was eventually relocated from Brickdam to 104 - 107 Regent Street, Lacytown where it established a thriving business selling goods imported from China, India and Eastern Europe. Prices were affordable to poor families.

Dress materials sold at 3 yards for $1 called '3 for D.' was extremely popular with the ladies in town and country.

In 1979, I was appointed a member of the Board of Directors of the company. The company leased part of its upper flat as offices to the Guyana Agricultural and General Workers' Union (GAWU) Later, another part of the building was leased as office space to the Guyana Rice Producers' Association (GRPA).

Much later, a private security guard service subleased a smaller portion of the same building as their office.

A large section of the building was destroyed by fire in 2001 but the bottom section of the building was saved and continued to be occupied and rented to Indian nationals conducting mostly retail businesses. In the late 2014, the entire structure was demolished.

Part of the land was sold to a private entrepreneur while an empty lot now exists where the poor man's store in the city once stood.

Most of GIMPEX's former staff members have since migrated or passed away.

As General Secretary of the Party and Member of GIMPEX's Board of Directors and based on a decision of the Board in 2013, plans were drawn up to construct a modern shopping mall with offices to lease, but this was shelved after the national economy went into the doldrums following the 2015 elections.

Alternatively, plans were initiated to establish a car park at the vacant lot owned by the company.

The realization of this project would have brought in handsome profits to the company. However, this effort was frustrated due to the bureaucratic never-ending demands for more and more paperwork by the Georgetown City Council.

MIRROR SALESMAN

Selling the Mirror newspaper in the afternoons after work around the East Coast car park and Stabroek Market was a political eye opener for me. It brought me into contact with people who held all kinds of opinions, from supporters to non-supporters who would either buy, or refuse to buy a copy of the four-page daily, evening newspaper. A weekend edition was published on Fridays.

Some Friday nights we would be called upon to work overtime whenever there were leaflets as paid ads or a centrespread that had to be inserted in the weekend edition of the MIRROR.

A substantial snack would be provided along with overtime pay which the team looked forward to receiving at the end of the month.

To understand the system of distribution and collection of money from the Mirror agents I would accompany from time to time, either Chitlall or Ramnarine the two comrades who were assigned the responsibility to do so.

While selling the Mirror newspaper people would gather around to ask lots of questions.

I had to provide answers on my own. There was no Party leader to turn to for help. I had to represent the policies of the Party as best as I could on my own. That meant I had to be well informed and be able to articulate those policies in 'plain and simple' language.

To misinform would be disastrous, if not embarrassing politically. In retrospect, I saw this as part of my political upbringing.

I knew the exercise was a political one and though I could keep the commission from the sale of each paper sold I nevertheless handed over the entire sum to the Party.

Saturday mornings were special in that Dr. Jagan and a team of us would walk in an Easterly direction on Robb street all the way down to Bourda Market. On the way, we would shout MIRROR! MIRROR! selling copies of the newspaper as we went along. Some mornings we would bump into Burnham at the Bourda market. He too would be selling the 'New Nation' his party's newspaper.

On one occasion while we were engaged in Mirror sales Bourda Market, Burnham hailed out to Dr. Jagan in a jocular manner telling him; 'Cheddi boy, you ain't got no supporters here!' Dr. Jagan responded with his trade mark smile, ignored him and continued with his mission.

ROLE OF THE MIRROR

In retrospect, this particular aspect of party work taught me that a cadre or party leader who depreciates the task of going out to sell his/her party newspaper, lacks appreciation of cadre building in preparation for leadership as well as its usefulness in nurturing public relations skills aimed at reaching out to people from all walks of life.

A Party newspaper is not just another newspaper, it plays the twin role of organizer and educator. Try as best as he or she can, the Party activist or organizer cannot be everywhere, but the newspaper can. It can help mobilize, educate and bring people together organizationally to discuss matters of interest to them. It will be counterproductive for the leadership of any political party not to promote a practice whereby party leaders and cadres would go out together to vend the Party newspaper and to depend exclusively on social media and television. All three are important, save that selling a newspaper puts you in physical contact with people.

Experience has shown that during community outreach exercises organized by the Party, when Party publications including its own newspaper are made available free of cost to all participants present, they deeply appreciate such gestures.

JAGAN THE COMMUNICATOR

Being with Dr. Jagan whenever he went out into the fields was both fun and educational.

The way he communicated with his supporters and non-supporters, the depth and simplicity of his analysis, his knowledge of historical facts, his awareness of international developments as well as his use of statistics was made easy for his listeners to understand. It was a joy to listen and learn from him, whether it was at a public or bottom house meeting, a public lecture, a press conference or an internal discussion on a topic of interest.

Dr. Jagan worked during the morning hours at his dentistry on Charlotte Street just around the corner West of Camp Street. By midday, he would be at Freedom House for internal committee meetings or to meet with people to offer solutions to their problems. Later in the afternoon just after four o'clock, along with one or two Comrades, Dr. Jagan would leave the city in his Austin Cambridge PN 201 and much later, in his Lada PZ 9338 for public or bottom house meetings at villages outside the city.

I recall accompanying him to a bottom house meeting at Dundee, Mahaicony. A huge crowd had gathered awaiting him. Villagers sat on rice bags made of jute of a brownish color. Others stood and listened attentively as Dr. Jagan spoke.

When Dr. Jagan was finished, questions and comments were entertained. The Party organizer at the time for the Mahaica/Mahaicony area was a man by the name of Mohammed Saffee.

Saffee got up and passionately professed his love and admiration for Dr. Jagan. And as though that was not enough, he unbuttoned his shirt jac exposing his hairy chest and told the villagers present as if he was about to cry, that were he to tear open his chest Dr. Jagan would bee seen emblazoned on his heart. The crowd roared with laughter.

Some months after, Saffee defected to the ruling People's National Congress (PNC). This was an important political lesson for me. It taught me to beware of the sycophants and those who engage in idolatry and hero worshipping in politics. Saffee had no ideological training, he was basically an opportunist and a racist driven by religious conviction.

Another afternoon, Dr. Jagan invited me to join him on a field trip to West Coast Berbice. It was a regular practice of his to take a young Comrade or two along with him on such trips except when he left for extended periods in the interior of the country such as the North West District or the Rupununi or some other far flung interior location.

Dr. Jagan would discuss the political situation with his companions while driving, suggesting what should be done by the party and how it should be done. He would take the opportunity to explain to us International politics. He taught us that it was important to condemn or criticize when necessary, but that at the same time, we should to put forward alternative proposals that would be doable and which people would find attractive.

Before embarking on field trips, Dr. Jagan would make sure that his car trunk was laden with Party publications including the Mirror and Thunder. He would also bring along copies of Moscow News, Granma, Soviet Weekly, New Times and China Today or Peking Review. We would tie one of each into a bundle and sell as a super pack for $1.00 at meetings.

On arrival on the West Coast of Berbice, Dr. Jagan stopped at a village named Hopetown. He approached three Afro-Guyanese male senior citizens who were leaning on an old fence as if preventing it from falling apart.

Dr. Jagan: Hi there! How things Comrades?

Villagers: No response, they exchange glances with each other;

First villager: 'well Comrade we're here holding on;'

Dr. Jagan: what about you Comrade? Pointing to another of the three men;

Second villager: 'We are here hanging on;'

Third villager to his two colleagues: 'Why y'all doan tell de man de truth; Doc, things bad like rass!!

And with that, a conversation started that lasted for about two hours.

In the meantime, many curious villagers on learning that Dr. Jagan was in the village, had gathered around to listen to what he had to say and to ask questions to which answers were provided to the satisfaction of all.

Dr. Jagan was a teacher of politics, economics and international relations. It was not unusual to find him at shopping centres, market places, street corners, car and bus parks with huge crowds gathered around him.

A closer look would find him with members of the youth organization holding a chart depicting economic and financial indicators on issues such as the 'debt trap' and its impact of Guyana's economy. He could be heard explaining in simple language what the foreign debt burden meant for each Guyanese. He would then answer questions.

A GLIMPSE OF THE PARTY IN THE LATE 1960'S

At the time when I joined the Party in 1968, it's leadership was made up of Cheddi Jagan, Ranji Chandisingh, Harrylall, Fenton Ramsahoye, EMG Wilson, Vincent Teekah, Rudy Luck, Ashton Chase, Philomena Sahoye, Bhola Persaud, Janet Jagan, Iris Persaud, Narbada Persaud, Moulvi Yacoob Ally, Ramkarran, Pandit Reepu Daman Persaud, Roshan Ali, Moneer Khan, CV Núnes, HJM Hubbard and Dr. CR Jacobs.

Later, following congress some new faces were elected to the leadership of the party they included; Ivan Remington, Balchand Persaud, Maccie Hamid, Hublall Ramdass, Edgar Ambrose, Derek Jagan, Harry Persaud Nokta, Clinton Collymore and Sheik Feroze Mohammed.

These were mature, experienced individuals, some of whom had served in the 1957 to 1964 PPP Government and had been in detention at Sibley Hall, Mazaruni prisons because they had fought courageously for Guyana's independence.

I had the honour and privilege to work with many of them, and through them, I was able to learn considerably about the vagaries and complexities of day- to- day politics. With others especially Dr. and Mrs. Jagan, I was shown the bigger global picture into which the smaller picture national version must fit.

Moneer Ahmed Khan was one of the Party leaders and Freedom House functionaries I came into contact with almost on a daily basis. He came from a rice farming family at Leguan, one of the many islands in the Essequibo river.

During the disturbances of 1962-1964 Moneer was Chairman of the Guyana Rice Marketing Board. Rice and railway sleepers were exported to Cuba but rioters and saboteurs were laying dynamite and homemade bombs to sabotage the ships and to destroy the wharves with the aim of preventing badly needed shipments fuel from being unloaded and at the same time, to prevent shipments of rice and railway sleepers being loaded onto waiting Cuban vessels.

Moneer's main task was to keep the port functioning. He accomplished this with the support of his comrades in the midst of all the challenges confronting him.

Khan was among thirty-four PPP political detainees held at Sibley Hall at the Mazaruni prisons.

Following his release, Moneer participated in the historic Freedom March across Guyana in April 1965 demanding the release of all political prisoners.

He later became manager of Freedom House in the late 1960's. It was during this period that I was assigned a shop assistant at the Michael Forde Bookstore named after Michael Forde who was killed by the terrorist bomb that exploded at Freedom House on the morning of July 17, 1964.

The PPP at that time was a loose mass party led by leaders who were Marxists though some in the leadership could be described as revolutionary democrats, nationalists as well as patriotic capitalists.

The nature of the struggle allowed for the involvement of all sections of the population thus the national and mass character of the PPP.

Since the principal objective at the time was independence every aspect of struggle at the time was directed at achieving that goal.

With the winning of independence on May 26, 1966 Guyana began to assert itself as one of the leading members of the Non- Aligned Movement (NAM).

INDIRA GANDHI VISITS

On October 14, 1968, Mrs. Indira Gandhi, Prime Minister of India visited Guyana.

Dr. Jagan held discussions with her at Herdsmanston House on Lamaha street.

It was a momentous occasion for the party and its Indo-Guyanese supporters, it reinforced their awareness and reassured all Guyanese that Dr. Jagan's international stature was recognized beyond the shores of Guyana.

Indira Gandhi's visit to Guyana was aimed at solidifying Guyana's role in the Non-Aligned Movement which, because of the cold war's East-West confrontation politics, had developed into a powerful international political alliance of governments of developing countries.

PROMOTING INTERNATIONAL CONTACTS

Whenever Dr. Jagan returned to Guyana from his overseas engagements, he would hand me a number of calling cards he had collected while overseas. My task was to add the information contained on the cards to a mailing list that already contained hundreds of names and addresses of well-known international personalities.

The mailing list was used to despatch copies of an 'Overseas Bulletin' to those persons whose names and addresses were on the mailing list. The bulletin contained the party's analysis of the latest political developments in Guyana as well as a synopsis of its position on a topical international issue. Mrs. Jagan drafted the monthly edition of the Overseas Bulletin. It was principally for overseas consumption.

My task was to reproduce copies of the bulletin after it was typed on stencil for reproduction on a Gestetner duplicating machine. My job was completed only after the hundreds of bulletins had been mailed overseas through the General Post Office in Georgetown.

CAP OF VENEZUELA VISITS

When Carlos Andres Perez, the then President of The Republic of Venezuela visited Guyana on October 20, 1978, Dr. Jagan, in his capacity as Opposition Leader took me along with him to the meeting that took place at Castellani House.

For me, it was a memorable meeting.

As a good listener, I was able to gain for the first time, and at first hand, the complexities of our country's border controversy with Venezuela.

The exchange of views between the two men revealed to me how skillful Dr. Jagan was at navigating around some rather tantalizing proposals made by Perez, the principal proposal being to grant Venezuela access to the Atlantic. It appeared as if Perez was laying diplomatic traps for Dr. Jagan to make a commitment to one proposal or the other. Dr. Jagan never yielded 'a blade of grass.'

Some how, this move by Perez was leaked to the press either by the Venezuelans themselves or a local fifth columnist who deliberately set out to make mischief and to embarrass Dr. Jagan and the PPP.

There is no truth whatsoever in the claim that a future PPP/C Government was prepared to bargain away a sliver of its national territory of land or sea to facilitate Venezuela's access to the Atlantic. To this day, forces hostile to the PPP continue to harp on this blatant falsehood based on sheer misinformation and speculation.

Little did I know at the time of Perez's visit that fourteen years later, I would be our country's Foreign Minister, tasked with the responsibility of overseeing Guyana's fragile bilateral relations with Venezuela and working with Facilitators appointed by the UN Secretary General.

On leaving Castellani House we concluded that the Venezuelan President's visit was carefully choreographed to suit a Venezuelan audience since the crafty Perez was nearing his first term in office and was seeking re-election for a second term.

The visit was useful to Burnham, he used it to bolster his image as a statesman inclined to friendly relations with Venezuela, the controversy was notwithstanding.

What I admired about Dr. Jagan was that notwithstanding Guyana's fragile relations with Venezuela, he maintained friendly personal relations with the political leaders of all the major political parties in that country; The Christian Democrats in COPIE, the Social Democrats in the Accion Democratica, The Communists in the Partido Communista and the Revolutionary Left in the Movimento Hacia el Socialismo.

Later, when Chavez came to power, consistent with this policy, Dr. Jagan reached out to him as well. With Suriname, Brazil and Colombia the approach was the same. When Janet Jagan was elected President in 1997, she pursued a similar foreign policy.

123

JAGAN THE INTERNATIONALIST

'Faced with repression and denial of rights at home, I had long felt the need for international solidarity. As often as I could, I made trips abroad to establish links through personal contacts.' Cheddi Jagan – The West on Trial

As our country's Opposition Leader for almost three decades, Cheddi Jagan's international stature and fame as a former Premier and champion for Guyana's independence allowed him to engage cordially with political personalities in Guyana's neighboring countries. This he did based on mutual respect knowing how important personal contacts were for the maintenance of good neighborly and friendly relations between Guyana and its neighbors, the controversy with Venezuela and the dispute with Suriname notwithstanding.

Dr. Jagan had many friends and overseas contacts. He made sure that they were kept abreast with political developments in Guyana. Many of them would come to Guyana from time to time to meet and exchange views and experiences with him. Some of those encounters were held at his home at Bel Air while others were held at Freedom House. Those held at his home would assume a more relaxed, intellectual and sociable character. I along with a few party leaders would be invited to be present to listen in to the conversations.

I recall being invited to his conversations with Ronald Dathorne, Professor, Department of English, University of Miami; Ken Bodhoo, Chairman, Department of International Relations, Florida International University and Dr. James Millette, Department of History, Mona campus, University of the West Indies just to name a few.

These conversations helped broaden my perspective of world politics and ideological trends that were competing with each other in Europe, Asia, Africa the Middle East and Latin America.

In Europe it was 'Euro-communism,' in Africa it was 'Ujama socialism,' in the Middle East it was 'Arab socialism' in Asia it was the rise of Maoism and in Latin America it was 'democratic socialism' vs armed struggle and liberation theology.

THE GUYANA PEACE COUNCIL

Dr. Jagan was staunch fighter for national and social liberation, peace and social progress.

His life-long contributions to the just struggles of the peoples of Asia, Africa, Latin America were known the world over.

Dr. Jagan participated in many international gatherings where peace, development and international solidarity were discussed and called for.

In 1973 together with a number of like-minded individuals including Dr. Clarence Drayton, Dr. Perry Mars, Attorney-at-law Khemraj Bhagwandin, Dr. Joshua Ramsammy, Annette Ramrattan, Harrry Ramdas and Lionel Seepersaud, the Guyana Peace Council (GPC) was established.

The GPC's establishment was preceded by the establishment of a Steering Committee comprising of the above-mentioned individuals who formulated a draft Constitution and took it to the first members meeting of the organization for adoption. An Executive Committee was then elected with Dr. Jagan as President, Dr. Clarence Drayton as Vice President, Harry Ramdass as Secretary and Lionel Seepersaud as treasurer.

I was elected Assistant Secretary along with five committee members.

Though some members of the GPC were sympathetic to the PPP, the GPC was neither an arm nor a branch of the PPP, rather it was an affiliate of the World Peace Council (WPC) with headquarters at the time in Helsinki, Finland.

The GPC organized a number of lectures, symposia, poster exhibitions around the country but more particularly on the coastland.

High level delegations from National Peace and Solidarity Committees from around the world visited their Guyanese counterparts in Georgetown to share experiences. On one occasion, Mr. Romesh Chandra, the then President of the WPC visited Guyana with a high-level delegation for talks with the local affiliate and the government of the day.

Dr. Jagan served at one time as a member of the Presidium of the WPC. This required him to travel frequently to many countries as part of WPC delegations.

I was fortunate enough to accompany him to some of the WPC's international gatherings in Eastern Europe, Ethiopia, Mauritius and Cuba.

In the run-up to the 1992 elections, emphasis on the GPC began to wane but the worse was yet to come. When Dr. Jagan assumed the office of President of the Republic in October 1992, the GPC and its activities faded away since many of us were called upon to work in institutions of state or government.

It was not until 2013 when I became General Secretary of the PPP that I took the initiative to bring together a number of like-minded persons with a view to establishing a Steering Committee whose primary task was to formulate a draft Constitution for a re-established GPC.

The members of the Steering Committee were C. Rohee, J. Edgehill, O. Satynand, B. Kuppen, M. Constantine, I. Ramtahul, B.S. Shadick, M. Ali, R. Benn, R. Ramraj, R. Gilbert and E. Bassoo.

Soon after the establishment of the Steering Committee in September 2014, I invited Raj Singh the then CEO of the Guyana Sugar Corporation (Guysuco) who at that time was a regular visitor to Guyana to join the Steering Committee and to assist in the formulating the rules and a constitution for the organization.

Raj Singh was unable to fulfill his responsibility. No draft constitution nor draft rules for the GPC was ever drafted and presented.

Following a change in government in May 2015, Singh left Guyana for the USA permanently.

A claim that Raj Singh was the President of the GPC, and that he was unilaterally removed from that position is a misrepresentation of the facts.

With the process left in limbo, I took on the task as head of the Steering Committee to prepare a draft constitution and the rules of the organization. Other requirements such as the election of an Interim Executive Committee, a step that was necessary before the organization could be relaunched were initiated.

The Interim Executive Committee was established on August 17, 2016. Its Members were Clement Rohee, Juan Edgehill, Andrew Bishop, Indra Ramtahul, Bibi S. Shadick, Mark Constantine, Omesh Satynand, Bishram Kuppen Mitra Ali and Robeson Benn.

The GPC was relaunched at its first meeting of the general membership on March 15, 2017 at the Sleepin Hotel on Brickdam, Georgetown.

Election for office holders were held and the following persons were duly elected: C. Rohee, President, J. Edgehill, Vice President, M. Constantine, Assistant Secretary/Treasurer. Six committee members were elected as follows; B. Kuppen, O. Satynand, M. Ali, A. Bishop, C. Duncan and H. Ally.

Later, Badrie Persaud, Khame Sharma, Peter Persaud, Norman Whittaker and Anna Correia were incorporated into the Executive Committee based on a unanimous decision of the majority Executive Committee members present.

The GPC's annual calendar of activities was based on the United Nations annual calendar of international events for observance by member states.

Speakers representing a wide cross section of Guyanese society have addressed gatherings of the organization. Activities held include; International Day Against Violence, Symposia on the Interconnection between Peace and Development, International Day marking the fight against poverty, World Environment Day, World Press Freedom Day and International Day of the Indigenous Peoples to mention a few.

The GPC regained its membership in, and affiliate status with the World Peace Council now headquartered in Athens, Greece.

At a duly constituted meeting the Executive Committee, members unanimously expressed their desire for cooperation in joint activities with the People's Progressive Party.

LONDON - MOSCOW

My first ever trip to Moscow was in 1974 via the United Kingdom, the country of my mother's birth. I was among a group of nine young Party members on our way to the capital of the then USSR to pursue studies in political science.

Janet Jagan was responsible for arranging our itinerary and coordinating with Lall Singh of the PPP UK Branch and Billy Strachan, a very good friend of the party with whom we were to make contact in case we had difficulties with the British Immigration Authorities while in transit at London Heathrow.

Fortunately, we did not encounter any problems. Though while awaiting our flight to Moscow, we were interviewed separately by persons whom I suspected were MI5 operatives.

My suspicion was aroused based on the nature of the questions we were asked like; who paid our airfares, where would we be staying while in Moscow, who will be paying for our stay in Moscow, and what will we be studying while there.

I consider Jan Carew's 'Moscow is not my Mecca' as a valuable piece of literary work but his work from a philosophical and ideological perspective clashed with my understanding of how a socialist society functioned and for whose benefit. My own experiences while living in Moscow for close to ten months taught me otherwise.

I met Jan Carew on one occasion when he came to Guyana sometime in the mid-eighties. Mrs. Jagan had an appointment to meet with him one evening at the home of a friend or relative of his in Queenstown where he was staying. Me and Gail Teixeira were invited to accompany Mrs. Jagan to the rendezvous.

We sat and listened to the conversation between the two. It was enjoyable as it was educational. I was happy that Mrs. Jagan took me along with her.

Later in life, I was to have the good fortune of accompanying Mrs. Jagan at similar meetings between herself and other Caribbean literary giants and artists.

STUDIES IN MOSCOW

Classes at the institute in Moscow were held in morning and afternoon sessions.

Professors from the Institute of Social Sciences delivered lectures on philosophy, political economy, the history of the international working-class movement and the history of the ruling party in the USSR.

With Dr. Jagan in Moscow - 1974

A comrade with whom I shared a room furnished for two, once jokingly told me while I was deep in study late one wintry night that, I needn't study too hard since he claimed, "Nobody fails here all of us will pass."

Assignments were handed to us from time to time. There were a number of inter-active sessions with the Russian professors as well.

There were students from Angola, Bangla Desh, Chile, Ethiopia, Mozambique and Yemen. We had a great time interacting and exchanging experiences with each other.

Week-end outdoor activities such as visits to and meetings with factory and state enterprises officials, workers and trade union representatives were organized with view to bringing us up to speed about how theory is put into practice at the work-place.

We enjoyed ballet performances at the famous Bolshoi theatre, the Circus of Moscow, ice hockey tournaments. And extended visits to other republics making up the USSR made our stay very interesting. The building in which we were housed for our studies had a great gym and a fantastic library. I took advantage of both facilities. A gym instructor would wake us with a whistle at 5 am each day week except week-ends. For many of us, it was a painstaking to rise at that time of the morning in the middle of a Russian winter.

A MOLE UNCOVERED

While I Moscow, I received a letter from Janet Jagan. It was sent via a comrade who was traveling to Moscow on holidays. Every year the party was invited to send about eight deserving activists to the USSR for rest and medical attention.

Because Janet Jagan knew who was abroad, she would send letters to those persons who she wanted to 'keep in the loop.'

In her letter, Mrs. Jagan informed me that Balchand Persaud, a long-standing member had been expelled from the party for "his involvement in activities inimical to the interest of the party."

Balchand was a member of the Central and Executive Committees of the Party. He had access to classified information and highly confidential records of the party. He held the key position of Organizing Secretary of the Party.

On my return to Guyana, Mrs. Jagan informed me that while Balchand was in detention along with other detainees at Sibley Hall at the Mazaruni Prisons in the 1960's he was recruited by the British intelligence services to carry out espionage activities on his own party. Balchand managed to work his way up to the top of the party and from there he provided the Brits with valuable information about the PPP.

The Party's success in uncovering Balchand's destructive role was of great importance for the maintenance of its independence and its political integrity. It was for these reasons, Balchand was expelled from the Party after he was confronted and admitted to his anti-party activities.

Because there were many PPP-sponsored students pursuing academic studies at the Patrice Lumumba People's Friendship University in Moscow, we were encouraged by the Party to meet with them from time to time.

These meetings were facilitated through the administration of our school and that of the university. The university campus was the usual venue for such meetings. At those meetings, we would discuss the political situation in Guyana and share our analysis of political, economic and social developments in the USSR and the Eastern block countries.

After our meetings, because the university students were financially better off than we were, we were invited to a nearby restaurant where we would be treated to chornee kleb with kolbasa and syr,(black bread with sausage and cheese) which we would 'chase' with pivo or kvass and, if available or affordable, the popular Russian morozhenoye or ice cream.

HOME 'SWEET' HOME

On our return to Guyana, we were pulled from the queue with arriving passengers and escorted to a small room where separately and individually, we were asked a number of political questions. I refused to answer most of the questions put to me by the two ranks who I suspected were from the Special Branch of the Guyana Police Force. All the books I had brought back with me were seized. I was told to report after two weeks to the Central Police Station at Brickdam.

On reporting to the police station on the time stipulated, the books were returned to me.

Being met by Special Branch ranks on my return home from subsequent overseas trips as I moved up the ranks of the Party, had become a routine occurrence. Not only would the ranks ask politically motivated questions, they would rummage through my luggage and take possession of literature they considered subversive.

On one occasion, I got so angry at this persistent abuse of power and personal harassment that I refused to have my suitcase searched. I was escorted to a separate room where I was confronted by two politically ugly looking individuals.

With truncheons in hand, they threatened to beat me if I did not open my suitcase and allow them to search its contents. I refused, and as they were about to start lashing out at me with their truncheons, a senior police rank in khaki uniform entered the room and shouted out aloud; "No beating ain't taking place here under my watch!" The men backed off and left the room sulking. I was told to take my belongings and leave which I did.

ON HOME GROUND

Looking back, I believe that because of the PPP's historical experience, coupled with its evolutionary maturity, the Party was successful in framing a unique philosophical and ideological outlook peculiar to the local conditions obtaining in Guyana.

That approach was critical in preparing its cadres for further ideological training overseas. Earlier training at the Party's Accabre College, put us in good stead to understand and appreciate what was taught to us at the school in Moscow as regards the applicability of theory to the praxis.

On returning to Guyana, the Moscow-trained cadres served the Party in an outstanding, if not extraordinary manner. They proved to be the most reliable politically, the best prepared ideologically and were the most effective, Party organizers in the field.

The ' Moscow graduates' as they were then called, executed their responsibilities in a highly efficient and disciplined manner. Above all, they were not loyal to any particular individual, on the contrary, they were loyal to the cause of country, people and their Party.

Cheddi Jagan never demanded loyalty to him personally from his Comrades. As far as he was concerned, loyalty to the cause for which the Party was fighting was good enough.

In any event, hero worshipping, back slapping as though we were in a Mutual Admiration Club as well as promotion of the cult of a personality was vigorously discouraged by the Party at that time and at all levels.

For Dr. Jagan, trust was to be based on commitment to the Party's ideology, its programme and policies. Honesty and transparency in the conduct of one's political and financial undertakings were of great importance to him when balanced with personal interests.

Cheddi Jagan rejected the notion of the Party being perceived as a group of 'yes' men and sycophants who simply 'followed the leader' blindly. Robust polemic on various issues of national interest was encouraged. Vigorous but constructive criticism and self-criticism were hallmarks that characterized the Jagan era.

Article 5, of the Constitution of the PPP under Rights and Duties of Members states:

'Every Member of the Party has the right within the Party, to openly express his or her view on any question under discussion. After a decision has been adopted a Party Member who disagrees has the right to appeal successively to the next higher body, including the Congress...'

Visionary he was, Dr. Jagan recognized the importance of investing in his Party's future. In this connection, cadre development, their placement and promotion were essential if the Party was to grow in both quality and quantity.

SEARCHING FOR MOM

Since passing through London on my way to Moscow in 1974, I have had the opportunity to be in London many times.

However, it never dawned upon me to visit the location where my mother lived at the time of her marriage to my father.

But, as someone once told me somewhat fatalistically, 'Nothing happens before it's time.'

And so, it was on February 1st, 2009, I arrived in London once again. This time, in my capacity as Minister of Home Affairs, to attend a Commonwealth Parliamentarians' Seminar on Human Trafficking and Migration.

On that occasion, I had in my possession, my mother's birth and marriage certificate as well as her British passport.

Before setting out for London, I had determined it was necessary for me to rid myself of a guilt feeling that had from tormented me for years simply because I did not exert any effort whatsoever to find my mother's place of residence at the time of her marriage to my dad even though I had been in her country of birth on numerous occasions.

My Mom Kathleen Rohee: 1925 - 1959

It was on a cold and wintry afternoon at about four o'clock when me and Marion Herbert, First Secretary at the Guyana High Commission in London set out by train for Wimbledon, South West London.

I knew Ms. Herbert during my tenure from 1992-2001 as the first Minister of Foreign Affairs of the PPP/C government.

It was during that period that Ms. Herbert was posted to the Guyana High Commission in London.

Since I did not know my way around London and worse yet, outside London City, Ms. Herbert was gracious enough to offer to accompany me to my destination.

We arrived at Wimbledon just after five o'clock that afternoon. The journey by train took approximately forty-five minutes.

From Wimbledon we took a cab which Ms. Herbert had pre-arranged to meet us at the train station. We proceeded to the Borough of Hendon, South West London.

Hendon is the Borough where the Parish Church of St. Paul is to be found at Mill Hill.

When we arrived at Mill Hill just after six o'clock, shades of night were already upon us. We decided to return the following day, February 2nd.

Once again, traveling the same route, accompanied by Ms. Herbert we arrived at Mill Hill at about 1400hrs. This time we proceeded straight to the church of St. Paul.

There we were welcomed by a senior member of the church and the Town Council of Hendon.

The Church of St. Paul was built and completed on August 8, 1833 under the supervision of William Willberforce. The church was consecrated on May 20, 1926.

The Church of St. Paul is where my mother and father were married on July 27, 1946, one year and three months after the end of the Second World War.

At the time of their marriage, my father was 28 years of age whilst my mom was 21.

THREE SIGNIFICANT EVENTS

Three important events occurred while I lived at the small apartment at Middle Road, La Penitence.

The Cuban embassy was established for the first time at High street Kingston, Georgetown.

Bilateral relations between Guyana and Cuba were on the upswing. Ivan Cesar Martinez, the first resident Cuban Ambassador was accredited.

The first modern dance school in Guyana was established with the help of professional Cuban dancers.

Cuban teachers in the Spanish- English language opened evening classes at the North Georgetown Secondary School. Me and Moses Nagamootoo enrolled immediately.

Cubana de Aviacion began weekly flights to Guyana with stops at Trinidad and Tobago Barbados and Jamaica. A Commercial Office along with an Office for Guyana-Cuba Cooperation in Fisheries was established in Georgetown a few doors north of the Cuban Embassy. In a matter of months, the Cuban presence in Guyana grew exponentially.

THE CUBANA AIRLINE DISASTER

I remember very well the day October 6, 1976 when we received the horrific news that the Cubana airline CU 455 had crashed into the Caribbean Sea off the coast of Barbados killing all 73 passengers on board including eleven Guyanese

It was a normal Wednesday afternoon at Freedom House when the news broke just after 3pm.

At first the news was sketchy, then it became clear that the crash was due to an explosion of two bombs placed on the aircraft by anti- Cuban terrorists.

It was a sad day for the entire English-speaking Caribbean and Cuba. The bombing of the aircraft was meant to deal a blow to Cuba- CARICOM relations and to scare off the governments, four of whom, a mere 4 years ago, had established diplomatic, trade and cultural relations with Cuba,

CARICOM-Cuba functional cooperation continues to this day notwithstanding the absence of a once vibrant CARICOM-Cuba Joint Commission

JONESTOWN

News about the Jonestown massacre was revealed to the Guyanese nation through the BBC. This angered many Guyanese from all walks of life. The Burnham Government had kept a lid on the mass suicide for almost seventy- two hours without the Guyanese people having an inkling about the matter.

The regime was embarrassed and had panicked. Its leading propagandists at the time, were at their wits end about how to handle the devastating international news that a US Congressman had been shot and killed in the interior of our country and, worse yet, how were they to explain the mass suicide of over 900 American citizens deep in Guyana's jungles.

To many Guyanese, what was not surprising was yet another expose' of the Burnham regime's penchant for 'tieing bundle' with shady and disreputable characters such as Jim Jones and his quasi, cultist People's Temple outfit. The end result being shame and disgrace brought upon a young nation still struggling against under-development and to find its way in a hostile international environment.

The news black out that enveloped the country and the restriction of foreign and local journalists who wanted to visit the location, made whatever little information that was available about the mass suicide a scarce commodity.

But PPP as always, had its feet on the ground. With the support of its activists and supporters in the area, the party received valuable information about the circumstances leading up to the mass suicide. Moreover, through contact made with the American survivors, who were part of the management of the Peoples' Temple, but who were unsupportive of the suicidal mission of Jim Jones, the PPP received even more valuable information and photographs of the terrible incident at Jonestown.

Contact was made with the party by its friends in the Caribbean who wanted first had information about the situation. In the circumstances, I was despatched by the Party on a mission abroad to provide updates to those in and out of government who had requested information and photographs of the horrific occurrence.

THE GRENADA REVOLUTION

Another historic event that occurred during this period was the overthrow of the Eric Gairy government of Grenada by the New Jewel Movement led by Maurice Bishop.

Maurice Bishop rose to prominence in the Caribbean as an outspoken critic of the despotic Gairy regime. He was a popular attorney-at-law and charismatic political leader in his country. Together with other like-minded countrymen they established, through the alliance of three organizations, the New Jewel Movement (NJM) in 1973.

The NJM emerged as the vanguard for democracy and the economic and social up-liftment of the Grenadian people.

Gairy had established himself as a buffoon on the international arena. He became the laughing stock of the Caribbean. He founded the Grenada United Labour Party (GULP) and Manual, Mental and Maritime Workers' Union. He used both to entrench himself in government making it appear as if he is the Prime Minister for life.

Gairy resorted to a combination of voodooism and political criminality characterized by the beatings and jailing of his political opponents. A pro-government, terrorist group called the 'Mongoose Squad' was established for that purpose.

In mid-November 1973, leading members of the NJM including Bishop had to be hospitalized as a result of police brutality. Gairy had established a Secret Police to augment the ranks of the country's regular police force.

The deterioration of the political situation on the island and harsh economic conditions of its populace, coupled with total control of the electoral machinery lead the leaders of NJM to conclude that only with the overthrow by force of arms of the oppressive regime could freedom and democracy be won. Moreover, according to the NJM, this decision was arrived at after they had received intelligence that Gairy had ordered the physical liquidation of their leaders

The rigging of elections in 1976 was a case in point, soldiers and police ranks were made to vote on more than one occasion. On a list of 60,000 registered votes 10,000 were bogus names. For those elections, the NJM had formed the 'People's Alliance' with the Grenada Nation Party and United People's Party

And so, it was on March 13, 1979, the day after Gairy had left the country, that thirty odd members of an armed detachment of the NJM swooped down on the army barracks in South St. George's and within a matter of minutes took control of the military. They went on to seize control of key and vital points in the country as well as the only radio station on the island.

The radio station became known as 'Radio Free Grenada' and it began broadcasting news bulletins justifying the actions of the NJM as well as appeals to the populace to support its programme and policies.

Guyana's and the rest of the English-speaking Caribbean's the response to the overthrow of the Gairy government was mixed, but basically no one regretted the fact that Gairy was gone.

The progressive, anti-imperialist governments, opposition parties and movements in Guyana, Jamaica, Suriname, Nicaragua, Cuba and in other Caribbean countries welcomed the revolutionary change in Grenada.

The revolution in Grenada took place during the 1970-1980 period when progressive/ revolutionary developments were unfolding in the Caribbean and Central America.

Electoral victories in St. Lucia, Aruba and Curaçao, the overthrow of the Patrick John government in Dominica and the Somoza dictatorship in Nicaragua as well as the progressive, nationalist military coups in Suriname in February 1980 and December 1990 respectively were manifestations of the wind of change.

The Burnham and Manley governments in Guyana and Jamaica respectively, openly voiced their support for Maurice Bishop and the change of political administration in Grenada. Bishop had visited Guyana on more than one occasion. On those occasions, I was sent by the party to welcome him on arrival at the airport and to accompany him to Georgetown from the airport.

Maurice Bishop: 1944 - 1983

One of his visits had to do with him being part of an international legal defense team engaged in a legal battle to free Arnold Rampersaud, a PPP activist who was framed for the murder of a police constable.

141

Another occasion had to do with him being on a mission to meet with Dr. Jagan to discuss bilateral relations between the PPP and the NJM as well as other matters of mutual interest.

It was during one Bishop's visits to Guyana that he met and held discussions with Forbes Burnham, the then President of Guyana.

It soon became an open secret that Burnham had agreed to provide military training in Guyana to some of Bishop's trusted lieutenants.

Following the seizure of power by the NJM, the PPP issued a statement in support of the revolutionary process initiated by the NJM. The Party however, went a step further. I was instructed to make preparations to travel to Grenada.

I departed Guyana on the night of the March 14, spent the rest of the night in Port of Spain and left early the following morning of the 15th on a LIAT flight to arrive in Grenada a mere three days after the takeover by the NJM.

I arrived in Grenada on the day before my 29th birthday.

Dr. Jagan had given me a sealed envelope containing a message to be hand delivered to Bishop.

At Grenada's International Airport I was met by representatives of the Provisional Revolutionary Government, I requested that I be taken straight away to hand the envelope to Maurice Bishop.

We drove to the radio station, the temporary headquarters of the new administration. On arrival at the radio station, I was warmly greeted by Bishop himself.

I was told that I was the first from overseas to arrive in Grenada since the events of March 13.

I handed Bishop the envelope which he quickly opened and read with great interest.

In his letter Dr. Jagan wanted to know from Bishop himself what was his new government's immediate priority.

Bishop offered me a seat, in the office he occupied, and in my presence, he put through a call to Guyana and spoke to Dr. Jagan directly telling him that his immediate priority was recognition of the new government.

Within a few minutes of that call, Bishop received a call from Michael Manley, the then Prime Minister of Jamaica. From the conversation, I gleaned it was about the same issue of diplomatic recognition of the new government.

My stay in Grenada for the next three days was hectic. Along with members of the NJM, I visited a number of places associated with the rule of former Prime Minister, Eric Gairy including the official residence of the Prime Minister on Mount Royal.

As an observer, I attended community meetings where members of the PRG interacted with residents explaining the programme and policies of the new administration. Questions were raised and answered to the satisfaction of those present.

Between the 16 and 17 of March many foreign correspondents began arriving in Grenada. Rickey Singh was among those who arrived. I bumped into him on the evening of his arrival at the same hotel where I was staying.

Diplomatic recognition of the PRG of Grenada was no easy task.

Though the majority of Caricom governments felt relieved with Gairy no longer being a member of the club, though they were not happy with the NJM's route to power. They probably feared that were they to endorse the new government in Grenada they would be sending a wrong message about the road to political power in their respective countries.

In the meantime, from all indications, Michael Manley had taken on the task of lobbying governments in the Socialist International, while Burnham targeted governments in the Non-Aligned Movement and Dr. Jagan sought the support of the USSR and the socialist countries in Eastern Europe.

On my return to Guyana from Grenada, between 20-30 March 1979, I wrote a series of articles for the MIRROR newspaper about the events in Grenada among them were; 'Exit Gairy,' 'Millionaire/witch-craft Gairy,' 'Reflections on Mount Royal' and 'Grenada- countdown to revolution.'

I never returned to Grenada since those eventful days though many of my colleagues travelled to the island to participate in conferences, workshops and other activities sponsored by the Bishop government.

General elections Westminster style was rejected by the PRG of Grenada.

Their argument was that the Westminster model was a failed model of governance and had to be replaced by a model best suited for Grenada but only after a new constitution had been promulgated following a national referendum.

In the meanwhile, Maurice Bishop assumed the responsibility of Prime Minister of the country, a cabinet was appointed. The Governor General remained in situ as the titular Head of State.

In just four and a half years, Grenada achieved many successes at the diplomatic, economic and social levels. New low-cost housing schemes were built, tremendous strides were made in public health, education became free of cost, agricultural development assumed a transformative feature in Grenadian society. A new, modern international airport to be built with the help of the Cuban Government was in the pipeline.

A fresh and new dynamism driven by the working people, the professional, intellectual and farming communities was evident for all to see.

Relations between the PPP and the WPA continued on a cordial basis throughout this period. On March 10, 1980, Dr. Jagan and Bonita Harris of the WPA were leaving by plane for Grenada to join in the first anniversary of the Grenada Revolution.

While the aircraft was on the tarmac, Harris was removed from the aircraft by security personnel. On seeing this, Dr. Jagan promptly deplaned and stood directly in front of the aircraft preventing it from leaving as a sign of protest.

Eventually, the authorities relented, no doubt because of instructions from higher up and both Dr. Jagan and Harris were allowed to leave for Grenada.

In just a matter of four and a half years after the triumph of the revolution, the rapid improvement in the lives of ordinary Grenadians was brutally interrupted by the unfortunate divisions that emerged at the leadership level of the ruling party and government.

From 23 to 25, November 1981 the First International Conference in Solidarity with Grenada was organized by the NJM and Government of Grenada. Cheddi Jagan represented the PPP at the event where he delivered an address.

In his address Dr. Jagan challenged the Guyana Government to "put the state-owned radio station and newspaper at the service of the people of Grenada to counter the lies, half-truths and slander against the Revolution."

He went on to say that as far as the PPP is concerned, "the Party is prepared to put its printing press at the service of fighting Grenada."

I left Prague permanently in the summer of 1983 only to find myself following with deep concern the dramatic unfolding events in Grenada.

The NJM leadership became embroiled in quarrels over an agreed ideological path and on strategy and tactics. So intense were the differences amongst the leaders that it resulted in a split at the leadership level of the party and government.

Proposals and counter proposals about joint leadership or power sharing between Maurice Bishop on the one hand, and his deputy Bernard Coard on the other assumed an organizational character. Hearsay and rumors became truths that began influencing policy formulation and digression from the March 13th Programmatic Platform began to be felt in social practice.

The end result was, the revolutionary process in Grenada became pregnant with ideological extremism, sectarianism, aloofness from the political realities and lack of a scientific appreciation for the role of the individual in history.

Cumulatively, the way was opened up for the implosion of a revolutionary process that had bright prospects, save for the short-sightedness and left-wing extremism by those who professed to be the 'brightest Marxists' in the English-speaking Caribbean.

The unraveling of all the socio-economic achievements that had been fought for and won by the people of Grenada in a relatively short period of time soon became a living reality, if not a nightmare for the people of Grenada.

Having not resolved the question of power, a disastrous sequence of events followed resulting in the execution/murder of Maurice Bishop and several others at True Blue on October 19, followed by the US-led invasion on October 25, 1983.

I recall during the tense period when Bishop was held under house arrest, Cheddi Jagan received a phone call from his very good friend, Dr. James Millette Professor at the Department of History UWI, and one of many progressive Caribbean academics, who asked him to act as mediator between the Bishop and Coard factions. Millette explained that he had spoken to Dr. Trevor Munroe, General Secretary of the Workers' Party of Jamaica encouraging him to join Dr. Jagan in fulfillment of that request.

Chartering an aeroplane to take Dr. Jagan from Guyana to Grenada posed a number of problems.

Dr. Jagan was reminded of his responsibility and role as 'Dean of Socialism in the Caribbean' as Maurice Bishop had once described him publicly.

In response to the call, Dr. Jagan summoned an emergency meeting of available members the Executive Committee of the Party to discuss the request and our options.

Time was of the essence. Events in Grenada were moving at a rapid pace. A decision had to be arrived at quickly.

There were many suggestions. We examined all of them as well as other options. In the end, we agreed that Dr. Jagan should not take on the role of mediator unless the two warring factions in Grenada were in agreement that he should. That position was transmitted to the parties concerned.

Bishop's supporters had no difficulty with Dr Jagan playing the role of mediator but the Coard faction was hesitant believing they had the upper hand as the crisis intensified. Moreover, they were consulting with Trevor Munroe of the Workers' Party of Jamaica (WPJ) whose role in the crisis was highly questionable.

With Coard's Revolutionary Military Council holding firm to their position and based on reports about confusion on the ground, the PPP decided it would not be safe for Dr. Jagan to travel to Grenada.

Instead, the party decided to despatch a message to both sides appealing for compromise and reconciliation in the interest of the people of Grenada and the unity and for consolidation of the progressive, democratic and anti-imperialist movement of the Caribbean.

But alas! It was too late!

A memorial service was held at the Brickdam Cathedral in honour of Maurice Bishop. The party sent representatives.

It was a very sad period for the entire Caribbean. The lessons are too many and the accounts too voluminous to be recounted here.

Suffice it to say that sometime in 1998, a communication came to the party from one of its long standing friends residing overseas enquiring whether the PPP/C government would be favorably disposed to receive those prisoners who were jailed in connection with the overthrow of Bishop and who were due to be released from prison. Having discussed the matter thoroughly the party responded saying it was not inclined to do so.

NEIGHBOUR SURINAME

The progressive, democratic contagion that had swept across the Caribbean onto South America did not leave Suriname untouched.

Some had branded the process as 'A wind of change'

Just five years after gaining independence on November 25, 1975 from the Netherlands the political situation in Suriname had reached boiling point.

Surinamese workers and farmers led by trade unions among which was Fred Derby's Progressive Labour Federation or C47 had become restless to the point of engaging in street protests in the capital city of Paramaribo.

Surinamese has grown frustrated and disillusioned with the non-delivery of goods and services as well as rampant corruption on the part of the traditional political parties; the National Party of Suriname led by Henk Aaron, the Progressive Reform Party of the VHP led by Jaggernath Latchmon and the People's Party of Indonesians in Suriname known as the Javanese Party led by Salikin Mardi Hardjo.

And in the interior of the country, armed groups led by Ronnie Brunswijk were waging guerrilla warfare.

On February 25, 1980 a group of sargeants belonging to the Surinamese military, who came to be known as the 'Group of 16' led by Dési Bouterse overthrew the Henk Aaron Government.

The military take-over of the country marked a new experience in governance for the Surinamese lasting for five years.

The NJM's road to power in Grenada seemed to have repeated itself in Suriname almost one year later.

During this period of military rule political opponents were detained, tortured and eventually executed on the ground that they were plotting to overthrow the military establishment.

The murders became known as the 'December Murders.' as of December 8, 1982.

Sometime after the February events, the PPP sent a party delegation to Paramaribo. The delegation comprised of Moses Nagamootoo, Shree Chand and myself.

The decision to send a delegation to Suriname, was in keeping with the Party's policy of establishing and maintaining Party to Party relations with whoever was the ruling party in any of Guyana's neighboring countries.

Prior to the military coup, in pursuit of this policy Dr. Jagan had visited and maintained friendly relations with the leaders of the three main political parties in Suriname.

Apart from the exploratory mission of the delegation, we were to meet with the Guyanese community in Paramaribo to determine whether they had any major concerns about their future in Suriname.

We met with Bouterse and some of his close lieutenants in a building just across the road from Fort Zeelandia.

We were given a background to the February events and on the situation at the time of our visit. We asked questions and were given answers.

We subsequently met with an appreciative number of Guyanese residents in Suriname and provided them with an update of the political situation in Guyana. We allayed their fears about their stay in Suriname.

Seven years after the coup, elections were held in Suriname under the condition that Bouterse would remain head of the military.

But by 1990, just three years after the elected government led by the VHP had been in office, the government was again overthrown by the military.

The National Assembly and the government were disbanded and replaced by military rule.

Following the coup, another PPP delegation comprising Moses Nagamootoo and Shree Chand left for Paramaribo. The objective of their mission was basically the same as it was on the previous occasion.

Between 1984 and 1990 following the visits of several delegations to Suriname, the PPP established an unofficial, presence in Paramaribo. The Surinamese authorities did not stand in the way of the PPP's request to do so since the raison d'etre was principally, to make representation on behalf of the hundreds of Guyanese resident in New Nickerie and Paramaribo, who had raised their issues and concerns with Dr. Jagan during his frequent visits to Suriname but which the Guyana Embassy in Paramaribo and the Consulate in New Nickerie at that time, had either ignored or fooled the people that they had taken up their issues with the Surinamese authorities when this was not the case.

Central Committee member, Shree Chand was identified to fulfill that responsibility.

Shree Chand served in Paramaribo until 1991 up to the time of the holding of national elections in Suriname. He was subsequently recalled to Guyana by the Party to assist in the campaign for free and fair elections in 1992.

Long after the tragic events of December 1982, in Suriname, the authorities in the Netherlands had issued an international arrest warrant for Bouterse claiming that he was behind the killings that took place in 1982.

I recall sometime between 1993 and 1997 while I was Guyana's Minister of Foreign Affairs, the non-resident Dutch Ambassador based in Suriname accredited to Guyana paid a courtesy call on my office.

During our conversations he raised two controversial issues.

The first had to do with an international arrest warrant for Bouterse issued by his government. The Ambassador wanted the Guyana government to give effect to the warrant by arresting Bouterse during a stop over he was scheduled to make at our international airport at Timehri where the Dutch authorities would have a plane waiting to fly him to Holland.

I rejected the request on the ground that first, we did not have in our possession any official arrest warrant for Bouterse; secondly, that such a move would prove harmful to Guyana-Suriname relations and, thirdly that it have could have dire repercussions as regards the huge Guyanese population in the neighboring country.

The second issue the Dutch Ambassador raised was concerning the presence in French Guyana of Gregory Smith the alleged assassin of Walter Rodney.

He raised this matter in the context of the extradition laws of the European Union.

The Ambassador appeared to be very much aware of the call to have Smith extradited to Guyana to stand trial, though he was quick to draw to my attention that so long as the death penalty remains on our statute books Smith could not be extradited to Guyana. In other words, the Ambassador was telegraphing to me the need to abolish the death penalty.

The discussion ended without any agreement on the two matters.

When I briefed President Cheddi Jagan on the two matters he supported my position and suggested that the positions be maintained.

Elections have since been held in Suriname on Monday 22nd May 2020. After more than two decades in government, Bouterse's New Democratic Party, lost the election to the Progressive Reform Party, an electoral alliance led by Chan Santokhi.

The collapse of the Grenada revolution had a negative impact on the national democratic process that had begun in Suriname under Bouterse. Soon after the US-led invasion the Surinamese Government expelled the Cuban Ambassador and a number of Cuban nationals from the country.

OFF TO PRAGUE

One morning, after settling down at my desk at Freedom House to begin the day's work, I was invited to Dr. Jagan's Office to meet with him.

After the usual pleasantries and exchange of views about party work at home and abroad, I was informed by Dr. Jagan that the party Secretariat had selected me to be its representative on the Editorial Board of the magazine 'World Marxist Review' which was based in Prague, Czechoslovakia.

I was shown the invitation letter signed by Konstantin Zaradov, Editor-in-Chief of the magazine which provided details about travel arrangements and accommodation for me and my family in Prague.

Dr. Jagan encouraged me to accept the decision, to advise my family and to begin making preparations to travel.

I agreed.

Soon after, Mrs. Jagan invited me to her office to talk about my responsibilities while in Prague.

My party responsibilities at home would be taken care of by herself and Kellawan Lall. Mrs. Jagan was kind enough to advise of her willingness to provide any help I may need.

My selection to be the Party's Representative at the magazine in Prague took me completely by surprise. I surmised that it must have been based on the confidence the party had in me to be assigned such an important responsibility.

What was even more puzzling to me was, why I was selected when there so many other senior and capable comrades at the leadership level of the party.

To this day, I have not been able to figure that out.

Preparations to travel was made easy because we did not have much in terms of furniture nor other earthly possessions.

What we had as our earthly possessions been either sold, given away or stored for safekeeping. Books that I had accumulated were packed in wooden crates and stored at the New Guyana Company Ltd. where the Mirror newspaper was printed.

Obtaining travel documents such as passports for my wife and my five-year old daughter, income tax clearance and approval for intransit visas for the UK while awaiting the airline tickets took sometime.

Of interest to me was when I returned to the British High Commission to uplift our intransit visas, the then High Commissioner advised me that in view of the fact that my mother was a British citizen by birth, I was entitled to British citizenship and if I so desired I can apply and receive it.

My response to him was I will think about it and will get back to the High Commission on my return. I never took up the offer.

A small farewell party was kept for me and family at Party headquarters the evening before our departure on October 31, 1979

Our route to Prague was Georgetown- Barbados-London-Prague.

Our arrival at London Heathrow on the morning of November 1st 1979 was problematic. We were asked a ton of questions by immigration authorities, like why didn't we have visas for Czechoslovakia, who sponsored our travel, who paid for our tickets, how long will we be in Prague, where will we be accommodated, who will pay for our accommodation and so forth.

Notwithstanding my answers to all the questions, we were never the less separated from other arrivals and placed in a room with others passengers from mainly from Third World countries who appeared to be faced with a similar situation.

We were detained for several hours but were eventually released and given seventy- two hours to get our Czech visas, rebook our flight and leave the UK for Prague.

With the help of a female Immigration/Welfare Officer we managed to rebook our flight. The airline gave us one-night free accommodation and meals at a hotel near the airport and provided transportation to the hotel and back to the airport.

It was already late in the evening of November 1st when we checked in at the hotel. Refreshing baths, a sumptuous dinner and early rest helped us regain our confidence and determination to push ahead.

While my wife and daughter were having breakfast at the hotel, I left by taxi for the Czech Consulate where the visas were easily uplifted.

We returned to the airport, checked in and not too long after were on our way to Prague.

The journey so far had been tough for my wife and daughter both of whom had never travelled before but I was happy to note that they had persevered and was keeping up with the journey thus far.

It was a cold wintry evening of November 2, 1979 when we arrived in Prague. And because we had missed our flight in London, there was no one at the airport to meet us. Fortunately, we were provided with sufficient warm clothing for the cold winter season before leaving Guyana. The 'winter coats' especially, were used by students who had returned to Guyana after completing their studies in the USSR.

With the help of a Czech Good Samaritan we were provided with tickets free of cost for the tram that would take us to 3, Thakurova street, Prague 6, where after walking a little distance we would reach the building where the Editorial Board was housed.

In Prague - 1979

Having arrived at the location, and after introducing ourselves, we were provided with transportation which took about twenty-five minutes to arrive at Bohnice, in Prague 8, Lesenka 547, apartment 30 where we would live for the next three years.

My work at the Editorial Board of the magazine entailed authoring or co-authoring articles after participating in study tours to countries who had representatives on the Board; Taking part in round table discussions, seminars and conferences sponsored by the theoretical organs of fraternal parties and of the magazine itself.

Further, I was expected to respond to requests from my party to attend and address congresses and other events such as newspapers festivals of fraternal parties in Europe as well as international conferences to which the party had been directly invited but could not attend because of distance and financial constraints.

In effect, my responsibilities entailed theoretical work, representation and writing articles for both the magazine and the PPP.

At the journal, otherwise known as "World Marxist Review" or 'Problems of Peace and Socialism' we were expected to be critical but constructive in identifying the problems of socialism and its various expressions.

Critical analysis from a Marxist perspective was what mattered in our discussions and in our writings for the magazine which was circulated in over 70 countries.

It was a general understanding among the Representatives, that their respective parties looked to the magazine to bring out the social, political and economic problems inherent in socialist societies. Problems swept under the carpets by officialdom in those countries, yet discussed hush-hushed by ordinary folk also formed part of our discussions.

We who lived and worked for a while in socialist country and, who paid working visits to others from time to time, knew that contrary to the official positions published by the ruling communist and workers' parties, there was another side of the coin. We recognized that there were two realities, one reality seen through the prism of the ruling parties and the other, seen though the eyes of the common man and woman.

Ours was the task to write about these problems in such a way that we did not appear to be critical nor offensive to the ruling parties who had representatives on the Editorial Board of the magazine. This was no easy task.

Living in Prague helped my wife gain deeper insights into the social and economic challenges obtaining in a socialist society and their impact on the common man and woman.

At the kindergarten school my daughter attended, manifestations of social and racial prejudices were to be felt. Some Czech kids encouraged by some parents made every effort to marginalize my daughter, the 'Little Black Girl' who was the only one of her complexion and race at the school.

Many afternoons she would come home from school crying, demanding not to be sent back.

It was only after several complaints by my wife, assisted by a sympathetic pensioner, who lived in our apartment building, and who had befriended my wife, that the disgusting behavior ended.

Pensioners in Czechoslovakia, who escaped the clutches of the Nazis and survived the Second World War, are recognized as War Heroes and Heroines. They are respected and listened to by younger persons who never experienced the ravages of a war.

Recognizing that my daughter would have problems adjusting to conditions back home and that enrollment at a Guyanese school was necessary if her education was to be advanced, we returned to Guyana to address the problem.

My efforts to meet with officials at the Ministry of Education to explain our predicament and to arrive at a mutually agreeable solution proved futile. In the circumstances, I came to the conclusion that, because of my political affiliation, the officials at the Ministry of Education avoided me like the plague.

Left without any help from the Ministry of Education, I turned to some friends who were in the teaching profession for advice. Very useful advice was offered which me and my wife accepted and enrolled our daughter at a primary school where she was graded and placed appropriately.

I returned to Prague for one more year leaving my family behind.

DEATH OF MY FATHER

During my second year in Prague, I learnt that my father had died on September 13, 1982. The cause of death was cancer of the stomach.

This was sad news for me. Regrettably, I could not return home for his funeral, the Party could not afford to fund my return nor could I on my own.

In a telephone conversation with Mrs. Jagan she conveyed her sympathies as well as those of Dr. Jagan and all my party Comrades back home. Mrs. Jagan gave me her assurances that the Party will provide whatever help that was needed for his burial.

Later, I was informed that Dr. and Mrs. Jagan attended his funeral.

At the time of his passing, my dad lived alone with the Bacchus family in Kitty, Greater Georgetown.

He and Mr. Bacchus had worked together as mechanic/ fitters at the Torani Irrigation scheme.

When the DeGroots emigrated to Canada, Dad went to live with the Bacchus family who were kind enough to accept him as a member of their family.

'RR' as he was popularly called, never took another woman during the twenty-three years since his wife Kathleen had passed away.

His death brought back the image of a surprise visit he paid to my office at party headquarters. He came to tell me that he was suffering from a terrible pain in his stomach after eating a banana. He had visited a medical doctor who advised him to do an endoscopy after which he would determine what next should be done.

Dad told me he had agreed to be admitted to the hospital and to undergo the operation.

Before leaving for Prague, I visited my dad with my wife and daughter at the Georgetown hospital's Seaman's Ward.

He was happy to see us and as usual, he had a task for me. He wanted me to massage his feet which I gladly did. Also, he asked for a glass of fresh orange juice which I brought the following day. He drank it all with a happy and satisfied look on his face

When I told my dad, we were leaving for Prague he said nothing. He just looked away. I took that as a sign of disapproval but then he looked back at me and wished us well. That pleased me.

Leaving the hospital, I knew I would not see him again, it was a painful feeling but the die was already cast. As destiny would have it, I was leaving to go in one direction while my dad would be leaving this life forever.

But there were happy moments while I lived and worked in Prague.

Dr. Jagan was the first to arrive in August 1980. He came to participate in a congress of the World Federation of Trade Unions (WFTU) with headquarters based in Prague.

Those were happy moments for me. Chatting with Dr. Jagan about the latest developments in Guyana and Europe much of the which he already knew since he read widely and kept abreast with world news by way of a small portable transistor radio, he always had with him.

During his short stay in Prague, I had the pleasure to accompany Dr. Jagan to the courtesy calls I had arranged prior to his arrival. The exposure these meetings gave me, and the knowledge I gleaned from the conversations thereat, was a great experience for me.

While in Prague, visiting General Secretaries and or Chairmen of political parties were given the opportunity to address the full Editorial Council of the magazine. The session included a question and answer period during which members of the Council were afforded the opportunity to pose questions to the distinguished visitors.

Dr. Jagan's visit to Prague was followed by separate visits for different occasions by, Sheik Feroze Mohammed, Education Secretary of the Party; Janet Jagan, International Secretary and Harry Persaud Nokta, Organizing Secretary, all members of the Central and Executive committees of the Party.

To be with Janet Jagan on a visit to any country was always fun-filled politically, culturally and educationally. There was always something to learn. Her visit to Prague was no exception. An ardent lover of culture she enjoyed every moment being in Prague, the heart of Central Europe. She was great at combining her political responsibilities with cultural excursions to museums, castles, theatre, visits to bookstores and souvenir shops as well as to historical sites. She always carried with her a little note book in which she pencilled in the birth dates of her relatives, close friends and those Comrades for whom she had a deep appreciation.

Moving around with Mrs. Jagan, while allowing her, her space and privacy is something only those who knew her could do.

I enjoyed walking in the summer time from Thakurova 3, Praha 6, where I worked, to the apartment building where we lived at 547, Lesenska, Bohnice, Praha 8.

A leisurely walk which took approximately one two hours through Prague's Central Park was relaxing as it was refreshing. Inside the park there were some huge ponds where ducks and swans swam around. And the flowers were just gorgeous when in full bloom.

Along the way, there were small hospices or vinarnas snugged neatly between six feet high grassy hedges where workers still in their blue overalls could be seen imbibing vino or pivo and eating sausages with mustard and black bread.

At small restaurants, the traditional klenedlik with stewed meat and steamed cabbage would be served. And a schnapp or two of the famous Becherovka would go along nicely along with that dish.

As I passed by, I would hail out 'ahoy, dobry den' to the Czechs sitting on long wooden benches, this was the typical way of saying hello and good day to the ordinary Czechs.

While in Prague I took every opportunity to learn the Czech language and to sharpen my skills in the Russian language which had diminished since my days in Moscow.

I took the opportunity on weekends to visit many of the ancient castles, walk along the Charles Bridge, visit the Old Town square to observe the movement of the famous astronomical clock that attracts thousands of tourists from all over the world. Window-shopping and eating out on Saturdays on Wenceslas Square where hundreds of small and medium size shops, department stores and outdoor restaurants can be found proved to be relaxing and entertaining.

ESPIONAGE ON PPP LEADERS

It was during my stay in Prague, the Party received reliable intelligence indicating that the British Secret/Intelligence Services M15 and M16 had been collaborating with Special Branch of the Guyana Police Force since the pre-independence period. This collaboration continued until the 1980's. Evidence was provided to show how telegrams and cables sent by Dr. Jagan to relatives and friends in the UK were intercepted, read and analysed. The analysis was shared from contact to contact.

The general assumption was that this collaborative, secretive intelligence gathering on the activities of the Jagan's must have been more widespread covering all areas of active communications depending on the location of Dr. Jagan and his relatives, comrades and friends.

In fact, when the official records of the British Intelligence Services concerning Dr. and Mrs. Jagan were declassified and released in March 2014, a perusal of the records show that since the 1950's, the movements of the Jagan's were being closely monitored, and their communications with friends abroad intercepted and read by the British intelligence services and passed on to Special Branch in the then British Guiana long after independence.

While in Prague, I spent many hours reading and studying the Marxist classics on my own.

Thanks to my studies in Moscow, I did not find it difficult to go further from where I had left off, first in Guyana, and later in Moscow.

Life in Prague gave me the opportunity to study the experiences of political parties in other countries particularly in Latin America. I was able to study their experiences in conjunction with ours as regards our common struggle to improve the living and working conditions of the people in our respective countries.

As the Party's Representative in Europe I represented the party at many international conferences, newspaper festivals and congresses of fraternal parties in Greece, France, Portugal, Finland, Sweden, Denmark, Austria, the USSR, Bulgaria, Romania, Mongolia, The German Democratic Republic, Italy, West Germany, Yugoslavia, Poland and Hungary.

By the time I returned home from Prague, the party had built up a formidable network of connections with fraternal parties which was critical for support and solidarity in our fight against the Burnham dictatorship, for the restoration of democracy and for free and fair elections

My visits to and conversations with fraternal parties in those countries complemented the on-going efforts at home by Cheddi and Janet Jagan. Collectively, our efforts helped to cement the relationship with the parties based on international friendship and solidarity.

Cumulatively, my international engagements put me in good stead and preparedness for the political and ideological struggles at home and for my party.

DONALD RAMOTAR

I finally left Prague for home in the summer of 1983. I was replaced by Donald Ramotar. Comrade Ramotar was born in the same year as I was. He is few months younger than I am.

Donald and I joined the party in the late 1960's.

I knew Donald while he worked as a sales clerk at GIMPEX. We became close friends and comrades.

On many occasions during budget debates in the National Assembly we would walk from Party headquarters to Parliament buildings to listen to the speeches by Parliamentarians from both sides of the House. Dr. Jagan's and Burnham's speeches were the most interesting to listen to but our own MP's were always well prepared to hammer the government ministers.

MP 'Boysie' Ram Karan was the best at poking fun at government ministers and extremely witty with his heckling at times

Ramotar liked singing calypsos and knew the lyrics of many by heart.

He married Deolatchmee aka 'Vejai' on November 5th, 1974 at a simple civic ceremony at the Office of the General Register in the presence of Feroze Mohammed and Narbada Persaud as witnesses.

Because Dr. Jagan wanted leading party activists to learn to drive motor vehicles the party decided that arrangements be made for me and Donald to take driving instructions together. Arrangements were made with an instructor who had a small motor car painted in yellow.

We started our 'driving lessons' together taking turns at the wheel, but soon after, I left for Prague while Donald completed his instructions and tests successfully.

To this day, I never learnt, and do not know how to drive a motor car.

While still a political activist in the Kitty/Campbelville area of the city, Donald later became active in the trade union movement and played an important role in the initial activities of the Federation of Independent Trade Unions (FITUG) - break-away of four Trade Unions from the Guyana Trades Union Congress (GTUC) which was dominated by government-controlled and company unions.

Like most Party cadres, Donald was sent in 1972 to the Soviet Union for training in political science.

After spending some years as a political and trade leader at home Donald and his family left for Prague in October 1983

After spending three years working at the magazine World Marxist Review, he returned home in 1987 and took up the job as manager for the Party headquarters.

Between 1989 and 1990 Ramotar attended the University of Guyana to study for a Bsc in Economics.

When I became a Minister of Government in 1992, Donald took over as Executive Secretary of the Party. In 1997, he was elected General Secretary of the Party and, in 2011 he was elected President of the country.

On my return to Guyana from Prague, I found myself and family without a home of our own.

My wife and daughter who had returned a year earlier were staying with her sister at Leonora village on West Coast of Demerara.

I took up lodging at Party headquarters for a few months until my wife managed to locate for rental, a small one-bedroom apartment at Vreed-en-hoop village on the West Coast village life in Guyana at that time was not easy.

There was no running potable water at the upper level of the apartment. Water for washing, bathing and cooking had to be fetched from a tap located deep under the parapet by the road side.

A make shift hut for use as a bathroom was built for us by the landlord. And, an outhouse a little distance behind the building was made available to us. While living under those rather cramped and insanitary conditions, completely different from the far more comfortable and hospitable conditions we enjoyed in Prague, we continued our search for a more comfortable but affordable dwelling place.

Two issues had to be settled on my return home from Prague was the question of my responsibility at Party headquarters and a salary. It appeared that the Party was faced with three options. First, to appoint me manager at Freedom House. Second, to put me in charge of party work in Georgetown and thirdly, to appoint me International Secretary of the Party. Following discussions first, at the Secretariat and then at the Executive levels it was decided that I should be appointed International Secretary. However, for that to happen, it meant that Janet Jagan would have to step down as International Secretary and assume the newly created post as Executive Secretary. As I was already a member of both the Executive and Central Committee, the transition was not problematic. A recommendation by the General Secretary on behalf of Secretariat to the Executive Committee and then from the Executive Committee to the Central Committee for the creation of the new post of Executive Secretary and then for me to be appointed International Secretary was unanimously agreed. By 1983, my salary was fixed at $550 per month. Before I left for Prague in 1979 it was $289 per month.

With D. Ramotar & Frank Anthony at a Party Congress

RIMA ARRIVES

My second daughter was born on April 18, 1985 while we lived at Vreed-en-Hoop, on the West Coast of Demerara. Janet Jagan suggested the name Rima, the forest nymph in the book 'Green Mansions' authored by W.H. Hudson. We agreed. And, as is traditional, she received her second name Amila after Comrade Reep a Hindu Priest, opened the 'Patra' or 'Book' to find a suitable Hindu name for the newborn.

My Second Daughter; Rima

The Demerara River separates West Demerara from the capital city of Georgetown where I worked.

Crossing the river early each morning and late evenings was a pleasure for me since it gave me the opportunity to meet people and to chat with them about politics and challenges of every day life.

After awhile, the 'regulars' on the ferry looked forward to seeing me to give them updates on local political developments they in turn would offer their opinions most times grounded in the reality of the communities where they lived.

While residing at Vreed-en-Hoop, I was afflicted with a bout of typhoid due to the living conditions. My good friend Dr. Moti Lall who had his clinic not too far from were we lived came to examine me and recommended that I be hospitalized

166

immediately. He was good enough to take me in his car to the West Demerara Public Hospital and saw to my immediate admission.

Dr. Madan Rambarran took very good care of me and saw to it that I was administered with regular injections which I was beginning to complain about but which put me back on my feet after about two weeks in hospital.

SEARCHING FOR A NEW HOME

Unknowing to me, Mrs. Jagan made enquiries about my living conditions at Vreed-en-Hoop and after being briefed by Dr. Moti Lall she suggested that I relocate immediately.

On my resumption to work Mrs. Jagan, Mike Persaud, the manager of Freedom House and I, visited about four houses on the East Coast that were up for rent. Mike lived at Success Village, on the East Coast, he had scouted around earlier making enquiries and had identified the houses.

What touched me most of all was the humanitarian character of Mrs. Jagan who took time off from her usually busy schedule and to drive herself in her Volkswagen to all four locations.

We eventually settled for a house at Courbain Park at La Bon Intention (LBI), a village on the East Coast.

Mrs. Jagan helped me pay the rent from of her personal savings.

Having found a suitable place to live with enough living room I was able to retrieve more of my personal belongings which were stored at the building housing the Mirror newspaper and others which we had accumulated during our stay in Prague

Later, on the party decided to invest some of its resources by purchasing a few properties. One such property was a house at Atlantic Ville about three miles outside the city. I was granted permission to live in that house with my family.

Consequently, we relocated from LBI to Atlantic Ville. A few years later, a two-bedroom apartment was added to the bottom of the building. Comrade Kellawan Lall, a journalist at the Mirror newspaper and his family were granted permission to occupy the apartment.

LIFE AT ATLANTIC VILLE

I lived at Atlantic Ville from 1988 to 1992. Those were extremely difficult years. My eldest daughter, Renate, attended the Cummings Lodge Secondary school, a stone's throw away from where we lived.

My younger daughter Rima, attended the St. Roses nursery school on Church street, Georgetown. My task was to take her to school in the mornings and to take her home from school. This was done on my way to work and from work.

Later, after sitting what was then known as the Common Entrance Examination, she attended St. Stanislaus College and later, at St. Joseph's High School where she ended her secondary school education. A shot at a government scholarship to pursue studies in Cuba was aborted due to the difficult circumstances obtaining in Cuba at that time as well as challenges with the Spanish language.

The transportation situation in Guyana at the time was horrendous due to constant shortages of gasoline, me and Rima would stand on the roadside for a considerable amount of time before we could get a squeeze in one of the minibuses heading for the city.

On some occasions, we would hitch a ride with friends or party comrades who would pass our way on their way to Georgetown.

My wife Rajdai decided that she wanted to do something profitable. She took some of our small savings and bought a few dozen small-sized packets of black pepper, curry powder and baking powder. She would walk from stall to stall at Bourda market offering her products for sale.

Eventually, she built up a reasonable clientele who bought her stuff on a regular basis. She saved part of the earnings and invested the other part in her business. Small and tiresome her business was, she nevertheless took on the task of collecting Rima from school some afternoons when my political work took me out of the city.

One afternoon while I was still at work Rima surprised me when she suddenly appeared at the door of my office. On enquiring who brought her she replied telling me that she walked all the way from her school on Church street to Freedom House on Robb street.

A feeling of anger mixed with admiration gripped me. I immediately packed my things and took her home.

Rajdai was a great cook and homemaker. She always wanted her own home and was quite satisfied with the little we had. We pooled what little savings we had accumulated and bought new, additional furniture for our home including a second-hand refrigerator.

During a trip to Cyprus I bought a three- burner table model gas stove. I packed it in my suitcase and brought it home much to the pleasure and satisfaction of my wife. A good cook is always pleased with a good stove.

We were struggling but things were slowly improving.

The banning a basic food items by the Burnham government was wreaking havoc in the country, all classes and social strata in the country were affected. Smuggling and black- marketing of the prohibited items became a big business.

Persons would walk from house to house, quietly selling potatoes, onions, garlic, flour and a variety of canned stuff such as sardines and corned beef for sale at prices many could ill afford.

My wife could only afford to buy small quantities of basic food items at prices she could afford.

Because I was International Secretary of the Party, I was required to travel overseas frequently to attend conferences, congresses and other international events on behalf of the party. Rajdai took care of everything while I was away. And even when I was at home, participating in Party political activities in the countryside, which sometimes lasted for an entire week-end or more, it meant spending time away from family and home.

WHEN DEATH STRIKES

Rajdai became pregnant once again. An examination by her gynecologist found that the fetus was badly located. She had to be hospitalized to undergo minor surgery. The surgery was successful but she had to remain in hospital for a few days to undergo medical observation by her doctor. Rajdai returned home safely and soon after was back to normal and started with her vending once again.

About three weeks later, she fell into a state of depression and began talking about being infected by blood from the blood bank of the hospital. She was advised by doctors close to the family not to worry because if that was the case any infection would have shown up in blood tests she would have done already. My wife appeared happy to hear that but a few days after she was again in a state of depression. I tried my best to talk her out of it hoping that conversation would help, but this was not to be.

Returning home one afternoon in late November of 1991, with my youngest daughter, I noticed the back door to our home was wide open, this was highly unusual. In the yard, a huge amount of laundry fresh from washing still hung fluttering in a cool breeze on the 'clothes lines' and a plastic tub with yet another set of clothes was left to soak. This was also unusual.

On entering the house, I called out for my wife, my daughter called out for her mom but there was no answer. We looked around the rooms but found no one, however, when I pushed the door to enter the bathroom, I found it was partly blocked by a chair behind the door. I pushed harder and managed to pass through, I looked up and there was my wife hanging from a rafter of the roof with a skipping rope around her neck. She looked as if she was dead.

I called out to a neighbor who came over and helped me cut her loose with a kitchen knife and lift her onto our bed in the master bedroom. We tried to resuscitate her but she was cold, rigor mortis had taken over the body. Luckily, my daughter did not witness this dreadful sight until her mother's lifeless body lay on the bed.

My wife Rajdai had committed suicide, as she lay on the bed, I sat next to her with tears in my eyes and I kept asking why? All the beautiful memories beginning from the day I met her, all through the difficult days we shared together, the years we spent in Prague, the birth of our two daughters, all these memorable events flashed though my mind as I sat and looked at her totally devastated.

It was another shocking and painful experience in my life. On a table in the sitting room I found a note she had written with a wild flower placed on it.

In her note, she said she regretted doing what she did but that she did it for the sake of the betterment of the family. She asked that I take care of our two girls especially Rima. By this time, neighbors were alerted about what happened. People began gathering outside our house. I asked a neighbor to call Mrs. Jagan at Freedom House and ask her to come. She came with her car filled with comrades.

Next came the police, then the people from the funeral parlour, then the journalists. My eldest daughter arrived home from school only to find the situation confusing. The police in the presence of a newspaper journalist asked my permission to take the note. I consented.

My wife's sisters accompanied by their husbands came. The House was filled with screams and loud weeping for a long while.

I retired to my room to rest and to try to understand what had happened while my wife was alone at home and why she did what she did. I just could not. The period of mourning, the wake nights, the funeral arrangements and the burial were held in keeping with a mix of Hindu and Christian traditions.

My comrades especially Mrs. Jagan and Rev. Dale Bisnauth of Burns Memorial Church were extremely helpful throughout the entire period.

My sisters-in-law, 'Dats,' 'Chand' and 'Toolsie' stayed at our home in turns to prepare meals and to attend to the needs of my daughters and other friends and relatives who dropped by to extend their condolences.

Because I had already emerged as a public figure and was in the news due to my political activities and a member of the Elections Commission, my wife's death was given wide coverage in the local media. But the worst was yet to come.

The government- controlled Guyana Chronicle somehow got hold of my wife's suicide note. I suspected all along, that the culprit who passed the note to the newspaper, was the police detective who came to do the investigation. He claimed he needed the note as 'evidence.' It must have been him who passed either the contents, or the actual note to the editor of the Chronicle newspaper at that time. There was no other way the contents of that note could have found its way in the pages of the government-controlled newspaper. Its contents were published along with a horror story speculating over the cause of my wife's death.

Janet Jagan brought the story to my attention and sought my agreement on a course of action she had contemplated. I concurred.

She called for a meeting with the editors-in-chief of the Guyana Chronicle, the Catholic Standard, the Stabroek News and the Mirror newspapers, the existing newspapers at the time, to discuss publication of the story concerning my wife's death and a course of action that could be agreed upon.

Those attending were Adam Harris, Father Andrew Morrison, David DeCaries and Janet Jagan.

The meeting agreed to a Code of Ethics concerning publication of deaths by suicide and how such occurrences should be reported in the press in future. The code was published in all four newspapers. The Chronicle newspaper eventually published an apology on the distorted story it had carried about my wife's death. This was just another manifestation of the greatness in spirit and humanity of Janet Jagan.

Mrs. Jagan was firm in her convictions about certain matters concerning the political and social life of her comrades and the wider community. Sadly, Rajdai did not live to see the day she had looked forward to, the victory of PPP/C at the polls on October 5, 1992.

IDEOLOGICAL SOMERSAULTING

My days in the Progressive Youth Organization (PYO) were the formative years of my political life.

Throughout my entire political life and work I have always sought to share my experiences with younger comrades hoping they would understand and appreciate what is meant to be politically and ideologically steeled.

In today's world, fraught with ideological confusion, convulsions and diversions, young people are the prime targets. They are viewed by populist demagogues as victims to be waylaid. The populist prowlers unabashedly proselytize tantalizing promises of the so-called 'good life' and/or that they stand in support of 'government for all the people.'

At the same time, getting into the action are the ayatollahs of the free market economy and free trade who openly proclaim neo- liberalism as the flavor of the day.

These charlatans boldly declare that any other economic model is anathema to and of no relevance in today's world.

Worshippers at the altar of unbridled capitalism are actively engaged in a campaign to discredit politically and intellectually any other model for economic development.

IDEOLOGICAL CHALLENGES FACING YOUTH

Regrettably, many young people in our midst are incapable of recognizing the fierce ideological battle currently taking place at a global level. And the local media has been totally unhelpful in this respect.

173

Had it not been for the Internet and the World Wide Web one can very well imagine how misinformed and poorly informed many of us would be.

Today's young generation know little or nothing about economic theory and practice nor about alternative models of socio-economic development.

Neither have they been schooled in the belief that people-centered models, practiced by clean and lean government, can bring about radical, all-round improvements in the living standards of working people.

Our young people have grown up in a uni-polar world. Multilateralism is under attack and every effort is being made to undermine and replace it with unilateralism, a reversal that can prove harmful to the national interests of developing countries like Guyana.

General knowledge of societies once called the Union of Soviet Socialist Republics (USSR) and the socialist bloc of countries in Eastern Europe is basically unknown. Not that they were the best examples, but they were nevertheless historic alternative models of economic development to be studied at least academically and from which lessons could be drawn.

Moreover, those who once proclaimed an unadulterated commitment to establish an economic alternative to the free market economy found themselves experimenting with developmental models that, by and large, were quite the opposite to what their founder leaders preached during the heady days of the 1970's and '80's.

CHINA, CUBA, VIETNAM AND THE NEWLY LIBERATED STATES IN AFRICA

In China, Vietnam and to some extent Cuba, the ruling parties, have adopted economic policies that, are socialist in form but fundamentally capitalist- oriented in content. In this respect, China is leading the way under the euphemism that it is 'Building socialism with Chinese characteristics.'

China's 'One Belt, One Road Initiative' is objectively developmental, but in effect, it is the Chinese version of neo-liberalism and market economics being promoted at an international level.

The Democratic People's Republic of Korea (DPRK) has downplayed the 'Juche Idea.' Its current leaders look to the Chinese model as a means of facilitating the building and sustaining its own indigenous brand of socialism with Korean characteristics. It wants to maintain the extant political-juridical system of governance but to promote capitalist development without dismantling the status quo.

In other words, the DPRK wants to eat its cake and have it.

The United States, South Korea and Japan are unsupportive, they want North Korea to denuclearize and open up to the West. Kim Jung Un's response was, "No way!"

Following the assumption to power in the mid- '80's by national liberation movements in Southern Africa viz; Mozambique, Angola, Guinea-Bissau, Namibia, as well as in Kampuchea and Laos, the preferred non-capitalist path to development adumbrated by progressive, anti-colonial, anti-imperialist leaders of that time led by Amilcar Cabral, Sam Nujoma, Oliver Tambo, Agostinho Neto and Samora Machel. With their passing, the alternative and developmental non-capitalist model was dumped by their successors and replaced by free market economies, fully integrated within the world capitalist system.

Corruption and nepotism are rampant in these countries and the state has become a vehicle for personal enrichment and accumulation of money and properties by the ruling elites.

Cuba is exceptional in many respects. Because of the economic blockade imposed by the USA, Cuba is unable to take full advantage of what the world capitalist system has to offer to build its brand socialism on the island.

However, with the implementation of numerous imaginative economic policies and a range of 'local heresies,' implemented by the Cuban authorities' ways and means have been found to sustain and advance up to a certain point, the socialist project initiated in 1959.

Stagnation would have become imminent had significant reforms not been initiated by the Cuban government.

A new constitution has been promulgated in Cuba to address the deficiencies and to apply corrective measures to ensure the sustainability and viability of Cuban society in all its manifestations.

Incidentally, many new leaders who now hold office in the countries that once proclaimed a preference for socialist-orientation, had, in their younger days, pursued academic studies in the Soviet Union and other Eastern European socialist countries. However, with the collapse of the world socialist system, the resurgence of global capitalism and the emergence of neo-liberalism as the dominant ideology globally, those cadres, claiming ideological evolution and maturity, have since abandoned their once held progressive, national democratic convictions and have been transformed into born again neo-liberal, free market converts.

In Africa for example, by way of ideological acrobatics the new African elites in the former national democratic states have somehow managed to reconcile their Marxist economic schooling with the customary wheeling and dealing praxis of free market economics.

NO IDEOLOGY IS AN IDEOLOGY

To many of our young cadres, these historical antecedents are but mere abstract notions of a world that closely resembles the lost civilization of Lemura, consequently, lessons on historical materialism are meaningless.

176

In fact, any suggestion encouraging them to study the historical evolution of society from a scientific perspective makes no sense whatsoever, save and except that, while in pursuit of a university degree, it becomes compulsory for them to do so during their POL.100 tutorials.

To make matters worse, courses in the social sciences at the University of Guyana are conducted by lecturers who are general supportive of the neo-liberal ideology and are prejudiced against any alternative model to the capitalist mode of development.

REJECTION OF THE 'ISMS' - A FORM OF DE-IDEOLOGIZATION

The current ideological convulsion taking place at the global level is manifesting itself at the national levels as well and Guyana is no exception.

With the neo-liberal ideologues now ruling the roost, today's young generation has been consumed by an ideology that is inherently anti-socialist, pro-capitalist and opportunistic in world outlook.

In the circumstances, given the dominance of neo-liberalism, the way has been opened up to promote the false belief that there is 'no need for adherence to any 'ISM' save and except the 'ISM' associated with capitalism. This particular matter is conveniently overlooked by the 'ideological modernists' because of their conviction that market economics is the 'be all and end all' of life on earth.

The campaign against any 'ISM' save and except the 'ISM' associated with capitalISM is ideological by its very nature.

Any proponent of this argument who claims otherwise is being obtuse and deceptive to say the least. Only those who do not know better will fall for such utter nonsense.

In the course of the de-ideologization process of political parties in developing countries their search for an ideological middle ground in effect, places them in the camp of liberal democracy.

The sum total of this de-ideologization process, meaning, transitioning from one ideology to another, is bound to result in a 'lost generation' of cadres, within parties that once had as its reservoir, a well equipped, rounded collection of cadres who were once ideologically prepared to effectively counter any negative political and or ideological eventuality.

Any political party whose leaders have convinced themselves that the only ideological orientation necessary is one aimed exclusively at winning elections, will find that after consistently failing to win elections after elections, their party's membership will end up losing faith and becoming disillusioned the longer that party remains in the political wilderness.

Moreover, organizational malaise is bound to seep into the structure of the party resulting in serious deficiencies.

Only a new reinvigorated, ideologically prepared leadership with a high degree of charisma, the ability to imbue a spirit of confidence and optimism and with fresh, rational policies will be able to energize their party members and supporters.

Experience has shown that political parties who historically, were deeply rooted in left-wing politics but decides to makes a radical shift to liberal or social democratic politics and ideologically oriented ends up politically marginalized and distrusted.

DE-IDEOLOGIZATION OF THE PPP

With the radical change in the balances of forces at the global level in favour of globalization and trade liberalization, the PPP initiated a process of gradually returning to what it started out to be in the 1950's. As the transformation process continued to evolve, those in the leadership of the Party who remained supportive of scientific theory and revolutionary democracy constituted a minority. They were made to 'shift down' and were labelled 'old guards' whose thinking is outdated and not in keeping with the exigencies of 'modern times.'

Experiences of political parties of a hue similar to that of the PPP, has shown how, in order to win or regain acceptance of erstwhile internal and external allies, the leadership of those parties had to demonstrate their evolution from what they were in the past to what they are at present.

The closing of the Party's ideological school ACCABRE and its classes, the termination of THUNDER, the Party'official organ as well as the shuttering of the Michael Forde Bookshop is indicative of the PPP's de-ideologization process.

IMPACT OF 'NO TO IDEOLOGY' ON YOUNG PEOPLE

The 'No ideology' assertion is, by its very nature, a self-serving ideological position. Its aim is to trap unsuspecting youths into a confused, dependent state of mind.

Under these conditions, the ideology of adventurism, opportunism, and terrorism take root pitting the newly found and exuberant converts against the rest of society.

The strategic objective of these new converts is to disrupt, by any means necessary, the peace, good order and cohesive development of society.

It is precisely this extremist ideology that has contributed enormously to the germination of international terrorism making it one of the foremost challenges in the current global dispensation.

Experience has shown that once the self-serving agendas of the pseudo democrats, the demagogic populists as well as that of the self-styled leftists are accepted by exuberant youngsters, they will be manipulated politically and personally because of their ideological immaturity.

In the final analysis, for the young people to be protected from the modern-day charlatans, the more experienced political leaders are expected to help them recognize the root cause of and cure for the ills of capitalist society including racism, unemployment, poverty, social dislocation and the increasing pauperization of the working people.

Efforts must be made to help the younger generation understand that there is a sociological and structural phenomenon of cause and effect inherent in the extant socio-economic model of development and that it is this model that perpetuates exploitation of man by man.

Ultimately, it is that society that wreaks havoc in the lives of millions of working people around the world. In this regard, the Guyanese working people are no exception.

THE CHEDDI JAGAN RESEARCH CENTRE

The Cheddi Jagan Research Centre (CJRC) was officially opened to the public on March 22, 2000.

The Centre is suitably placed to play the role of an institution that promotes by way of lectures, and discussions on alternative models of economic development such as the national democratic state and its main features, why democracies fail, the main characteristics of a failed state, people-centered developmental challenges and the challenges of nascent oil and gas economies.

The CJRC, being the only Centre of kind in the whole of Guyana has the responsibility to promote scientific theory advanced by Cheddi Jagan, pertaining to the historical development of societies, dialectical materialism, the history of the international working class movement and above all, the history of the Guyanese working people's struggle for national and social liberation. The Centre can also play a role as a forum for intellectual thought and discussion on progressive, democratic ideas and lessons drawn from the experiences of other peoples in their struggle for national liberation and social emancipation. As a research centre, the CJRC can establish functional cooperation with the University of Guyana and the Cyril Potter College of Education for the benefit of researchers. International linkages can also be established with Centres having a similar ideological genre in other countries of the world. Finally, it is my considered opinion that evening classes for a variety of subjects delivered by qualified, active or retired persons, can be offered free of cost by the Centre for the benefit of interested persons. The whole idea is to have at the Centre, a constant flow of persons, young and old, who are hungry for knowledge of both an academic and political/ideological nature.

The Centre would benefit enormously were it to utilize the wide variety of human resources available to it on a pro bono basis as well as the facilities at its disposal to advance the cause for which it was established to the benefit of all Guyanese.

The Cheddi Jagan Research Centre

PUSHING FOR A FRESH APPROACH

It is not surprising that neo-liberalism has impacted the progressive, democratic forces in the English-speaking Caribbean. In this regard, the PPP was no exception.

Between 2007 to 2015 while I served as General Secretary of the Party, I sought to strengthen, in a creative fashion, the foundation principles of the Party as reflected in its Constitution and Programmatic Platform.

My objective at that time was to execute this task in conformity with Guyanese realities and the long-standing traditions of the party.

In this connection, efforts were made to re-establish a Cadre Commission - an internal mechanism within the party - for the development and promotion party cadres. To facilitate this, classes at the Accabre College of Social Sciences were held on a continuous basis.

Further, efforts were made to place the party on a new and re-invigorated approach to party building, this resulted in a resurgence in membership and a greater understanding and appreciation of the foundation principles of the party.

From my own knowledge and experience, similar situations of this kind were experienced at one time or another, in different parts of the world, by political parties of various ideological shades and hues

National liberation movements and communist and workers' parties were not immune to these developments.

Attempts by these organizations to adjust or re-adjust their ideological and philosophical orientations resulted in the emergence of fundamental internal differences on tactical and strategic issues. The end result was deep divisions and even splits at the leadership and membership levels of those parties.

It is to be recalled that the split in the PPP in 1955 resulted on the one hand, to the re-affirmation of the pro-socialist, internationalist orientation of the Jagan- led faction while on the other hand, the Burnham-led faction held to a social democratic, nationalist ideological outlook.

This was a classic manifestation of the type of ideological and philosophical turmoil that erupts from time to time in political parties and nationalist movements.

At the beginning of the mid-1980's, the PPP began a strategic push for political power following the death of Forbes Burnham in 1985 and the emergence of positive changes in the international arena.

THE HISTORIC EMPIRE CINEMA CONGRESS

Burnham died on Monday August 6, 1985. The PPP had just concluded its 24th congress at the Empire Cinema in Georgetown held under the theme "Towards a Democratic Government." It was first time the Party would have held a congress in Georgetown since the 1950's.

The congress was highly successful. A record number of delegates and observers participated. And over fifteen overseas delegates from fraternal parties and movements attended. It was the largest ever foreign representation at a congress of the party.

It was at that congress that the party endorsed the recommendation that it contest the next elections as PPP/ CIVIC with Sam Hinds as the Prime Ministerial candidate.

History was in the making.

Assessing the political situation in the country at the time, I had advanced a suggestion at the Secretariat level of the party that the next constitutionally due congress be held in Georgetown. I reasoned that the balance of forces in the country had shifted in favour of the party and consequently, the political situation favored a return of party congresses to the city. The recommendation was supported and I was tasked with the responsibility to find the venue and to head the committee whose task was to make all arrangements for the successful realization of the congress under the direction of the Executive Committee.

The metropole Cinema was my first choice given its proximity to the headquarters of the party which made logistics manageable and resources easily accessible. However, the manager of the Cinema when approached advised that he could not make that cinema available but was prepared to make another of his Cinemas available. That cinema was the Empire Cinema located a short distance away from our headquarters. The Executive Committee accepted my recommendation that the Empire Cinema be the venue for the congress.

Prior to and after the convening of the congress the Party's Constitution and Programme maintained language that reflected the Party's adherence to a scientific world view and international working class solidarity, however following the Congress, a marked shift away from the hard line ideological positions the party once extolled in the 1970's and 80's was to be found in its public pronouncements and official press releases

As the prospects for winning the 1992 elections became obvious, publications such as 'Thunder' the theoretical and discussion organ of the party and Mirror the Party's weekly newspaper focused increasingly on the fight for free and fair elections.

Cheddi Jagan eventually captured his renewed and reinvigorated ideological appreciation of Marxism in the epoch of the late 1980's and mid-1990's in his call for a New Global Human Order.

THE GUYANA-SOVIET FRIENDSHIP SOCIETY

The first and last time I met and shook Burnham's hand was in the mid-1970's at a reception hosted by the Guyana- Soviet Friendship Society held at the Critchlow Labour College on Woolford Avenue.

The Guyana-Soviet Friendship Society had been established in 1972 to help press the Guyana Government to establish diplomatic relations with the USSR and to foster friendly relations between the peoples of Guyana and the Soviet Union. Heading the Organisation were Sidnauth Singh and Komal Chand among others.

The society played an important role as an NGO in disseminating Information about the achievements of the Soviet Government and people. Through pictorial exhibitions, lectures, cultural programs and receptions the society was able to bring a greater awareness and understanding among Guyanese people about developments in the USSR.

At that time, the Burnham administration was playing the game of equi-distance from the two superpowers and had become deeply involved in the Non-aligned Movement.

This foreign policy was of great benefit to the PNC, the Party was awarded scholarships for its young members to attend the Patrice Lumumba Friendship University in Moscow as well as training for military officers and pilots barter agreements were signed with Yugoslavia, the GDR, Hungary, Romania,the USSR and the Democratic People's Republic of Korea. Loans, military hardware, helicopters were exchanged for locally produced products because of the shortage of foreign exchange.

In December, 1972 Guyana along with Jamaica, Barbados and Trinidad and Tobago jointly established diplomatic relations with Cuba.

Earlier, in December 1970, Guyana established diplomatic relations with the USSR. At that time, those steps were considered progressive and anti- imperialist from a foreign policy perspective.

THE GUYANA/GDR FRIENDSHIP SOCIETY

During the 1974 to 1976 period, though a Guyana-German Democratic Republic Friendship Society was established it took many years before Guyana established diplomatic relations with that Eastern European country.

EMG Wilson, Boyo and Bridgette Ramsaroop and Eddie Rodney were the leading lights in that organization. Boyo had studied in the GDR and was married to Bridgette a German National.

The society held picketing exercises and demonstrations calling on the Burnham government to establish diplomatic relations with the GDR. Cultural activities, panel discussions and photographic exhibitions were held to foster a better understanding of developments in the GDR.

Years later, the Guyana Government established diplomatic relations with the GDR and a Trade Mission was established in Georgetown.

Many Guyanese specialists and technicians who had been awarded scholarships by the Jagan government had returned from the socialist countries in Eastern Europe but were not given jobs by the government of the day even though they were highly qualified academically.

PPP/PNC RELATIONS & CRITICAL SUPPORT

The contradictory anti-imperialist foreign policy of the Burnham administration between the 1974 - 1976 period, was reflected in its contradictory domestic policy. It was during this period that rapprochement between the PPP and the PNC had become a reality.

That was period when the PPP extended 'Critical Support' to the PNC because the latter had begun pursuing a number of forward looking foreign and domestic policies including what was described as 'nationalization of the commanding heights of the economy.'

 The party held a number of consultations with its membership across the country to hear their views on the intended policy. Although the greater number of members supported the change in policy towards the Burnham regime, there were smaller numbers of comrades who were not supportive.

The Comrades called openly for armed struggle on the ground that a change in policy could not be justified in light of the many atrocities that had been committed by the dictatorship and that the way to political power was not through the ballot box but 'through the barrel of a gun.'

It was not until it was clear that the majority view had prevailed amongst the general membership that the leadership of the party finally settled on its new policy branded 'Critical Support.'

'Critical Support' was not meant to be unconditional support for the government, it basically meant unity and struggle.

Unity in support of policies that benefit the working people while criticizing those that negatively impact their working and living conditions.

This new policy came into force in 1975, just about two years after the army had intervened in the elections held in 1973.

At a public lecture on the subject held at the auditorium of Freedom House, Cheddi Jagan came under fire from a small group present who expressed racial and extremists' sentiments in opposition to 'Critical Support.'

They accused him of 'selling out the Indians' and were opposed, not only to any support whatsoever to the Burnham dictatorship, they even called for armed struggle to overthrow the dictatorship and the partitioning of Guyana citing India and Pakistan as an example of the way to go.

A few days later, following a meeting of the party's executive committee Dr. Jagan invited key personalities who had publicly opposed the party's line for an exchange of views. The meeting was held at his home at Plantation Bel Air.

Those invited were Doodnauth Singh, Jailall Kissoon, Dr. Ganraj Kumar, and Ayube McDoom.

From the PPP side were Cheddi and Janet Jagan, Reepu Daman Persaud, Ram Karan, Feroze Mohammed and me.

The discussion was held in a rather cordial and informal atmosphere with each invitee providing their analysis of the political situation in the country.

While discussions were taking place, Janet Jagan served soft drinks and fruit cake. Dr. Jagan did most of the talking from the PPP side.

Eventually, a general understanding among the men on why the new policy was necessary and what were its objectives was arrived at. Public disagreement on the subject subsided.

But 'Critical Support' brought about internal differences on the question of strategy and tactics within the leadership of the party.

Ranji Chandisingh, Halim and Zahir Majeed and a few comrades from the Corentyne took the line that what the party ought to have extended was 'Unconditional Support' rather than 'Critical Support' for the Burnham administration. They further argued that members of the party should feel free to join the government in order to demonstrate how committed the party was to the 'anti-imperialist process.'

The Chandisingh clique argued that with 'Unconditional Support' it would be difficult for the ruling PNC to reverse any of the gains Guyana had made on the domestic and international fronts.

That approach was roundly rejected by the leadership of the party since in effect, it meant the dissolution of the party and loss of its organizational identity as an alternative political force in the country.

Weeks later, Chandisingh and others announced their resignation from the party. Vincent Teekah, a former member of the party's Executive Committee and Chairman of the PYO had left earlier and was appointed Minister of Education.

At that time, it was widely rumored that Moses Nagamootoo was planning to leave the party and to go over and join the others who had jumped ship.

This rumor gained wide circulation within the membership of the PPP and PYO on the eve of a congress of the youth organization that was scheduled to be held at Grove on the East Bank of Demerara from 17-19 April 1976. The matter was openly discussed and settled at the congress. Nagamootoo never left, he remained with the party to champion whatever differences he had internally.

Chandisingh was appointed a Vice-President in the Burnham administration and later, under Hoyte, as Ambassador to Moscow.

I enjoyed conversing with Chandisingh over 'Brown Betty' ice-cream which we both enjoyed. He was a knowledgeable Comrade and made Marxism easy to understand. On several occasions he and his wife Veronica invited me to New Amsterdam in Berbice to assist in fundraising activities.

Traveling to New Amsterdam from Georgetown by hire-car or mini-bus was always a pleasure for me. And at the fundraising activities I had the opportunity to meet with Comrades and well-wishers from the New Amsterdam and Canje areas in Berbice.

An earlier effort encouraging me to leave the party was made by Vincent Teekah who, after returning from law school and spending sometime at the leadership level of the party, had crossed the floor to become a government MP and later a Minister of Government. The incident occurred one night after a reception held at Freedom House.

Vincent Teekah offered to take me home in his vehicle. At that time, I was living at my in-laws at Kingston, Georgetown. On arrival at my destination Teekah engaged me in a conversation about my personal future and prospects for improving the welfare of my family.

I sensed the conversation was headed in the direction of me leaving the party and following him where ever he might be going, though that itself he did not make clear to me. I guess he didn't want to be clear either since we were members of the same political party nor was, he sure what my response would be.

I sat and listened to the senior comrade. What I could not under was why me. Afterall, I was not as prominent as he and other leaders were in the party. This to me, was 'small fry' Teekah was fishing for. At least so I thought at the time. The conversation ended with him asking me to consider what he told me and suggesting that we will talk again. That was a Friday night.

By Monday Dr. Jagan received a resignation letter from Teekah and the following day the contents of the letter was in the press. Teekah was soon appointed a minister of government.

And though it was never investigated, rumours had it that Teekah was involved in an amorous affair with a female foreign national as a result of which he was killed by an unknown assailant.

Teekah's flip from PPP to PNC was not an isolated event. Burnham was 'head hunting' at the time to enlarge his parliamentary strength. He used all kinds of subterfuges, stratagems, threats, pressures and carrots forcing a number of PPP MP's to cross the floor over to his side. They include; Maude Branco, Harry Lall, Yacoob Ally, Edgar Ambrose, Ivan Remington and Peter Scarce among others.

This was a serious blow to the party but it showed that those who were not ideologically grounded could easily be bought and later sold. As Burnham once said, "Every man has a price."

PPP/PNC INTER-PARTY TALKS

Critical Support laid the basis for inter-party talks between the PPP and the PNC. Though I was involved in the formulation of the new policy at the leadership level, I was not involved in the Party to Party talks.

The Party's representatives were restricted to a few members of the executive committee. Its composition was Cheddi and Janet Jagan, Ram Karan, Reepu Daman Persaud and Feroze Mohammed.

The talks were held at Belfied village on the East Coast of Demerara where Burnham lived at the time in a huge two-story wooden Mansion

Details of the talks were shrouded in secrecy. A few of us were briefed from time to time by Dr. Jagan about progress made and agreements reached during the talks.

Among the agreements were PPP representation on state boards, representation on the Board of Governors of the University of Guyana, and representation on the Guyana Elections Commission and that the PPP would encourage its members to join the People's Militia.

The militia was established for the purpose of making 'Every Citizen a Soldier' with membership down to the smallest community. The PPP had recommended that the militia's membership be broadened to include every village, factory and city block. The Party expressed its opposition to the militia being used in industrial disputes.

As regards PPP representation on the Board of Governors of the University of Guyana, Sheik Feroze Mohammed and me were selected to serve on the Board. And concerning representation on the Elections Commission, I was selected to be the Party's representative on the Commission.

It was during this period of rapprochement between the two parties that agreement was reached to the effect that representatives of the PPP and PNC would go to the towns and villages to participate in organized outreach meetings to sensitize the people about the two leaders' versions of socialism. These events were held countrywide and both parties fielded representatives.

I spoke some at some of these events with Henry Jeffery who at that time was the Head at the Cuffy Ideological Institute on the Linden-Soesdyke Highway. Years later, Jeffery gravitated to the Civic component of the PPP to become its first Minister of Housing in the newly elected PPP/C government of 1992.

Inter-party talks between the PPP and the PNC in the 1974 - 1976 period was proceeding well until news came that the government had imported a huge shipment of arms and ammunition costing millions of dollars. The party, through the MIRROR news paper published an editorial headlined 'Money for guns not for bread!' According to Dr. Jagan, at a subsequent meeting between delegations of the two parties, Burnham drew attention to the editorial and called for its retraction.

Dr. Jagan told the Party's Executive Committee that the delegation refused to retract the editorial. Burnham was reminded that publication of the editorial was consistent with the spirit of critical support.

Burnham disagreed. The talks broke down in December of 1976 and was never resumed until years later.

The party to party talks was instructive for the PPP, it reaffirmed that from a class point of view, how defending the interests of the working people could easily be frittered away if leaders were not strong and assertive enough to stand up to threats from an elite representing the reactionary petty and bureaucratic bourgeoisie.

Prior to the break down of the talks, Burnham attended many locally organized solidarity activities with the socialist counties and national liberation movements.

L.F.S. BURNHAM

Burnham rarely wore a suit and tie in Guyana or abroad save in exceptionally unavoidable circumstances. His mode of dress was either a neatly custom-made shirt jac suit made of expensive suiting or a beautifully embroidered shirt jac or guayabera tailored specially for him. He was in the habit of wearing high top boots of various colours.

Burnham smoked John Player's Special - the most expensive cigarette at the time packed in a black cylindrical plastic container.

While at social functions and under the watchful eyes of his close-men, usually dressed in white shirtjacs and dark trousers and with threatening expressions on their faces, one of them would be nearby with the black cylindrically shaped container with his cigarettes inside and a gold plated lighter.

With the click of his fingers he would signal the close man to bring up the cigarette container. He would pluck one and insert it between his lips. The close man would then proceed to light the cigarette with the cigarette lighter with LFSB etched on its left side much to the delight of the smoker.

While puffing away Burnham would engage in idle and meaningless chit-chat with those around him while cracking a few political jokes in between.

It was in this kind of jovial and relaxed environment that Burnham would peddle a persistent falsehood to those around him.

He could be heard saying that he and Cheddi would 'knock glass together' meaning that irrespective of the political animosity between the two, they would have drinks together. Burnham would seek to impress upon his audience that Jagan's avowed commitment to the working people was superficial and that he should not be taken seriously.

Many found this to be untrue because Dr. Jagan's day to day political life was quite to the contrary. Jagan was not a drinker of alcohol, he loved fresh fruit juices. He was not known to have any 'drinking partner' relationship with Burnham.

To persons around him Burnham seemed a rather affable and sympathetic person but to many like me who knew him politically, we were not to be fooled, we knew Burnham as a ruthless and deceptive dictator. His sister, Jessie Burnham, did a great service to Guyanese during her lifetime, she alerted us to the idiosyncrasies of her brother Forbes in her historic publication; 'Beware of my Brother Forbes!

CIVIL RESISTANCE AND NON-COOPERATION

Just before the 1973 elections, Desmond Hoyte, the PNC's representative on the Elections Commission had declared that the votes would not be counted at Queen's College, the central counting place but this was soon reversed. The elections were blatantly rigged and in response, the PPP launched a campaign of CIVIL RESISTANCE AND NON-COOPERATION. The regime's response was to initiate wave of arrests of party leaders and leading activist's victimization and discriminatory. In 1973, Dr. Jagan's firearm license was revoked and one year later he was charged and placed before the court for unlawful possession of ammunition and the component part of a firearm/pistol. This action by the security forces so enraged his supporters that it gave rise to spontaneous countrywide protests. The sugar workers, backed by their union called a one-day strike across the sugar industry in solidarity with Dr. Jagan.

On the morning of Tuesday, July 30, 1974, a number of police ranks belonging to Special Branch turned up at Freedom House with a warrant to search the premises.

I was assigned to accompany them while they searched high and low. They found nothing of evidential value. The took away a copy of Lenin's 'State and Revolution' many copies of which were on sale at the Michael Forde Bookshop just below Party headquarters.

Cartoon by Hawley Harris depicting security forces rummaging through files at Freedom House, Party HQ

Fearing a deterioration in the political situation, on Wednesday, October 9, 1974, the magistrate moved rapidly. He found Dr Jagan guilty of possession of illegal ammunition but reprimanded and discharged him. And in the case of possession of a component/part of a firearm he was fined $25,000 or one-month imprisonment. His lawyers agreed to appeal both decisions.

In the meantime, outside the court on that same day, a huge number of Party supporters had gathered. Some greeted the news with loud shouts of "victory!" Others, were vehement in their condemnation.

Amongst the crowd was Dr. Walter Rodney and the catholic priest, Father Campbell- Johnson. Dr. Jagan was lifted shoulder high and he led a procession back to Freedom House where he thanked the huge crowd for the support while the trial was ongoing. It was around this period that a controversy arose over government's refusal to employ Dr. Walter Rodney at the University of Guyana.

Dr. Rodney had returned to Guyana in 1974, and had applied for the job to Head the Department of History at the University of Guyana but was persistently refused on political grounds. The dispute pitchforked Rodney into prominence and triggered a political tidal wave that created persistent headaches for the Burnham dictatorship.

For the first time in many years, unity among the opposition forces on this issue. The unity was manifested at public meeting held in October of that the very year, where BH Benn of the Working People's Vanguard Party (WPVP), Eusi Kwayana of the African Society for Cultural Relations with Independent Africa (ASCRIA) Moses Bhagwan of the Indian Political Revolutionary Association(IPRA) and Cheddi Jagan of the PPP spoke on the 'Rodney affair.'

ARNOLD RAMPERSAUD ON TRIAL

During that same year, on July 18, 1974 to be exact, police constable, James Henry was shot and killed at a toll station located at the Number 62 village on the Corentyne, East Berbice.

In response, the police carried out raids and searches at the homes of a number of PPP activists on the Corentyne. The government linked the killing of the policeman to the protests the PPP had launched against a number of toll stations government had mounted along the Corentyne public road placing an unaffordable cost to vehicles passing through each station. Farmers, parents of school children and the travelling public were severely affected financially.

Within 48 hours of the shooting incident, on July 20, 1974 Arnold Rampersaud a taxi driver, father of five children and a known supporter of the PPP was arrested and charged with the murder of Henry.

The trial began first in Berbice in November 1976 but owing to the strong protests and the anger of the people over Rampersaud's arrest case was transferred to the Georgetown Magistrates Court.

So long as we knew the next court day for Rampersaud's appearance at the Berbice Magistrates Court, a group of us would journey the day before to Berbice. We would pass the night at the Party's office on Main Street New Amsterdam. The next day we would be in the picket line before 9 am long before the case was called. The court room would be packed to capacity with Rampersaud's relatives, friends and well wishers. The court orderlies would have a difficult time controlling the crowds in the court.

A broad-based Arnold Rampersaud Defence Committee was established comprising a battery of top Guyanese legal luminaries including B.O Adams, Doodnauth Singh, Ashton Chase, Miles Fitzpatrick, Ralph Ramkarran, Moses Bhagwan, Jailall Kissoon and C.M.L. John instructed by Solicitor Ayube McDoom.B.O. Adams led the team.

Later, following the internationalization of the case a group of outstanding legal experts from overseas joined the team to assist in Rampersaud's defense.

From the Caribbean came Morris Bishop of Grenada, Frank Solomon and Sash Parmanand of Trinidad and Tobago and Denis Daly of Jamaica, all prominent lawyers. Margaret Burnham, and Max Stern two distinguished Black American attorneys came from the USA while John Bowden, a British Solicitor representing the Haldane Society of the U. K. Amnesty International was represented by a distinguished Professor of the University of Minnesota Messages of support and solidarity from all around the world flooded the offices of the Prime Minister and the Attorney General and Minister of Legal Affairs

On the home front, vigils, picketing exercises, public meetings, freedom marches and rides were organized. Of great significance was a 'march in solidarity with Arnold' from Linden to Georgetown by bauxite workers. Cheddi and Janet Jagan, Dr. Walter Rodney, Fr. Malcolm Rodrigues and Eusi Kwayana were deeply involved in all these political activities.

Working at Freedom House in those days, I would be involved in all the political activities. Also, from time to time I came into contact with our overseas friends who had come to assist in the case. Because Morris Bishop was the political leader of the New Jewel Movement of Grenada, I became acquainted with him during the course of a bilateral meeting with him Dr and Mrs. Jagan.

As Executive Secretary of the PPP: 1980-1992

The local and overseas team was unmatched in the history of Guyanese legal jurisprudence.

The case became a national and international embarrassment for the government so much so that in the end, Arnold Rampersaud, having spent three years in prison as a political prisoner was acquitted and set free. The defense team at the trial had declared that;

"The accused was a victim of a conspiracy, hatched against him because of his political conviction and because he is a member of the opposition PPP."

In his famous five-hour address before the 12-member jury at the conclusion of the third trial B.O. Adams said;

"The Defence does not condone the shooting of a policeman. But the Defence condemns any attempt to convict the accused by leading false, and fabricated evidence. Let me say right now that Francis is lying. And there is nothing more wicked than to swear false testimony against your fellow man who is fighting for his life. The moral guilt is tremendous."

Rampersaud was the first Guyanese to face three trials on a murder charge. This is unprecedented in the history of Guyanese jurisprudence.

Two trials had ended in disagreement by the jury. At the third trial the jury arrived st a unanimous decision of not guilty against Rampersaud.

This was a great victory for the progressive, democratic forces who had joined ranks at home and abroad to secure justice and fairplay for a man who was framed by the police working hand in glove with a brutal dictatorship.

DR. WALTER RODNEY

The controversy concerning the University Guyana's refusal to employ Dr. Rodney continued to develop momentum. Rodney became a central, if not a popular rallying figure for all those who opposed the Burnham dictatorship.

A fundamental point to note in the resistance and rebellious climate that emerged at time was the fact that Rodney was Black, he was a world renowned intellectual, a progressive historian a brilliant and articulate speaker.

If Burnham thought he was the best, then, according to Guyanese jargon, "He had met his meter." With Rodney entering the political arena, the battle lines were drawn. Co-incidentally, it was around this period that Dr. Walter Rodney had returned to Guyana. Many felt that Rodney had a big influence in transforming the WPA into a robust political party in 1979.

Three years after Dr. Rodney's return to Guyana, in August 1977, the PPP made its call for a National Patriotic Front and National Front Government. The call was premised on a 'Winner does not take all' policy adopted by the party after lengthy discussions.

Soon after the call was made public, the WPA published a paper and launched a campaign calling for a Government of National Unity and Reconstruction. Unlike, the call by the PPP, the WPA's paper did not envisage inclusion of the PNC in the government in its proposal.

At a meeting held in the same year at the head office of the Clerical and Commercial Workers Union (CCWU) on Murray now Quamina Street, and attended by Dr. Jagan and Dr. Rodney,

Dr. Jagan argued strongly that the PNC should not be excluded from a national unity government.

So strong was the resentment of the PNC by the WPA at that time, Dr. Jagan's proposal did not get far. Ironically, the ruling PNC, once described as the WPA as the Worst Possible Alternative, the PNC also rejected the notion of being part of any national unity government.

As it turned out, the attempt by the PPP and the WPA, both individually and collectively, to arrive at a consensual position on some form of unity government to replace the PNC's was in a sense, a precursor to another attempt made between

1982-1983 by the PPP, the WPA and the VLD. On that occasion, the parties concentrated more on areas of convergence rather than areas of divergence.

Owing to public attacks by the VLD on the PPP, and notwithstanding efforts by the party to encourage the VLD to desist from publicly attacking the PPP, the VLD nevertheless, persisted in their attacks.

Maybe this was the VLD's way of wriggling out of the all-party talks.

THE BACKGROUND

The situation in Guyana had reached a boiling point politically. Guyanese were experiencing their toughest days ever since independence. The prohibition and extreme shortage of basic food imports such as flour, potatoes, onions, caned food and milk, cooking oil, chick peas/ channa made life difficult for working class as well as the middle class.

The Government resorted to lies and excuses claiming that the shortage of foreign exchange was the reason for the country's economic problems. People were encouraged to buy local foodstuff of which there was little or none available and to use rice flour instead of the imported wheaten flour. Long lines particularly of housewives and working women sprung up outside grocery stores and supermarkets in the city. In the country side it was worse. It was during this period that smuggling of basic food items became a national industry.

Our borders with Venezuela and Suriname suddenly became alive as a new breed of entrepreneurs aka 'traders' emerged. The traders were in effect smugglers who were actively engaged in smuggling prohibited/banned food items across the borders from neighboring countries. The ranks of the traders included; teachers, police rank and a large number of persons from the professional class who joined in the lucrative illegal trade only to become rich overnight.

Meanwhile, the pavement at Water street Georgetown, on the western side of the Betancourt now Muneshwar's store became a thriving financial centre or the local 'Wall Street' as the illegal buying and selling of foreign currency emerged as a profitable financial activity for money-changers who began to populate the vicinity.

And the long lines of Guyanese, outside the Central Passport Office and, by extension, the US and Canadian Consulates, applying for visas to flee their country of birth became an everyday spectacle. It was under these conditions that the PPP waged a lone, heroic struggle for the removal of government-imposed ban on basic food items; for a living wage and for better living and working conditions of the Guyanese people.

The announcement of Dr. Walter Rodney's imminent return to Guyana was welcomed by most Guyanese especially those living in the city where the economic crunch was felt the hardest.

At a mass public meeting held at the Parade Ground on the eve of Rodney's return to Guyana PNC thugs invaded and broke up the meeting where Eusi Kwayana, Cheddi Jagan and others were scheduled to speak. It was a sign of things to come.

On September 8, 1974, a public rally jointly sponsored by the PPP and ASCRIA was held at the La Penitance market square. The speakers were Joshua Ramsammy, Eusi Kwayana and Cheddi Jagan. Over one thousand persons attended.

Similar public meetings were held in various parts of the city where a combined number of political leaders spoke including Eusi Kwayana, Cheddi Jagan, Brindley Benn and Moses Bhagwan.

At all these meetings the main topic was the banning of Dr. Rodney from employment at the University of Guyana and the fight against dictatorship for democracy and civil liberties.

Discriminatory practices by the government-controlled Board of Governors at the University had affected lecturers at the institution including Drs. Joshua Ramsammy, Kathleen Drayton, and Mohammed Insanally.

In July 1975, Dr. Jagan and Dr. Rodney met for the first time. They embraced each other warmly at a function marking the July 26, attack on the Moncada Barracks hosted by the Guyana-Cuba Friendship Society held at Freedom House, headquarters of the PPP. It was an embrace that would last until, and even after the death of Rodney.

The PNC recognizing the threat Rodney posed to its administration, made sure that his movements were closely monitored by the Special Branch of the Guyana Police Force. Rodney's public meetings were continuously disrupted and broken up by PNC and House of Israel thugs combined.

On many occasions, Rodney's meetings, especially those held on Merriman's Mall to the north of Bourda market, were so huge that an attack by PNC thugs would have resulted in the thugs themselves being assaulted and chased out of the meeting.

It was at those meetings that the captivating drumming and chanting of two young WPA activists belittling Burnham and branding him 'King Kong' and warning that liberation has to pass, and that the PNC will run like 'rass.' That must have really angered Burnham.

Because of the huge popularity of Rodney and the way he spoke to the people, it became obvious to those of us who had been on the political hustings for sometime, that trouble was brewing. Burnham was certainly not going to rollover.

In early June 1979, Rodney and three of his colleagues were accused of burning down the building housing the Office of the PNC General Secretary and Ministry of National Mobilization situated at the time on the western half of Camp street, between Quamina and Middle Streets. Some members of the WPA were arrested, charged and placed before the court.

Huge crowds gathered outside the Georgetown Magistrates' Court when the trials began. On June 14, 1979 a large crowd had gathered in solidarity with the accused, outside the courts, PNC and House of Israel thugs turned up in full force armed with sticks and long knives.

They attacked the crowd lashing out with their sticks at every one in sight. Those armed with long knives or 'jukkas' began stabbing at defenseless persons in the crowd. People began running for safety helter skelter, some ran along South Road, others ran into Brickdam yet other ran towards Stabroek market. I was in the crowd that ran towards Brickdam.

A group of thugs came running behind us as if chasing us. As I ran, I looked back and saw a group of thug's pounces upon a White man on the parapet on the southern side of St. Stanislaus College. The man was among those of us running from the armed attackers of the crowd outside the courts. The man appeared to fall after being stabbed several times about his body by a man wearing an African style dashiki.

I ran towards Magnet Place, the street to the east of the then Ministry of Home affairs. From Magnet Place I ran across to South Road and Croal street into King street then across Regent street into Robb street ending up at Freedom House.

At Freedom House I related to the Comrades there what had occurred. Later, we gathered that the man who was stabbed on Brickdam was Father Darke, a catholic priest and photographer for the Catholic Standard newspaper. Freedom House was put on the alert in case of an attack.

Throughout the entire period of Rodney's political activism in Guyana, Burnham continued to threaten to physically eliminate the leaders of his organization. He urged them to sign their wills because the dogs of war would be unleashed on them. The tense political situation at the time was characterized by blatant state-sponsored terrorism, thuggery, political harassment and victimization.

There was much talk that the military hierarchy was likely to move away from pledges of loyalty it had made at PNC party congresses. The downfall of the Burnham dictatorship seemed inevitable.

Sometime between 1981-1982, Cheddi Jagan had cause to write to David Granger, the then Commander of the Army concerning GDF's relations with the PNC and involvement in industrial and party-political issues.

Granger's response was that he would discuss Jagan's concerns with his Commander-in-Chief and get back to him. Jagan never heard back from Granger.

Walter Rodney and Cheddi Jagan held regular consultations during this period. It was only natural that dialogue should take place in the existing circumstances.

With the PNC seemingly weak and isolated, the question was how should the PPP and WPA cooperate to unite the people in order to achieve the desired goal of removing the PNC from government. This was a matter of strategy and tactics.

In meetings with Dr. Rodney, Dr. Jagan advanced the view that the PPP's support base was highly organized and politically conscious and therefore well prepared to answer to the call for action at anytime by the leadership of the Party. Dr. Jagan further contended that what was needed was intense political/ideological work among the mass of Afro-Guyanese since they had been duped for years by the PNC under Burnham. He pointed out that although the PPP had done a considerable amount of political work over the years among Afro-Guyanese, much more was needed among them. With this in mind, Dr. Jagan was of the view that it was in that particular area that the PPP and the WPA ought to concentrate their efforts.

The WPA was opposed to Jagan's approach. They held to the view that notwithstanding the work the PPP had done and continued to do among its supporters, the WPA should do political work amongst the sugar workers in particular if racial and working-class unity is to be realized.

While these discussions continued the WPA appeared to shift its focus towards an approach that would spell disaster for the organization and the popular struggle as a whole.

The assassination of Dr. Walter Rodney by means of a bomb blast on June 13, 1980 sent shock waves from Guyana throughout the entire world. It brought the WPA to its knees never to recover from what turned out to be a devastating political blow.

Why the WPA, an organization that had successfully brought the peoples' struggle to the cusp of political change in Guyana, would choose to embark on a form of struggle that was fraught with immense dangers is a puzzle only the surviving WPA leaders of that era could explain.

And though they were given every opportunity to do so at the Commission of Inquiry into the assassination of Dr Rodney, many of the key leaders who are still around did not come forward to explain why the WPA chose to embark on a form of struggle that claimed the lives of its leader and many others.

As for the PPP, its leaders had, from time to time done many an analysis of the pros and cons of carrying out such forms of struggle in Guyana.

In so doing, the party took into consideration Guyana's national peculiarities and more specifically, its ethnic make-up as well as the experiences in Asia, Africa, Europe, Latin America and the Caribbean when it opted for a revolutionary approach to mass struggle combined with parliamentary and extra-parliamentary struggle as the way forward.

On several occasions' agent provocateurs posing as 'friends of the party' came forward from time to time wanting to 'help' the party. They discreetly approached individual party leaders claiming they had arms and ammunition either to donate or to sell to the party. These so-called 'friends' who were no doubt agent provocateurs were politely but swiftly rebuffed and sent packing by those whom they had approached.

Internally, especially after the 1973 elections, voices within the party could be heard calling on the party to take up arms against the dictatorship in light of the persistent rigging of elections. Those voices though in a minority, were vocal and reflected the restlessness and impatience of some members and supporters, who felt that a change of government through the ballot box seemed well nigh impossible and that the only way out was to overthrow the dictatorship by force of arms.

The leadership of the party at that time, had to fight off the extremist and racist tendencies that had sprung up within its ranks at that time. The disaster that befell the WPA following the death of Rodney was instrumental in hammering home the message to the comrades supportive of that form of struggle that that was not the way to go in the struggle against the dictatorship and for democracy.

Following the death of Rodney, the PPP maintained friendly and cordial relations the WPA notwithstanding the differences between the two parties on strategy and tactics. As the struggle continued, the PPP/WPA relationship was consummated with the formation of the Patriotic Coalition for Democracy (PCD) prior to elections that were due in 1990.

The run-up to those elections was dogged by a host of shenanigans orchestrated by a PNC-controlled Elections Commission. The humpty-dumpty preparations for the 1990 elections ended up with a two-year postponement because of a botched voters list and the refusal by the Hoyte administration to implement electoral reforms demanded by a united opposition and friendly external forces who had publicly expressed their support for the reforms.

The ruling PNC tried every trick in the book to hoodwink the electorate during the two- year postponement. But the pressure at home and from overseas was unstoppable. When elections were finally held on October 5, 1992 the PPP/C romped home with a commanding majority.

THE CUBAN FACTOR

The Cubans were very influential during the period of rapprochement between the PPP and the PNC, in fact, together with the communist and revolutionary democratic parties in Latin America, they had formulated the theoretical and practical basis that advanced the need for fraternal parties like the PPP to work with socialist parties like the PNC.

It was during this period a National School of Dance was inaugurated with the help of the Cubans. Medical brigades became an institutional feature of the country's Public Health Service, and an agreement was signed allowing a cuban fishing fleet to fish in Guyana's territorial waters.

Later, Cuban instructors began evening Spanish-English classes at the North Georgetown Secondary School. Moses Nagamootoo and I joined the class.

Some of the PPP's fraternal allies like the Socialist Unity of Germany, the United Workers Party of Yugoslavia, the Workers Party of North Korea and the Communist Party of Cuba put the PNC and the PPP on the same level when it came to party to party relations.

In other words, when it came to participating in certain international events where hitherto the PPP was the only party from Guyana present, this was no longer the case because the PNC had become a permanent fixture at international gathering previously attended only by the PPP.

The relationship between the governments of Guyana and Cuba had grown so strong that the Cuban Government decided to bestow on Burnham its highest award, the José Marti National Award much to the displeasure of the PPP and other political and social forces in Guyana.

The political backlash came when Fidel Castro paid an official visit to Guyana en route to a Conference of Non-Aligned Movement in Algeria. The PPP picketed Castro with placards stating 'Down with Burnham Batista Regime'

The excrcise was meant to embarrass the Burnham and to send a signal to Fidel.

PARTY WORK IN GEORGETOWN

Party work in the city Georgetown, as I suppose it is in any capital city was, on the one hand, difficult and frustrating because the PNC threw every possible obstacle in our way. Moreover, they used racism and the bogeyman of communism to keep their supporters garrisoned politically, organizationally and ideologically.

On the other hand, working in the city was rewarding because it was in Georgetown where, apart from the sugar estates, the overwhelming majority of the Guyanese working class are to be found.

And since the PPP and Cheddi Jagan were perceived as champions of the working class, the party in many instances achieved great successes working among the inhabitants of Georgetown.

THE GEORGETOWN COMRADES

I first got to know Shirley through Cyril Belgrave, an experienced stevedore and a key man at the 'Calling on Centre' on Lombard street where stevedores would, on a daily basis, report for work on the waterfront.

And it was through Cyril that I became acquainted with Gladwyn Levius, Víctor James, Louis Mitchell aka 'coffee', Clement Snell and all Afro-Guyanese party members, many of whom, while working as stevedores, played exemplary and courageous roles supportive of the 1957 to 1964 Jagan government.

Shirley was also a close friend of Maurice Herbert another Black party stalwart who came through the ranks of the Party ending up as an employee at GIMPEX on Regent street where he worked as a customs clerk.

Maurice Herbert owned a FIAT motor car. GIMPEX was the local agent for those cars.

On one occasion, when Dr. Jagan was returning from home, after receiving medical treatment abroad, large numbers of Comrades were mobilized to go welcome him home at the Atkinson Airport as it was known then.

Maurice invited me to accompany him along with Shirley. It turned out to be a memorable trip to and from the airport. We discussed party work and local politics. And bilateral along the way between Maurice and Shirley enabled me to glean a lot about the party's history.

On arrival at the airport, hundreds of party members and supporters had gathered to welcome home Dr. Jagan who, on deplaning, delivered a rousing and enthusiastic speech about his trip abroad and his expectations of Comrades in the struggle that lie ahead.

STALWARTS AND SACRIFICES

I was in the thick of the struggle along with many party stalwarts who made enormous sacrifices of a personal, professional and otherwise nature. It is impossible to list them all in this book.

I Recall the contributions of Narbada Persaud, Cyril Belgrave, Gladwin Levius, Shirley Edwards, Doris Awah, Moneer Khan, Philomena Sahoye-Shury, Harold Snagg, George Lee, Vernon Fung. Charlie Casatto, Roshan Ali, Arai Thantony, Christina Ramjattan, Balchand Persaud, Reepu Daman Persaud, Maccie Hamid, Isahack and Sabra Basir, Naseeb Gafar, Arthur Joseph, Ricabdeo Chowbay,

Churchill, Bhojwan Lall, Rohit Persaud, Feroze Mohamed, Pooran Molai, Winston Madramootoo, Carl Douglas, Kumkarran Ramdass, the Hassan Family, Kawal Ramessar, Budhram Mahadeo, George David, Luis Mitchell , Yacoob Ally, Stella Dac Bang, Basil and Eula James, ignatius Charlie, Una Mulzac, Anand Sewdarsan, Carl Douglas, Hardat Ramdass, Isaac Fraser, Premchand Dass, Pariag Sukhai, Janki, Reuben Wade, Beatrice Casatto, Harry Lall, Maurice Herbert, Arthur Cumberbatch, Ramesh Balsingh, Gerald Beaton and many, many more unsung heroes and heroines too numerous to mention.

These were all fighters of the highest caliber who spared no effort in giving their best to the party at different periods of the party's struggle to achieve its goals.

Other Comrades who had served as Ministers of Government along with Comrade Cheddi as Premier in the 1957 to 1964 Government including; C.V. Nunes, Charles Jacobs, H.J. M. Hubbard, Ashton Chase, B.H. Benn, Ram Karran and E.M.G. Wilson stayed with the Party until their passing or departure from Guyana for health reasons.

Ashton Chase, one of the founders of the PPP, is the sole survivor of that generation of leaders.

And even though some of these stalwarts would have fallen by the wayside, immigrated, flipped to the other side or died, irrespective of what the new kids on the bloc were told about them, my point is that each of these individuals contributed in one way or another to the glorious struggle making October 1992 possible in so many ways.

For this they must be recognized and saluted because had it not been for their sacrifices as well as their patient and consistent efforts at party building, many of us, who were either ministers of government or permanent secretaries in the PPP/C government of 1992 to 2015 as well as those of us who today hold top positions at the leadership of the Party would not have been there had it not been for the valiant efforts of our predecessors.

The thirty-five members of the Central Committee who now sit atop a solid foundation built by many unsung heroes and heroines of the PPP ought to pay homage to those stalwarts and their sacrifices during those difficult days.

Out of government after 1964, Cheddi Jagan never ceased in his efforts to seek out allies in support of the struggle for free and fair elections and a return to democracy. He recognized that support for that struggle had to be broad-based irrespective of the mix of ideological views.

Throughout the years while working with Dr. Jagan, I gained the unassailable impression that he was a firm believer in alliances. This belief manifested itself up to the time of his becoming the President of the Republic after twenty-eight years in the political opposition During those years the PPP was always in an alliance with different social and political forces on many different issues.

To Dr. Jagan, the interests of the broad masses of the Guyanese people were paramount. And if alliances, whether tactical or strategic can help advance the interests of the working people, as far as his thinking was at the time, the party should engage since we were in a struggle for Guyana's second independence.

MY FIRST ENCOUNTER WITH DAVID GRANGER

It was during this period that the PNC decided to embark on a project aimed cultivating white potatoes at Kato, a mountain village located at the Pakaraima mountains in Region 8. A man by the name of Mittleholzer was contracted to implement the project. A lecture was organized at City Hall to sensitize the public about the benefits of producing white potatoes as part of the ruling PNC's Feed, House and Clothe the Nation campaign launched in 1972.

I decided to attend. A question and answer period followed the lecture, I decided to ask a few questions which appeared embarrassing to Mr. Mittleholzer the Chairman decided that enough questions had been asked and brought the event to an end.

As I was leaving City Hall, I met David Granger I had read about him and his association with the Guyana National Service (GNS) I shared my impressions about the lecture with him as we walked along Regent Street. He didn't say much save for asking if I belonged to any organization, when I told him of my membership in the PYO he suggested I leave the organization and join the YSM.

I did not respond; I made my way over to Regent and King streets and headed for Freedom House on Robb Street.

By 1976, because of poor infrastructural planning and development, the white potatoe project ended up as a colossal failure in the same way the GlobalAgri project at the Berbice River failed

THE COMMITTEE IN DEFENCE OF DEMOCRACY

The boycott of the referendum in 1980 helped create the basis for unity among the opposition parties as was the case five years earlier in the 1973 elections.

This unity was exemplified in the creation of the Committee for Defence of Democracy (CDD).

It was the first time after many years that a united front was created amongst social, political and trade union organizations to fight a single issue - a referendum that nobody wanted.

The entire country knew that the referendum was bound to be rigged, but they also knew that what was needed was a united opposition to thwart, if not expose the rigging.

The holding of the referendum had three fundamental objectives; First, the postponement of general and regional elections that was due in 1978. Second, to extend Burnham's dictatorial rule over Guyana. And third, to give the ruling PNC a two thirds majority in the National Assembly.

The CDD's campaign against the Bill calling for a referendum on the constitutional amendments was remarkably successful save for the government's response which was characterized by violence and brutality against opponents of the Bill.

Applications to hold public meetings organized by the CDD and to use loud speaking equipment were routinely denied by the PNC-controlled, Guyana Police Force.

Whenever CDD street corner meetings were held in the city PNC thugs accompanied by goons from the House of Israel, a religious sect with connections to the PNC, would turn up and unleash attacks with sharpened sticks and knives on the listening crowd.

One such public meeting took place early afternoon of May 30, 1979 in Georgetown at the corner of Orange Walk and North Road. Suddenly, a band of thugs armed with sticks and pieces of wood known as '2x3' turned up and launched a merciless physical attack on the crowd that had gathered.

Pandemonium broke loose, the meeting broke up with people running for safety in different directions. I was standing next to a catholic priest. As things started to quiet down, the priest advised me to move away with him. I took his advice. Eusi Kwayana joined us. The three of us walked in a southerly direction towards Regent Street. On arrival at the corner of Orange Walk and Regent Street, we branched off in different directions.

GAIL TEIXEIRA

Gail Teixeira, a Guyanese born Canadian of Portuguese descent, whom Dr Jagan had met while on one his regular visits to Toronto, Canada was offered the job as his personal assistant at Party headquarters.

She left Guyana with her entire family in July 1966 just after our country was granted independence on May 26, 1966.

While in Canada she became politically involved with the Communist Party of Canada and the Association of Concerned Guyanese (ACG).

Teixeira returned to Guyana on January 2, 1977 to take up the job with Dr. Jagan.

The Party Secretariat agreed to Dr Jagan's recommendation to employ Teixeira mainly because of her membership in the Communist Party of Canada and the Association of Concerned Guyanese (ACG). Her academic qualifications played a major role as well.

Almost immediately, soon after her arrival, she became immersed in political work associated with the PPP and its women's arm the Women's Progressive Organization (WPO).

Teixeira helped form the 'Workers Stage' a small but energetic cultural group made up of many talented, budding amateur artistes.

The group performed at street theatre depicting satirical skits and short plays of a political nature as well as social commentary.

The biggest and most successful performance put on by 'Workers Stage' was held at the Theatre Guild in Kingston, Georgetown Because of her activist orientation, Teixcira could be found in almost every party activity. Teixeira replaced Janet Jagan at GECOM in February 1979

Together we established a Committee for Solidarity with the Peoples of Southern Africa. That committee organized solidarity activities in support of the liberation struggles waged by the ANC of South Africa; SWAPO of Namibia; the MPLA of Angola; FRELIMO of Mozambique and the PAIGC of Guinea-Bissau Dr. Walter Rodney addressed one of the Organization's solidarity activities held at the St. George's Anglican School in Georgetown.

Gail Teixeira was actively involved in the activities of the Committee for Defence of Democracy (CDD). Eusi Kwayana, Tacuma Ogunseye, Teixeira, me and other PPP and WPA activists were present at a CDD public meeting held on May 30, 1979 at the corner of Orange Walk and North Road when House of Israel and PNC thugs descended on the meeting and attacked the people present with sticks

Teixeira ran in a westerly direction on North road and then onto Church street but was cornered by some of the thugs who had chased her all the way to St. Roses high school where they pounced upon her and gave her a sound thrashing. So terrible was the beating she got that it left some reddish welts on the whitish skin of her arms and legs.

A REFERENDUM IN PLACE OF ELECTIONS

As was predicted, the elections that was due to be held in 1978 was postponed and the referendum held on July 10, 1978. The referendum was boycotted by the United opposition.

As anticipated. the referendum was massively rigged. Less than 20 per cent of the voting population turned out to vote 'YES.'

The Burnham dictatorship did secure by fraudulent means, the two thirds majority it so badly wanted in the National Assembly, but like the king in his new clothes, the farcical referendum exposed Burnham and his acolytes to the outside world.

The CDD had accomplished its main objectives, it had exposed 'down to the bone' how through a combination of force and fraud the PNC had negativized the will of the electorate. At the same time, it had drawn to the attention of the world, the corrupt and dictatorial nature of the Burnham regime in Guyana.

THE CROOKED BARBED WIRE ELECTIONS

After the two-year postponement of the election that was to be held in 1978 and because of the fraudulent referendum that was held in that same year, elections were finally held on December 15, 1980.

By that time new non-government organizations and political parties had emerged on the local political scene. A broad-based Civil Liberties Action Council (CLAC) has been formed, David Westmaas and Attorney-at-Law, Khemraj Bhagwandin were the leading lights in that body.

In the run-up to the elections, CLAC submitted a memorandum to the United Nations charging that the PNC had violated the right of citizens to elect a government of their choice through rigged elections.

Later, in early 1980, the PPP petitioned the United Nations, the Organisation of American States (OAS), the Commonwealth Secretariat and the CARICOM Heads of Government drawing to their attention the threat of rigged elections and calling on them to support the right of the Guyanese people to free and fair elections.

In the build up to the elections, the People's Progressive Party (PPP), the Working People's Alliance (WPA) and the Vanguard for Liberation and Democracy (VLD) formulated and published a joint 21-page memorandum on Civil and Political Rights and Free and Fair Elections

The joint memo demonstrated once again, the readiness of the PPP to be party to an alliance with other political parties to fight unitedly for free and fair elections.

The joint efforts of the political parties went a step further. International observers were invited by the parties to travel to Guyana to observe the 1980 elections.

Among those who came were, Lord Avebury, Chairman of the UK Parliamentary Human Rights Group, Lord Pratap Chitnis, Member of the latter UK parliamentary group. Observers from Canada, Jamaica, University of the West Indies, and the United States formed part of the international team of observers.

A team of foreign journalists were present as well. As was anticipated the elections were blatantly rigged.

Gail Teixeira the PPP Representative on the Elections Commission resigned in protest after denouncing the fraudulent elections. She served on the Commission from 1979 to 1980.

As far as the delegation was concerned the elections was "as crooked as barbed wire."

DEATH OF BURNHAM

Before his demise, Forbes Burnham had grown dismissive of, and reluctant to heeding the call by his colleagues to accept a proposal to approach the international financial institutions particularly the IMF for assistance in the form of a stabilization programme to extricate Guyana from its excruciating economic ,financial problems and the rapidly deteriorating social conditions in which the

215

country had found itself after many years of wasteful economic and social experimentations with 'Cooperative Socialism.'

Sometime in the first quarter of 1984, faced with the extant political and economic conditions obtaining in the country, Burnham decided to send out feelers for party to party talks once again with the PPP. The PPP for its part, in and out of parliament, had signaled its interest in re-engaging with the ruling PNC. However, neither of the two parties were favourably disposed to re-engaging immediately nor directly. The PNC was feeling its way towards that goal, while the PPP was probing to ascertain the prospects for re-engaging. The different approaches notwithstanding, both sides had a common objective. However, the challenge to both parties was to find a vehicle that would make their common objective achievable.

It was around this time, that constructive and cordial relations developed between the Guyana Peace Council (GPC) and the Guyana Committee for Peace and Solidarity (GCSP), two local organizations that promoted solidarity and peace activities in Guyana. Over the years, representatives of these two organizations had been attending international gatherings sponsored by the World Peace Council (WPC). It was in the context of their frequent meetings at international gatherings that representatives from the two bodies managed to develop personal and cordial relationships.

As the relations between the two organizations became cozy and as the representatives of the two bodies became more comfortable exchanging views and ideas among themselves about the political situation in Guyana, a suggestion arose about formalizing the conversations on a bilateral basis.

Although it was an established fact that neither the GPC nor GSPC were arms of the two political parties, nevertheless, in the two organizations there were individuals who were leading members of the two parties.

Subsequently, formal talks began between representatives of the two organizations on the prospects for engaging in joint solidarity and peace related activities in Guyana. The team from the GCSP included; Elvin McDavid, Halim Majeed and Patrick Denny, while from the GPC it was Clement Rohee, Harry Ramdass and Feroze Mohamed or alternatively, Roger Luncheon. At the end of our formal meetings, we would engage in informal conversations about the political situation in Guyana and the prospects for the two political parties re-engaging in bilateral discussions on matters of mutual interest.

When it became obvious, that the informal political discussions had matured and was taking precedence over international peace and solidarity matters, the leaders of the political parties were informed. That triggered an exchange of correspondence between the two political parties. Two teams were established to engage in formal party to party talks. On the PPP side, it was me and Feroze Mohamed, while on the PNC side it was Ranji Chandisingh and Elvin McDavid. Halim Majeed performed the function of a scribe.

Our first meeting was held on July 19,1985. We met in one of the committee rooms at Parliament Building. Most of our meetings dealt with a Terms of Reference, procedural and house-keeping matters. But at one meeting, it became clear that for the PNC their goal was to have the two parties coalesce under the banner of paramountcy to form what they called a 'Fatherland Front.' I discerned this model was based on the Bulgarian and Vietnamese experience. At another meeting, the idea of forming a National Progressive Front based on the Iraqui experience was floated. In either of the two scenarios, Burnham was to be President and Chairman of cabinet while his party would play the leading role. For its part, the PPP was to play a secondary and supportive role. We in the PPP could not support any such role for the PPP.

Two days after, on July 21, 1985, a joint press release about the meeting was issued with the understanding that a comprehensive statement on the talks would be issued at a later date. The statement published in the local newspapers read; 'Following upon the exchange of letters between the PNC and PPP with respect to talks between the two parties, the Preparatory Committee, which was mutually agreed to, met for the first time on Friday 19th July. This Committee's task is primarily to work out the procedures, the agenda and the general framework in which the two-party talks are to proceed. At its first meeting, the Committee discussed broadly several questions related to its task. Both sides advanced views on the structure for the talks and offered suggestions for their positive development. In the course of the discussions, there were several points of coincidence while others are to be further discussed.'

Between July and October,1985 the two sides met on two occasions. During this period, representatives of the two parties were grappling with the text of the comprehensive statement. And, following approval by our party's executive committee, I submitted to McDavid our party's proposals with respect to the structure of the talks envisaged. While all this was going on, the PPP was busy preparing to host its 24th congress to be held on the 3,4 and 5 of August in the city of Georgetown. On Monday August 6th 1985 President Burnham died.

On assuming the mantle of President, Hoyte killed the talks. The last meeting between the two sides, but with depleted participants was held on October 29, 1985. The PNC side was represented by McDavid alone while the PPP was represented by Feroze Mohamed and Reepu Daman Persaud. My absence was due to the fact that I was preoccupied with my work as the sole representative of the PPP's on the Guyana Elections Commission. The election was just one month and two weeks away, due to be held on December 15th 1985.

In his last public speech delivered during a rainy morning from a balcony on the Southern side of the National Cultural Centre, facing the tarmac, Burnham, warned his followers present including the Heads and other ranks of the 'Joint Services' as well as cabinet ministers, all of whom were 'bused in,' that approaching the IMF in search of a solution to the country's economic and financial crisis would be a 'recipe for riots.'

Burnham refused to accept the advice of his then Finance Minister to the effect that the country had become 'uncredit-worthy' due to a wrecked and bankrupt economy.

Earlier, in speeches at public events, Burnham called on Guyanese to "eat less, sleep less and work harder," and as if to add to insult to injury, he confessed to his supporters that he had "nothing to offer them but hard work"

Moreover, with the economy in dire straits, Burnham's cynicism appeared limitless. He 'stuck his neck out' promising the nation that "the small man would become the real man."

Forbes Burnham found himself locked in a battle with self-denial in the face of mounting disillusionment on the part of his own supporters and the population as a whole. Their stomachs were empty, and they were becoming increasingly restless.

To offset any potential social and political turmoil, Burnham engaged in a series of rabble-rousing speeches to his supporters around the country. He promised that his government would provide every Guyanese with "free milk and cassava"and that "not a single Guyanese would go to bed hungry."

On one occasion, Burnham was invited to speak at a May Day rally held at the National Park. Joseph Pollydore, the then TUC General Secretary addressed the crowd before Burnham spoke; he called on Burnham to pay the workers $14 per day as the basic minimum wage,

For his part, while delivering his speech, President Burnham asked the ecstatic crowd that was swooning with his flowery language whether they preferred the $14 per day or hydroelectricity, the majority of his listeners responded lustily; "We want hydroelectricy."

That was precisely the response Burnham was looking for. Tons of Free food and drinks came next but, in the end, the workers got neither the $14 per day nor hydroelectricity.

Guyanese were to later look back and mock at this sad experience recalling that all they eventuality got was a massive, if not burdensome hydrocele. Such was the cynicism and deceptiveness of the man that Hoyte had succeeded.

I had the opportunity of meeting Burnham on one occasion, even though I saw him on many occasions in the past, riding on horseback riding from east to west on North Road. That was in the late sixties. At that time, I lived at 13 North Road.

DESMOND HOYTE

Hugh Desmond Hoyte assumed the Presidency of the country after President Forbes Burnham died.

Hoyte became President at a time when the Guyanese economy was nearing economic collapse.

On assumption to office, Hoyte wasted no time in dismantling the Burnham apparatus and to put in its place, a technocratic bureaucracy.

Hoyte immediately opened talks with the IMF and the World Bank aimed at putting in place a Structural Adjustment Programme (SAP) to take Guyana out of the economic and financial morass into which Burnham had plunged the country with his misguided and so-called 'cooperative socialist' policies.

The harshness of the (SAP) Hoyte had negotiated with the international financial institutions had a terrible anti-social and economic backlash on the Guyanese working people and the business community. According to a former supporter of his party and government, Hoyte's economic policy caused "Afro-Guyanese civil servants, his own political constituency to suffer."

In light of his background as an economist, Hoyte favoured a technocratic approach to solving Guyana's economic and financial problems more particularly its foreign debt overhang.

PROTESTS AND POLICE ARREST

Hoyte's economic reforms were branded the Economic Recovery Programme (ERP). The program was in effect a Structural Adjustment Programme supported by the World Bank and the International Monetary Fund. (IMF).

But the loan the government received came with a heavy price viz; the devaluation of the Guyana dollar. The exchange rate was to be ten Guyana dollars to one US dollar.

As a response to the crushing pressures on the working people in particular, the PPP and the trade unions organized a march and a massive demonstration in front of the parliament to coincide with the presentation of the1989 estimates of expenditure.

I was assigned the responsibility to lead the march from Party headquarters to the parliament buildings and there the picketing exercise would begin. At that time, I was International Secretary of the Party.

Everything went well until the police arrived and began harassing the demonstrators. Then they began making efforts to break up the picketing exercise. I got caught in the efforts to resist the actions of the police. Then suddenly, I was grabbed from behind and beaten with police truncheons.

I fell down but refused to stand up. The police decided to drag me while on my back from the parliament buildings to the Brickdam police station where I received another sound beating, cuffs and kicks by police ranks and was thrown into the lock-ups.

Later that night, I was removed from the Brickdam lock ups and taken to another lockups at police headquarters compound at Eve Leary.

The stench of urine and filth at that lock ups were unbearable. I had no choice but to try my best to sleep it off.

The following morning, I was taken to the Georgetown Magistrates Court presided over by Mr. Stephen Knights. The prosecutor was Ms. Clarissa Rheil, a closeted member of the ruling party. Rheil was later appointed a member of Parliament when the PNC lost power in 1992 and much later, High Commissioner to Canada on the return of the PNC to power in 2015

I was charged with disorderly behavior, obstructing a peace officer in the execution of duty, resisting arrest, and assaulting a peace officer in the execution of duty and for leading an illegal procession.

Notwithstanding pleas by the lawyers representing me, the magistrate refused bail and remanded me to the Georgetown Prisons.

The prosecutor told the magistrate that her instructions were that I was not to be released until parliament had completed consideration of the estimates for the 1989 budget, an activity that could take as long as three weeks.

I spent three weeks at the Georgetown Prisons at Camp street. I was placed in the section reserved for condemned prisoners far removed from the rest of the prison population.

I was allowed to be on 'self-support' meaning that meals prepared by my wife was allowed to be in brought from outside the prisons.

It was clear to me that, perhaps because of my politics, I was not allowed to mix nor to communicate with the rest of the prison population. It was for this reason I assumed; the prison authorities placed me in one of isolated cells reserved for condemned prisoners only.

On my return to court after Parliament had finished its business, I found myself before a different magistrate. Three of the charges were dismissed while I was fined for the other two. We decided appeal the latter two. I was told by the presiding magistrate that I was free to go. Mrs. Jagan, who was present in court at the time, gave me a lift in her Volkswagen PZ379 to Party headquarters, from there I went straight home to have a good rest.

The team of lawyers who represented me at the time were; Bayne Karan, Jainarine Singh Jnr., Khemraj Ramjattan and Stanley Moore.

Earlier in the process while I was at the Brickdam lockup's Mr. Ralph Ramkarran made an official request to the police to see me but was refused.

Similar treatment was meted out by the police to two medical doctors, Roger Luncheon and Deane Sharma who requested permission from the police to examine me following the beatings I received.

Balram Raghubir, the then Commissioner of Police was at pains to explain the actions of the police who had received a negative press and a bad image in respect to treatment of peaceful protestors.

HOYTE BATTLES FOR SURVIVAL

Hoyte's tenure in office was not made easy as a result of the emergence of an international climate that favored regime change in countries ruled by 'Little Caesars' who maintained themselves in office through rigged elections.

Guyana was one of such countries that was ripe for 'regime change.'

Notwithstanding his efforts at economic reform, Hoyte came under tremendous political pressure internally and externally.

At the level of CARICOM, the Commonwealth Group of countries, and the Organization of American States pressure began to mount for free and fair elections.

The US, Canada the UK and the European Union's support for 'regime change' became increasingly vocal.

And in Guyana itself unity of the political and social forces was stronger than ever before in their demands for electoral reform as exemplified in the formation Patriotic Coalition for Democracy (PCD).

In effect, Hoyte was riding an elections tiger.

Regional and General Elections were held in December 1985. And notwithstanding the presence of international observers, the elections were no different from those that were rigged in 1968,1973, the referendum in 1978 and the elections held in 1980.

As on previous occasions, the army was brought out to patrol the streets and were again engaged as escorts for the ballot boxes.

Before leaving Guyana, the international observers declared that the elections "Were as crooked as barbed wire."

Hoyte, thinking he had gotten away with another fraudulent election, soon found himself in hot water.

A number of Caricom member states had grown tired of having within the grouping a member state with a reputation for rigging elections and was ruling by fraudulent means. Moreover, with the Commonwealth Secretariat obligated to upholding its commitment to free and fair elections Mr. Hoyte found himself cornered by the very organizations to whom he had declared his government's commitment.

Hoyte' attendance in January1986 at a specially convened meeting of Caricom Heads of Government at Mustique, St. Vincent and the Grenadines, following his 'victory' at the December 1985 elections dealt a serious blow to the legitimacy of the election results. The Heads expressed their deep concern over the assurances and explanations offered by Hoyte as regards the situation in Guyana. Caricom Heads threatened to suspend Guyana from the regional body in the event that an end was not brought to elections rigging in Guyana.

ATTEMPTED COUP IN TRINIDAD

On the eve of the Jamaica meeting of Heads, in fact, on July 27, 1990 during a meeting of CARICOM Foreign Ministers, news came about an attempted coup in Trinidad and Tobago and the holding hostage of the then Prime Minister ANR Robinson by the Jamaat al Muslimeen.

It was under this ominous cloud that the 11th meeting of Conference of Heads was convened at the Jamaica International Conference Centre.

At the end of the conference, a communique was issued condemning the coup and welcoming the efforts by Caricom member states in resolving the tense situation in Trinidad and Tobago.

It was only after the situation in Trinidad had returned to normalcy, that delegations began departing Jamaica for their respective destinations.

In the meanwhile, the US-based lobbying firm of Paul Reichler was intensifying its lobbying activities in the USA.

ATTEMPTS AT A JOINT PCD PROGRAMME

On our return to Guyana talks resumed among the PCD parties about the prospects for a pre-electoral alliance. During the talks initiated in 1987, it was agreed that before a pre-electoral alliance could be considered, a Joint Programme would be necessary.

In light of the fact that following the 1985 rigged election, the PCD had formulated a memorandum entitled 'Elections Crooked as Barbed Wire,' it was generally agreed that attempts be made at formulating a Joint PCD Programme. With this in mind, a team comprising representatives the various constituents of the coalition were assembled to begin work on a first draft of the Joint Programme.

Picture shows a PCD demonstration and march from the East Coast, Demerara, to the City, highlighting the demand for free and fair elections. It also brought into focus demands for respect for human rights and overall improvements in social conditions.

Navin Chandarpal, the First Secretary of the Party's youth arm was selected to be the Party's Representative on the team. However, owing to pressure of work at the level of the youth organization, Navin asked to be relieved of the task. The Party agreed that I would replace him as the Party's representative on the team.

Tacuma Ogunseye represented the WPA, Claudius London represented the DLM. Representatives from two parties, one based at Linden, the other in Georgetown were also on board.

As the work in the Joint Programme proceeded rather painstakingly, the group was eventually reduced to just me and Ogunseye.

On completion of the first draft, the document was circulated to the PCD parties. There was general agreement on the text. The next question however, was whether the document should be made public and if so, when.

The PPP was of the view that the document should be made public well in advance in anticipation of an agreement on a pre-electoral alliance.

Moreover, the party was of the view that releasing the document would help the populace understand what the PCD parties stood for collectively and how their interests would be protected.

The WPA and the DLM disagreed. Ogunseye and London conveyed to the PPP, through me, the reasons why their parties were not in agreement to have the document published.

This was conveyed to the Executive Committee of the Party who, after some discussion, decided that a high-level meeting of the PCD parties should meet to discuss the matter with a view to arriving a solution. No agreement was reached.

In the meanwhile, the question of a Consensus Candidate for all the opposition parties within the PCD became the central issue.

When it became obvious that the PCD parties were opposed to the candidate coming from the PPP, the debate shifted to a candidate from outside the PCD.

Dr. Jagan worked tirelessly day and night putting forward a number of consensus-type formulas aimed at arriving at a workable solution, but to no avail.

In the midst of all these happenings a broad-based civic organization by the name of 'Guyanese Action for Reform and Democracy' (GUARD) emerged and was making some waves on the political front.

The question of the Consensus Presidential and Prime Ministerial Candidates had by now become a hotly debated political issues in the country. Names floated for the Prime Ministerial position were Clive Thomas and Paul Tennessee while names for presidential candidate were Cheddi Jagan and Ashton Chase

The PPP had lengthy internal discussions on all the issues in respect to both positions. In the end, notwithstanding tremendous pressures from different constituents insisting that Cheddi Jagan drop out of the race to be the Presidential candidate, the party held firmly to its position and in the end agreed that Cheddi Jagan would be the Presidential Candidate while Samuel Archibald Hinds would be the prime ministerial candidate of what became know as the PPP/Civic.

Dr Jagan had arrived at the conclusion that since the remaining PCD parties, amongst others, did not support him to be the consensus presidential candidate, he proposed the formation of a civic grouping, which in alliance with the PPP, would contest the elections.

We went about identifying a number of outstanding Guyanese from various walks of life who were not members of the PPP but who had indicated their support to the party. The response was overwhelming. At the leadership level, a discussion took place about how to brand the alliance in readiness for the elections. The comrades present put forward various options. Some suggested a total rebranding of the Party with the initials 'PPP' not being mentioned. But it was Janet Jagan's advice to us that won the day.

She calmly but jokingly asked; "Why change a brand that is already a household name like Colgate or Heinz with its fifty-seven varieties? Keep PPP and include Civic by adding either a plus, dash or slash sign to the PPP brand name", she suggested. Thus emerged, PPP/CIVIC.

The next stage was for the leadership of the party to initiate country-wide consultations with its entire membership to put them in the picture and to win their support for the positions the leadership was recommending as the way forward.

Members of the CIVIC component accompanied party leaders to various parts of the country so that our members could familiarize themselves with the CIVIC members and vice versa. This process proved to be tremendous success.

Later, a two-day seminar was held at Party headquarters where civic members presented papers under the theme; "Human Development - A New Direction in Policy Formulation and Implementation" for discussion.

While all this was going on, the PCD had receded into the doldrums.

For its part, the WPA supported a proposal that Mr. Ashton Chase be the consensus candidate for another opposition grouping.

Convinced that the only path to success at the elections was to go forward in alliance with civic-minded individuals grouped in a CIVIC component in alliance with the PPP, Dr. Jagan persevered and won.

Throughout the years in opposition Dr. Jagan fought for cross-party alliances. In fact, at every meeting of the Party's Central Committee and Congress a permanent agenda item has been the search for alliances and the building of national unity.

It is in the context of the pursuit and significance of alliances that Dr. Jagan's call for a National Patriotic Front and National Front Government, the efforts to create the Patriotic Coalition for Democracy and finally, the formation of the Civic component in alliance with the PPP must be viewed.

THE PPP LOSES ITS TRADITIONAL FRIENDS

For the PPP, the collapse of the Soviet Union and with it the world socialist system, meant the loss of support from fraternal parties in Moscow and Eastern Europe.

Mikhail Gorbachev and his inexperienced opportunistic cohorts who had by that time assumed control of the Communist Party and government in the Soviet Union by 1985 began the process of dismantling the command-type, socio-politico and economic structure in the USSR under the guise of what was called "glasnost and perestroika or " reform and openness."

REFORM AND OPENNESS IN THE USSR

In effect the reform process meant embracing of the free market economy through greater economic liberalization, privatization of state enterprises and political freedoms.

Opening up the country to the West to facilitate greater foreign investment and economic and military/nuclear cooperation with the USA and the European Union was seen as the panacea to the socio-economic problems confronting the Soviet Union.

The ultimate strategic goal was to overcome economic stagnation in the USSR which Gorbachev and his opportunistic gang claimed the country was experiencing.

This was in effect a smokescreen to allow the corrupt and the nouveau riche bureaucratic bourgeoisie that had emerged in Moscow and other Soviet Republics to occupy more and more economic and financial space in the political, economic and social life of the USSR.

The architects of the 'reform and openness' process, openly rejected the view of the more conservative wing of the ruling CPSU led by Yuri Andropov and Konstantin Chernenko who were of the view that the system built up over the years in the Soviet Union possessed, by its very nature, solutions or 'local heresies' that could be tapped to address the problems the country was facing. They were of the view that it was not absolutely necessary to go the 'full monty' vis-a-vis the aggressive liberalization approach Gorbachev was pushing.

In this regard, those in the conservative wing of the Party who did not give unconditional support but gave what was tantamount to 'critical support' to Gorbachev's aggressive liberalization initiatives were branded 'old thinkers' and were gradually eased out of their positions in the leadership of the party and cabinet.

Ironically, while there was general all-round support for reforms and openness in the Soviet Union what was lacking was a measured and calculated pace of the said reforms within the constitutional arrangements of the USSR.

Yuri Andropov who had succeeded Leonid Brezhnev together with like-minded colleagues at the leadership level of the Party supported measured reforms guided by the Soviet Constitution, but with Andropov's death and that of other older stalwarts in the Party such as Konstantin Chernenko who had succeeded Andropov, that cautious approach to reforms ended up dead in the water.

By the 1990's Gorbachev and his gang followed by Yeltsin went on a wrecking spree which had a snowballing effect through out the Union. They eventually lost complete control of glasnost and perestroika resulting in the collapse of the socialist system in the Eastern European countries in 1989, and eventually culminating in a similar but even more dramatic collapse of the USSR on December 26, 1991.

Unlike the popular revolt in Czechoslovakia when Warsaw troops and tanks entered Prague in August of 1968 to safeguard the socialist bloc, twenty-three years later, there were no tanks nor troops to occupy the Red Square to safeguard socialism in the USSR.

The plan to destroy the Soviet Union and the socialist community of states was well orchestrated, and executed.

The first objective was to undermine and destroy its socialist allies; Having weakened its external support base, objective number two was aimed at undermining and destroying the system from within.

Objective three, was to wipe from the world map the USSR the bastion of socialism and the only economic and military rival to the USA.

The PPP's response to the dramatic developments in the Soviet Union and Eastern Europe was at best measured and characterized by a high degree of political and ideological pragmatism.

As the then International Secretary of the Party I took it upon myself to propose that the Party organize for an entire week-end, an in- house political/ideological seminar to discuss developments in the USSR and Eastern Europe.

I suggested that such an activity would help with our analysis of the situation in Eastern Europe and from that analysis we could draw certain political conclusions before making any public policy statement on the matter.

This recommendation was agreed at the Secretariat level and later, endorsed by meetings of the Executive and Central Committee of the Party.

It was further agreed that two key departments of the Party viz; the International and Education departments, the former headed by me and the latter by Feroze Mohammed respectively, would collaborate to successfully realize the event.

The seminar was held from 2-3 December 1989 at Freedom House. It brought together all members of the Party's Central Committee as well as leaders of its women's and youth arms. All the cadres who had studied in Moscow, Bulgaria, the German Democratic Republic and Cuba were invited to attend.

The seminar was a great success, all the participants were highly motivated. Presentations by those to whom topics were assigned were well researched, informative and educational.

The seminar concluded on a high note, it helped clarify many misconceptions and misunderstandings. It demystified many obscure notions peddled by the local and international media.

At the conclusion of the seminar, the party was in a better position to make public its views on the matter. Later, at a public lecture, Dr. Jagan offered insights into the party's position on the unfolding developments.

TEMPERING THE PPP'S IDEOLOGICAL VIEWS

It was from here on that tempering of the party's language on ideological issues began. However, while the fundamentals remained intact, it was a slow, moderated process.

The hardline, ideological public posture the Party had adopted following its declared transformation in 1969 from a loose mass party to a more disciplined, Marxist- Leninist type of party, gradually shifted to reflect more and more what it had been in the early 1950's. And greater attention was paid to realpolitik locally and internationally.

Two factors influenced this tactical and strategic shift by the Party.

First, was the lost of support from the CPSU and other powerful Communist and Workers' parties in Eastern Europe. That support evaporated with the collapse, and effective disappearance of the socialist bloc.

Second, the epochal developments in Europe and the ending of the 'cold war' at the end of the 1980's created the external conditions for the PPP's return to office after twenty-eight years in the political wilderness.

That historic opportunity was not lost to an ever-vigilant PPP.

But more importantly, was the domestic situation.

A key factor, was the growing isolation and unpopularity of the PNC regime internally, this was compounded by widespread disenchantment and demand for free and fair elections by the broad masses of the Guyanese people.

PREPARING FOR THE FIGHT

These two factors, combined with Dr. Jagan's evolving ideological views helped create the perception that Jagan and his Party had 'changed.' Moreover, these factors resulted in the lowering of the party's ideological rhetoric in its public messaging.

General elections in Guyana were due to be held in 1990 and the prospects that the PPP would win, were those elections free and fair, became a real possibility, if not a foregone conclusion.

Elections were however postponed due the production of a discredited voters' list by the Election Commission and the absence of long fought for electoral reforms which the PPP, and much later, which the Patriotic Coalition for Democracy (PCD)began pressing for.

In the same year of 1990, in response to an invitation received from the Frente Sandinista por la Liberacion de Nicaragua (FSLN) I was despatched by the party to Nicaragua to observe the elections scheduled to be held on February 25, 1990 in that Central American country.

My two-week stay in Nicaragua turned out to be educational and instructive. I was exposed to a country that was ravaged by civil war which lasted several decades and cost that country millions in US dollars.

Following the overthrow of Somoza in 1979, the FSLN managed to gain complete control of the political process by 1981 after ousting some of its allies who disagreed with the ideological orientation of the revolution.

Elections held in 1984 was won by the Sandinistas but by February 1990, the tables had turned and the United Nicaraguan Opposition (UNO), an opposition alliance led by Violetta Chamorro won the elections.

Three elements of the Nicaraguan electoral process struck me as I moved around the country with other NGO's who had arrived in the country to observe the elections.

First, was the decentralized electoral process where each of the 15 geographic departments and 2 autonomous regions of the country had their own electoral councils with their own electoral roll and arrangements peculiar to each particular department and region.

Second, was the presence of a large number of international observers who covered almost every polling station at each department and autonomous region.

The most prominent and largest contingent of the international observers represented the Carter Centre whose officials were to be found at almost every department and autonomous region.

Third, was the fact that after the counting, tabulation and verification of the votes, provided there were no disputes nor demand for recounts, all ballot papers were collected, sealed accordingly and escorted by departmental and autonomous elections officials, party agents and international observers to designated areas where they were burnt and buried in the full view of all present.

The Sandinistas lost the elections because of the large number of 'el voto sancionada' or the 'punishment vote' as well as 'el voto de abstencion' meaning the abstention vote.

The Nicaraguan electorate had grown tired of war and more so, because the 'contras', or armed groups opposing the revolution, funded by local big business and external sources, had managed to penetrate Managua, the capital city and other important towns in Nicaragua.

The 'contras' were wreaking havoc throughout the country, militarily and economically.

The Sandinistas appeared overwhelmed. They were under increasing pressure to run the government effectively, administer the affairs of state and at the same time, provide basic goods and services to the Nicaraguan people.

The cost of the war waged by the Sandinista army against the 'contras' amounted to more than half of the country's national budget

The cumulative effect of these developments was the lost of confidence in a liberation movement that had promised a better, securer life to the Nicaraguan people.

A mere five years after liberating the country from the hated Somoza military dictatorship the FSLN's popular support had plummeted to an all time low.

In the view of a tired Nicaraguan electorate, the alternative was to turn to the right-wing US- sponsored electoral alliance with the hope of bringing an end to the war and to usher in peace and alleviate the suffering of the Nicaraguan people.

On my return to Guyana, I shared my experiences and observations with the Executive Committee of the Party. I recommended that for future elections in Guyana we should press the government to invite the Carter Centre and other international observers.

Also, I recommended that we should press for the adoption of some of the electoral arrangements along the lines of the Nicaraguan model.

The Executive Committee agreed with my recommendations. Later, the party pushed for the acceptance of my recommendations in the Patriotic Coalition for Democracy (PCD) a loose anti-dictatorial, pro-democracy alliance of political parties.

With 1990 elections postponed for two years, the PPP under the leadership of Dr. Jagan decided to mount during that period, mass protests actions to press for electoral reforms.

These reforms included: 1) counting the votes at the place of poll, 2) inviting overseas observers to observe elections, 3) polling agents to accompany ballot boxes, 4) abolishing overseas and postal voting and 5) establishment of an independent Elections Commission with an independent chairman.

The struggle for free and fair elections in Guyana was a long and difficult one.

Elections in Guyana became synonymous with fraud by vote rigging and a padded voters' list beginning from 1968 up to 1990.

Starting from 1968, the ruling PNC for the first time, introduced postal and overseas voting and the abuse of voting by proxy.

TAKING THE DEBATE ON RACE TO ANOTHER LEVEL

It was because of my experience working in Afro-Guyanese communities and knowledgeable of the Party's efforts at gaining a better understanding of the evolving socio-economic and socio- psychological conditions of Afro-Guyanese that I proposed that the party sponsor a symposium on 'Race and Class - The National and International Dimensions'

The party accepted my suggestion that the symposium be hosted by THUNDER, the official theoretical/discussion journal of the PPP on the occasion of the 39th anniversary of the launch of the journal.

With the agreement of the party, I wrote Professor Ali A. Mazuri, Dr. Phl. (Oxon), Dept. of Political Sciences at the University of Michigan inviting him to be the guest speaker at the event.

The good professor replied accepting our invitation to participate at the event billed for December 9, 1989, however due to ill health he wrote again saying he was no longer available.

Donald Ramotar, Vincent Alexander and Ravi Dev addressed the symposium as panelists.

I chaired the event which was highly successful, it attracted an audience comprising a wide cross section of the city population as well as lecturers and students from the University of Guyana.

The event shored up the image of the party. It showed that the PPP was finally prepared to move its activities out of Freedom House as the preferred venue, and to host an event at a prestigious hotel. It further showed that the party was prepared to confront the issue openly and share a platform with persons known to hold non-PPP views but who nevertheless, held constructive positions on the racial problem.

THE PATRIOTIC COALITION FOR DEMOCRACY (PCD)

With elections once again on the horizon for 1990, the opposition political parties began strategizing regarding the way forward.

It was to be first elections that would be held with Forbes Burnham out of the picture. Burnham was dead and gone, Hoyte had assumed the mantle of the Presidency and, by extension, was now being put to the test as regards the holding of free and fair elections.

By now, all opposition political parties at the time, had considerable political experience under their belt individually, and collectively, as regards the question of alliances.

the long years of struggle against dictatorial rule, for democracy and free and fair elections while in the political wilderness had taught the political parties that unity of the political opposition is a vital perquisite if victory at the polls was to be achieved.

Based on the success an earlier political formation known as the Committee for Defence of Democracy (CDD), the opposition parties at the time, namely; the PPP, the WPA, the DLM and the PDM agreed to establish the Patriotic Coalition for Democracy (PCD). This development was welcomed by the Federation of Independent Trade Unions (FITUG), the Guyana Council of Churches and a host of other social organizations in the country.

With limited financial resources, the PCD mounted a series of well-organized public meetings and an intense letter writing campaign to governments and overseas based organizations. The private sector and local manufacturers were lobbied for their support. Mr. Yesu Persaud, Vickram Oditt, Vic Insanally, Ronald Ali and many others from the business and professional class threw their support behind the PCD with Dr. Jagan playing a leading role.

Bishop Randolph George of the Anglican Church and Bishop Benedict Singh of the Catholic Church were invited to be consultants and advisers to the PCD.

It was clear to many of us in the leadership of PPP at the time, that the political situation was rapidly changing in our favour.

And what was significant about the process was that Party General Secretary, Cheddi Jagan was very open with his comrades at the leadership level about the results of his engagements with non-PPP well-wishers, the diplomatic community and representatives of the business community. He provided full disclosure to us about his discussions and the outcomes, of his engagements with various entities.

And whenever he was scheduled to hold discussions or negotiation with persons or entities outside the party, he always made sure that he was accompanied by a comrade or two. And he encouraged internal debates on the outcomes of his meetings because he wanted to ensure consensus, safeguard the unity and collective decision-making at the leadership level of the party.

In this way, there was rarely any disagreement among ourselves on strategy and tactics.

The WPA's and DLM's role in the PCD was critical in the sense that apart from the class and ethnic nature of their respective constituents, they brought a semblance of ideological and political balance to the persona of the PCD.

This was important in terms of attracting broad national and international support in the fight for free and fair elections.

In its effort to achieve its objectives, the PCD wrote to then President Hoyte requesting a meeting with him. Mr. Hoyte responded saying he is prepared to meet with the PCD on condition that the organization names its leader.

No meeting took place since the PCD refused to engage Hoyte in a matter that had no relevance to its request for a meeting with him.

The PCD decided to launch a lobbying exercise among the CARICOM member states.

The lobbying exercise was to culminate at the time of the convening of the meeting of conference of Heads of State and Government of CARICOM in Kingston, Jamaica.

I was asked to go as the sole advance party representing the PCD with letters to deliver to the Governor Generals, Prime Ministers and Foreign Ministers of Trinidad and Tobago, Barbados, St. Vincent and the Grenadines, the Commonwealth of Dominica, St. Lucia, Grenada and Jamaica.

Apart from making a case for the lobbying mission, each letter, save those to the Governor Generals (which was basically for information), requested individual bilateral meetings with each Head and a PCD delegation on the margins of the summit in Kingston.

The responses to my courtesy calls to the offices of these officials were mixed. In Trinidad and Tobago, the government's response was luke-warm though the then Opposition Leader, Patrick Manning, welcomed me warmly at his office and engaged me in a rather enlightening conversation.

In Barbados, the response to my call was cool to say the least, with brief meetings held with permanent secretaries at the Offices of the Prime Minister and the Ministry of Foreign Affairs.

In St. Vincent Prime Minister Mitchell's Office apologized for his unavailability and offered a meeting with the Permanent Secretary to the PM's office to which I readily agreed.

In Roseau, the responses to my calls on both the PM's and the Opposition Leader's Office were mixed with no commitments being made.

I experienced similar responses to my calls on the offices of the Prime Ministers and Foreign Ministers in St. Lucia and Grenada.

The reception in Jamaica, the host country for the conference of Heads was exceptional in many respects.

Jamaican officials at the Office of Acting Prime Minister P.J. Patterson was warm and understanding.

Commitments were made to meet with the PCD delegation. Assurances were given that invitations would be extended to the PCD delegation to attend the opening session of the summit and to all social functions hosted by the government of Jamaica.

Arrangements to have bilateral meetings with different Heads attending the conference was left to the PCD.

Dr. Jagan arrived in Jamaica as the sole representative of the PCD, ultimately, the PCD delegation was just the two of us. For one reason or another none of the leaders of the other parties could have made the trip.

Soon after Dr. Jagan had settled in at the hotel where he was staying, I met and briefed him about the entire lobbying exercise starting from Port-of-Spain to Kingston.

We discussed and settled on a programme for the duration his stay in Jamaica.

His priority was to tackle the Caricom Heads who were favorably disposed to meeting with him and to ask those with whom he met to encourage others who were not convinced that meeting with him was in their best interests.

At a reception following the Official Opening of Conference Dr. Jagan and me mixed and mingled freely with the dignitaries' present. We were both doing our political work. Dr. Jagan was lobbying Heads while I was lobbying Caricom government officials.

President Hoyte and his delegation spotted us at the function, I was told later, that they had enquired of the Jamaica officials why we were there. An explanation was offered to them but they objected.

Dr. Jagan met with several Heads and their officials at a hotel in Kingston, I was fortunate enough to sit in at some of those meetings. Later on, while Dr. Jagan met alone with other Heads individually, I went off to arrange other bilateral. Having completed the main task. Dr. Jagan met the Private Sector Organization of Jamaica (PSOJ), Mr. Oliver Clarke of the Gleaner Newspaper and much later, the Guyanese diaspora in Jamaica. The following day, he was interviewed by local radio stations, newspapers and TV stations.

I recall during one of the many interviews Dr. Jagan was asked about his party's position on the invasion of Kuwait by Iraq which was dominating world news at the time.

Dr Jagan denounced Iraq's action putting his opposition to the invasion in the context of the party's long held position that support for the inviolability of national borders and, protection of the territorial integrity and national sovereignty of states was a matter of policy for the party.

In that regard, Dr. Jagan reminded of the stand adopted by the party regarding Turkey's invasion, and partial territorial occupation of Cyprus and Britain's colonialist occupation of the Malvinas. Dr. Jagan's declaration made international headlines.

Years later, following the election of the PPP/C to office a high-level Kuwaiti delegation travelled to Guyana to convey to President Jagan their gratitude for his government's and party's support and solidarity at a time when their country needed it.

On the eve of our departure from Jamaica we paid a visit to Asgar Ali a Guyanese national who had taken up residence in Jamaica. Asgar worked in the financial sector of Jamaica and was helpful to Dr. Jagan in making contact with some Jamaican personalities.

We visited Asgar at his office in Kingston and later in the evening at his home because Dr. Jagan had received a phone call earlier in the day from Paul Reichler in Washington informing that he should be at a location to receive some very important faxes concerning support for free and fair elections in Guyana.

We were chatting and having light refreshments in Asgar's study when the phone rang around 6pm. Dr. Jagan was told by Asgar that the call was for him.

Following a brief conversation between the caller and Dr. Jagan, the fax machine in Asgar's study began beeping. A stream of faxes began coming through. The faxes were coming from Reichler's office.

They were separate letters bearing the official letterhead and respective signatures of eight congressmen and six senators, all addressed to the US State Department requesting that aid from the USA to Guyana be tied to free and fair elections in Guyana.

This was great news that was made public following Dr. Jagan's return to Guyana.

VICTORY OF '92

With the electoral reforms and a fresh voters' list, a solid basis was laid for the holding of free and fair elections in Guyana. Years of hard, painstaking work by many patriotic Guyanese at home and abroad had finally paid off.

Just as he did in the fight for his country's independence, Dr. Jagan emerged as the undisputed and indefatigable champion of democracy and for free and fair elections in Guyana.

In his push for free and fair elections Dr. Jagan used effectively the 'Harare Principles' that emanated from the 12th Meeting of Commonwealth Heads of Government Meeting (CHOGM) held in Zimbabwe in October 1991.

The principles included; adherence to democratic principles, good governance and the rule of law.

President Hoyte had attended the CHOGM meeting in Zimbabwe and had committed to the Harare Principles. The Harare Principles were however, at variance with the political realities obtaining in Guyana at the time. The elections held in 1985 were blatantly rigged and those due to be held in 1990, had been postponed for two years because of the flawed voters list and a tainted commission in place at the time.

Hoyte found his government in a political dilemma. There was no wriggle room allowing him to reconcile his undemocratic rule in Guyana with the lofty principles enshrined in the Harare Principles.

Three years after the PPP/C had assumed office, at the 14th CHOGM held in November 1995 in New Zealand, Heads moved a step further to institutionalize the Harare Principles.

In their 'Millbrook Action Programme' CHOGM agreed to 'impose bilateral and multilateral penalties for intransigent members up to and including expulsion from the Commonwealth.' Further, the Heads agreed to establish the 'Commonwealth Ministerial Action Group' (CMAG) to enforce the 'Millbrook Action Programme'

Cheddi Jagan kept himself abreast with international developments around the world. That, together with his wide- ranging contacts with personalities in almost every country enabled him to take advantage of global ideological and geo-political changes taking place world- wide and to turn the tide, as it were in his favour. Jagan's persistent political struggles at home and abroad as well as his diplomatic efforts to win free and fair elections at home, eventually paid off when free and fair elections were held finally on October 5th, 1992.

The presence of the Carter Centre along with other teams of International Observers who did a quick count, concluded that the PPP had won the elections. At first, Hoyte refused to accept the results but after much persuasion he capitulated, conceding defeat.

Hoyte's miscalculation that the PPP had lost the election was premised on his party's examination of the 'number of East Indian names' on the voters list, which, according to him 'did not add up'. Hoyte did not take into account the significant number of cross -over votes as well as the Amerindian vote that contributed to the PPP's victory.

In this regard, Cheddi Jagan in Epilogue Three to his book 'The West on Trial' makes the point that; 'Even if all the East Indians had voted for the PPP, we still could not win the elections,' he concluded therefore that a significant number of cross-over votes from disillusioned PNC supporters as well as votes from the Amerindian communities had contributed to his Party's victory.

THE PPP/C IN GOVERNMENT- THE BACKGROUND

The PPP/C came to power following the much anticipated regional and general elections held on October 5, 1992.

Because of a flawed voters' list and pressure from the opposition, Patriotic Coalition for Democracy (PCD) for much needed electoral reforms, the elections were postponed for almost two years.

Speaking at an Elections Campaign rally - 1992

I served on the Elections Commission as the Representative of the PPP from 1984 to 1991.

The Commission at that time, comprised of a Chairman and a Secretary, two representatives of the ruling party and one representative of the political opposition.

The Chairman, at the time was Sir Harold Bollers, a retired Judge.

Meetings of the Commission was a struggle in itself. At almost every meeting of the Commission, the Chairman would shoot down any recommendation I made. Further, he ruled that my recommendations not be recorded in the minutes of the meeting. His aim was to frustrate me and force me out of the Commission.

The two government- sponsored members of the Commission took a cue from the Chairman's line of argument and supported him at all times.

When I decided to reveal proceedings of meetings of the Commission to the press, the Chairman became very angry and wrote several threatening letters to me pledging to debar me from future meetings. However, when I turned for meetings, Mr. Bollers was like Gentle Jesus, very meek and mild.

My assertiveness and exposure to the press about his behaviour at meetings had payed off.

My novel approach caused the Chairman to be much more cautious and cleverer when discussing matters, I submitted for discussion. He made sure that the matters were put to the vote knowing that I would be defeated by government's built-in majority on the body.

Then a break- through came. On the invitation of President Hoyte and Opposition Leader Cheddi Jagan, a high- level delegation led by President Jimmy Carter arrived in Guyana.

Hoyte had refused to recognize the Carter Centre asking "Who is Carter?" Later, under pressure he relented.

Robert Pastor, a skillful negotiator and consummate diplomat was a key man in the delegation.

Backed by President Carter, Pastor and a small technical team, were successful in pushing through all the reforms the opposition had been demanding for years. Hoyte agreed to the reforms that were eventually passed into law.

Two of the key reforms called for the reconstitution of the Elections Commission with an independent chairman and six persons, three from government and three from the political opposition. The Chairman was be selected by the President after the Leader of the Opposition would have submitted the names of six persons not unacceptable to the President.

Rudy Collins, a Guyanese diplomat of long and distinguished career at the Ministry of Foreign Affairs and the CARICOM Secretariat was one of the six names 'Not unacceptable to the President' that Dr. Jagan, the then Leader of the Opposition had recommended to replace Harold Bollers. The five other names listed were;

David Yankana, Jules DeCambra, Joey King, Ronald Luckoo and Brynmore Pollard.

Of the six persons listed, Collins' was selected by then President Hoyte. Subsequently, Collins and the six commission members, took up their seats on the newly re-constituted Guyana Elections Commission. Under immense pressure, Bollers was forced to resign in 1991.

I resigned, and was replaced by Ralph Ramkarran. Bud Mangal, a medical doctor, and Moen McDoom, an attorney-at-law, joined Ralph as the two other representatives of the political opposition.

THE TRANSITION

One of the first tasks of the Party on being officially declared winner of the elections was to name its representative to negotiate the transition from the outgoing PNC/R administration to the incoming PPP/C administration. Dr. Roger Luncheon was identified as our representative while Dr. Cedric Grant represented the outgoing administration.

The transition process went smoothly save for some bureaucratic elements at the then Department of International Economic Cooperation (DIEC) whose Head, offered some resistance on the grounds that the DIEC is an autonomous body funded by UNDP.

This intransigent posture was abandoned after Juan Larrabure, the Resident Representative of the UNDP publicly declared that the DIEC was a government project, and that in any event, the project had come to an end with exhaustion of resources for the project.

Next came the naming of cabinet ministers. To this end, a meeting of the Executive Committee was convened.

Dr. Jagan presented his proposals which closely resembled the portfolios held by the Party's shadow ministers in the National Assembly prior to the elections However, following discussions some adjustments were made in respect to the portfolios for Home Affairs, Health and Head of the Presidential Secretariat.

Dr. Jagan named me his Minister of Home Affairs but was opposed by Mrs. Jagan, who countered Dr. Jagan's proposal. She recommended Feroze Mohammed instead.

This surprised many since the general expectation amongst the leaders gathered, was that Feroze was best suited for the post of Minister of Education since he had done a great job in the National Assembly as shadow Minister of Education for many years.

Mrs. Jagan's argument was that the party should appoint someone who would give the police assurances about the new government policies towards the police force. She suggested that the person appointed should play the role of a supporter and consolidator rather than someone who may be prone to rock the boat. It was clear that the 'someone' she was referring to was me. In her estimation, rather than putting Feroze at the Ministry of Education he should be assigned the Home Affairs portfolio.

Dr. Jagan did not agree, but in the end, he conceded, indicating that he would designate me, Minister without portfolio in the Office of the President with responsibility for the Foreign Ministry.

Dr. Roger Luncheon was nominated to be our Minister of Health but he declined stating he had a preference to be Head of the Presidential Secretariat and Secretary to the Cabinet. After some discussion on the matter, the meeting agreed that Luncheon would fill the two positions.

THE CHEDDI JAGAN SWEARING IN

After twenty-eight years in the political opposition Cheddi Jagan was sworn in as President of Guyana on Thursday, October 9, 1992.

His swearing in ceremony was simple but impressive not only because of the small gathering of people from all walks of life, but also because it was held at State House, the former residence of the British Governor and of the former Ceremonial Head of State.

Swearing in of President Cheddi Jagan: President: October 1992- March 1997

Patrick Manning, the sitting Chairman of CARICOM flew over from Port-of-Spain to Georgetown to attend the swearing ceremony.

In a statement read at his swearing in ceremony Dr. Jagan said; "We will once again build national, racial-ethnic and working people's unity. The unity of our entire nation is our goal."

Dr. Jagan went on to add; "I expect the fullest cooperation not only of our many friendly countries and our overseas brothers and sisters but also of progressive-minded personalities and organizations: investors, experts and advisers."

A NEW LEASE OF LIFE; A NEW HOME AT QUEENSTOWN

When the PPP/C assumed office, I had been a bachelor for about one year since my wife's death.

During that period, I was father, mother and friend for my two daughters. Making sure they had breakfast, a good snack for lunch and a reasonable dinner, were not easy tasks.

More importantly, I had to ensure that they attended school on time, did their home-work, kept their room tidy and ensure that their school uniforms were always ready. These were house-keeping chores we all shared.

Just a few days after the election victory, I was advised by Dr. Luncheon, our new Head of the Presidential Secretariat that he had received instructions to have me and my two daughters relocated with my belongings to a government-owned property at New Garden Street, Queenstown. Faith Harding, a former government minister had been living there before the change of government.

The House was an old fashioned, but beautiful wooden building located on the western side of the street. It had a high roof that made the interior of the house rather cool. A large verandah, and a reasonably size sitting and dining room made the interior of the house comfortable. There were three bedrooms, a comfortable kitchen and modern toilet and bath.

I subsequently converted a bottom flat of the house into my study.

Having been assigned responsibilities for the Foreign Ministry it became necessary for me to travel abroad very often. This compelled me to hire a good friend of my late wife to undertake housekeeping duties at home while I was on travel duty.

Before converting the bottom flat of my new residence into a study, 'Chand" one of my sister-in- laws and her small family were invited to occupy the flat temporarily. Chand was of great help during my absence and when our helper was not available.

It was during my first trip abroad that I met the girl who was to be my second wife.

In preparation for my first official assignment abroad, I began by perusing the personal files of the home-based staff of the Ministry of Foreign Affairs attached to each of Guyana's diplomatic missions and consulates. My mission was in keeping with a campaign and manifesto promise of the Party to assess and make recommendations to reduce staff and other expenses at the various overseas diplomatic missions

MY SECOND MARRIAGE

In so doing, I came across the name Chamalee, which I found intriguing. It was a one-word name I had I never heard before.

According to the personal file of the individual, who I assumed to be a male East Indian, the Chamalee worked as the accountant at the Guyana Embassy in Washington DC.

On arrival at our Embassy situated at 2490 Tracy Place, I was introduced to the staff only to find that the Chamalee was a young, very slim well-dressed, female East Indian

Some overtures to the young lady resulted in an invitation to lunch being extended to me.

One Saturday morning I promptly found myself at the entrance of the high-rise apartment building at 4850 Connecticut Avenue where Ms. Chamalee resided.

Her apartment was a one bedroom with sitting room, a kitchen and washroom that suited a single person.

We ate curried chicken with rice and dhol which she had just cooked specially for me. I thoroughly enjoyed the meal after which we sat and talked about Guyana and life in Washington.

Throughout my trip from one capital city to another, I maintained telephone contact with my newly found friend in Washington. I continued to do on my return home.

To take matters a step further, 'Ronnie' Nawbatt, a close comrade of mine had alerted me of an impending business trip he was scheduled to make to Washington. I called Chamalee telling her to expect a call from Ronnie my close friend.

On his return to Guyana, Ronnie informed me that his visit went well and that he was treated to a sumptuous traditional Guyanese meal at the young lady's apartment. He shared his impressions with me of Chamalee ending with the words "Go for it!"

Meetings with Chamalee's mother 'Sattie' Singh and 'Savo' one of her four sisters assured me of the correctness of an important personal decision I was about to make.

I broached the matter with my two daughters who seemed happy over my decision and the prospect of having a step-mother in the home.

The next step was to call Chamalee. I called and jokingly told her that she had two options; either she marries me or be re-posted to Headquarters in Guyana. She said she understood that to mean marrying me would mean the other.

She accepted my request which implicitly meant she would be returning home.

First Lady Janet Jagan was informed of these developments as well as President Jagan. Knowing my personal situation, they approvingly wished me good luck.

The marriage took place on Saturday, May 7, 1994, at a simple ceremony held at State House courtesy of President and Mrs. Jagan. The Minister of Education and Presbyterian priest Rev. Dale Bisnauth officiated at the ceremony.

Our simple wedding ceremony was held at State House - 1994

Regrettably, President Cheddi Jagan couldn't be there. He left Guyana accompanied with Presidential Adviser, Kellawan Lall for President Nelson Mandela's inauguration in South Africa which dates coincided with our marriage.

A few days later, another function was held at the home of the bride's mother at the village of Maria's Lodge on the Essequibo Coast. Many invitees from villages on the coast were invited.

My marriage to Chamalee gave me, and my daughters a new lease of life. That new lease of life coupled with the dawn of the new era with a new government in power meant that Guyana was on the cusp of transformative changes with the Guyanese people at the centre of these changes.

THE CHEDDI JAGAN PRESIDENCY

The tasks ahead for the newly President Jagan were monumental, but with his experience in government, his international stature plus the formidable team he had assembled from both the party and the civic component and whom he had appointed to serve as ministers in his cabinet, nothing was impossible.

Good governance - a lean and clean government with equity; democracy in all its aspects - political, social, and cultural - and the empowerment of the people at all levels; debt relief; a mixed economy with the private sector being the engine of growth; economic growth with social and ecological justice; balanced agricultural/industrial and rural/urban development; an integral programme of human resource development; multiculturalism- unity in diversity and a progressive foreign policy based on mutual respect for the sovereignty and territorial integrity of states, non-interference in the internal affairs of nations and peaceful co-existence between states with different political systems, were the main policy objectives of President Cheddi Jagan's administration.

In his speech at the ceremonial opening of the Six Parliament on Wednesday, December 17th, 1992 President Jagan pointed out:

"It is true that a fundamental characteristic of democracy is that the will of the majority prevails over the minority. But the minority must be able to rest assured that decisions have been taken only after opposing views have been expressed. That alone must be a cause for comfort. And that alone must assure the electorate that parliamentary democracy is being practiced for the collective good of the nation."

Dr. Jagan's first overseas mission was at a conference of CARICOM Heads of Government held in Port of Spain, Trinidad and Tobago from October 28-31,1992.

The conference was called to discuss a document entitled "Time for Action." The document called for certain fundamental reforms in the operations of CARICOM more or less in line with what existed at the European Union and the Commission. One of the principal recommendations in the document was the call for the establishment of a supra-governmental Commission similar to the European Commission with similar powers to ensure implementation decisions adopted by Heads and to hold them accountable. Having regard to the principle of sovereignty of states which member states were not prepared to surrender to a supra-national body that proposal ended up dead in the water.

I attended that conference with Dr. Jagan along with Nigel Gravesande, the then Permanent Secretary at the Ministry of Trade and Gillian Rowe a Foreign Service Officer at the Foreign Ministry.

During the meeting, President Jagan met with Prime Minister Patrick Manning to explore an initiative floated by the T&T Prime Minister at the conference which became known as; 'The Manning Initiative.' Basically, the initiative had to do with the joint sharing of office space at overseas missions to accommodate more than one Caricom member state so as to cut down on expenses. According to the Prime Minister, the initiative envisaged sharing office space either at one of the T&T missions or the renting of a new building. The over-head expenses would be shared jointly between the occupants.

President Jagan liked the idea because at home, his administration was engaged in cost cutting exercise at the Foreign Ministry and the Office of the President because of the heavy debt burden and servicing of the foreign debt.

Back home we analysed the financial and international legalities of the initiative and found that it was for us at the time not feasible. Nevertheless, I was sent to Port-of-Spain on two occasions to negotiate on the matter and found to my surprise that the Foreign Affairs official who was negotiating with me was stalling and in some instances putting stumbling blocks along the way as the negotiations proceeded. When I reported the situation back home, we decided to call it a day. The matter never came up again. I doubt whether the initiative ever became a reality.

While on the aircraft returning to Guyana from the Heads of Government conference, Dr. Jagan informed me that he would appoint me his Minister of Foreign Affairs.

My Instrument of appointment & swearing in as Senior Minister of Foreign Affairs - 1992

One of the toughest decisions President Jagan made during his meetings with Caricom Heads of Government was to hold to the view that there had to be a change of the Guyanese nominee to Preside over the proceedings of the 48th Session of the United Nations General Assembly.

In place of Former Foreign Minister Rashleigh Jackson's nomination, Ambassador Rudy Insanally's name was endorsed by the Government of Guyana to be President of the 48th Session of the United Nations General Assembly.

Because I had to rush off to another overseas assignment soon after my return from Trinidad, my swearing in as Senior Minister of Foreign Affairs was postponed pending my return from overseas.

I was nevertheless granted full powers to execute my assignment as Minister without Portfolio within the Office of the President.

As the Jagan administration rolled out its plans for national development, they brought rays of hope to thousands of Guyanese working men and women.

People knew Jagan as a decent, honest and modest man. His name was not synonymous with corruption and he shunned squander-mania and racism.

It became self-evident that there was goodwill all around.

Many Guyanese who had not been home for years returned looking either for investment opportunities or to determine what they could give back to their country in terms of resource mobilization.

In and out of government, Dr. Jagan was a staunch fighter against corruption, squandermania and nepotism.

He made it clear to the nation long before being elected that he would not tolerate any of these three evils in his government. He committed to 'a lean and clean government' and mentioned several times that political leaders in poor, debt-ridden countries should not live 'Cadillac-style in a donkey cart economy.'

Because of his stand against corruption and nepotism one government minister was sacked because he managed to secure a job for his son at a Washington-based international financial institution without the knowledge of the President, nor the approval of cabinet. Another minister was shifted to another ministry where contracts for infrastructure projects and contact with contractors were not easily available.

Another Minister was called in and requested to cease appending 'doctor' to his name since it was firmly established that he had no such academic qualification

I recall the occasion when I was invited by the President to explain how I was able to purchase a plot of land at Eccles and to build a house in just three years as a government minister.

I was astonished when confronted with the question but nevertheless had no difficulty responding since, as I explained, it was my wife and her sister, not me, who put their hard earned money as an investment to purchase the land and to build the house on the said land. Incidentally, because my wife had served at the Guyana Embassy in Washington for a number of years and her sister, who was living and working in New York, for a number of years. I suggested to the President that they were in a much better financial position that I was to purchase a plot of land and build a house. That brought the matter to an end.

To bring about greater accountability, Dr. Jagan met weekly with his ministers individually and on a rotating basis for one-on-one consultations with him on issues pertaining to their sector. Ministers were required to go out on community visits regularly and meet-the-people walk-abouts with a view to sharing with them government policies and to receive feed- back from them on the performance and the quality of services delivered by government.

A number a cabinet sub-committee were established to address the more complex issues facing government. The subcommittees proved to be useful since they spared cabinet time-wasting discussions and effort to dispense with what would have been time consuming and tedious discussions.

Moreover, the President insisted that each minister put in place at their respective ministries, an 'Oversight Team' comprising of persons from civil society and in good standing. The team would be informed about the ministers' portfolio responsibilities, but must be favorably disposed to assist in ensuring the dynamism and people-centered activism of the ministry in fulfillment of government's programmes and policies.

The Constitution of Guyana stipulates that the President of the Republic shall Chair meetings of Cabinet, however, Dr. Jagan put in place a system whereby each cabinet session was chaired by a different minister on a rotating basis.

This innovative approach assisted Ministers to master the technique of chairing important meetings where complex issues were ironed out.

Dr. Jagan held regular meetings with the trade unions and other stakeholders who made representations to government on issues of concern to their constituents.

At the end of these meetings, it was always a question of more money, and where it was to come from.

Compounding the situation, just two years after acceding to office, was an eleven-day strike in 1994 by nurses called by the Guyana Public Service Union (GPSU). Negotiations took almost one year from 1995 to 1996 during which, a bipartisan body was established by President Jagan to investigate government's financial wherewithal, and its capacity to pay the increases demanded by the union.

On one occasion, President Jagan called on his Minister of Finance to 'open the books' at the Ministry of Finance so that union leaders could see for themselves the precarious financial situation facing the government.

The union and the Jagan administration had reached, according to Patrick Yarde, President of the GPSU, "an agreement on reasonable pay increases and a commitment to do other things including an agreement to negotiate a wages policy."

President Jagan's death brought further complications to a rather sensitive negotiating process which was far from completion.

By the time Janet Jagan assumed the Presidency in December 1997, the non-resolution of outstanding issues with the union had become a festering sore.

JAGAN'S FIGHT FOR DEBT RELIEF

Cheddi Jagan was an ardent fighter for debt relief and debt cancellation on behalf of the underdeveloped and the highly indebted poor countries. He waged a relentless campaign far and wide. His knowledge of the issue was remarkable and the solutions he advanced were deemed reasonable, if not acceptable, by all those who heard him speak on the subject.

While Jagan was in opposition, Fidel Castro had launched a vigorous campaign world- wide on the question of the foreign debt and debt relief.

259

So committed was Castro to the search for a solution that in August 1985 in Havana, Cuba he hosted a Continental Dialogue on the foreign debt under the theme; 'La deuda externa no es pagable.' viz; the foreign debt is unpayable. Dr. Jagan along with two of his colleagues were invited to the international gathering in Havana. Me and Kellawan Lall were selected to accompany Dr. Jagan.

The dialogue saw an impressive gathering of politicians, intellectuals, economists, developmental experts, scientists, academics, legal experts and priests. Progressive writers from Latin America were also present.

Dr. Jagan made a masterful presentation. He pointed out that the;

"US $10 billion debt of the Commonwealth Caribbean countries imposed a crushing burden on, and inhibits sustainable development of those countries."

He stressed that; "The net outflow of capital from Latin America and the Caribbean in the 1981-85 period was US$36 billion yearly in the form of profits, dividends and debt payments."

President Jagan called on the participants at the dialogue to; "Launch a campaign for debt relief through cancellation, long term re-scheduling and debt-for-nature swaps."

The event attracted the attention of the international financial institutions and governments of the G7 countries as well.

The clock had started to tick. Debt relief in one form or another was firmly on the international agenda.

THE JAGAN, CASTRO ENCOUNTER

At the conclusion of the continental dialogue, a bilateral meeting was arranged between Fidel Castro and Dr Jagan.

Dr Jagan took me along since Kellawan Lall had gone off on another mission outside Cuba. We were transported by car from the protocol house in Miramar to Fidel's office located at the Plaza de la Revolucion.

It was about 11 pm when we entered Fidel's office. In a small room suited for about five persons a small dinner with light refreshments was served over an exchange of pleasantries between Cheddi and Fidel.

Seated in the room were Cheddi and me, Fidel, Manuel Pinero and Fidel's personal interpreter. At that time, Pinero was the Head of the Departamento de Americas y el Caribe of the ruling Communist Party in Cuba.

The conversation began with an assessment of the dialogue and suggestions regarding implementation of the recommendations. Then the two men began exchanging views about international cooperation. The conversation then moved to ways and means of improving agricultural production and exportation of rice, sugar, tobacco and the by-products.

Discussions moved on to energy and innovative means of producing energy to cut costs such as the utilization of bagasse, and the use of energy saving bulbs manufactured in and exported from Cuba.

Issues pertaining to the environment and how to address environmental challenges were discussed in great detail.

How Cuba succeeded in its public health and education sectors were explained. Challenges facing the Cuban government by sending its medical specialists and trained teachers overseas to developing countries particularly in Africa was a topic that Fidel dealt with extensively.

As I sat and listened throughout the discussion, I imagined myself in a University learning from these two intellectual giants.

The meeting ended with calls to meet again sometime in the future.

When the doors opened for us to leave the building, the sun was just rising. It was around 6am in the morning. Seven solid hours of discussion with a number of decisions and recommendations left to be implemented either at the bilateral or multilateral level.

While being transported back to the protocol house, I turned to Dr. Jagan and asked; "Comrade Cheddi, how is it that Fidel is a lawyer and you a dentist by profession and yet both of you are so knowledgeable about all those things you both spoke about?"

Dr. Jagan turned to me with his famous smile and patting me on the back replied; All you have to do is to apply yourself."

Those words of wisdom remained with me to this day.

TAKING THE FIGHT FOR DEBT RELIEF TO ANOTHER LEVEL

I recall, as Foreign Minister, following the PPP/C's victory in the 1992 elections, I had recommended to President Jagan that his new government establish diplomatic relations with the Vatican. Such a move I suggested, would send a strong signal to religious community in general, but more particularly, to the Catholic community at home as well as to the international community just in case there were any lingering concerns about the ideological orientation of the new government. The matter went to cabinet for consideration and the recommendation was unanimously approved. Following the arrival in Georgetown in 1996 of the Apostolic Nuncio representing the Holy See based in Port of Spain, Trinidad and Tobago, a private bilateral meeting took place between President Jagan and the visiting dignitary. Present at the meeting were myself as Foreign Minister and the Director General, Ministry of Foreign Affairs.

In response to a question from the distinguished visitor about how the Holy See could be of help to the new administration, Dr. Jagan proposed assisting in the campaign for debt relief. He pointed out that while bilateral loans could be negotiated, rescheduling or write-offs for multilateral debts were almost impossible. To this, the Emissary calmly and politely replied; "But the debt is not an act of God it is an act of man and therefore can be undone."

Left to Right- Fazal Ali, President Cheddi Jagan, Pope John Paul & Clement Rohee – 1996

Photo courtesy: L'Osservatore Romano, Citta Vaticano, Servizio Photograficio

The Vatican's diplomat resolved to take up the matter with his principals in Rome.

Later that same year, addressing the World Food Summit held in Rome, from 16 to 17 November 1996, Dr. Jagan emphasized;

"Debt relief must be seen as an investment not only in the development of poor countries but also in the security of rich nations."

Situating his call to the gathering to support his call for debt relief within the meaning one of the Pope's earlier encyclicals, Dr. Jagan advised the gathering;

"The Pope's call for a solution on moral and ethical grounds to Third World's debt must be heeded."

Soon after his participation in the World Food Summit, a commentator by the name of David Bacon had this to say about President Jagan's presentation:

"None of the new participants in the world food debate had any simple solutions to offer. But they made it clear that pieties are no longer enough. Guyana's President Cheddi Jagan, once the target of the CIA de-stabilization efforts, offered the most eloquent example testimony for the countries of the South when he called the idea of privatization, free markets and foreign investment would lead to food security "a myth.""

At a meeting of the Central Committee of the party held sometime in 1997, the Party recognized the great success Guyana had achieved in debt reduction and rescheduling. Congratulations were extended to Dr. Jagan, Bharrat Jagdeo and me for our respective roles played as President, Finance Minister and Foreign Minister in accomplishing these goals.

In a January 1998 interview with veteran St. Lucian journalist Earl Bosquet, Janet Jagan pointed out;

"President Cheddi Jagan was very much involved in negotiating the IMF/World Bank debt write-off approval. This negotiation has been going on for two years and finally our Finance Minister has told us that it is now concluded and by 1999 the actual relief will flow into our budget."

SUPPORT FROM POPE JOHN PAUL

During his stay in Rome, on November 18, President Jagan, me and Fazal Ally of the Guyana Rice Producers' Association (GRPA) paid a courtesy call on Pope John Paul at the Vatican.

The backdrop to that meeting is noteworthy.

The establishment of diplomatic relations between Guyana and the Holy See in June 1997 laid the basis for that historic meeting.

Following our participation at the World Food Summit, the Foreign Ministry, in accordance with my instructions, had scheduled a meeting with the Pope the day before our departure from Rome.

As is customary with Dr. Jagan, before important bilateral meetings he would consult with colleagues on matters of interest to him. Consistent with this tradition, President Jagan solicited my views as to who among the delegation should accompany him to the meeting with John Paul.

The delegation to meet the Pope was restricted to only three persons.

Apart from Dr. Jagan, the rest of the delegation comprised of me, Havelock Brewster, Fazal Ally and Lall Singh, Guyana's Ambassador to the Holy See.

I recommended that me and Lall Singh accompany President Jagan to the meeting.

Following our consultation, President Jagan indicated that instead of Lall Singh, Fazal Ally would be the third person.

This was a smart move by the President. It demonstrated that, for him, the meeting with the Pope was more political that prolocular. He also wanted to demonstrate to rice farmers at home how he held them in high esteem by taking along their representative to the meeting with the Pope.

This was an important lesson for me as regards the politics of diplomacy

The Pope proved very knowledgeable about challenges facing developing countries and asked a number of questions about food production and the agricultural sector in Guyana.

Called upon by President Jagan to make some remarks, Fazal Ally's intervention treating with the agricultural sector in general and, the rice sector in particular tickled the interest of the Pope.

The meeting was highly successful, John Paul was fully supportive of the call for debt relief.

While we were in Rome, President Jagan took the opportunity to meet with the Italian President Oscar Luigi Scalfaro for an exchange of views on enhancing bilateral relations between Italy and Guyana. President Jagan had requested the Foreign Ministry to make the arrangements for the meeting before we left Guyana to attend the World Food Summit. The President wanted to discuss the activation of a million Commodity Aid Grant to the tune of US$4 million dollars for the procurement of heavy-duty agricultural machinery and drainage and irrigation equipment. However, due to the fact that the Government of Italy was rocking

from crisis to crisis, the disbursement of the funds became a victim of the ongoing crisis until it ended up dead in the water.

President Jagan meets with the Italian President- 1996

CHEDDI JAGAN: ECONOMIST AND POLITICIAN

As President of Guyana, Dr, Jagan continued to wage an all-out battle for debt relief for his country as well as the heavily indebted poor countries.

At the 16th meeting of Heads of Government of CARICOM, the Heads; 'Noted Guyana's willingness to assume the lead responsibility for the debt issue within the context of the follow-up to the Summit of the Americas.'

Dr. Jagan eventually succeeded in securing debt write offs and debt relief at both the multilateral and bilateral levels but not after putting in place stringent measures to cut public expenditures.

Dr. Jagan was essentially a developmental economist. He had established formidable relations with internationally recognized academic institutions, universities, economists and political scientists in many countries. He could speak authoritatively at international fora on political and economic theory and practice.

He was often invited to address international seminars and conferences and to share his experiences of being in government while Guyana was still a colony of Great Britain.

What stirred the interest of many, was the fact that although he was perceived to be a communist, he nevertheless was capable of interpreting and articulating global problems and developments in a manner that people came to accept him not as the orthodox, die-in-the-wool communist-type, but as a progressive, left wing democrat who skillfully and creatively used the Marxist methodological approach as an analytical tool.

In this connection, President Janet Jagan in an address at York University, Toronto Canada had this to say about Dr. Jagan:

"His world outlook cannot be understood within the limited confines of any particular ideology, while he was committed to a Marxist outlook, he saw the development of Guyana within the context of its own historical experience and modern systems of democracy"

She went on; "

"He believed in national liberation, a staunch fighter in the struggle against colonialism, and an internationalist, joining the fight against injustice and poverty all over the world".

DEVELOPMENT INITIATIVES UNDER JAGAN

During the Cheddi Jagan Presidency, releasing land for housing development, opening up more lands for agriculture, improving the delivery of goods and services in the public health and education sectors and unblocking of resources accrued from the donor community for use in a timely and efficient manner were some of the day-to-day challenges that faced the new PPP/C administration.

Out of his deep concern for the need to address racial discrimination and inequality, President Jagan took steps to establish A Race Relations Commission with the late Anglican Bishop Randolph George as Head of the Commission. The Commission functioned at a sub-optimal level principally because the opposition PNC refused to cooperate in the realization of its mandate.

The political obstacles notwithstanding, the Commission was instrumental in the realization of important anti-discrimination legislation that sought to protect workers from any form of discrimination on the basis of race, gender or religion.

Cheddi Jagan and his ministers did their level best, under very difficult national and international circumstances, to lift the country and its people from the extremely difficult conditions inherited from the previous administration.

To get badly needed social and economic projects moving on the ground, Dr. Jagan established Community Development Councils (CDC's) involving residents in every town, village and community.

The basic task of the CDC's was to identify urgently needed community development projects to help in the formulation of project proposals for the improvement of roads, public health issues, sanitary conditions, cleaning of drains, disposal of garbage and environmental matters in general.

President Jagan made regular visits to communities around the country to familiarize himself with problems of the ground.

The visits helped him in the decision-making process at the various levels of government.

Reaching out to Guyanese in the diaspora, Dr. Jagan introduced a Remigration Scheme aimed at encouraging them to return home with their tools of trade, vehicles and other household items.

The scheme was highly successful. Guyanese re-migrated and took advantage of the duty-free concessions inherent in the scheme.

The Jagan administration's policies were fundamentally developmental and people-centered. To my understanding, though he was not a development economist by profession, he was, for all practical intents and purposes, one by the way he formulated his plans and executed his government's programmes and policies.

The goal of the State to which his efforts were directed, was national democracy. In effect, the day- to-day policy initiatives and government programmes were national democratic in character. In other words, with Jagan in the driving seat, the process of moving Guyana towards a national democracy was already in motion.

AT THE WHITE HOUSE, MEETING PRESIDENT CLINTON

I accompanied President Jagan to Washington twice for meetings with President Bill Clinton to discuss the situation in Haiti and the Summit of the Americas. The President wasn't happy staying at the exclusive Mayflower Hotel he preferred a more modest hotel such as One Washington Circle or at the home of a friend where he usually stayed whenever in Washington. However, Secret Service and White House security and protocol arrangements combined, militated against his desire to shift to another location.

Because of the tremendous public education work that preceded his accession to the Presidency as regards the oppressive nature of the foreign debt, for the period while he was President, Dr. Jagan gained the support of many world leaders including President Bill Clinton of the United States with whom he had met twice on two different matters.

The first occasion was in August 1993 at the invitation of President Bill Clinton who invited five CARICOM leaders to meet with him at the White House to discuss CARICOM-USA bilateral relations. I had the honour and privilege to accompany President Jagan at that historic meeting.

Among the leaders attending the meeting were; PJ Patterson of Jamaica, Erskine Sandiford of Barbados, Patrick Manning of Trinidad and Tobago, and Hubert Ingraham of The Bahamas. The leaders were accompanied by their respective Foreign Ministers.

The meeting proved to be extremely successful. Areas discussed included challenges facing small economies, Trade and development, the fight against illegal drugs, strengthening democracy, the restoration of democracy in Haiti and closer partnership with the USA.

The White House meeting laid the basis for the CARICOM-US Summit scheduled to be held in Barbados on May 10, 1997.

Sixteen Heads of Government from CARICOM plus the Dominican Republic participated in the summit including President Samuel Hinds who had assumed the presidency following the death of President Cheddi Jagan.

I had the privilege of accompanying President Hinds at the summit.

Out of summit came the 'Bridgetown Declaration of Principles and Plan of Action' which reflected agreement in principle on, trade and development, development financing, the environment and democracy.

Meeting President Clinton at the White House on September 16, 1994

Cheddi Jagan and I visited Washington for a second time early in December 1994 for preparatory talks with President Clinton on the First Summit of the Americas (SOA) scheduled to be held in Miami, Florida in December of the same year.

President Clinton had initiated the SOA process by calling for the convening of a hemispheric meeting in the United States, of Heads of Government and State.

The US President convened a series of bilateral meetings in Virginia, with hemispheric and regional groupings to jump start the SOA. Those consultations resulted in the convening of the first SOA in Miami, Florida.

At the first SOA, Dr. Jagan made a fantastic presentation which impressed President Clinton who chaired the summit. The US President made references from time to time to Dr. Jagan's presentation.

Following the Miami meeting, President Clinton wrote to President Jagan stating, 'I was impressed by the arguments advanced by CARICOM leaders regarding the special problems of small states. I will urge the new Congress to pass the Interim

Trade Programme as promptly as possible and Ambassador Kantor will continue his dialogue with Caribbean countries to find a solution to the banana issue. We recognise our extraordinary interdependence., and we must consult with greater frequency to find common solutions to our shared concerns.'

THE CALL FOR A REGIONAL DEVELOPMENT FUND

It was at that summit that Dr. Jagan called once again for debt relief. He floated the idea of a mini-Marshall Plan for Small economies and a Regional Development Fund (RDF) similar to what obtains in Europe for CARICOM countries.

The mini-Marshall plan was situated in the context of North/South cooperation to address the foreign debt, reduce poverty and underdevelopment. The call for the establishment of an RDF eventually found its way in Dr. Jagan's call for a New Global Human Order.

As far the RDF was concerned, Dr. Jagan and I worked hard to promote the idea within CARICOM and CARIFORUM, the latter being the mechanism for enhanced development cooperation between the CARICOM countries plus the Dominican Republic and the European Union.

At first, there was some apprehension among CARICOM member states about the efficacy and applicability of the concept, but more critically, was the concern over the question of the source of financing for the Fund.

Dr. Jagan used his considerable knowledge about the operationalization of the RDF within the European Union, to demonstrate by way of example and comparative analysis, why it became necessary for the more developed countries in Europe to create a RDF to pull the least developed countries in Europe, that included Ireland, Greece, Portugal and Spain out of underdevelopment.

Dr. Jagan suggested to his colleagues that a similar financial arrangement should be put in place within region to help lift the least developed CARICOM member states out of their LDC status.

The matter was left to ministers to formulate, settle and return to Heads for agreement.

In the meantime, while the matter was before CARICOM, I suggested to Dr. Jagan that we organize a government- sponsored a seminar on the RDF in Georgetown.

We solicited the support of the Delegate of the European Union to Guyana whose support was almost immediate.

Three technical specialists from the European Commission on RDF matters arrived in Georgetown to participate in the Seminar.

With the support of the Caricom Secretariat, invitations were sent out to all member states inviting them to send representatives to attend the event.

Dr Jagan delivered the opening remarks at Seminar and Dr. Richard Bernal, Head of the Caribbean Regional Negotiating Machinery (CRNM) participated fully as well.

The seminar was a great success and contributed enormously to the Region's acceptance of the concept and operationalization of a RDF for CARICOM. Little did I know at the time that the RDF concept was to become a major issue later on within the Councils at Caricom.

That seminar was to be the last public event in the life of President Cheddi Jagan.

At the ministerial, level I made a case for Guyana to be designated an LDC because of the heavy debt overhang impacting the country's economy, the GDP per capita ratio, the levels of industrial depression, and the high levels poverty and unemployment in some regions of the country.

At first, there was some reluctance from my ministerial colleagues to accept my argument, it was only after a rather lengthy discussion, they eventually relented and agreed that Guyana be included as a beneficiary of the RDF.

The then Prime Minister of the Commonwealth of Dominica, Mr. Edison James had this to say on the matter;

"The Regional Development Fund which became known as the Regional Integration Fund was seen by Jagan as a crucial and indispensable tool to take this region to a higher level of development."

The Fund was eventually agreed and established by Heads after a study was done to determine the annual financial contributions that was needed from regional and extra- regional sources and which member states would qualify to draw down from the Fund's resources based on established criteria.

A Resource Mobilisation Unit, attached to the CARICOM Secretariat was established to assist in the mobilisation funds. In 2008, the Fund became known as the CARICOM Development Fund (CDF).

Located in Barbados, the CDF's mandate is; 'To provide financial or technical assistance to disadvantaged, countries, regions, and sectors in the Community.' The Fund supports infrastructural development, sustainable energy, capacity building, Small Medium Enterprise (SME).

Cheddi Jagan would be pleased to know that his idea has become a living reality from which CARICOM member states are now benefitting.

Addressing Parliament -1994

GETTING THE MESSAGE OUT

President Jagan was a busy man on the international arena. I accompanied him on state and official working visits to India, China, Malaysia, Singapore, Brazil, Venezuela, Suriname, Syria, Bahrain, Kuwait, the United Arab Emirates, Cyprus, Canada, several CARICOM members states and the United States. Successful bilateral meetings were held with the governments of those countries.

At all his engagements while in these countries, President Jagan promoted his call for a New Global Human Order much to the interest and approval of his audiences.

I recall in preparation for his trip to New York in September of 1994 to participate in the Session of the United Nations General Assembly, Ambassador Insanally and I arranged for President Jagan to deliver lectures at Medgar Evers College, Howard, Columbia and Princeton universities in the United States. I accompanied the President to these events. I found the President quite at ease and professorial when delivering his lectures at each one of these institutions.

Many questions on global politics and development economics were asked by both students and academic staff, all were answered by Dr. Jagan to the complete satisfaction of all present.

To me, it seemed that the President was at Accabre, his party's school of social sciences.

I recall sometime in mid-1973, Michael Manley, former Jamaican Prime Minister visited Guyana for talks with the CARICOM Secretariat and Dr. Jagan about a proposal to establish an Association of Caribbean States (ACS).

I received a call from the Office of the President inviting me to join the President at a meeting he was having with Manley at his office.

On entering the President's office, I was introduced to Mr. Manley by the President. It was the first time I was meeting face to face with Mr. Manley. Little did I know that the next time I would meet with him would be at his funeral.

Mr. Manley had been contracted by the CARICOM Secretariat, following a recommendation by Heads of CARICOM and the Presidents of Colombia, the Dominican Republic, Mexico and Venezuela.

The Heads of State and Government had recommended that an association of states bordering the Caribbean Sea, be established to facilitate political consultations as well as technical and economic cooperation among the littoral states of the Caribbean Sea.

President Jagan told Manley that while he was favorably disposed to the concept, he was more inclined to supporting a loose form of association without any organizational structure similar to what obtains at the OAS or CARICOM. He considered that would be too burdensome financially and from a human resource standpoint, for the highly indebted poor countries in the region.

President Jagan voiced support for rotating chairmanship per member country who would be responsible for coordinating with other member states, and they in turn, would have shared implementation responsibilities with support from a small Pro-tempore Secretariat assisting with coordination. The Secretariat would be based in the country chairing the association.

Manley took note of President Jagan's concerns and recommendations and assured him that he would share them with other governments to benefit from their reactions.

The closing session of the 25ᵗʰ Party Congress at Queen's College - 1994

MICHAEL MANLEY MEETS RAMNARESH SARWAN

At the end of their official deliberations, Manley, being very knowledgeable of the game of cricket, shared with President Jagan an observation he made while watching a junior Caribbean cricket match in Jamaica. He said he spotted a young Indo-Guyanese batsman who he discerned had excellent batting skills and who possessed the potential for playing first class cricket. He said he recalled the name he heard was "Sarwan?"

Manley wanted to meet with the young cricketer before he left Guyana. I was assigned the task to set up the meeting.

The meeting was arranged for the next day with the assistance of the efficient staff at the Office of the President.

The ACS came into being July 24, 1994 at an official signing ceremony at Cartagena, the port city on Colombia's Caribbean coast.

Prime Minister Samuel Hinds and I participated in the signing ceremony. Sam as we called him, signed onto the historic Agreement on behalf of the Government of Guyana.

OFF TO INDIA, CHINA, MALAYSIA AND SINGAPORE

Between mid-December 1993 and mid-January 1994, President Jagan embarked on his second and longest overseas trip on government business. The journey included State Visits to India, China, Malaysia and Singapore. The President's delegation included; me as Foreign Minister, Bharat Jagdeo as Minister of Finance, Dr. Roger Luncheon, Head of the Presidential Secretariat, Pauline Sukhai, Vickram and Dawn Odditt, and Nadia Jagan-Brancier.

Throughout the entire visit, the President and his delegation were well received. And while the President did his level best to woo foreign investors in the different countries to explore investment prospects in Guyana he had a keen eye for the more low cost, indigenous cottage industries which in his view could employ large numbers of Guyanese, and in so doing, help significantly to reduce poverty at home. His visits to India and China were extremely useful in this regard. Incidentally, while we were in India, President Jagan despatched Bharat Jagdeo to Japan to negotiate debt relief and other financial matters with the Japanese authorities. Arising from the talks, the Japanese Government, in 1995, provided US$100,000 worth of spare parts for one of the power stations and a Grant Aid package from a 1994 US$1.4 million Grant Aid Agreement.

Though Malaysia and Singapore did provide us with some of the areas of particular interest to Dr. Jagan, the two countries offered us a first hand opportunity to appreciate how these once under-developed countries were able to move by leaps and bounds to become modern and highly developed economies in South East

Asia. The answer is to be found in the model of economic development adopted by both countries albeit with fundamental differences peculiar to their respective and specific local conditions.

I was happy to be on the trip to these countries with Dr. Jagan. For me, the trip provided me with another opportunity to listen, look and learn. These three 'L's' I believe, were the reasons why Dr. Jagan took other younger colleagues, like myself, along with him on these journeys. To me, the local heresies and unconventional ways of improving the livelihoods of people that Dr. Jagan was looking for in China and India were both intriguing and enlightening. The problem was the cultures and work ethics in those countries, especially when it came to labour intensive productive enterprises, the practices and customs are radically different from what obtains in Guyana; thus, the question of applicability arose as a major challenge. What was of interest to me what the fact that our visit to India took place over the Christmas holidays and while we Guyanese are accustomed to spending the holiday season in a traditional way, in New Delhi there was no sign of any jollification whatsoever as an indication that there was something to celebrate.

In the case of Singapore and Malaysia, what I learnt in the course of our visits was that the island of Singapore had no natural resources, though Malaysia, which was once part of as a federation, had its rubber and balata plantations. But both together, and later, as separate states, had high levels of poverty yet, not long after attaining independence as separate states, were able to move rapidly from poverty to prosperity becoming the fast-developing economies in Asia.

Singapore's success, and to a large extent Malaysia's as well, is founded on an economic model characterized by strong control over wages and labour, a huge influence of the business sector in government, what appears to be authoritarian rule, a highly developed banking and services sector, heavy dependence on manufactured exports and a highly educated work force. There was no doubt in my mind, based on our conversations and observations with government officials and private sector representatives, that there is ownership all around for a clearly defined, government-sponsored national development strategy. Further, it appeared to our delegation, that the state's control over key domestic markets and institutions were key to achieving government's economic goals. It seemed to me that, notwithstanding certain fundamental differences in their socio-economic architecture, the Singapore and Malaysian economic models were patterned after what obtains in Japan, China and South Korea as well as the USA.

When I hear people ask, why since Guyana is well endowed with an abundance of natural resources yet the country was not able to make the transformative changes as Malaysia and Singapore did, my answer is short and somewhat simplistic, those countries did not experiment with utopian and failed concepts such as 'Cooperative Socialism'as Guyana did.

ENGAGEMENTS IN VENEZUELA

President Jagan made Official State Visits to Venezuela in February 1993, Brazil in November 1993, Colombia in April,1994 and Suriname in June,1994

Before embarking on his visit to Venezuela, I brought to the President's attention an agreement between the Guyana Energy Authority (GEA) on behalf of the Government of Guyana and Petroleum of Venezuela (PDVSA) on behalf of the Government of Venezuela.

The agreement stipulated that a mutually agreed portion of the usual quantity of petroleum, bought from and supplied by PDVSA to the GEA would be held back and not be shipped to Guyana. The mutually agreed quantity of petroleum would be quantified in the US dollars and the money would be utilized to purchase a fleet of luxury motor cars for government ministers and other bureaucrats. In other words, at a time when the country was experiencing severe and lengthy bouts of power outages or blackouts, the then Hoyte administration intentionally and uncaringly, shortchanged the Guyana Electricity Corporation (GEC) now Guyana Power and light (GPL) of badly needed supplies of fuel so as to provide a reliable service to the populace. To them, what was more urgent was the fleet of luxury cars for government ministers and certain privileged bureaucrats in the governance system.

The President discussed the matter with the relevant ministers of government and the Head of the GEA at that time. A decision was taken at the level of Cabinet to adjust the agreement. Instead of luxury motorcars, low cost prefab houses manufactured in Venezuela would be procured. I was instructed to meet with the

Venezuelan Ambassador to Guyana and to advise him about the wishes of the Government of Guyana.

In February1993, accompanied by me, Gail Teixeira and a number of public and private sector representatives, President Jagan travelled to Caracas, Venezuela where he met with President Carlos Andres Perez fifteen years after he had met with the latter in Georgetown. The meeting between the two leaders was friendly and cordial. It was like two old friends meeting and reminiscing and analysing developments in Latin America and the world at large.

During the meeting, President Jagan raised the agreement between PDVSA and the GEA. President Perez said he had seen the request for a change in the agreement and had issued instructions stating his concurrence with the request. A fresh agreement was subsequently drawn up and signed by the appropriate representatives. The agreement, entitled 'The Guyana/ Venezuela Investment for Housing Fund Project' called for the immediate disbursement of US$6 million towards Guyana's much anticipated housing programme.

In less than three months, the prefab houses arrived in Guyana and Guyanese contractors, along with their Venezuelan counterparts worked together to assemble fifty four low cost houses at a small housing scheme at Uitvlugt, at the West Coast of Demerara, one hundred at Enterprise at the East Coast of Demerara and sixty six at Experiment, Bath Settlement at West Coast Berbice. This marked the first steps of the PPP/C's 1992 manifesto commitment to provide low-cost housing to the people of Guyana.

At the end of their official engagements, the two Presidents issued a Joint Communique. Within the ambit of the Guyana/Venezuela Joint Commission, the communique captured all the agreed areas of cooperation including health, the environment, transport, trade, agriculture and joint ventures.

After being decorated with the Collar of the Liberator, Venezuela's highest National Award, President Jagan travelled to the State of Bolivar where he met with the Guyanese community who turned out in large numbers to listen to him talk about the situation in Guyana and the new government's plans for the country's future development

During Perez's Presidency, Fernando Ochoa Antich served as Venezuela's Foreign Minister. Antich came from a military background. He did not speak much, but whenever he did, he was brief and straight to the point. Diplomatic niceties were not his forte. Antich came with an agenda which emphasized procedures that should characterize the relationship between the Facilitators themselves and between the Facilitators and the Ministers. He wanted a 'practical settlement of the controversy based on the provisions of the Geneva Agreement.' Antich also raised concerns over the granting of concessions to oil companies by Guyana off-shore the so-called 'Zona de reclamation.'

I met with Antich on two separate occasions. First, was on September 1, 1993 at the United Nations. Together, with our respective Facilitators, Ralph Ramkarran being ours and Alister McIntyre, the UN Secretary General's Personal Representative, I had my first meeting with the UN Secretary General, Boutros Ghali to brief him on the status of Guyana/Venezuela relations. Ochoa did the same from his government's perspective. The meeting was uneventful, save for a vague, passing reference made by Antich about 'foregoing the legalities' inherent in controversy and the need to 'strengthen the search for a negotiated solution.' The Guyanese side did not give much credence to the reference since, as far as we were concerned, it was clearly ultra vires to the UN Good Offices process.

My second meeting with Antich was in late September of the same year during the 48th Session of the UN General Assembly. At that meeting, again with the Secretary General, I basically reaffirmed and updated the Secretary General what was agreed to at my early September meeting.

Following President Jagan's visit to Venezuela, for the next ten months in 1993, political turmoil rocked the country for several months. President Perez was charged for misconduct in public office. He was placed under house arrest but was allowed to leave for the Dominican Republic where he remained in exile. Hugo Chavez spearheaded a failed coup after which elections were held in December of the same year which was won by the COPEI Party led by Rafael Caldera.

President Jagan met President Caldera for the first time in August,1995 at Port of Spain, Trinidad and Tobago on the occasion of the launch of the Association of Caribbean States (ACS). Caldera was accompanied by his recently appointed Foreign Minister, Miguel Angel Burelli. I accompanied President Jagan briefly to that meeting. The meeting between the two Presidents was basically of an informal nature, their discussions focused on border cooperation in the fight against smuggling of contraband. It was at that meeting that the concept of 'Globality' was first introduced by President Caldera without any specificities being mentioned. A general reference was made to the maritime boundaries between the two countries without any understanding or decision being reached.

Later, in the same year, President Jagan and the First Lady travelled to the Venezuelan island of Marguerita for a brief vacation. During their stay on the island, newly appointed Venezuelan Foreign Minister, Miguel Angel Burelli, paid a courtesy call on the Guyanese President and First Lady.

At the end of his vacation, President Jagan flew to Cartegna, Colombia via Caracas, where he made a stop-over, during which he met briefly with President Caldera. At Cartegna, President Jagan participated, along with fifty other leaders, in the Eleventh Summit of the Non-Aligned Movement held from 18 to 20 of October. From Colombia, President Jagan flew to New York to address the 50th Session of the UN General Assembly in the same month of October.

The local Stabroek News newspaper, made a song and dance about President Jagan's engagements with Presidents Perez and Caldera accusing him of engaging in 'secret meetings' with the Venezuelans and 'selling out' Guyana's national interests by 'appeasing' or 'pandering' to Venezuelan interests The newspaper went so far to make the ridiculous claim that I was being 'sidelined' in the process as if it had ever expressed any support for the PPP/C's approach to, and its policies or engagements with the Venezuelan authorities. Had the Stabroek News been monitoring my activities closely, they would have recognized that I could not be at four places at the same time.

In his address to the 50th Anniversary Session of the United Nations, President Jagan made reference to the foreign debt problem stating; "Third world debt is strangling our reconstruction and human development efforts. Although we paid more than $1.3 trillion between 1982 and 1990, our countries were 61 per cent deeper in debt in1990 than they were in 1982. During the same period, there was a net South-to-North outflow of $418 billion – not including outflows such as royalties, dividends, repatriated profits, underpaid raw materials and so on – a sum equal to six Marshall Plans…at the same time, our Third World countries lose about $500 billion annually in unfair non-equivalent international trade, a sum equal to 10 times the official development assistance from the developed world."

President Jagan called for the establishment of a New Global Human Order; "The unjust economic order must be replaced by a just new global human order for international and individual security and peace. The human development paradigm must be established on a basis of empowerment of our people, accountability, productivity and sustainability. Economic growth must be linked to equity, with social justice and ecological preservation."

THE CALL FOR A NEW GLOBAL HUMAN ORDER

It was President Jagan's progressive approach to analyzing global problems that allowed him to formulate a concept which in essence, revealed the 'true colors' of his ideological orientation and the extent of its evolution.

President Cheddi Jagan addressing the United Nations – 1995

UN/DPI Photo/G. Kinch

This new thinking was reflected in his call for the establishment of a New Global Human Order (NGHO).

With the help of his ministers and a consultant, Dr. Jagan convened on August 2-4, 1996 at the Sophia Convention Centre a hugely successful International Conference on the New Global Human Order.

One of the recommendations that emerged from the conference was the call to establish a Secretariat whose main task would be to push for the internationalization and global acceptance of the concept principally by governments.

Two years before, through the Ministry of Foreign Affairs, I managed to accomplish several tasks relative to the call.

First, was to have a motion on the NHGO passed in the National Assembly. This was accomplished successfully during the First Session of the Sixth Parliament on June 27, 1994 by way of resolution No. 37.

Next, I took the motion to my colleagues at the Council on Foreign and Community Relations (COFCOR) of CARICOM for consideration.

My colleague Foreign Ministers were somewhat reticent about the agenda item, so were some members of the technical staff at the CARICOM Secretariat.

That did not bother me since I knew the ways and means of getting matters through an organization tethered to multilateral diplomacy.

My next step was to suggest to Dr. Jagan that we take the matter to a meeting of Conference of Heads of Government of CARICOM. He agreed.

First, he took the matter to an Inter-sessional Meeting of the Heads of government held from 11 to 12, March 1994 in St. Vincent and the Grenadines where, after much discussion it was adopted, subject to ratification by the Meeting of Conference that was to be held in Guyana from 4-7 July, 1995.

In the communique issued at the end of the July, 1995 conference held in Georgetown, the Heads of Government stated:

'In this regard, they(the Heads of Government) supported the call by the President of Guyana for the establishment of a New Global Human Order, which not only challenges the international community to make the next fifty years a time dedicated to social and ecological justice, but also that each nation needed to set in place a new order of society that expresses concern for the security of nations and individuals and, which prescribe a common set of values that must be adhered to for the attainment of a just, peaceful and secure society.'

On 24, October 1995, Dr. Jagan introduced the call for the establishment of a NGHO at the United Nations General Assembly on the occasion of the 50th anniversary of the world body.

The matter was forwarded to the United Nations Economic and Social Council (ECOSOC) for further deliberations and adoption.

Multilateral diplomacy within the UN, given its wide and numerous members has a way of slowing things down.

Two years later, in my capacity as Guyana's Minister of Foreign Affairs, and in an effort to build momentum to the call, I took the matter to a Summit meeting of the Rio Group held in 1997 in Asunción, Paraguay. Thanks to the diplomatic leg work done prior to the summit by our Permanent Representative to the United Nations, the call was unanimously adopted and was viewed as a shot- in- the- arm for the complicated process at the UN.

With a view to popularizing the concept at the country level, I took the initiative to have established; 'Circles of Friends for the Promotion of the NGHO' in London, Washington, Caracas and Suriname where our government had pro-active Heads of Missions as well as Guyanese grouped in Associations of Concerned Guyanese.

The idea behind the initiative was to reach out to academics, intellectuals and other interested individuals as well as NGO's, to promote the NGHO in various institutions in capital cities around the world, but more particularly, in those

286

countries where a significant number Guyanese resided and who could form the nucleus of the 'Circles of Friends' on a voluntary basis.

In 1999, Dr Jagan's daughter Nadira, in collaboration with her mother Janet, published a booklet on the subject.

At their request, I agreed to write the foreword to the publication. In the foreword I pointed out:

"Interestingly, with the emergence of the global financial crisis, many world leaders are now advocating, albeit in different ways, precisely what Dr. Jagan had proposed since the early 1990's. This situation vindicates the visionary approach of Dr. Jagan."

The booklet was of great assistance in popularizing the concept. Where we could not be physically, the booklet served the purpose.

With the death of Dr. Jagan and later Mrs. Jagan, concrete and active support for the concept from our own PPP/C government dwindled, save for the half-hearted support that was given, which me and Navin Chandarpal valiantly strove keep alive.

I did not expect our government to drop the ball. It was my general expectation that government would continue to pursue vigorously, the matter at the international level. But alas! it was not to be. The concept was perceived to be too ideological by some, and to be associated with the Jagan era. It became anathema and had to be down-played, eventually becoming an issue of least concern for the Party.

With the advent of the APNU+AFC coalition government in May of 2015, the new government effectively killed the initiative.

TACKLING THE GLOBALITY ISSUE

In keeping with a long-established practice, our Foreign Ministry is called upon to prepare a brief on Guyana/Venezuela relations for the President's consideration in preparation for upcoming Conferences of CARICOM Heads of Government. Among the issues the Ministry included in its brief was the concept of Globality introduced by the Venezuelans and its implications for the McIntyre Process.

At a meeting of CARICOM Heads of Government held in July 1994 in Georgetown, President Jagan spoke to the brief and alerted his colleagues to the 'new initiative' by Venezuela and its far-reaching implications. In the final communique issued at the end of their deliberations, 'The Heads took note of Guyana's apprehension of the concept of Globality being advanced by Venezuela to guide Guyana/Venezuela relations.'

The CARICOM communique angered the Venezuelans to the extent that Burelli despatched letters to both me and Sir Alister accusing me of misrepresenting their position on the Globality issue. I responded clarifying Guyana's position. I stood by the text on the Globality issue in the CARICOM communique. My gut feelings told me this was not the end of the matter as far as the Venezuelans were concerned.

In November 1993, President Cheddi Jagan paid an official State Visit to Brazil. I accompanied the President on his visit. During his stay in Brazilia, official talks were held with Itamar Franco the then President of the neighbouring country. Arising out of the talks it was decided to resuscitate the Guyana/Brazil Joint Commission which had been dormant for years. An innovative step was taken to establish a Guyana/Brazil Group on Consular Cooperation- a permanent mechanism for the evaluation and resolution of consular matters. The two leaders examined ways and means of bringing the two countries closer, in this connection, a bridge across the Takatu River linking the two countries was further explored. And the construction of a deep-water harbour, as a companion project to the bridge that would allow for the export of Brazilian goods through the Atlantic from those states that border Guyana. President Jagan further explored the possibility of purchasing aviation fuel from Brazil and have it trans-shipped by road to the border town of Lethem in Guyana so as to help bring down the cost of air transport from the coastland to the interior of the country. A communique issued at the end of what can be described as a highly successful visit, made reference to trade, energy, agriculture and other areas of functional cooperation.

Geographically situated next to Brazil the largest and most populous country in South America (208.3 million) and the fifth largest economy in the world by Nominal Gross Domestic Product, Guyana's geo-strategic location makes it a gateway for countries of the Caribbean Community (CARICOM) to South America. Successive governments of Brazil particularly those with an eye to continental integration like the governments of Itamar Franco, Fernando Henrique Cardoso, and Luiz Ignacio Lula DaSilva took concrete initiatives to bring Guyana closer to Brazil and the rest of South American fulfillment of Guyana's once proclaimed 'Continental Destiny.'

These concrete initiatives were reflected in Brazil's sponsorship of Guyana's membership or association with the Rio Group, a Latin American political consultative group, the European Union/Latin American and Caribbean countries (EU/LAC), the Union of South American Nations (UNASUR) and the South American trading bloc (MERCOSUR and 'The Initiative for the Integration of the Regional Infrastructure of South America' (IIRSA). Regrettably, it was only in the early 1990's, with the assumption to office of successive PPP/C administrations (1992-2015) that our relations with Brazil gained momentum and brought about tangible results bilaterally and multilaterally.

More recently, with the signing of Agreements and/or Memoranda of Understanding between the People's Republic of China and a number of CARICOM member states including Guyana vis-a-vis the Belt and Road Initiative, it is hoped that Guyana will one day, with a favourable improvement in the international situation as well as the correlation of political forces in Latin America and the Caribbean, Guyana be able to play its strategic role as the gateway to South America for CARICOM.

In June 1994, President Jagan paid a State Visit to Suriname. Ronald Runaldo Venetiaan was the President of Suriname at the time. The visit, which I was part of, had more to do with signalling the new PPP/C government's interest in promoting friendly and good neighbourly relations with the government and people of Suriname as well as to demonstrate the Jagan Administration's interest in safeguarding the well-being of the thousands of Guyanese nationals resident in Suriname.

In and out of government, Dr. Jagan was consistent in promoting friendly relations with neighbouring countries irrespective of the party or coalition of parties in government.

Arising out of the discussion between Presidents Jagan and Venetiaan was agreement to encourage meetings of the Guyana/Suriname National Border Commissions and the resuscitation of the Guyana/Suriname Cooperation Council. The Cooperation Council is similar to a Joint Commission to promote functional cooperation between like-minded countries. President Jagan's interest in cooperating with Suriname in the bauxite industry, hydro-power, Suriname's petroleum industry, agriculture development and cross border security found expression in a Joint Communique issued at the end of his official visit.

President Jagan's visit to Suriname, paved the way later in the same year, for representatives of the Guyanese private sector to visit Suriname and for officials of Suriname's State Oil Company (STATSOLIE) to visit Guyana. In retrospect, it is interesting to note that during his visits to Venezuela, Brazil and Suriname, President Jagan paid special attention to the energy sectors in those countries naturally because he was looking for innovative ways to solve the energy problem obtaining in his country.

In September 1994, because of his deep and abiding interest in developmental issues, but more particularly, environmental and energy issues as well as the need for support for his campaign for debt relief, poverty alleviation, mobilization of grant aid and to strike a balance between development assistance for physical infrastructure such as sea defence works, critical for Guyana as a low-lying costal state, and social infrastructure President Jagan was invited to meet with the European Commission in Brussels. Mr. John Callighoru, the EU Delegate to Guyana at that time had arranged the meeting for Dr. Jagan. Then then EU Commissioner for Environment and Energy Kristof Papoutsitis had a made a specific request to meet with President Jagan.

In a paper he presented to the Commission, President Jagan pointed out; "We must elaborate a rational model of development not simply for economic growth but also for human development. We need growth with social justice and eco-justice. There will be no solution to environmental questions, for instance, if the boundaries of poverty continue to expand."

President Jagan exhorted the Commission to "Let us now move fully towards the preparation of a development agenda by a panel of distinguished experts and experienced persons to prepare a practical report based on experience in diverse countries and on close, critical analysis to possible options. Such a report must deal with the international competitiveness of the Third World, the basis of new modalities for international cooperation for development financing of development." The President's paper was well received and helped lay the foundation for increased development assistance from the EU not only for Guyana but for the CARIFORUM countries as well.

HAITI

In 1994, the question of Haiti was firmly on the international agenda especially that of CARICOM. The democratically elected President of Haiti, Bertrand Aristide had been overthrown in September 1991 by a bloody and brutal military coup, led by army general, Raoul Cedras. Efforts at various levels, including a raft of sanctions throughout out the period 1992 to 1994 to restore Aristide to the presidency had failed. Haitians were fleeing their country in large numbers. Efforts to stem the flow of Haitian refugees did to meet with much success. When this failed, a plan to establish 'Safe Havens' in some CARICOM countries were canvassed by the Clinton Administration. President Jagan and I traveled to Barbados, to meet with the Special Envoy of the US President to discuss the plan.

President Jagan, like his CARICOM colleagues advanced the position that the answer to the coup makers in Haiti, did not lie in the establishment of 'Safe Havens' for the resettlement of the refugees, rather, he posited there was an urgent need to restore democracy in Haiti and to create the necessary conditions for the democratically-elected government and President of Haiti to be re-instated. The Special Envoy, did not press the issue, although he did mention that at least one member-state had agreed to establish a 'Safe Haven' in their jurisdiction. His bottom line was his mission was to consult and to gather views on the project not to impose.

CARICOM Heads of Government at their 15th meeting held in July 1994 in Barbados, decided that member states would be part of a United Nations Mission to Haiti. The Mission's task was to facilitate the conditions required for the return of Haitians who had fled their country and for the early implementation of appropriate measures towards the resolution of the Haitian crisis. Subsequently, at the end of July (1994), the UN Security Council adopted Resolution 940 whose operative paragraph stated:

'Authorises member-states to form a multinational force under unified command and control, and to use all necessary means to facilitate the departure from Haiti of the military leadership, the prompt return of the legitimately elected President and the restoration of authorities of the Government of Haiti, the cost of implementing this temporary operation is to be borne by the participating member-states and approves the establishment of an advance team of the UN Mission to establish appropriate means of coordination with the multinational force...'

On September 16, 1994 President Clinton extended an invitation to all the CARICOM Heads of State and Governments to a White House meeting on Haiti. Unfortunately, President Jagan had committed himself to another engagement that coincided with the date of the White House meeting as a result, I was deputed to Represent him at the White House encounter.

By that time, Guyana had agreed to be part of a Multinational Force to implement UN Resolution 940. The PPP/C government, in keeping with its commitment to consultative democracy, decided to consult with national stakeholders as to whether it should participate or not in the multinational force. Towards this objective, consultations were held with a wide cross-section of civil society and across the political spectrum as well as at cabinet and the Defence Board.

We were given a warm reception by President Clinton. His speech at a luncheon hosted in our honour was full of praise for the CARICOM governments that had agreed to be part of the multinational force in pursuit of the UN resolution which the US had played a major part in promoting and sponsoring at the Security Council. Guyana had joined with Antigua and Barbuda, Barbados, Belize, Jamaica, and Trinidad and Tobago, to form a CARICOM contingent in the multinational force.

On my return to Guyana, on September 22,1994 following, consultations with the President and approval by cabinet, I moved a motion in the National Assembly calling on the House to approve the deployment of members of the Guyana Defence Force (GDF) outside of the national territory but more specifically to join the CARICOM contingent as part of the UN multinational force to restore democracy to Haiti.

In my contribution to the debate in the National Assembly, I pointed out:

"Sometimes one hears negative talk about non-interference in the internal affairs of states. This argument has been conveniently used as blanket prohibition to any kind of international scrutiny, whether partial or impartial, of the conduct of national affairs, including; protection of human rights and fundamental freedoms. Matters such as elections rigging, political assassinations and victimization have been conducted behind the shield of non-interference in the past. We recall, when we were fighting in the opposition to have international observers come to this country to observe our elections, our demand was deemed an invitation to foreigners to interfere in the internal affairs of this country.

I emphasized that; "Those who stand dogmatically on the lofty principles of non-interference in the internal affairs of countries, must bear in mind that the practice on non-interference is being continuously eroded as a result of changes in global economic conditions as well as the removal of territorial barriers to international trade".

I went on to point out that, in respect to foreign intervention in Haiti "We stand in support of the multinational force because we believe that it is the preferable to go the multilateral way rather than the unilateral way. Past experiences show that this is the correct position to adopt. We have even said to those who oppose intervention for the sake of opposing it, that in many instances intervention may be legally and morally unjustified but politically correct."

I concluded my intervention by stating; "Guyana has a long history in supporting the peoples' struggles for national liberation, social emancipation and their right to self-determination. Haiti must not be the exception'. The motion tabled in my name in the National Assembly was read and passed without amendment. The operative paragraph of the motion read; 'Be it resolved that the National Assembly hereby approves of the employment of troops of the Guyana Defence Force outside of Guyana to participate in the implementation of United Nations Security Council

Resolution 940 in compliance with the decision of the CARICOM Heads of Government.'

Within a matter of days, following passage of the resolution, a contingent of Guyanese troops departed our international airport to join their CARICOM counterparts as part of the UN multinational force bound for Haiti. President and I were at our international airport to see our troops off and to wish them well.

Exactly nine months after, I attended the 25th Regular Session of the OAS held in the first week of June 1995 in Montrouis, Haiti. This was my first visit to Haiti which I had heard and read much about. The hosts of our meeting chose Montrouis for security reasons as well as for suitable accommodation purposes. Montrouis is a communal section in Haiti and is one of the most important beach tourism locations in Haiti. The town is located some sixty-six kilometres or one and an hour drive outside of Port-au-Prince.

Save for a visit to the camp where the CARICOM military contingent was stationed, my stay for the entire duration of the meeting was restricted to the hotel and nearby surroundings, delegates were warned not to go beyond the boundary. I was happy to meet and greet the Guyanese soldiers and to have a brief chat with them. Edward Collins, the then Chief of Staff of the Guyana Defence Force was visiting at the time, he was pleased to meet with me and later, paid me a courtesy call at the hotel to meet and greet my colleagues from other CARICOM countries.

At the end of its deliberations, the meeting issued 'The Declaration of Montrouis'. The declaration contained a paragraph that was relevant to the situation obtaining in Guyana at that time and with which I was pleased; 'That at the request of each state concerned the Organization of American States, has conducted notable efforts to defend democracy where it has been undermined by promoting the restoration of constitutional order. In some cases, it has also participated in national reconciliation or institution-building process, including electoral observation;'

Another paragraph that reflected Guyana's contribution to the restoration of democracy in Haiti read as follows; 'The meeting, also noted that the unflagging efforts of member states and the Secretary General in support of the determination of the Haitian people to defend their sovereignty and to apply the provisions of resolution AG/RES. 1080(XXI-091) contributed to the restoration of Haiti's democratically elected government following the coup d'état in September 1991.'

GUYANA JOINS THE ORGANIZATION OF ISLAMIC CONFERENCE (OIC)

In September 1995, I took a recommendation to cabinet requesting approval for Guyana to join the Organization of Islamic Conference, now Organization of Islamic Cooperation (OIC).

I felt this was a necessary step for Guyana to take considering the fact that a considerable part of our population are practicing Muslims. In this regard, I considered it important to have the Muslim population of Guyana represented at the OIC, an international grouping of 57 countries with a collective population of over 1.8 billion where the interests of Guyanese Muslims, together with their brothers and sisters around the world, would be represented as an integral member of the International Muslim Community or Ummah.

Following cabinet's approval, Guyana applied and was admitted to membership in the OIC with observer status. Three years later, on October 1, 1998 under the Janet Jagan administration, Guyana became a full member of the OIC.

In addition to pursuance of his international policies on the global stage, President Jagan was equally pro-active on the domestic front in respect to constitutional reform.

President Jagan proposed that the Fundamental Rights Section of Guyana's Constitution be preserved and strengthened and that the directive principles be reviewed and abandoned where irrelevant, inapplicable or inappropriate.

President Jagan advocated that the powers of the Elections Commission (GECOM) be more adequately and unambiguously defined and its composition reviewed. Further, he called for the powers of the President be reduced.

In the circumstances, a Constitution Review Commission was established. I was called upon to be a member of the PPP delegation to the public hearings of the Commission held at the National Assembly in May 1997.

Confirmation of Bharrat Jagdeo as Senior Minister of Finance - 1995

WORKING WITH PRESIDENT JAGAN

I was happy to work with Dr. Jagan at the Office of the President. I had grown accustomed to working with him over the years at Freedom House.

I served as the interlocutor between the President and the Director General at the Ministry of Foreign Affairs (MFA). This was because President Jagan had not identified anyone whom he was comfortable with at the time to fill the post of Minister of Foreign Affairs.

Any correspondence from the MFA that required the attention of the President had to pass through me. And, all correspondence requiring the signature of the President was treated with in similar fashion.

Throughout the entire 1992 elections campaign, Dr. Jagan had emphasized the point that more money was allocated in the budget to the Office of the President, and the Ministry of Foreign Affairs compared to the sums allocated to the health, education and security sectors. He promised that on his assumption to office, he would cut the budgetary allocations for the Office of the President and Ministry of Foreign and reallocate badly needed resources to the social and security sectors.

To achieve this goal, it meant that staff and other charges to those two Ministries had to be drastically reduced. Contributions to international organizations were suspended until such time that payments were affordable.

About one month after the new government had assumed office, I was sent on an assignment to our overseas missions, save those in China, Cuba, Russia, Suriname, Brazil and Venezuela since the staff at those missions at that time were very slim. We decided that those six missions would be visited later, in two other rounds since visits to them would take me away from home for a very long time.

In respect to the Missions I planned to visit, my instructions were to assess the staff strength at each Mission relative to the extant responsibilities of each Mission or consulate and make recommendations about staffing needs that would be required to undertake the declared policy directions and foreign policy priorities of the new PPP/C administration.

As a first step, I requested all the personal files of members of staff of each Mission.

I went through each file with great care and made notes of the job descriptions of each member of staff as per the instructions I had received.

I visited Guyana's diplomatic Missions and Consulates at New York and Washington, Toronto and Ottawa, London and Brussels.

My specific instructions with respect to the Ambassadors and Consul Generals were that after interviewing them, to convey my recommendations to Dr. Roger Luncheon, Head of the Presidential Secretariat. He would take it from there.

My recommendations with respect to the Home-based and locally recruited staff were conveyed to the Director General and Head of the Administration and Finance Department at the Ministry of Foreign Affairs for action in accordance with the conditions of service of the staff members affected.

The office of the President was kept abreast with my recommendations as I moved from Mission to Mission.

While visiting our High Commission in London, I received a call from the Office of the President requesting that I travel to Miami to join President Jagan to participate in the Conference on the Caribbean and Latin America (CCLA), an annual event organized by the Washington-based Caribbean and Central America Action (CCAA) and traditionally held in Miami, Florida. The annual event is usually attended by Caribbean and Latin American Governments, businessmen, politicians NGO's to promote private sector growth and to influence the 'powers that be' in US administration. President Jagan was accompanied by a number of Guyanese Captains of Industry and Commerce. Among them were Yesu Persaud, Pat Thompson, Vic Odditt and others.

By engaging in a series of non-stop meetings with private sector representatives, President Jagan took full advantage of the presence of business leaders from the Caribbean and Latin America. President Jagan held a number of bilateral meetings with political leaders from many countries to promote the new government's policy that Guyana was open for business and welcomed foreign investors. The President was pleased with his participation in the conference and so were the Guyanese businessmen who accompanied him. What lay ahead was the big question of follow up or, as some call it; 'After Sales Service.'

OUR OVERSEAS SUPPORT GROUPS

It was always an honour and pleasure to accompany the President on his travels and visits to other countries. my conversations with him while on the aircraft or intransit at an international airport always turned out to be an educational or a learning experience for me. We would share our analysis concerning the situation in Guyana and governance issues. We would also share our observations concerning the conversations he had with the leaders with whom he met, the places of interest we visited as well as the town hall meetings we had with the Guyanese community. President Jagan had visited Canada many times before in his capacity as Opposition Leader in Guyana's National Assembly. His visits were instrumental in bringing together, Guyanese resident in Canada to lend support to the struggles at home for free and fair elections and the restoration of democracy during the 1964 to 1992 period. These efforts resulted in the establishment of the Association of Concerned Guyanese (ACG-Canada). It was through his efforts and regular visits to the USA that a similar organisation, the Association of Concerned Guyanese –USA (ACG-USA) was established.

With the exception of the PPP-UK Branch, which was established since the late 1960's as a branch of the PPP with card bearing members, these associations were not branches of the PPP, on the contrary, they were broad-based organizations though they did have in their rank's persons known to have been members of the Party while they lived in Guyana.

Owing to the persistent political activism and outstanding leadership of Sash Sawh as President of the ACG-Canada and Arjune Karshan in New York, USA, both individuals were appointed ambassadors to Venezuela (1996-2006) and Suriname (1994-2009) respectively. Ambassador Karshan was expecting that with his recall from Suriname, he would be given a second posting but when this did not happen, he was deeply disappointed and hurt, so were his family and close relatives consequently the Party lost not only the Karshan family but his extended family as well.

In November 1996, on our way back to Guyana from a conference in Italy, President Jagan and I met with the more prominent leaders and activists of PPP-support groups in New York city. The aim of his meeting was to bring the disparate organisations, groupings and individuals together under one umbrella while maintaining their respective organisational and leadership structures. The President put forward is proposal to the meeting which was followed by a general discussion. The majority of those present agreed wholeheartedly while one individual held out that they would have to consult with the members of his organization. A commitment was given to provide the President with a response in two weeks. When the response did come it signalled a rejection of the President's proposal

IN CANADA

In pursuit of Guyana's political and economic interests abroad, President Jagan paid his first official visit to Canada in June 1996. At the start of his visit, the President held discussions with Prime Minister Jean Chretien and several cabinet ministers from different provinces of Canada. During their conversations, the two leaders explored opportunities to support economic development, capacity building and institutional strengthening, and investment opportunities in mining and energy for Guyana. The President held meetings also with Canadian businessmen and non-governmental organizations. And in keeping with his intellectual pursuits, President Jagan paid a visit to the International Development Research Centre (IDRC) where he met with a good friend, Mr. Keith Bezanson with whom he collaborated in preparation for his participation at the UN-sponsored 'World Hearings on Development' held in New York from early June 1994.

Prior to his visit to Canada and following his participation in the World Hearingson Development in New York, President Jagan wrote to Canadian Prime Minister Jean Chretien expressing his support for a 'Business Advisory Project' funded by the Canadian International Development Agency (CIDA) and implemented by the Canadian Executive Service Overseas (CESO) in Guyana. Chretien in his response of July 1994, reassured President Jagan that the Canadian Government will continue its support for the project.

RACISM AND BIGOTRY AT WORK

On my return home, after completing my assignment in respect to Guyana's diplomatic missions overseas, the then Opposition Leader, Desmond Hoyte sought to impugn my assignment as malicious, discriminatory and vindictive. He went so far as to make a ridiculous claim that persons were profiled and targeted for dismissal based on their ethnicity.

Truth be told, Hoyte and the PNC were upset because we were killing four birds with one stone, cutting costs, trimming staff, dismantling a bloated staffing compliment and fulfilling our manifesto promise.

I did not mind the politics of criticism, what bothered me was the spurious allegation that I had terminated the service of only Black members of staff employed at our country's overseas Missions.

It was a contrived racist lie aimed at galvanizing the sympathies of Afro-Guyanese at home and abroad, who had lost confidence in Hoyte's party, the PNC.

To this day, the PNC propagandists keep repeating this falsehood as though they have nothing else in their arsenal of lies to utilize.

Mr. Hoyte must have been a convert to the Gobellian view that the more a lie is repeated the more it is likely to be believed.

It is against this backdrop that in October 1996 a terrible swipe, packed with racist innuendos and hostility was levelled against President Jagan.

During a speech delivered at the Travelodge Hotel in Toronto, President Jagan spoke extensively about his experiences with racial bigotry while living and working in the United States.

He told his audience;

"The PPP is not an Indian party and the British and Americans did not remove me and put in Burnham because of race. In fact, if they were using race I should have been kept there and Burnham should have been kept out forever because as we know Black people are generally at the lowest scale of the social ladder."

These remarks were cherry picked from the totality of the President's entire speech and twisted to give it a racist slant in a Guyanese context. The allegation was clearly aimed at bringing Jagan's outstanding reputation into disrepute.

At first, the President was defiant when pressed to make a public apology. His response was "I do not know that I have to apologize, I said what I meant to say."

Subsequently, after internalizing and commiserating with party leaders on the subject, the President issued a public apology.

The vicious and unwarranted attack on Dr. Jagan came as a complete surprise to many inside and outside Guyana. President Jagan in and out of government was not known to harbour nor expound racist sentiments.

OFF TO FIVE ARAB STATES

In November 1996, President Jagan embarked on another of his extensive overseas trips. On this occasion, his destination via Toronto was; Syria, Kuwait, Sharjah, Abu Dhabi and Bahrain ending in Rome, Italy then back home via New York. Following consultations with George Hallaq, his good friend who resided in Athens, Greece, an itinerary was worked out and sent to me detailing his journey.

In Toronto, the President was scheduled to deliver a lecture at conference at York University. He would take sometime out to spend sometime with his daughter Nadira and her family before starting out on his journey to the Middle East.

I left flew out to Damascus, Syria as an advance party to join our Middle East Envoy, Ambassador George Hallaq and the protocol personnel at the Syrian Foreign Ministry to ensure that the programme was settled and all the arrangements were in place

President Hafeez al-Assad (father of Bashir) himself and some members of his cabinet including his Foreign Minister were at Damascus International Airport to greet President Jagan on his arrival. For me it is always a pleasure to see Dr. Jagan smiling and in a happy and relaxed mood. That was precisely how he looked as he deplaned the aircraft.

The visit was highly successful in many respects especially the conversations with the Syrian President. I was very impressed with President Assad. He appeared urbane but was very witty when referring to the politics of the Middle East. He struck me as a very astute politician, he was deeply knowledgeable of the history, politics and economic and cultural realities of the Middle East. Listening to his conversations with President Jagan, I could discern his profound awareness about the intricacies of Arab diplomacy and his stewardship of the Umaah in respect to relations with Israel, the United States and other Arab countries.

While in Damascus, and at his request, the Syrian Foreign Ministry arranged to have President Jagan meet and brief the diplomatic resident in Damascus about his Guyana's call a New Global Human Order. His presentation was followed by an animated discussion on the topic since, from all appearances the ambassadors present seemed to be senior diplomats and old hands of the theory and practice of international relations.

President Jagan held meetings with the Syrian business community where he promoted his country as an investment friendly country open for business. A Memorandum of Understanding on technical and functional cooperation between Guyana and Syria was signed cementing the friendly relations between the two countries.

From Syria, the President and his delegation flew to Sharjah, the third largest and third most populous city of the United Arab Emirates. President Jagan and the Ruler of that State met and held discussions on promoting mutually beneficial relations between Sharjah as part of the United Arab Emirates (UAE) Visits were paid to places of interest to the Guyanese delegation including visits to institutions of higher learning and cultural sites since Sharjah is considered to be the cultural capital of the UAE. At the end of the official visit, the delegation went on to the State of Kuwait.

Kuwait City with a population of 1,134,000 (1996) impressed me as a busy place compared to Sharjah with a population of 334,000 (1996). I surmised that the city's business at that time, especially in the construction of infrastructure, was due to the fact that our visit took place just six years after a war with Iraq its neighbour to the north. The war was provoked as a result of Iraq's invasion of Kuwait in August 1990 and occupation for about six months. The US-led 'Operation Desert Storm' launched in January 1991, and lasting for approximately two months drove Iraq's occupationist forces from Kuwait and liberated the country.

The opposition PPP in Guyana viewed Iraq's attack, invasion and occupation of Kuwait as an act of aggression against Kuwait. The Party publicly condemned Iraq's actions and called for the immediate and unconditional withdrawal of all Iraqi forces from Kuwait. The PPP made it clear that it does oppose acts of aggression of a sovereign state for the sake of opposing, rather its position is one of principle and based on Guyana's geo-political reality exemplified by

Venezuela's and Suriname's claims to significant portions of Guyana's territory and by extension the threats to the country's national sovereignty and territorial integrity. It is precisely for these reasons that the PPP opposed Turkey's invasion and occupation of Northern Cyprus in August 1974 and, Britain's war of aggression against Argentina over the Falkland/Malvinas islands in April 1982.

It was from this background that our visit to Kuwait took place. The Kuwaiti's were very aware of the PPP's position. In preparation for our visit to Kuwait Our Permanent Representative to the United Nations, Ambassador Insannaly, had met and briefed his Kuwaiti counterpart in anticipation of our visit to his country.

Kuwait's Ruler, Sheik Sabah Al Ahmad Al Jaber Al Sabah, was happy to receive President Jagan. He knew, probably from the briefing he received from his Foreign Ministry, that Dr. Jagan, as opposition leader, had personally condemned Iraq's acts of aggression against his country. I recall a Kuwaiti diplomatic mission arriving in Guyana in August 1993 to convey the Emir's gratitude to the President and government of Guyana for the support and solidarity extended during the period of the invasion In this regard, it was quite noticeable that President Jagan was given what could be described as 'Royal Treatment.' Our programme in Kuwait City was an intensive one since the Kuwaiti's wanted us t o see the efforts; they were making to rebuild what was destroyed during the war and to construct a modern society.

At the end of our visit, a number of agreements on technical and economic cooperation between Guyana and Kuwait were signed.

The next stop in our itinerary was Abu Dhabi, the capital of the United Arab Emirates and the second most populous city of the UAE. It is also the seat of the government of the UAE. I found this island city most fascinating. Rich in oil and awash with commercial enterprises with a population just over one and half million, it was clear to see from its skyline how well endowed the city was economically and financially.

President Jagan and the Emir of Abu Dhabi, Sheik Zayed bin Sultan Al Nahyan met and held talks on a wide range of subjects including energy, the environment and questions of development. Considering the history of the country's evolution from a commercial, trading post in pearls to a highly developed modern island city in the Persian Gulf following the discovery of oil and gas, the ruler expressed great interests in these topics having regard to the fact that Abu Dhabi owns massive oil and gas reserves and with the highest GDP per capita in the world. The two leaders exchanged views on challenges of development for some time during which the Emir shared with the President Jagan his plans for the establishment of Free zones, tourism and the real estate business in the island city. With oil and gas GDP constituting 34.2 % of total GDP and non-oil and gas constituting 65.8 % of the country's total GDP, there was no doubt in our minds that the goals set by the Emir were achievable. Finally, a critical issue that emerged from the discussion, at least from my perspective, was the importance of transparency, accountability and firmness in negotiating with foreign investors.

Our delegation's last stop was The Kingdom of Bahrain, another island nation in the Persian Gulf comprising of an archipelago of small islands of which Bahrain is the largest in land mass. Bahrain's population is about 1.2 million. What struck me as the aircraft was on its descent onto the runway of the international airport just outside Manama, the capital, was that all the dwelling houses had one thing in common, they were all painted in white, or so it appeared to me.

Because I found this this phenomenon puzzling, I decided to ask one of the interpreters assigned to our delegation for an explanation. I was told that the walls of the traditional Bahraini house are usually plastered with burned limestone called 'Noora' which produces the white colour. I was told further, that one of the useful qualities of the burned limestone is that it is absorbent to water and makes the interior of the house cooler. Moreover, unlike white paint, the applied burned limestone does not fall off walls as paint would tend to do after some years and because of weather conditions. Bahrainis are gradually replacing the traditional 'Noora' with concrete blocks and white paint.

Our visit to Bahrain took place at a time when an uprising called the 'Dignity Uprising' was taking place. The 'Uprising' was initiated by a coalition of forces in the country who were demanding democratic reforms.

In conversations between the Emir of Bahrain and President Jagan, the President was given an overview of the Bahraini economy and the kingdom's future plans for the country's economic and social development. Passing reference was made to the uprising and those who were behind it. The Emir chose to place emphasis on his plans to expand the banking and financial services sector, the modernization of the country's aluminum smelting and production capacity and to make the export of petroleum products, the country's second largest export. At the end of the conversation, it was clear to us that this was a small country with a booming economy that was headed for fantastic growth rates. The country however, seemed to be headed for democratic reforms down the road.

Strangely, although we moved around the capital city, there were no signs of any protest demonstrations. From all appearances, it seemed as though it was business as usual all around. A visit I paid to a downtown market place or bazzar to do some purchases was uneventful.

The Emir of Bahrain at that time was Isa bin Salman Al Khalifa, an intelligent but jovial monarch. He wasn't stuck up on protocol and preferred to discuss in a relaxed, informal atmosphere. On the lighter side of the discussion, the Emir was very up to date with the latest American movies and offered his bewilderment at the digital advances of the movie industry in the United States. Two particular movies were of interest to him, one was 'Jaws' and the other was 'Twister.' Making quips about both movies, the Emir wanted us to know that it was how the human factor was depicted in the movies that was of interest to him.

Our Visit to Bahrain brought the curtains down on President Jagan's three-week visit to the four Middle East countries. At the end of the visits, several agreements and Memoranda of Understanding were signed bringing the countries visited and Guyana closer under the rubric of functional cooperation. The visits to the countries resulted in the Rulers becoming better aware and knowledgeable about Guyana and the rest of the Caribbean and the prospects for cooperation and investments beneficial to each country.

From Bahrain, President Jagan and his delegation flew to Rome, Italy to participate in the World Food Summit organized by the United Nations, Food and Agriculture Organisation (FAO)

IN PURSUIT OF ECONOMIC DIPLOMACY

306

Basing its Mission Statement on the progressive domestic and foreign policies laid down by the Jagan administration, the Foreign Ministry formulated a policy of Economic Diplomacy, the objective being, to mobilize as much technical and material assistance as possible for the purpose of capacity building and institutional strengthening.

The Foreign Ministry through its diplomats at our Foreign Missions were tasked with this new responsibility.

In the foreword to a 'Economic Diplomacy Manual for Foreign Service Officers and Heads of Missions' I pointed out;

'In partial discharge of its mandate, the Ministry of Foreign Affairs has prepared this Manual on Economic Diplomacy. It is essentially a synthesis of ideas expounded during several brainstorming sessions on issues such as; trade, investment, private sector-government relations, rapprochement with Latin America and capacity building initiatives, as well as ideas from other sources.

The major areas of focus of our Economic Diplomacy policy initiative and roles to be played by personnel at the Ministry of Foreign Affairs in order to ensure success were outlined as follows:

'Use as a tool that supports the aims of the National Development Strategy; To become more active in the domain of economics, external economic relations/negotiations and private sector development and, assuring the preservation of Guyana's sovereignty; To support policies aimed at developing external trade and investment flows; To solicit the participation and views of the local private sector and; To forge and consolidate relationships with countries and organisations that would serve to enhance the Economic Diplomacy process.'

To accomplish these goals, Heads of each of Guyana's Overseas Missions were instructed to put in place internal arrangements at his or her Mission. A Foreign Service Officer at the Mission was to be assigned specific responsibility to ensure the implementation and active pursuance of the goals set out in the manual. The Foreign Service Institute in Georgetown was to assist in reorienting staff to the aims and objectives, as well as their preparedness to pursue like eager beavers the Economic Diplomacy policy initiative.

Regrettably, due to institutional inertia, compounded by the absence of what should have been, a complete overhaul or reform at the Ministry of Foreign Affairs, limited success was achieved in pursuit of this lofty endeavour.

Heads of Overseas Mission & Consulates in Georgetown - 1996

SELECTING HEADS FOR OVERSEAS MISSIONS AND CONSULATES

I was tasked with the responsibility to recommend nominees to fill vacancies that had opened up with the change of government for our country's Overseas Missions, Consulates and Honorary Consulates.

In consultation with Janet Jagan I made the following recommendations; Odeen Ishmael as Ambassador to the United States and the OAS; Lalleshwar Singh as High Commissioner to the Court of St. James and the Commonwealth Secretariat in the UK and Ireland; Satyadeo Sawh as Ambassador to Venezuela; Karshan

Arjune as Ambassador to Suriname; James Mathieson as Ambassador to Belgium and Brindley Benn as High Commissioner to Canada.

Our missions in China, Cuba, India and Moscow were left in the hands of Charge D' Affaires.

Following the submission of my recommendations and the subsequent discussion that ensued, President Jagan recommended Brentnol Evans from the Bauxite mining town of Linden to fill the post of Consul General to the Consulate in New York.

Based on recommendations made, cabinet approved appointing a number of new Honorary Consuls for a number of countries. Some Honorary Consuls who served under the previous administration remained in their positions.

My recommendations, including those from the President were subsequently approved by cabinet.

Our Foreign Ministry's request to its counterpart in Venezuela for agreement to facilitate Sash Sawh's appointment as Ambassador to Venezuela encountered some unforeseen obstacles. Opposition Leader Mr. Desmond Hoyte accused the government of selecting a known felon as an ambassador. He was referring to Sash Sawh. From all indications, one of Mr. Hoyte's 'dirt diggers' based in Canada, had dug up an old case involving Sash Sawh who had appeared in a Toronto Court to give evidence in a minor court case and was accused of giving false evidence.

The case was eventually dismissed but Hoyte and sections of the media 'went to town' on the matter. They mounted a vicious and wicked campaign aimed at discrediting Sawh and at the same time, disparaging President Jagan for selecting him as an ambassador. One member of the President's Cabinet raised the matter at a cabinet meeting suggesting that the President withdraw Sawh's name and identify a replacement. President Jagan would have none of it, he rejected the suggestion on the ground that the allegation was spurious and without foundation. I supported the President's position and called on my cabinet colleagues to 'hold on head' in the matter until it blows over.

Eventually, the Venezuelans granted Agreement to our request and Sawh was accredited Guyana's Ambassador to Venezuela in Caracas.

Sash turned out to be one of Guyana's best ambassadors to Venezuela. He built up excellent relations with Venezuelan government officials and the diplomatic corps in Caracas. Also, he established strong relations with the Guyanese community in Venezuela helping them in many ways. He pushed for commercial, cultural and all forms of cooperation between Guyana and Venezuela. At the end of his tour of duty, he was awarded the Order of Francisco Miranda, one of Venezuela's highest National Awards.

In a note written to me by President Jagan in October 1996, on the eve of the annual celebration on the lawns of State House marking the victory of the PPP/C at the polls in1992, the President informed me that he had spoken to Sash Sawh about recalling him to Georgetown to serve as a minister and that he had agreed. I was instructed to provide the Ambassador with early notification.

I spoke to Sash on the phone the following day, he repeated what he told the President but made one request, he wanted at least one month to pack and ship his earthly possessions to Guyana and to make the farewell rounds in Caracas and to the Guyanese community. We agreed. I passed on the details of our conversation to the President who concurred.

Sash served as our Minister of Agriculture for almost ten years. Then disaster struck, a heavily armed marauding criminal gang, inspired by an absurd racist and revanchist ideology emerged. Its leaders proclaimed that the path to 'African Guyanese liberation' is one that must be travelled separately from others and must be achieved by any means possible including killing those who do not share their racist ideology. It was this gang that attacked the home of Minister Sawh and brutally shot and killed Sash along with two of his siblings and a security guard. The murder of the minister aroused national and international condemnation. Sash's murder dealt a serious blow to the governance of the country under the PPP/C. The incident ramped up public safety and security concerns, bringing into sharp focus questions pertaining to national security. The gang was eventually dismantled by the security forces. Regrettably, up to the time of writing neither a Coroner's Inquest nor a Commission of Inquiry was held to determine the circumstances that led to the murder of Minister Sash Sawh, his siblings and the security guard.

Following Sash Sawh's recall to Guyana, the President requested me to make recommendations for someone to replace him. Of the names I recommended, Bayney Karran was selected. The Venezuelan authorities granted Agreement and Mr. Karran was duly accredited Ambassador to the Republic of Venezuela.

THE FIRST LADY GOES TO THE UNITED NATIONS

It was sometime in mid-1994, during the Presidency of Cheddi Jagan that First Lady Janet Jagan indicated to me her interest to serve for three months as a member of Guyana's Permanent Mission to the United Nations.

At that time, Samuel Rudolph 'Rudy' Insanally, Guyana's Ambassador and Permanent Representative to the United Nations had assumed the position of President of the 48th Session of the UN General Assembly (UNGA) from 1993 to 1994.

Rudy needed help to 'man' the Mission as well as to assist him in executing his functions as President of the UNGA.

The Foreign Ministry with the assistance of the Office of the President provided the Ambassador with an experienced and competent team comprising Janet Jagan, Professor Dennis Benn, Dr. Bertrand Collins, Neville Bissember Jnr. June Persaud, Neil Pierre and Allison Drayton.

Ambassador Insanally and his small, energetic but professional team did a fantastic job. They performed creditably, much to the satisfaction of the member states of the world body.

One day, during Mrs. Jagan's stint at PR New York, I received a call from her suggesting that Guyana do the honor of ratifying the Convention on the Law of the Sea, better known as UNCLOS.

My response to her was that I needed at least one day, to consult on the matter with the relevant department at the Foreign Ministry and the Head of the Presidential Secretariat.

It took me almost two days to get the background work done and to prepare a brief for the President as well as a cabinet memo requesting approval to proceed with the ratification process. Luckily, Mr. Neville Bissember Jnr. who was at the Mission at the time, had participated in international preparatory meetings on the Convention and was au fait with all matters pertaining to the Convention, this made the process of ratification much easier than we had envisaged.

During its presidency of the General Assembly, Guyana's prestige and respectability had soared to great heights among the community of nations.

It was due to Mrs. Jagan's stewardship as Deputy Permanent Representative, that on 16th November 1994, Guyana became the 60th nation to ratify the United Nations' Convention on the Law of the Sea (UNCLOS) thus bringing the Convention into force.

Once again, Guyana's prestige soared at the United Nations for taking the bold step to bring the Convention into force. This act by its very nature, was to have a lasting impact in the comity of Nations and in global affairs.

On Mrs. Jagan's return Guyana, Opposition Leader, Desmond Hoyte sought to make a big issue about her stint at our country's Permanent Mission to the United Nations. He tabled a number of questions in the National Assembly seeking written responses from me, concerning remuneration to Mrs. Jagan, cost for accommodation, transportation and meals while she served at the UN. The questions were aimed at embarrassing Mrs. Jagan and the PPP/C administration. But his stand on the matter backfired because of our government's predisposition to be transparent and accountable with respect to use of government funds for such activities.

Three years later in 1997 Mrs. Jagan was elected President of Guyana. In that capacity, she addressed the 52nd Session of the United Nations General Assembly. After her participation in the session and, following in the footsteps of her late husband, she proceeded to deliver lectures to students at the universities of Columbia and Princeton. Her lectures were well received.

OVERSEAS VOLUNTEERS

I recall at a bilateral meeting with British Foreign Secretary Douglas Hurd, he asked me to explain what I meant by economic diplomacy. I did, and the end of my explanation he offered to have his staff discuss with the Volunteer Services Organization (VSO) of the UK, prospects of sending volunteers to Guyana to assist in capacity building in those areas where their expertise were badly needed.

Similar successes were scored in Canada with the Canadian University Services Overseas (CUSO) and the Canadian Executive Services Officers (CESO), international development organizations who were favorably disposed to providing invaluable assistance to our country

While lobbying in Washington for free and fair elections in Guyana, Dr. Jagan, Paul Richler and I paid a courtesy call on the headquarters of the Peace Corps Volunteers. At the meeting with the directorate of the Organisation, a commitment was made that, should the PPP/C win the 1992 elections, the new government would bring back Peace Corps volunteers to Guyana. Dr. Jagan did win the elections and the Peace Corps are back in Guyana.

Later, due to the acute shortage of draftsmen at the Attorney General's Chambers we turned to Nigeria and India for help. The responses in both cases were overwhelming.

During an official visit to Malaysia with Dr. Jagan we visited the Ministry of International Trade and Industry. It was during a tour of that ministry, I learnt that every Malaysian Embassy and consulate has a Trade and Investment Office staffed with representatives from that ministry. The officers there report directly to that ministry, not the Ministry of Foreign Affairs. Each office is given a target for investments in Malaysia that they must accomplish at the end of each year.

So successful was the Jagan government's resource mobilization efforts that, the 1992 programmes and projects began accumulating with pre-1992 roll over projects. This resulted in inordinate delays for the effective and efficient delivery of goods and services to the people. A major challenge for the Jagan administration had surfaced.

Arising out of a visit I made to Chile as part of a CARICOM delegation to participate in a meeting of the CARICOM/Chile Joint Commission, I shared with Dr. Jagan what I had observed in Chile.

My observation was that because the Chilean Government was faced with a similar problem as that of the government of Guyana, they had seconded to those ministries where projects were blocked, senior ranks of the Chilean army to help unblock the programmes and projects. This worked effectively because the ranks reported directly to the office of the President and not the subject ministers in those ministries where problems existed. We discussed the matter at length with the involvement of Dr. Roger Luncheon, Secretary of the Defense Board and Joe Singh the then Chief of Staff of the GDF. The proposal was agreed with the understanding that it would be taken to cabinet for consideration.

The discussion at cabinet was robust, some ministers were supportive while others were against. Eventually reality prevailed. The lack of institutional capacity to implement projects and as a consequence, denying the beneficiaries the benefits confronted the 'Resisters' who eventually conceded making the proposal acceptable to all.

Joe Singh was tasked with the responsibility to submit names of army officers.

The names were submitted and officers were interviewed and assigned to the ministries of Agriculture, Health, Foreign Affairs and Public Works.

Keith Lowenfield was identified as the coordinator of the team. Lowenfield submitted progress reports on a weekly basis to the Office of the President.

This is the same Lowenfield who at the time of writing, served as Chief Executive/Elections Officer of GECOM. In a matter of three months all outstanding matters were cleared up and tangible results were to be seen.

While at GECOM, Lowenfield was to prove himself a loyal servant of the People's National Congress by resorting to several nefarious activities at GECOM in order to have the APNU+AFC alliance illegally occupy the seat of government through electoral fraud.

Dr. Jagan was a 'People's President'. He never allowed his Presidential duties to interfere with his groundings with the working people. In fact, he combined his meetings with people with his Presidential duties. This twin track approach was a principal characteristic of his presidency.

President Jagan was faced with many challenges at the domestic level while in office. Two examples will suffice; Constant power outages and the economic viability of the Guyana Electricity Corporation; Pushing back against external pressures to privatize the power company and the Guyana Airways Corporation, the state entity overseeing the activities of the only national flag carrier airline. In addition, President Jagan was confronted with the task of determining the future of a number of failing and unprofitable state-owned enterprises.

President Jagan refused to privatize the Guyana Electricity Corporation (GEC) now Guyana Power and Light (GPL). He once told the nation that he was not elected to preside over the sale of the power company. He looked for alternatives in Canada and despatched a high-level delegation to Canada to negotiate an Investment Partnership Agreement with Saskpower, the principal electric generating utility in the province of Saskatchewan, Canada.

While those negotiations dragged on, Dr. Jagan turned to Wartsila, a manufacturer and supplier of diesel generators in Finland. He eventually struck a deal with Wartsila. In 1994, Wartsila signed its first Operations and Management Agreement with the local Guyana Electricity Corporation (GEC). Following the agreement, a modern turn-key electric generating plant was established at Garden of Eden, on the East Bank of Demerara This development brought some relief to the citizenry as regards the uninterrupted supply of electricity. Insofar as the national airline was concerned, the Guyana Airways Corporation was more a liability than an asset.

Apart from its international flights plying the Georgetown-New York route, the airline was carrying heavy loses financially and was uncompetitive with other airlines plying the same route. Compounding the airline's woes even further, its flights to the interior regions of the country were subsidized by funds provided by government. In the meanwhile, local small aircraft commercial operators, who by now, had developed the capacity to operate flights to the interior of the country were screaming discrimination and state monopolization since only the army's Skyvan was authorized to operate flights to the interior of the country on a commercial basis.

To help reduce the State carrying the costs for the internal flights, President Jagan advanced the suggestion that storage facilities be established at Lethem in the Rupununi, where aviation fuel bought from Brazil or Venezuela could be stored at the said facility.

Months of consultations and changes to the Board of Directors of the Corporation, aimed at making the airline profitable, dragged on. With no realistic results in view, a consortium of local businesses, in collaboration with some technical professionals stepped in and took over the failing flag carrier. This move soon became a failure, the airline collapsed and brought the much admired but failed airline to an end.

FATHER OF THE NATION STUMBLES AND DIES

Sometime on the afternoon of Friday, February 15, 1997 between 3- 4 pm, President Jagan was scheduled to chair a statutory meeting of the National Anti-narcotic Commission (NANCOM).

Based on invitations they had received, representatives from the relevant government agencies and departments gathered for the meeting in the cabinet room. I was present at the meeting in my capacity as Minister of Foreign Affairs.

After waiting for approximately forty-five minutes, we were informed by Dr. Luncheon, Head of the Presidential Secretariat and Secretary to NANCOM, who had left the room, but returned some twenty minutes after, that the President was indisposed and that he Dr. Luncheon wound chair the meeting.

The meeting ended sometime between 5-6pm.

My knowledge of the President's routine is that having returned to his office following his morning scheduled engagements, he would have his midday lunch which would be a sandwich, a small amount of local fruits and some tea. He would then retire for his usual midday nap for about forty-five minutes. That nap would have been in his private resting room adjoining his office. While he was Opposition Leader based at Freedom House, he would have his rest in a hammock.

Whether the President was diagnosed as showing signs of a heart attack at the time when Dr. Luncheon went to check on him between 3-4pm on the day of February 15, has not been established. Moreover, how ill Dr. Jagan was at the time when he left his office for his residence at State House, and, whether he had to be assisted was not established. In the circumstances, I will not speculate.

When I received a phone call at my home at Queenstown on the night of Friday February 15, at around 7pm informing that the President had been hospitalized. I was shocked. I immediately left my home to visit him at the Georgetown Public Hospital. On my arrival, I saw the President's son Joey Jagan, Dr. Luncheon, Dr. Hughley Hanoman and Gail Teixeira, the then Minister of Health. I was told that the President had suffered a heart attack early in the evening between 7-7:30 pm.

He had to be carried down the stairs at State House in a stretcher and was brought to the hospital by an ambulance since his physicians had advised against him traveling by car.

The persons present were in a huddled discussion as to whether the President should be taken overseas for medical treatment. Apparently, treatment at any of the local hospitals had been ruled out.

The President was lying in bed with an oxygen mask over his nose and mouth. He was listening to the discussion. He looked at me and I in turn looked at him with a sense of disbelief.

My tower of strength and source of inspiration had fallen, though he still looked strong and healthy.

After spending about two hours standing at the bedside with the others I left for home.

On my way home, I recalled how one afternoon during a break of a sitting of the National Assembly, Mrs. Jagan who was a Parliamentarian at the time had a quiet talk with me on the balcony of the parliament building. She expressed concern over the President's unwillingness to take up an offer to travel to the UK for a further medical check up.

I was told that earlier in the year, the President had travelled to Port of Spain, Trinidad and Tobago to do an angiogram.

That angiogram had indicated that all was not well and his physicians had recommended that a second opinion based on further tests be sought elsewhere.

Dr. Hughley Hanoman and Dr. David Dabydeen were instrumental in arranging for the tests to be done in the UK. The President kept postponing the visit but eventually agreed to travel to the UK on March 6, 1997.

He wanted the medical assessment to coincide with a lecture he was scheduled to deliver at the University of Warwick. The lecture was organized by David Dabydeen, Director of the Centre of Caribbean Studies and Professor at the Centre for British Comparative Cultural Studies at the University of Warick.

Incidentally, another offer had been made by Guyanese-born, Texas-based medical doctor and philanthropist, Dr. Tulsi Dyal Singh to have the second opinion done at Midland, Texas but that offer was turned down.

Tulsi was a very good friend of Dr. Jagan. He was of great assistance to him from a medical point of view and in establishing contacts with political personalities at Midland, Texas. Tulsi was instrumental in organising and bringing to Guyana, several badly needed teams of professional medical practitioner from Midland. On one of his regular missions to Guyana, Tulsi brought the Mayor of Midland, Robert E. Burns.

I had the opportunity of visiting Tulsi at Midland one two occasions. The first, was on a political mission, the second was with Mrs. Rohee.

Midland city is the seat of Midland County, Western Texas. It is situated midway between El Paso and Forth Worth. It is the financial and trade centre for the vast Permian Basin which contains large deposits of oil and gas. Midland has one of the most modern and highly technologically advance medical centres in the State of Texas.

During my conversation with Mrs. Jagan, she warned that the President was moving on in age but was nevertheless continuing with his hectic schedules. She anticipated that if he continued at the rate, he was going it would have a heavy toll on his health. She was concerned about the constant postponing of his trip to the UK.

The conversation ended there.

I guess Mrs. Jagan raised her concerns with me because she probably wanted me to raise the matter at the leadership level of the party. My dilemma however, was how could I do that while the President was busy going about his duties and when there was no visible sign of him being ill.

But now this unexpected crisis had fallen upon the Nation

On the morning of the following day, Saturday, February 16, I was informed that, following consultations with the President's physicians, his wife and two children, representation was made to the US government, through the US Embassy in Georgetown, to medi-vac the President by air to the United States via Panama. Arrangements were made for him to be admitted to the Walter Reed Army Medical Centre at Washington DC.

I was called upon as Foreign Minister to fulfill certain prolocular formalities since the arrangements to transport and hospitalize the Guyanese President in a foreign country were being made on a government to government basis.

I was in regular contact with Mr. Hugh Simon, the then Charge d'Affaires at the US Embassy in Georgetown who went to great lengths to put the necessary arrangements in place on the US side.

A US military aircraft flew in early on the morning of Saturday February 16. President Jagan was transported first by ambulance from the hospital, then by helicopter from the Guyana Defense Force's Camp Ayangana to our international airport at Timehri where the US army aircraft was waiting to fly him to Panama. There, he would rest overnight, and depart on the morning of Sunday,17 for Andrews Air force Base in Maryland thence to the Walter Reed Army Medical Centre at Bethesda.

According to Guyanese medical experts, the use of a turbo jet for a four-hour flight from Georgetown to Panama City with an ailing President on board and without any of the prescribed medication were deficiencies that were potentially problematic.

Further, whoever it was that insisted on the decision, contrary to advice of the President's physicians, to have the President transported by helicopter to the international airport, rather by road in an ambulance, must be held responsible for what turned out to be a potentially dangerous situation when, due to vibrations common to travel by helicopter, it was observed that sections of the President's skin and fingers were becoming cyanosed, a condition was that quickly addressed by his physicians on board.

Having been informed by Joe Singh, the army's Chief of Staff about the President's estimated arrival at the airport, I left home and arrived at the airport about half an hour before the chopper arrived with him on board.

Some of my cabinet colleagues were there already and were engaged in a huddled hush hush conversation.

I took it upon myself not to engage in any conversation with anyone nor to be distracted by anything, other than to stand at a conspicuous location on the border of the tarmac. I wanted to observe everything that was taking place from the President's arrival, his transferral to the US army aircraft, to it's takes off in a Northwesterly direction.

President Jagan arrived at the Walter Reed Medical Centre on Sunday afternoon. He underwent angioplasty surgery on the night of Sunday February 17, 1997.

Regular updates on the President's condition were provided to the nation. At one time, the good news came that he was recovering though still in danger. In the midst of the crisis, government business continued as usual. I was tasked with the responsibility to provide regular briefings to the diplomatic and donor community in Guyana.

A small Committee was established to make arrangements for a State Funeral, but the committee was quickly disbanded after we received news about an improvement in the President's condition.

Prime Minister Sam Hinds, while performing the duties of President, temporarily assumed chairmanship of cabinet meetings.

Republic Day celebrations on February 23rd went on as planned. Sam Hinds delivered a moving speech at the flag raising ceremony held at the National Park, said he:

"Our prayer is that the self-same Jagan spirit of toughness and resilience, fortitude and strength of character, that fighting spirit which has served Guyana so well, for so long, will serve him well in this time of personal trial to overcome this enormous challenge." And Mrs. Janet Jagan on behalf of President Jagan sent a televised message of greetings to the Guyanese people.

In her message she said; "In those fifty years, President Jagan has devoted his whole life to the basic ideals of freedom, democracy, human liberty, unity and struggle to eliminate poverty and suffering not only in Guyana but in the region, the hemisphere and the entire world. Mashramani greetings to one and all."

On the eleventh day, following Republic Day observances Guyana received the news that shook the Nation. President Cheddi Jagan, the Third Executive President of the country had died. Odeen Ishmael, the then Guyana Ambassador to the USA and the OAS sent the following message:

"It is my sad duty to announce that His Excellency President Cheddi Jagan died at 12:23am EST. on Thursday March 6, 1997 at the Walter Reed Army Medical Centre in Washington DC.

President Jagan was 78 years old. Guyana is all the poorer with the passing of this great Guyanese leader. But the Guyanese people are nevertheless enriched with his legacy of struggle for freedom, democracy and social justice - a struggle for which he dedicated his entire life. -March 6, 1997"

President Jagan died on the day he was scheduled to leave Guyana for the U.K. for his comprehensive medical checkup.

Asked by a Guyanese journalist how he should be remembered, - Janet Jagan said;

"Well, I think they must remember him as the Father of Independence. People also say he's the Father of the Nation. He gave his life to the betterment of the Guyanese people. He fought tirelessly for National Unity and he made such a tremendous contribution! I don't think he could ever be forgotten..."

On receipt of the sad news, the committee tasked with preparations for the State Funeral was re-established but with a much-enlarged membership comprising party and state representatives.

To accompany the body back to Guyana, a delegation comprising senior Party comrades and government functionaries travelled to Washington to join the Jagan family.

On receiving the news on radio and TV that the President's body had arrived at the airport and was about to leave for Georgetown, thousands of people lined the East Bank Highway from the airport to the city.

The President's body was brought to State House for viewing by members of the party's leadership. It was at that event that Indra Chandarpal, me and a couple other Comrades made a solemn pledge that we will remain faithful to the ideals and convictions of Cheddi Jagan notwithstanding his departure from this life.

The queue of thousands of persons who came to view the body at State House stretched for several blocks and lasted for two days.

The State Funeral ceremony was held at Parliament Building where Feroze Mohammed read the eulogy on behalf of the Party

A procession from Parliament to Freedom House and thence to Babu Jhan at Port Mourant, East Berbice, the birth place of Dr. Jagan was massive and stretched for several miles.

After almost two days of viewing by Berbiceans, and others who had travelled from other parts of the country, the cremation was finally held at Babu Jhan on March 13, 1997. It was one of the saddest moments in my life. Everyone present were sad, if not in tears. Mourners came in their thousands to pay their last respects to their fallen hero and leader. During the cremation, Mrs. Jagan invited me to sit next to her for a brief while. She did not go to witness the actual burning of the corpse on the pyre.

We chatted briefly about the future of the Party and government with Comrade Cheddi no longer with us. Her main concern was to keep his ideas alive and to keep the Party united. Delivering the final remarks on behalf of the Party at the cremation site Ralph Ramkarran told the thousands gathered there;

"Cheddi Jagan's journey through life has now come to an end. As we return his body to the winds of his native village, we try to understand what contributions of elements created such a life as his and what forces determined his unerring but uncharted course in service to his people."

Little did I know that, innocuous as Mrs. Jagan's concerns appeared to be at that time, years later it would come to pass, when I would be branded an "Old Guard," and a "Fake Socialist," whose time had come to "shift down in order to make space for others."

Immediately following the cremation of President Jagan, I was despatched as the Party and government representative to the funeral of Michael Manley, former Prime Minister of Jamaica. Manley died on March 6, the same day that Cheddi Jagan died.

Manley's funeral was held on March 16, 1997. While at the funeral, my mind went back to his visit to Guyana and his conversation with President Jagan. For me, that was indeed a memorable occasion.

My attendance at Manley's funeral, marked the second occasion I was to be at an historic occasion for the Caribbean on my birthday. The first being on March 16, following the seizure of power by the New Jewel Movement in Grenada on March 13, 1979.

Many Caribbean leaders in expressing their condolences on the passing of President Jagan spoke in glowing terms about the Guyanese leader. P.J. Patterson former Prime Minister of Jamaica remarked; "His political tenacity and intellectual contributions to the dialectics of our time can never be questioned." Owen Arthur, former Prime Minister of Barbados was quoted as saying; "Cheddi Jagan was a crusader for sovereignty and a champion of the Third World solidarity and development." And the Prime Minister of St. Vincent and the Grenadines, Sir James Mitchell had this to say; "Cheddi Jagan, perhaps beyond all politicians in this region, demonstrated the fortitude exceeded by none."

At the national level, Ian McDonald writing in the Stabroek News said: "Cheddi Jagan was at all times without compromise, a man of the people, completely free of the taint of corruption, dedicating his life to the cause..."

THE TRANSITION

It was just about two weeks after President Jagan had died that the party initiated internal discussions on the transition of political power from one President to another at the State level and from one General Secretary to another at the Party level.

During this period, a sense of great expectation prevailed throughout the country. The populace was anxious to know who will replace Dr. Jagan as General Secretary of the Party and as President of the country. Moreover, since elections were not far away, a hotly debated topic was, who will be the Presidential Candidate of the party for the next elections due to be held in 1997.

The transition process took place at two levels. First, was the constitutional process to have Samuel Hinds appointed President and for President Hinds to appoint Janet Jagan as Prime Minister. Those transitional steps proceeded smoothly, but not after lengthy internal discussions at the leadership level of the party.

Navin Chandarpal was selected to replace Samuel Hinds in the National Assembly.

While he was alive, Cheddi Jagan had reached a "gentleman's agreement" with Hinds to the effect that were he, President Jagan, be unable to execute his constitutional duties, Hinds would accede to the Presidency but ultimately, the PPP must hold the Presidency. Hinds concurred.

The transition process at the level of General Secretary of the Party proved to be somewhat more difficult because some Comrades saw the position of Party General Secretary, as a precursor for the position of Presidential Candidate for the 1997 elections.

It was decided that at no time, should one person hold both positions of President and General Secretary. Further, it was also agreed, that the General Secretary should not ipso facto be the Presidential candidate.

Several meetings of the Executive and Central Committee were convened to discuss and decide on the position of General Secretary.

In this connection, a number of suggestions were made, the principal one being that there should be a collective, rather than a single General Secretary or a General Secretary as the Presidential candidate.

Janet Jagan was of the view that the position of Party General Secretary should be held by an individual from among several comrades who were ideologically trained in Moscow. Among the names she mentioned were Sheik Feroze Mohammed, Donald Ramotar, Clement Rohee and Kellawan Lall. Mrs. Jagan also put forward Ralph Ramkarran as a possible candidate for the post.

Roger Luncheon's name was mentioned but due to him being Head of the Public Service his name was ruled out. Moreover, Janet Jagan ruled out herself for reasons that the job required a younger and more energetic Comrade. Sheik Feroze

Mohammed was recognized as the popular choice for the post of Party General Secretary but he declined holding the post. He nevertheless supported separation of the two top positions.

As far as my name was concerned, Mrs. Jagan asked that I be considered on that grounds that I grew up in the Party and was prepared for the job. She added that I had studied in Moscow, spent three years at the World Marxist Review and that I had a hard life.

She went on to point out that I spent sometime in Cuba, that I am trustworthy but that I tend to be controversial at times in my relations with my Comrades.

One Comrade took the position that in considering who should fill the position, consideration should be given to the social composition of the party.

Another Comrade stated that no Comrade should be excluded from contesting the post of either the General Secretary or Presidential Candidate. Reference was made to the Party's Constitution stipulating that every member has the right to be elected to leading positions in the Party.

Yet another comrade stated that I would not be suitable for the post because as Foreign Minister, I would be required to travel abroad frequently and because the General Secretary's position was a full-time job.

Recognizing that my ministerial portfolio responsibilities were irreconcilable with those of the General Secretary's, I chose not to fight the issue at the time though on reflection, I felt I should have countered some of the views that had a ring that seemed alien to the Party's philosophy.

Nevertheless, in the ensuing discussion, I said I was happy that my name was among the final three names proposed along with Donald Ramotar and Navin Chandarpal.

I expressed the view that it would be in our best interest to have a General Secretary who would uphold the aims and aspirations of the working class, be visible among the people and someone who would work with the leadership to arrive at decisions on a collective basis. I went on further to say that whoever is elected should uphold the principle of criticism and self-criticism. I ended by expressing my support for Donald Ramotar to be the next General Secretary.

Janet Jagan endorsed the consensual view that Donald Ramotar take on the mantle of Party General Secretary. In doing so, she drew to the meeting's attention, the emergence of various ideological trends at an international and national levels and stressed the need to have a Comrade in the position capable of maintaining the Party's ideological stature.

In the end, Ramotar got the nod, and, following a recommendation from the Executive Committee, to the Central Committee, he was elected General Secretary of the Party on March 29,1997.

With Sam's assumption to the Office of President, the seat of Prime Minister became vacant. Janet Jagan as an elected Member of Parliament was appointed Prime Minister and First Vice President with effect from March 17th 1997. Repu Daman Persaud was appointed Second Vice President on the same date.

With the transition completed at both State and Party levels, governance of the country continued in earnest.

THE SAM HINDS PRESIDENCY

The Sam Hinds Presidency with Janet Jagan as Prime Minister, legally and Constitutionally installed, continued to pursue policies adumbrated by the late President Cheddi Jagan.

The Sam Hinds Presidency lasted from March 1997 to December of the same year. His tenure can be characterized as a 'holding presidency' Though constitutionally, he did have and did exercise full powers as the President of the Republic.

In 1997, President Hinds signed into law the Termination of Employment and Severance Pay Bill and the Trade Union Recognition Bill. The latter had its genesis since1953 when the colonial Government, among other reasons, suspended the British Guiana constitution for fear of a communist take-over of the colony.

President Hinds represented the nation at the historic meeting between President Clinton and Caricom leaders held in May 1997 in Bridgetown, Barbados.

In June 1997, President Hinds attended and addressed the 19th Special Session of the United Nations General Assembly named the Earth Summit+5. And in July 1997, he attended the 18th Meeting of the Conference of Caricom Heads of Government held in Montego Bay, Jamaica. In a speech delivered at the opening of the conference, President Hinds told his colleague Heads; "We would fail the original architects of Caricom if we do not refine their vision in light of our experiences."

While in Jamaica, President Hinds signed on behalf of the Government of Guyana, the nine Protocols laying the basis for the creation of the Caricom Single Market and Economy (CSME). Following the signing, President Hinds had this to say; "Guyana is conscious that despite the distances separating us, we can find much benefit in a Single Market and Economy. It would be for us to find arrangements which distribute the benefits widely, leaving no one out."

President Sam Hinds: March 1997 – December 1997; Prime Minister: 1992-2015. Addressing United Nations General Assembly – 1997

Photo courtesy: UN/DPI by Eskinder Debebe

FRESH CHALLENGES AND NEW CONFIGURATIONS

With elections due in 1997, no fundamentally new policy initiatives were initiated during the two-year period.

It was during this period, that calls were made to strengthen the Party's alliance with the Civic component through regular consultations and to confront the charges of corruption that were hurled at the government.

If truth be told, already, while Dr. Jagan was alive several cases of corruption were brought to his attention involving senior party leaders. When investigated, these allegations were proven to be true, resulting in the removal of two ministers from their positions.

It was in this context, some Comrades felt that with the passing of Dr. Jagan, bribery and corruption would become more rampant and therefore the need for the Party to take concrete steps to nip it in the bud.

A small internal Party Anti-corruption Committee was established involving Comrades who were not office holders in government. That committee being a political body became still-born because it had no legal powers to investigate nor to sanction or dismiss any one proven to be corrupt.

It was during this interregnum, that robust debates surfaced at the leadership level of the Party about the efficacy of the Civic Component and whether it brought any proven political dividends to the Party's electoral fortunes. This matter was to become an ongoing debate at the leadership level of the Party on the eve of every election.

But the dominant view that the Civic Component has, and continues to play a mutually reinforcing role for the Party in its electoral alliance politics has always prevailed.

During the discussions, calls were made to expand the ranks of the Civic Component and to engage its members in regular consultations on policy issues. Meanwhile, considerations arose among some members of the Civic Component, to have the Component elevated to a more formal organizational structure with its own office bearers.

This suggestion was not supported by the majority within the Civic Component. At the Party level, there was lack of support for such a move.

By March 1997, elections preparations were in full swing. A vicious campaign targeting Mrs. Jagan was unleashed by the opposition People's National Congress (PNC) even though no decision had been in respect to the Party's Presidential Candidate for the upcoming elections.

With the decision that no one Comrade at no time, must hold both the Presidential candidate and General Secretary positions at the same time, with a new General Secretary in place, the way was made clear for the selection of a Presidential candidate.

Several configurations were proposed such as returning to the leadership structure of the 1950-1960 period and convening of a pre-elections Congress.

The names that emerged in the course of the discussion were Ralph Ramkarran, Roger Luncheon, Janet Jagan and Bharat Jagdeo.

The configuration finally arrived at was what became known as the "A" Team with Janet Jagan as Presidential Candidate, Sam Hinds as Prime Ministerial candidate and a Number Three from the PPP in the event Mrs. Jagan was unable to fulfill her duties as President.

Ralph Ramkarran was nominated to fill the Number Three position and he agreed on condition that he not be asked to join the government on a permanent basis but that in the eventuality that the Number One could not function he would take over as a replacement.

This did not go down well with a few members of the Executive Committee. Ramkarran eventually asked to be given time to reconsider his position.

Ramkarran subsequently, advised that he stood by his position because of family commitments which he was unprepared to surrender at the time.

A torrent of ad hominem attacks and allegations were hurled at Ralph particularly by Moses Nagamootoo whose aim, from all indications, was to bring down Ralph and ultimately, deny him the number three position on the 'A' team.

Many of us in the leadership at that time, were of the view that Nagamootoo behaved in this way because he had his eye on the Number Three position, though Ralph was a good choice. Our suspicion was fuelled by public statements Nagamootoo made while abroad claiming that at a meeting somewhere in the interior of Guyana, Cheddi Jagan had named him as his successor. No one believed Nagamootoo because, Dr. Jagan never mentioned such a view to the leadership of the Party and secondly, because Nagamotoo chose to raise his claim after Dr. Jagan's demise. In any event, during the transition period, Nagamootoo had already begun to display, vacillating, opportunistic, divisive and anti-party tendencies.

It became clear to the majority in the leadership of the Party and government at that time, that Nagamootoo had lied when he said that Dr. Jagan had identified him to succeed him as General Secretary of the Party and President of the country. Nagamootoo had also lied when he said that he was by-passed in favour of Jagdeo to be the number three in the 'A' Team. The fact of the matter is, we arrived at our decision on the composition of the 'A 'Team after many days of full, frank and open discussion at the leadership level of the Party. Worse yet, Nagamootoo publicly accused the Party of 'failing to offer vibrant leadership', that the Party 'lacked integrity honesty and honour' and that he has 'differences with the leadership,' All of this was done to create confusion within the ranks of the Party.

Compounding the problem further, Nagamootoo stated publicly that he was to be appointed a Presidential Advisor, claiming that he and Jagdeo had discussed his appointment to that position and that he was awaiting Jagdeo's return from overseas. Nagamootoo even claimed that Janet Jagan had promised to appoint him a Vice President during her presidency.

Responding to the verbal abuse primarily by Nagamootoo, Ramkarran informed the gathering that he would not continue to sit and to be attacked on scurrilous grounds by Nagamootoo. He requested to be excused from the meeting.

Nagamootoo was severely criticized by the Party's leadership for being insensitive and disrespectful to Ralph Ramkarran who, like other leaders, made untold sacrifices for the Party and in many and different ways.

Efforts were made but to no avail, to encourage Ramkarran to return to meetings of the Executive Committee and to agree to hold a position in cabinet.

After several hours of debate on numerous suggestions about who should fill the Number Three position in the 'A' Team, and with Ralph Ramkarran out of the picture, the meeting unanimously agreed that Bharat Jagdeo be named as the Number Three. Jagdeo agreed.

Donald Ramotar is on record for having pushed aggressively for Jagdeo to be the Number Three. But that notwithstanding, and independent of Ramotar's position, a number of prominent members including me, supported Jagdeo for the Number Three position.

With the 'A' Team in place, the PPP/C was ready to go to the polls.

Janet Jagan faced off against Opposition Leader, Desmond Hoyte of the newly created PNC/Reform alliance for the elections held on December 15,1977.

CAMPAIGNING FOR VICTORY IN '97

The political situation in the country was tense following the death of President Cheddi Jagan. The opposition PNC/R was calculating that the PPP would suffer tremendous losses with the absence of Cheddi Jagan for the first time.

Hoyte was banking on political returns from his Economic Recovery Programme (ERP) based on an IMF Structural Adjustment Programme (SAP).

The opposition PNC made Janet Jagan the principal target of their campaign, weaponizing race and nationality to accomplish their objective.

But with a strong team supporting our Presidential Candidate, the opposition's objective was thwarted throughout the entire campaign.

And, notwithstanding her advanced age, Mrs. Jagan travelled around the country speaking at numerous meetings and rallies.

Campaigning with Janet Jagan in Wakenaam - 1997

For the elections, 461,369 persons were the total number of electors registered to vote at a total number of 1,844 polling stations.

The PPP/C's Presidential Candidate won 55.5 percent of the total valid votes cast compared to the 42.3 won by the PNC.

In the previous elections held in 1992, with Cheddi Jagan as the PPP/C's Presidential Candidate, the Party won 53.3 per cent of the valid votes cast while the PNC won 40.5 per cent.

It was the first time in the PPP's history, it had won such an impressive number of votes at a free and fair election. Asked some years later, how she felt about being selected the Presidential Candidate of the Party and her victory at the polls, Janet Jagan told her interviewer; "I felt like I was going into a prison"

This massive win enraged the PNC's leadership so much so that they rejected the results of the elections.

The PNC threatened street demonstrations and to take legal action to block the swearing in of the newly elected President even after Doodnauth Singh, Chairman of the Elections Commission had declared her the winner. It was clear to everyone that the PNC had no intention of filing an Elections Petition.

The PNC sought and secured a Writ through the High Court aimed at preventing Mrs. Jagan from assuming Office and carrying out the functions of President of the Republic.

On December 19th, during a small Swearing-In ceremony held at State House in the presence of the Chancellor of the Judiciary, the Chairman and members of GECOM, a few senior party and government officials as well as the diplomatic community, a Marshall of Court turned up to serve a Court Order on Mrs. Jagan to block her from assuming the Office of President.

Mrs. Jagan accepted the Court Order but then she threw it over her shoulders much to the surprise of those present.

In an interview held with a TV journalist, Martin Goolsarran on January 18, 1998, Janet Jagan had the following to say concerning her action:

"Yes, I regret what took place and I wish to apologize for my action. At the same time, I would like to take the opportunity to show the other side of the coin so that people may understand the state of my mind and what had occurred. I also wish to mention very categorically, that it had nothing at all to do with dis- respect for the laws or our Constitution."

In deciding on the writ to prevent Mrs. Jagan from assuming office and carrying out the functions of the Presidency, the then Chief Justice on January 12, 1998, discharged the orders nisi of certiorari and prohibition.

The Chief Justice argued that while certiorari lies against the decision of the Chairman of the Elections Commission, the jurisdiction of the Court is ousted by Articles 177(4) and 177(6) of the Constitution.

Under Article 177(6) once a person named in the instrument is declared elected as President at an election held pursuant to the provisions of Article 60 (2), that Declaration shall be conclusive evidence that the person so named was so elected and no question as to the validity of the election as President of the person so named shall be enquired into in any court.

That article, the Chief Justice ruled, prevents direct scrutiny of such a Declaration, but not an enquiry by way of an Election Petition.

The PNC appealed the CJ's decision and subsequently presented a Petition to the Court contesting the validity of the results of the 1997 elections.

CRISIS AND THE HERDSMANSTON ACCORD

For one year the PNC kept up their street protests and demonstrations, as well as their boycott of sittings of the National Assembly. The Opposition Leader had declared that he will make the situation 'ungovernable' for Janet Jagan.

In the meanwhile, in response to an invitation from the Government of Guyana, CARICOM despatched a three-man mission to Georgetown. The mission included, Sir Henry Forde of Barbados, Sir Shridath Ramphal, and Sir Alister McIntyre.

The Mission had three objectives:

1. To enable CARICOM to formulate an independent position on the situation in Guyana;
2. To attempt to arrest the trend towards escalating violence;
3. To do everything possible to ensure that the people of Guyana are united in their quest for free democratic expression.

The Mission stayed in Guyana for five days during which time they held consultations with all stakeholders.

On the day before their departure, on January 17, 1998, the Mission brokered what became known as the Herdsmanston Accord, Herdmanston being a protocol housed owned by the State and used to accommodate visiting guests.

Soon after their arrival in Guyana Sir Shridath Ramphal along with Sir Alister McIntyre met privately with President Jagan at her home at Plantation Bel Air. Accompanying the President were Ralph Ramkarran and Dr. Roger Luncheon.

President Jagan had invited me and Kellawan Lall to the meeting but soon after we arrived, we were asked to wait at another section of the property.

The meeting lasted for about three hours. After all the guests, including Ramkarran and Luncheon had departed, me and Lall were briefed by the President about what transpired.

The news was shocking to say the least.

The Herdsmanston Accord called for an independent inquiry or Audit of the December 15, 1977 elections to be carried out in two stages:

According to the Report of the CARICOM Audit Commission,

In the first stage;

*An urgent review of the due process of the count on and after December 15, 1997, (including the role of the Elections Commission), to be completed within three months of January 17, 1998 with a view to ascertainment of the votes cast for the respective political parties;

In the second stage;

*An Audit of the systemic aspects of the electoral process, including the post balloting phase; An immediate moratorium on public demonstrations and marches will be declared and implemented. The ban on these activities will be simultaneously lifted. These arrangements will subsist for a minimum period of three months from January 17, 1998.

*Activities for sustained dialogue between the PPP/C and PNC;

*Establishment of a Constitutional Reform Commission with a broad-based membership and with a mandate to consult with society at large and conclude and present its report to the National Assembly within 18 months of January 17, 1998 and with:

*Post-reform elections to be held within 18 months after the presentation of the Report of the Commission to the National Assembly."

In effect, this meant that Mrs. Jagan's Presidency was to be reduced from five to three years.

In an interview with President Jagan by Earl Bosquet held on January 25, 1998

President Jagan had this to say;

"But most of all, the Accord brought us away from the brink. It was my view that we were on the brink of a disaster. If it had not been for the responsible behavior of the PPP/Civic, I am afraid this country may have gone into the abyss that we went into in the 60's.

I want the whole Nation to know how dangerous the situation was and it was due to the responsible attitude of the PPP/Civic government that we were able to make what necessary concessions were required to bring about peace to this land.

In specific reference to the denial of two years of her five - year term, President Jagan said;

"I think bringing back the Nation from the brink is what we have to deal with, and so far, we have achieved that. I hope that there will be no breach of the agreement. That will be regrettable. But I think you have left out an important aspect of the agreement and that is dialogue between the two parties, and that is very important. In the interest of preserving the nation and allowing our people to go forward to a peaceful existence, to earn their living, to educate their children and to have a normal life, we must have dialogue between our two parties, and that is very important."

President Janet Jagan went on:

"But while we are on the subject of the Accord, I want to quote from something I saw in the local newspaper, an article about our Foreign Minister, Clement Rohee, addressing the OAS. He made what, to me, was a profound analysis of the situation. He said, let me quote: "Countries that have just come out of dictatorial rule, have an extremely fragile democracy. He added that; "Despite the efforts put into setting up institutions, installing good governance and stamping out corruption at different levels, there are forces within the society who are determined to destroy that fragile democracy. He also referred to the former President of Haiti, Jean Bertrand Aristide, who said; "The real test of democracy comes out, not in the first elections, but in the second elections."

With Madeleine Albright in Guatemala, With Cesar Gaviria & With Surinamese Ambassador Albert Ramdin

From the inception Janet Jagan's Presidency was rocked by controversy and turmoil. Opposition leader Desmond Hoyte's remarks at a public meeting in Georgetown about "slow fyah, moe fyah" meaning, that slow fire and more fire would be added to his party's protests to unseat the "White American Jew who Guyana did not want as its president" only helped to whip up his supporters to resort to more street demonstrations and violet protests in the capital city.

To her credit, Mrs. Jagan had the foresight to alert her colleagues in the leadership of the Party about what could be expected from the political opposition were she to be selected the Party's Presidential Candidate and should she become the President of the Republic.

Having won the election and sitting at the Office of the President her worst fears came to pass.

Her government was confronted with street protests reminiscent of the 1962 to 1964 period and a general strike called by the Guyana Public Service Union (GPSU) to press for the early implementation of the agreement reached during the Cheddi Jagan administration and, in addition, for a forty percent increase in wages and salaries for public servants.

MISSION COMPLETED BUT ATTACKS CONTINUE

In the midst of the ongoing destabilizing events, by May 1998, within a matter of five months, the CARICOM Audit Commission managed to complete its mission in Guyana.

On May 30, 1998 Mr. Ulric Cross, Chairman of the CARICOM Audit Commission (CAC) submitted his report on the first stage of the Commission.

At a Handing-over of the Report Ceremony held on June 2nd 1998 in Georgetown, the then Chairman of CARICOM Prime Minister Keith Mitchell, said; "...there is no denying that the issue is a very serious one for Guyana and for the Caribbean Community. Anyone who thinks otherwise should be elsewhere. It is therefore of utmost importance that everyone – whatever their political persuasion recognizes the urgency of finding a solution to the current impasse."

In his Report, Cross stated:

"The CAC found that the results of their vote count varied only marginally from that of the final results declared by the Chief Elections Officer."

With the first stage of the Herdsmanston Accord completed, the process then shifted to the second stage which called for an end to the ban on public demonstrations; an end to public demonstrations for a period of three months; the commencement of political dialogue between the PPP and PNC; the establishment of a Constitutional Reform Commission and the convening of the National Assembly.

To initiate the second stage of the Accord, Opposition Leader Desmond Hoyte was invited to join CARICOM Heads of Government at their Summit meeting held at Castries, St. Lucia on July 2, 1998.

I had the good fortune of accompanying President Janet Jagan at that meeting. It was at that meeting that what became known as the 'St. Lucia Statement' was negotiated and signed on September 14, 1998 by President Janet Jagan, Opposition Leader, Desmond Hoyte and the then Chairman of CARICOM, Kenny Anthony, Prime Minister of St, Lucia, on behalf of the Caribbean Community.

The Statement called for the commencement of a dialogue between the PPP and the PNC; commitment to Constitutional Reform for completion by July 1999, allowing the parliamentary opposition to take their seats in the National Assembly by July 15, 1998 and the provision of a CARICOM Facilitator. Mr. Maurice King of Barbados was named Facilitator of the Dialogue Process.

February 26,1998 was set as the date for the opening of the 7th Parliament.

The opening of Parliament was graced with the presence of the Prime Minister Owen Arthur of Barbados and Keith Mitchell of Grenada. A huge demonstration of PNC supporters had gathered outside Parliament buildings. They were noisy and hostile. President Jagan was cool and stateswoman-like during the entire proceedings which was boycotted by the PNC.

In her address to the Members of Parliament, President Jagan said:

"The PPP/Civic government is committed to economic growth in an open economy where the state and private sectors play their respective roles. This growth must be distributed in such a manner that the end result must be continuing human development since we are committed to a vision in which people are at the centre of development"

President Janet Jagan went on to say;

"Devising a strategy for harmonious development of all Guyanese is of central importance. Tensions and divisions are not inevitable and realistic methods can be found to accommodate the needs of all our citizens. In the coming period we have to consider innovative and imaginative ways to hammer out appropriate arrangements for the development of all sections of the population."

As the President was preparing to depart Parliament Buildings, the crowd of people on the street outside parliament had swelled numerically. They had become increasingly hostile and vocal. Mrs. Jagan refused to depart via the Hadfield Street, Southern back entrance to Parliament Buildings. She considered that an act of cowardice.

The mob attempted to block the Presidential vehicle leaving the compound of Parliament through the official entrance and departure of the building, but the police did a great job in clearing the way using minimal force.

As the Presidential vehicle proceeded in a North-Easterly direction on Brickdam, and was about to turn left into Avenue of the Republic, a mob ran behind the slowly moving Presidential vehicle hurling huge rocks onto the vehicle thus endangering the life of the President and the chauffeur.

The police managed to escort the vehicle carrying the President away from the hostile crowd.

The incident incensed the PPP/C's supporters to such an extent that the Party had to call on its supporters to remain calm and to avoid getting involved in any acts of violence.

A subsequent police report on the incident revealed that a woman by the name of Patricia James was seen by a police sergeant carrying a haversack filled with rocks which were used by the mob to hurl at the President's vehicle.

The incident was witnessed by both Prime Ministers representing Caricom.

THE PUBLIC SERVICE STRIKE

The strike by public servants lasted for fifty-seven days. The government had offered a 4.6 percent increase in wages and salaries which was rejected by the union who in turn demanded a 40 percent increase for 1999 and a fifty percent increase for 2000.

President Jagan appealed to the workers for understanding and appreciation of the precarious financial situation the government was facing explaining that the amount in increases that being demanded by the union was unaffordable.

Bharat Jagdeo the then Minister of Finance described the union's demands as "unrealistic" stating that "ninety percent of government revenues was going to pay public servants and to service the foreign debt."

In the end with no solution in sight and with the economy reeling as a result of the strike, the government found itself fighting battles on the political, industrial, legal and parliamentary fronts. A way out had to be found.

Eventually, the Janet Jagan administration chose to go to arbitration to end the strike in 1999.

An arbitration panel headed by Dr. Aubrey Armstrong was established.

And much to the disappointment of government, but to the satisfaction of the union, the arbitrator awarded 31.6. percent salary increases for 1999 and 26.6 percent increases for 2000.

The impact of the strike cost the government; G$1.3 bln. more than was expected and $G5.5 bln, for the next two years.

THE JANET JAGAN PRESIDENCY

The administration of President Janet Jagan faced many challenges with every passing day. But the President insisted that notwithstanding the challenges in Court and elsewhere, her government must not only deliver goods and services to the people, it must continue to do so as efficiently and effectively as it can to the people. In other words, she insisted that government must be seen to be functioning.

To give life to this directive, ministers were instructed to go out into the fields and been seen among the people addressing problems and concerns consistent with their portfolio responsibilities.

Between March 1997 and the holding of general election in December of the same year, I was called upon to represent the government at the Commonwealth Heads of Government Summit at Edinburgh, Scotland held from 24-27 October 1997.

My participation in a CARICOM delegation to South Africa in January 1998, to inaugurate the CARICOM- South Africa Trade and Investment Mission was my first overseas mission on behalf of the newly elected PPP/C administration.

The trip was part and parcel of the President's wish that government be seen to be functioning. Great attention was paid to the newly established Ministries of Housing and of Culture, Youth and Sport as well as to the promotion of the arts including the Castellani National Gallery. The President also paid close attention to the Ministries of Health, Housing, Education, Social Security, Amerindian Affairs and Foreign Affairs.

In February 1998, on the occasion of the 25th anniversary CARICOM, President Janet Jagan, along with the Prime Ministers of Barbados, St. Lucia, Trinidad and Tobago and the Secretary General of Caricom, helped turn the sod to mark the start of the construction of the permanent headquarters of the CARICOM Secretariat at Liliendaal, Georgetown. In her speech the President stressed the importance of proper accommodation for the Secretariat to enable its effective functioning. Construction of the building commenced in May 2001 and the commissioning took place in February 2005 under the Bharrat Jagdeo administration

Through her respective cabinet ministers, the Janet Jagan administration continued to place emphasis on debt relief, rehabilitation of social and physical infrastructure, the development of the fisheries sector, the restoration of moral and ethical standards in society and the distribution of house lots for low cost housing as well as to fight against corruption.

At the parliamentary level, two important pieces of legislation were laid and passed in the, National Assembly, they were the Integrity Legislation Bill and the Trade Union Recognition Bill.

In1998 due to unusually heavy rainfall, Guyana's coastal regions experienced serious flooding. Over35,000 residents were severely affected. President Jagan declared a State of Emergency in the affected areas and national and international assistance and relief for the affected communities was mobilized. Thanks to the tremendous political goodwill extended to the recently elected President, criticisms over government's ability to respond quickly were few and the administration was able to address the concerns of the people speedily and efficiently.

In 1999, President Jagan signed the Petroleum Exploration Agreement with ExxonMobil.

In accordance with a mandate of the Herdsmanston Accord, a Constitution Reform Commission was established. With the agreement of the opposition, Ralph Ramkarran, was appointed chairman of the Commission.

The PPP delegation to the Commission comprised of Reepu Daman Persaud, Sheik Feroze Mohammed, Ronald Gajraj, Bernard DeSantos, Philomena Sahoye-Shury, and Edward Rodney.

Later, in October 1998, Ronald Gajraj a former lieutenant of the Guyana Defence Force was appointed Minister of Home Affairs.

Consistent with the 'St. Lucia Statement', Maurice King, an Attorney-at-Law from Barbados was appointed Facilitator to initiate the political dialogue between the PPP and the PNC in accordance with the mandates contained in second stage of the Herdmanston Accord.

The talks between the two parties focused on Constitutional Reform and Electoral Reform.

Talks at the Constitutional Reform Commission examined the bicameral form of parliament, an executive, versus a titular president with enhanced responsibilities for the Prime Minister, the establishment of Select Committees of the National Assembly and an Inter-Party Committee on Electoral Reform (IPCER) with its main focus on the holding of local government elections before the next general and regional elections due in 2001.

Among the more important recommendations agreed to by the PPP was that no person should serve for more than two consecutive terms as President.

President Janet Jagan and I, participated in her first meeting of CARICOM Heads of Government at the Ninth Inter-Sessional meeting held in St. Georges, Grenada from 2-3 March 1998. At that meeting The Heads engaged in a discussion on the situation in Guyana following the December 15, election. In a 'Statement on Guyana' issued at the end of the meeting, the Heads; 'Called on the political leaders in Guyana to remain faithful to Accord (Herdsmanston) in all respects, and on all Guyanese to support them in this course They attached particular importance to the role of the minor political parties in this regard and have valued the consultations with them.' The Heads further 'Welcomed most warmly the indication from the President of Guyana that her government will proceed with the expeditious enactment of the enabling legislation now textually agreed between the two main parties so that the agreed audit may begin as envisaged.'

Finally, the Heads agreed that; 'The long-term resolution of Guyana's problems was for the people of Guyana; but CARICOM would keep watch with its member countries through the arduous process leading to reconciliation,'

On July 2, 1998, President Janet Jagan and I attended her second CARICOM Heads Government meeting this time, in Castries. St. Lucia. The President addressed the Opening Session of the conference. In her address, she thanked the outgoing Chairman of CARICOM for his "leading role in the efforts aimed at surmounting the post-elections problems in Guyana"

AN ILLUSIVE TRUCE

This was an extremely important meeting for Mrs. Jagan since we were in the midst of the crisis that had arisen from the December 15 election and the 'Herdsmanston

Process' seemed to be running aground because of the non-cooperation by Opposition Leader Desmond Hoyte. CARICOM leaders had invited Hoyte to the St. Lucia meeting as a matter of urgency and with the intention of encouraging him, along with President Jagan and the sitting Chairman of CARICOM to sign on to an agreed statement.

In the end, after a robust discussion on the political situation in Guyana and the way forward, agreement was reached on a draft statement. President Jagan and I met separately in a private room to go over the draft for comments. The President made some minor amendments to the draft which called for the Constitutional Reform process to get started, the establishment of standing committees in the National Assembly, enabling legislation to facilitate the opposition to assume their seats in the National Assembly, acceptance of a 'High Level Facilitator' to facilitate Political Dialogue between the two main political parties and their recommitment to the 'Herdsmanston Accord' The draft which eventually became known as 'The St. Lucia Statement." was adopted and signed by Janet Jagan, Desmond Hoyte and Kenny Anthony. The document eventually became known publicly as the 'St. Lucia Statement.'

ON THE CARICOM BEAT

President Jagan met briefly with President Caldera of Venezuela who had travelled to St. Lucia, to pay a good will visit to the Caribbean Community for an exchange of views with the leaders on the occasion of its twenty-fifth anniversary. It was at that brief meeting that agreement was reached between the two Presidents that President Jagan would pay an official visit to Venezuela in July 1998.

As per norm, the final communique issued at the conclusion of the St. Lucia conference, contained a paragraph on the status of Guyana/Venezuela relations. In the communique, the Heads of CARICOM; 'Reaffirmed their support for the territorial integrity and sovereignty of Guyana and desire for a peaceful settlement to the controversy between Guyana and Venezuela.'

While in Castries President Jagan took the opportunity to invite to breakfast with her, the outstanding and world-renowned St. Lucian Poet Laurate and Playwright Derek Walcott, whose celebrated works include 'Omeros', 'Dream on Monkey Mountain' and 'White Egrets.'

I was invited to listen in to the conversation which reminded me somewhat of a conversation Mrs. Jagan had some years ago with the famous Guyanese-born poet, novelist and playwright Jan Carew author of 'Black Midas', 'The Wild Coast,' 'Death Comes to the Circus,' 'Streets of Eternity,' 'Moscow is not my Mecca' and many more

At the time when we met Walcott, he was sixty-eight years of age, President Jagan was seventy- eight and I was forty-eight. I thoroughly enjoyed listening to the conversation of the two individuals; one a literary giant, the other well versed in the works of Walcott and other West Indian writers. As I listened to the conversation, I could not help recognizing the connection between poetry and literature and politics. In the end, I drew the conclusion that neither of the two were neutral politically nor ideologically.

JANET JAGAN REACHES OUT TO VENEZUELA

During her brief period in office, President Janet Jagan made successful State Visits to Venezuela from 22-23 July 1998, Suriname from 30-31 October 1998 and Brazil from19-22 May 1999. In addition, President Jagan led Guyana's delegation to the first European Union, Latin America and the Caribbean (EU/LAC) Summit held from 28 to 29 June 1999 in Rio de Janeiro, Brazil.

Apart from her official engagements, President Jagan continued the practice started by her late husband to meet with the Guyanese community in each country. Town hall inter-active sessions were held much to delight and satisfaction of the Guyanese community in those countries.

Over in Venezuela, elections were held in December 1993 after a period of political instability. The Social Christian Party (COPEI) led by Rafael Caldera won the elections. Caldera was one of the more conservative, right wing political leaders with strong connections to Venezuelan big business and big landowners. For years, elections in Venezuela have been like musical chairs between the Centre-right, Social Democratic, Accion Democratica Party led by Carlos Andres Perez and the COPEI led by Caldera. What was peculiar however, was the fact that irrespective of which of these two leaders were in power, Cheddi Jagan, without compromising his country's territorial integrity and sovereignty, was able to maintain friendly and cordial relations with the two Venezuelan leaders.

Three years after Caldera came to power, Janet Jagan was sworn in as President of Guyana having won the election in December 1997.

Miguel Angel Burelli Rivas was appointed Caldera's Foreign Minister in 1994. Burelli contested unsuccessfully, elections in Venezuela in 1968 and the 1973 as a Presidential Candidate. In the 1968 elections, his Democratic Republic Union (URD) in alliance with three other parties gained the third largest number of votes after COPEI and AD that had formed electoral alliances with other parties as well. By 1973, Burelli had formed a new political party called the National Opinion. Without entering into an alliance with any other party, Burelli contested the election held in that year as the Presidential Candidate of his National Opinion, but lost significantly moving from the third, to the sixth political force in Venezuela.

His electoral demise notwithstanding, Burelli emerged as a skilled lawyer, politician and diplomat. It is because of his political experience, legal expertise and probably other personal considerations that Caldera chose him to be his Foreign Minister

Burelli came to Guyana in March 1995.He seemed very affable, friendly, charismatic and confident of himself. During his brief stay in Georgetown, Burelli paid courtesy calls on President Janet Jagan and Prime Minister Samuel Hinds. He and I had long discussions.

In the course of our discussions and, as was to be expected, Burelli came with his pet subject - the globality concept tucked under his arms. After some diplomatic palavering, he laid his cards on the table. He wanted to talk about maritime delimitation, recovery of part of the Essequibo territory, and a leasing regime to be defined and the concept of 'Globality.'

Burelli came touting Venezuelan large-scale financial contributions for the 'joint development' of the Essequibo region 'in exchange for a practical proposal' for the settlement of the border controversy. In effect, this meant ceding Guyana's national territory to Venezuelan exchange for Venezuelan financial development assistance. What the Venezuelans had in mind was precisely what Caldera's predecessor, Carlos Andres Perez had advanced some years ago, which was, Venezuela's access to the Atlantic through Guyana's coastland. I concluded from this offer, that the Venezuelans, irrespective of which party was in power, had certain agreed bipartisan positions in respect to their ambitions to Guyana's waters in the Essequibo region and by extension, its spurious claim to two thirds of Guyana's national territory.

In August 1995, Venezuela pounced upon a cyanide spill from a tailings pond, property of a Canadian gold mining company, into a section of the Essequibo River. The Venezuelan government deemed the spill an 'irrational exploitation of the Essequibo region.' This was clearly another manifestation of Venezuela's spurious claim that Essequibo is part of their so-called "Zona de Reclamation.' Burelli did not hesitate in letting me know that environmental degradation in the Essequibo region "is of great concern to his government".

Burelli further put to me the suggestion that Guyana/Venezuela bilateral relations should be situated in future under the ambit of a concept he described as 'Globality.' I recall hearing President Caldera mention the word during his informal conversation with President Jagan when they met two years ago in Port-of-Spain in August 1995. Caldera had made a passing reference to the concept without providing any details. It appears that his Foreign Minister was given the task to elaborate on the details. According to Burelli, Venezuela envisages Globality as the principle under which Guyana/Venezuela future relations would be interlinked. In other words, Guyana/Venezuela future bilateral relations was to be subordinated to the concept of Globality.

I thanked the Minister for his presentation and requested further amplification of the Globality concept. In the latter half of 1996, Burelli submitted to me through diplomatic channels, a paper setting out his thoughts on the Globality concept entitled; 'Summary for a comprehensive approval for the re-orientation of relations between Guyana and Venezuela.' I responded to Burelli's submission in September of 1996 expressing my concern over his linking his Globality proposal to the McIntyre process. I nevertheless requested that officials from both sides meet to discuss the concept further as well as the practicalities for its implementation. Burelli did not respond to my request but I knew that the matter did not end there and that it would surface again.

In my brief to President Janet Jagan on Burelli's visit, I surmised that the Venezuelan Globality proposal was aimed at moving away from the Good Officer Process and to shift the border controversy away from the multilateral to a bilateral level. Further, I advised that Venezuela's 'Joint Development' of the Essequibo proposal had as its fundamental objectives, first, a permanent presence of Venezuelan personnel in the Essequibo region and secondly, access to the Atlantic through Guyana's coastland which could only happen if Guyana were to cede part of its national territory to Venezuela in exchange for financial development assistance. I reminded the President that historically, Guyana had opposed Venezuelan's economic strategy of 'Joint development'.

Janet Jagan together with a small delegation including me, arrived in Caracas on 21, July 1998 at the start of a three-day visit to Venezuela. Apart from the prolocular aspects of the visit, President Jagan had meetings with the Venezuelan Chamber of Commerce, the Venezuelan Investment Fund and Petroleum Venezuela. The President had two rounds of meetings with President Caldera. Burelli and I sat in at those meetings. A draft communique was formulated for the agreement of the two Presidents. President Jagan passed her copy of the draft to me for my comments.

The text of the communique was generally innocuous, save for three paragraphs that caught my attention. The first was a paragraph which spoke to '…the sustainable management of the environment…' and that 'Both Presidents agreed that under the aegis of the McIntyre process Guyana and Venezuela will initiate negotiations leading to an agreement on environmental matters.'

The second matter had to do with a paragraph that read; '…In an effort to accelerate the promotion of bilateral relations, the Presidents agreed to adopt an integral and global approach to the bilateral agenda and to establish an integral framework for consultation and cooperation'.

And thirdly, was a paragraph that referred to '…the establishment of joint enterprises for the processing and marketing of living marine resources.

I immediately recognized the handiwork of my Venezuelan counterpart in the three paragraphs in which he managed to slip in the matters he had raised with me at our meetings in Georgetown. I drew the paragraphs to the President's attention, but she did not raise any objections, she simply reminded me that 'the devil is usually in the details.' I kept my opinions to myself. And though the Guyanese officials and Ambassador Karran knew what my views were I nevertheless instructed them to signal to their Venezuelan counterparts that the greenlight was given to prepare the document for signature.

At the conclusion of her of her official visit, President Jagan was awarded the Order of the Liberator – one of Venezuela's highest national awards. She then flew to the State of Bolivar where she met hundreds of Guyanese residents in the cities of San Felix and Puerto Ordaz to brief them about the developments in Guyana and the policies of the new PPP/C government. The reception Mrs. Jagan received was amazing as it was overwhelming.

Back home, the local media made a hue and cry over what was agreed concerning the environment. A total misinformation campaign was launched especially by Stabroek News in an effort to disparage the President's visit and her knowledge of the intricacies of Guyana/Venezuela relations.

At a press conference held to report on her visit, the President dealt effectively with the bits and pieces of misinformation that was being peddled in sections of the local media. The President made it clear that no agreement was made to monitor the environment in the Essequibo in collaboration with Venezuela nor to consult with Venezuela before granting any concession to foreign investors in Guyana's mining and forestry sectors.

Approximately four months after President Jagan's return to Guyana, President Caldera while on an official visit to Brazil in November 1998 made a public statement declaring that Venezuela would not renounce its rightful claim to the Essequibo. No doubt this was aimed at sending a signal to Brazil who had always stood by Guyana in support of its territorial integrity and national sovereignty. Moreover, I assumed from his statement, that the Venezuelan President was sending a message to CARICOM leaders who, at every one of their summits, found it necessary to include in their communiques support for Guyana's territorial integrity and national sovereignty.

SURINAME AHOY!

President Janet Jagan's visit to Suriname in October 1998, was organized to coincide with the inauguration of the EU- funded Guyana Suriname ferry service the MV Canawima that linked Guyana with Suriname. A communique issued at the end of the official visit listed three priority areas for

implementation namely; the resuscitation of the Guyana/Suriname Cooperation Council, convening of meetings of the National Border Commissions and the conclusion of a Guyana/Suriname Fisheries Agreement. It is interesting to note that between 1998 and 2000 very little was accomplished owing to a combination of two factors. First, was the political instability in Guyana stemming from legal challenges and the efforts at destabilization by the PNC following the December 1997 elections. Secondly, was the intransigence on the part of the Surinamese to cooperate notwithstanding the efforts by the Guyanese authorities. What was ironical however is that in 2000, a series of events would push Guyana and Suriname to return to the very three issues.

President Janet Jagan taking the salute with President of Suriname -1998

Following her official engagements in Paramaribo, Presidents Jagan and Wijdenbosch of Suriname travelled to Nickerie to jointly launch the ferry service on Saturday October 31,1998 President Jagan traveled to Guyana on the ferry's

353

inaugural journey across the Corentyne river to arrive at Moleson Creek, East Berbice.

CHANGES IN VENEZUELA

Hugo Chavez, came to power in Venezuela in December1998 after an attempted coup in 1992 and a Presidential Pardon granted by President Caldera in 1994. His political party called the Movement of the Fifth Republic won 56 per cent of the votes. In keeping with her policy that her government be represented at the inauguration of South American Presidents, President Janet Jagan, accompanied by me and Ambassador Karran attended the inauguration in Caracas of President Chavez on February 4, 1999. President Jagan had the honour of being the first Head of State to hold talks with the newly inaugurated President. Sitting in on their conversation, I discerned a certain chemistry between the two individuals that could be characterized as mutual respect, a sense of genuine friendship and camaraderie.

President Janet Jagan meets with President Chavez in Caracas - 1998

President Chavez appointed Jose Vincent Rangel his Foreign Minister in February 1999. By March 30, of the same year, Rangel was in Georgetown. Rangel made unsuccessful bids for the presidency of Venezuela at three successive elections in held in 1973, 1978 and 1983 as the presidential candidate for three different pro-socialist political parties. Though an active politician, Rangel is a lawyer and journalist by profession. He wrote for a number of different newspapers in Venezuela.

During his one-day visit to Guyana, Rangel was accompanied by a number of key government and parliamentary officials. Rangel met with President Janet Jagan and former President Hoyte. The newly-minted Venezuelan Foreign Minister and I, signed the Terms of Reference for the Guyana/Venezuela High Level Bilateral Commission (HLBC), that was agreed upon during President Jagan's visit to Venezuela. We also initialled the Final Act outlining the Work Programme of the various sub-committees falling under the HLBC. Co-incidentally, it was while Rangel was in Georgetown, that President Jagan signed an agreement awarding a number of petroleum exploration blocks to ExxonMobil.

From all indications, it seemed to me at the time, that it was the signing of that agreement, no doubt, that caused Foreign Minister Rangel, soon after his visit, to despatch a letter to me and Mr. McIntyre protesting the granting of concessions by Guyana in the Essequibo and, at the same time, claiming that Guyana was 'ignoring its obligations under the Geneva Agreement.'

Rangel made it clear that he will initiate negotiations with Guyana on environmental matters and that he has adopted the global approach to the Guyana/Venezuela bilateral agenda.

By September 1999, Sir Alister McIntyre had resigned. He was replaced by Sir Oliver Jackman who achieved nothing followed by Prof. Norman Girvan who suffered a similar fate in their respective roles as Good Officer.

At the end of her visits to the neighboring countries, Joint Communiques were issued and details of bilateral agreements signed were published in the local press.

President Jagan participated actively at many important meetings and conferences held in Latin American countries such as Argentina, Chile, the Dominican

Republic, Bolivia and Peru as well as well at CARICOM Heads of Government Conferences in a number of CARICOM member countries.

JANET JAGAN: THE LATIN AMERICANISTA

President Janet Jagan was an ardent supporter of Guyana's integration with both CARICOM and Latin America. It was with her support that I successfully navigated Guyana's association with the Rio Group, a Latin American and Caribbean political consultative grouping in which Guyana became a full member; Mercosul, a Latin American trading block in which Guyana was accredited Observer Status, ALADI, a South American Integration Association within which Guyana developed a close working relationship, and Parlatino - The Latin American Parliament in which President Jagan participated at one of its sittings in La Paz, Bolivia.

The strategic approach for advancing her government's interest to bring Guyana closer to the continental nations was formulated by Ambassadors Bayney Karan and Satyadeo Sawh, then Ambassadors to the OAS and Venezuela respectively, and me, with technical inputs from staff at the Ministry of Foreign Affairs.

President Janet Jagan with Venezuela President Caldera & With President Cardoso of Brazil

The strategic approach, was developed in accordance with President Jagan government's stated policy to actively pursue bilateral and multilateral relations with Latin American countries.

That policy was reflected in the Government of Guyana being represented at the inauguration of newly elected Presidents in Latin America.

One of our greatest accomplishments in the advancement of our Latin American diplomacy was our accession to membership in the Rio Group. I saw the importance of pushing to accomplish this goal in light of the strategic direction President Jagan had given to the Foreign Ministry.

The leadership role of the PPP/C government in regional and hemispheric affairs shone through when Guyana was assigned the role of spokesman for CARICOM in the Rio Group.

But this was only the beginning, more was to come.

At the 11th Summit meeting of Heads of State of the Rio Group held in Asunción, capital of Paraguay, in September 1997, I made a presentation to the meeting on Guyana's call for a New Global Human Order. My presentation was facilitated, thanks to the support extended by the Brazilian Foreign Ministry who ensured that it was included as an agenda item for the meeting.

At the end of my presentation, I appealed to the Leaders present to support the call. Fortunately for me, documents explaining the subject had been despatched to the Foreign Ministries of the Rio Group countries well in advance of the meeting, as such, there was little explaining to do since the Presidents from all appearances, had been fully briefed on the subject.

In the circumstances, the call was approved by the Presidents for onward transmission to the Office of the Secretary General of the United Nations for consideration. It was left to Guyana's Permanent Mission to the UN, to follow-up with the Permanent Missions of the Rio Group and to ensure that the matter was pursued.

President Janet Jagan attended the Summit meeting of the Rio Group held the following year in September 1998 in Panama City.

The Panama Meeting was dominated by discussions on the impact of the Mexican 'Tequila Crisis' and the global financial crisis that was wreaking havoc in Asia, Latin America and the USA. Proposals such as the 'dollarization of the Mexican peso' were advanced for discussion elsewhere with a view to resolving the crisis. A follow-up meeting was planned to be held in Mexico the following year.

Unfortunately, due to the difficult political situation at home as well as internal party discussions on transitional arrangements, President Jagan could not make it to the following Rio Group Summit that was held in 1999 in the Mexican port city of Vera Cruz, in the State of Vera Cruz, Mexico. I was asked to represent her at that meeting.

Both meetings served to strengthen Guyana's relations with the key players in South America.

Since the death of President Cheddi Jagan, the intellectual author of the call for a New Global Order, the support garnered for the Call at councils of major Latin American gatherings, was considered a significant diplomatic achievement for Guyana in its drive to promote the Call at various international fora. Thanks to the visionary leadership of President Janet Jagan we were able to accomplish this signal achievement.

As she pressed ahead with her Latin America Agenda, I recall the occasion when President Jagan enjoyed enormously, her participation at the first joint meeting between the Heads of State of the Rio Group and the European Union held in Rio de Janeiro, Brazil in June, 1999. This was to be her second visit to Brazil.

That meeting was organized with the aim of institutionalizing the European Union - Latin America and Caribbean Consultative Mechanism known as the EU-LAC Mechanism. It also served as a forum for political dialogue between the leader's present.

At the conclusion of the meeting, President Jagan expressed an interest to visit the colossal statue of Christ the Redeemer at the summit of Mount Corcovado.

The Brazilian President at that time, Fernando Henrique Cardoso, cautioned her about climbing the stairs to reach the summit since her vehicle could only take her up to a certain point, after which she would have to proceed on foot. Mrs. Jagan insisted saying she would make it.

And she did! She was happy she was able to achieve what appeared to be a life-long dream, but the exhaustion that came following the climb, had a toll on her ability stay up for the rest of the day.

Next day, President Jagan was back on her feet and in the evening, she was at the famous Veloso Restaurant and Bar, located Rua Aristides Espinola, Leblon in Rio where the well-known Brazilian composer, Antonio Carlos Jobim sang his popular "Girl from Ipanema."

President Jagan never ate much nor drank alcohol, but she enjoyed the company around her, the ambience and the history of the place where she happened to be at the time.

THE PRESIDENT FALLS ILL

On our return trip to Guyana from Rio, President Jagan fell ill on the aircraft. A medical doctor on board was summoned, he recommended that during our scheduled stop-over-stop at Port-of- Spain that she be hospitalized for short while medical tests are carried out. This is precisely what occurred when the aircraft arrived at Port-of-Spain. The President deplaned and was taken away by ambulance. I continued on my way to Georgetown.

As result of her illness, President Jagan was unable to participate in the 20th Session of the meeting of conference of CARICOM Heads of Government held in Port-of-Spain Trinidad and Tobago from 4-7 July 1999. I was mandated to represent Guyana at this meeting.

In its final communique, issued at the end of the conference, the Heads gathered at the conference wished the Guyanese President well and a speedy recovery

Under the Janet Jagan Administration, Guyana's bilateral and multilateral relations with CARICOM member states were strengthened after responsibility for CARICOM Affairs was added to my portfolio responsibilities.

Joint Economic and Technical Cooperation Commissions with Jamaica, Barbados and Trinidad and Tobago were established. Trade missions were despatched to a number of CARICOM countries as well as to the Dominican Republic to promote Guyanese products and to encourage bilateral trade between Guyana and other member states. A trade office was established in Port- of-Spain in Trinidad and Tobago.

Our diplomatic missions, consulates and Honorary Consuls were given specific instructions to promote our foreign trade and economic interests from the capitals where they are located.

On the home front, in early 1998, President Jagan and I, along with the Chinese Ambassador travelled to Lethem in the Rupununi to lay the cornerstone at the site for the construction of the Chinese funded Moco Moco run-of-the-river hydroelectric power station. On its completion in November 1999 the power station was commissioned by President Bharat Jagdeo.

President Jagan was at ease with the Chinese. She had visited China in August 1962 where she met with Chinese President and Chairman Mao Tse Tung and Chou en Lai the Chinese Premier. Thirty-four years later, in June 1996 she returned to China as head of a party delegation to that country.

Electricity generated from the Moco Moco mini-hydro power station, albeit for the few years brought great relief to the residents in the community. Not too long after, disaster struck with the collapse of the station because of a mudslide.

JANET JAGAN MEETS MANDELA

The President and I attended many CARICOM meetings together but the most enjoyable, if not interesting one for me was the 19th meeting of the Heads of Government conference held in St. Lucia from June 30 to July 4,1998.

At that meeting, President Nelson Mandela of the Republic of South Africa, was invited to address the Heads of Government, however, before doing so, a caucus of Heads plus one was held with President Mandela along with Alfred Nzo his Foreign Minister. I was present as the 'Plus One' as Foreign Minister.

President Nelson Mandela

Two matters of interest arose in the course of the discussion, both were initiated by Guyana long before at previous meetings of CARICOM Foreign Ministers.

The first had to do with a request to have a South African embassy established in one of the CARICOM countries but the question was, which member state was the most suitable location. I made a case for Guyana, stating that Georgetown would be a suitable location in view of the fact that Guyana was the host country for the CARICOM Secretariat and further, that economically it would be less costly to have a mission established in Guyana.

Jamaica expressed a strong interest in hosting the South African mission and since I had an interest in another pending matter I backed away from my earlier position and supported the appeal by our Jamaican friends

President Mandela's response to the matter was in typical Mandelian style. He pointed out that while he was incarcerated at Robbin Island, he received a letter from a small girl from a village in South Africa who asked him to promise her that on his release he will provide drinking water to her home and her village. Mandela told his CARICOM colleagues that since his release he fulfilled the girl's request, and that he is pursuing similar projects across South Africa. He emphasized that that was one of his priorities.

The message was subtle, but nevertheless, had its desired impact. Although President Mandela didn't say it, it was clear that the establishment of new South African embassies at various countries was not a priority for his administration. I looked across at President Jagan, we nodded at each other in agreement with Mandela.

The other matter had to do with a request that South African Airways consider stopping over at one the CARICOM country's international airports en route to North America.

President Mandela responded stating that although South African Airways is a state-owned enterprise, its Board of Directors will have to consider such a request. The Heads appeared satisfied with the responses from the South African leader.

Apart from an exchange of views on CARICOM-South Africa relations in particular, and with Africa in general the meeting ended on a cordial note with expressions of solidarity and mutually beneficial support as well as for the need to foster closer ties between CARICOM and South Africa.

Years later, a South African Embassy was established in Kingston, Jamaica, that embassy is accredited to Guyana, but in-transit, stop-overs by South African Airways at an international airport in a CARICOM country never materialized.

MEETING CASTRO

President Janet Jagan met with Fidel Castro briefly on three occasions, first was in Caracas in July,1998 for the inauguration of Hugo Chavez; in the Dominican Republic in August, 1998 for a conference of Heads of Government of CARIFORUM countries and in Rio de Janeiro, Brazil, in June 1999 for a Summit of European Union/Latin America and the Caribbean leaders. Her encounters with Castro were more perfunctory and informal rather than business-like and of a serious nature. While in opposition between the 1973 to 1985 period, Mrs. Jagan's attitude towards the Cuban government changed from being enthusiastic to nonchalant due to the active support the Cuban government had extended to the oppressive and dictatorial Burnham regime that had rigged elections for decades to hold on to political power in Guyana. However, the response from the Cubans while being diplomatically correct, at the same time, they nevertheless maintained fraternal relations with the PPP, a relationship which the PPP did not shun.

On September 22, 1999, President Janet Jagan addressed the 53rd Session of the United Nations General Assembly. She had arrived in New York accompanied by her Political Advisor, Mr. Kellawan Lall. I had arrived in NY a few days before to help with the programme for her visit.

President Janet Jagan addresses United Nations General Assembly & meets with the UN Secretary General Kofi Annan – 1998

Photos:Courtesy UN/DPI photo by Greg Kinch

In her address to the General Assembly, President Jagan pointed out; "The democratic system has emerged as a popular form of government for many member states of the United Nations. Guyana has rejoined this growing majority.

Unfortunately, this had to come after hard struggles and our people experienced three decades of lost opportunities under an undemocratic regime".

Turning her attention to the prevailing international situation at the time, President Jagan stressed; "Guyana has come a far way in over-coming poverty and maximising its full growth and potential. As such we continue to rely heavily on external assistance for our economic development. We are therefore particularly concerned by the rapid diminution of resources available for financing by both bilateral donors and multilateral agencies". President Jagan suggested to the world body that "Only through the establishment enlightened cooperation can the world enjoy the blessings of peace. I wish to therefore renew the plea by Dr, Jagan who called for an early agreement of a more just and equitable system of international relations"

While in New York, President Jagan addressed a huge gathering of Guyanese nationals at York College in New York where she updated them and answered many questions on the situation in Guyana. She also delivered lectures at Princeton and Columbia Universities on 'New and Restored Democracies - The Guyana Experience'

A TRIUMPH OF MULTILATERAL DIPLOMACY FOR GUYANA

Multilateral diplomacy is greater teacher of the ways and means of striking compromises, making accommodation and winning friends over to your side to take a stand on a matter that is close to the soul of the nation. Having spent years on the CARICOM circuit, I came to recognize the efficacy of multilateral diplomacy as an effective tool to advance Guyana's interest at other levels. The lesson learnt was not to sit, listen and learn or to file reports and to make diplomatically, nicely worded statements and or speeches. On the contrary, the most fundamental of all is how and when to apply what has been learnt to your own national circumstances given the realities and peculiarities obtaining at the time as well as the historical background to the issue at hand.

It was from this perspective that I formed the opinion that the governing PPP/C should take its quest to safeguard Guyana's territorial integrity in the face of a threat from its western neighbour to another level. My idea was to set up a type of contact group of member country of the Commonwealth to receive reports and to monitor the evolving status of our relations with Venezuela. From that perspective, a much wider and greater area of support and solidarity would be leveraged in favour of Guyana from like-minded countries in the Commonwealth of nations.

As I saw it, what is done at Caricom summit meetings, whereby reports on Guyana/Venezuela relations are provided to Heads, could be done at other multilateral gatherings where Guyana is a member in good standing. Commonwealth Summit meetings were, in my view, an appropriate forum where Guyana's interests can be safeguarded. All that was required was the necessary diplomatic legwork.

My first step towards the achievement of this goal, was to brainstorm the idea with top officials at the Ministry of Foreign Affairs, our Permanent Representative to the UN (PR-NY), and our High Commissioner in London (HC-London) to get their inputs and approval. When that was secured, I then proceeded to discuss the matter with the President, then to put the proposal for consideration and approval to the National Security Committee, the Central Intelligence Committee, the Defence Board and thence to Cabinet. Having gotten the proposal approved with some amendments all the way through, the next step was to despatch letters to PR-NY and HC-London advising them on the steps to be taken in pursuit of the matter.

The mechanism proposed to be established was a 'Commonwealth Ministerial Monitoring Group on Guyana/Venezuela Relations' The composition of the Group would be; Antigua and Barbuda, Bangla Desh, Belize, Canada, South Africa and the UK. Letters addressed to my counterparts in these countries were to be despatched explaining the proposal and requesting their support for the initiative. My suggestion to the Ministers was that we utilize the ECOSOC meeting during the 54th Session of the UN General Assembly (GA) to meet to address any issue they may wish to have clarified. I recommended to PR-NY that in furtherance of this initiative, meetings be arranged first bilaterally, and then collectively with the Ministers and Ambassadors of the six countries present at the GA to brief them about the proposal.

The meeting during the ECOSOC as well as the bilateral came off successfully. The stage was now set to advance the process, with an eye to the Commonwealth Heads of Government Meeting scheduled to be held in Durban, South Africa in November 1999.

ON THE HOME FRONT

Some time in 1998, President Jagan requested me to submit to her my recommendations to fill vacancies at the level of Heads of four of our diplomatic missions overseas. Following consultations at the political and Foreign Ministry levels, I recommended that Cheryl Miles be posted to Brazil as Ambassador, Critchlow to Cuba as Ambassador, Rajnarine Singh to Ottawa as High Commissioner, Danny Doobay to Toronto as Consul General, and Gail Lee to Brussels as Charge d'Affaires. President Jagan agreed with the recommendations after I pointed out to her that my recommendations reflected a good balance between the political and career appointees as well as gender and ethnicity which in a Guyanese context are   important factors in respect to local politics and public perception. The matter was taken to Cabinet as recommendations from the Office of the President and was approved.

Meanwhile, notwithstanding the PPP/C's efforts to stick to the time frame for implementing the Herdmanston Accord and the commitments made by the President and the Opposition Leader at St, Lucia, the Constitutional talks dragged on. Thus, with every passing day, it became clear that, at the Inter-party dialogue process, the PNC was not interested in local government elections being held before the next general elections due in 2001.

The PPP for its part, was keen on holding local government elections using the 1992 voters list and with a reconstituted GECOM. The Party recommended a fast track approach to the local government elections.

President Janet Jagan was of the view that local government elections should be held before the next general elections.

In fact, the PPP had agreed to proceed with local government elections in 1998 but the PNC called for the postponement of the elections to a later date on the ground that general and regional elections were too close.

Meanwhile, at the level of the inter- party dialogue the opposition PNC kept insisting that government policies should be formulated and settled within the meaning of the dialogue process, this was opposed by the PPP on the ground that government policies should be formulated and settled constitutionally by cabinet, although consultations on specific issues may be held from time to time and wherever necessary, before a Bill is laid in the National Assembly for consideration and approval.

At some point in time during the inter-party talks it was agreed that the CARICOM facilitator be present during the talks.

Among the agreements reached in the talks was the establishment of an inter-party body on reform of local government system.

By July 1999, the work of the Constitution Commission came to an end. The next step was to take the Report of the Commission to the National Assembly for consideration and approval.

JANET JAGAN STEPS DOWN

In early August 1999, President Janet Jagan indicated to the party's leadership her desire to resign as President of Guyana. Her reasons were that she did not have the strength carry on and was unable to offer vigorous leadership which the office demanded. Her failing health was offered as another reason. And even though she made no mention of it, it was clear to many that the hysteria which the political opposition had generated over her colour and Jewish-American origin were factors that had contributed to her decision to resign.

The President was of the view that with her resignation, the political situation would be better for the party and government if she goes.

In an address to the nation on August 8, 1999, Janet Jagan announced of her decision to resign. The announcement was more than the routine 'Breaking News' it came as a shock to thousands of party, members, supporters and sympathizers. In her address, Mrs. Jagan stated;

"The time has come for me to take a decision; I have been considering over the past month… I, therefore, wish to announce, that I intend to resign my position as President and to fulfill the promise I made during the 1997 election campaign." President Jagan went on;

"At the time, the PPP/Civic had announced the concept of the 'A' Team, made up of myself, Prime Minister Samuel Hinds and Finance Minister Bharrat Jagdeo. It was stated at public meetings and through campaign material that should anything happen to the President, clear cut means would be used to replace the President by the third member of the 'A' Team, Bharrat Jagdeo, with the Prime Minister retaining his position in the post allotted to the Civic Component of the PPP/Civic alliance... Dr Jagan brought dignity to this country. So did Mr. Samuel Hinds..."

Many Guyanese at home and abroad were in a state of disbelief. There was widespread anger and disgust over the way she was treated by a disgruntled political opposition as a democratically elected president, as a fighter for Guyana's independence and as a champion for women's rights and as outstanding leader of the PPP.

History would show that apart from the 1962 to 1964 period, the 1997 to 1999 period was one of the more difficult periods for the PPP while in government.

In both instances, Janet Jagan was forced to resign, first as Minister of Home Affairs in June 1963 while the PPP was in government and fifty-seven years later, this time as President of Guyana while the PPP was in government.

Janet Jagan resigned on August 8, 1999. Sam Hinds was sworn in as President and Bharat Jagdeo as Prime Minister.

Janet Jagan's elected tenure was to last from December 1997 to December 2001. However, in light of the Herdmanston Accord, her tenure would now last from December 1997 to December 1999. Mrs. Jagan resigned in August 1997 four months earlier.

Just a few days after, Sam Hinds resigned as President and on August 11, 1999 Jagdeo was sworn as President of Guyana. Sam was sworn in as Prime Minister on the same day.

The transition of process was smooth and uneventful. The ship of state was back on even keel.

Janet Jagan remained in Executive and Central Committees of the Party where she continued to play a leading role in the party.

Mrs. Jagan could be seen at party headquarters up to the time of her death.

THE JAGDEO PRESIDENCY

It is not my intention in this chapter to do a critical review of the Jagdeo administration nor to chronicle the achievements while he served out the remaining two years and his two consecutive five-year terms as President of Guyana.

I leave that task to others.

Suffice it to say that Bharat Jagdeo assumed the presidency at a time when the economy was reeling from blows because of the impact of the strike and the arbitral award to public servants.

President Bharrat Jagdeo : 1999 - 2011

On top of that, the high cost of servicing the foreign debt continued to be a millstone around the neck of the nation.

During the remaining two years of the 1997 elections victory, the Jagdeo administration maintained basically, the same domestic and foreign policy orientation as the previous three PPP/C administrations.

Issues such as privatization of public enterprises came the fore. However, because of the controversial nature of the subject, it generated a great amount of public interest as well as internal debates in the party and government.

Problems with the sugar industry began to crop up with the looming discontinuation of subsidies from the European Union and the uneconomic performance of some sugar estates.

Long before, the bauxite industry had been showing signs of a possible collapse with the consequence of thousands of workers being thrown onto the breadline. The toxic mix of race and politics at the bauxite mining town had come to a boiling point.

The negotiations with Saskpower fell though the cracks because of the volatile and unstable political situation that continued to prevail like a hangover from the Janet Jagan administration.

General and Regional elections were due in 2001, a mere year and a half after Janet Jagan's resignation.

Implementation of the agreements reached in the Herdsmanston Accord were still incomplete.

The PNC had agreed to discuss race relations but eventually adopted a foot dragging attitude on the subject.

They refused to participate in the Special Select Committee on Constitutional Reform

It was indeed trying times.

The results of the election in 2001 was again challenged in the court by the opposition PNC this time to block the swearing in of the new president.

The court eventually threw out the matter and, on August 11, 1999 Jagdeo was sworn in as the 7th Executive President of Guyana.

This experience marked the sixth occasion when the PNC, in collaboration with local and/or external reactionary forces sought to either block or interrupt the PPP's democratically elected right to govern the nation.

The first occasion was in1953 when, after just 133 days in office, the British colonial power suspended the constitution and sent troops to remove the PPP from office.

The second occasion was in 1964 when, after seven years in office, the British and American governments, at that time, conspired to remove the PPP from office on the ground that it posed a so-called 'communist threat.' to the hemisphere.

After twenty-three years in government, there was a further interruption of the PPP/C's rule. when the APNU/AFC 'won' the May 2015 regional and general elections, the result of which was contested in court by the PPP/C by way of an elections petition which after five years have not been heard.

It is my considered opinion that the 1964 to 1992 and the 2015 to 2020 periods respectively, were both aberrations of the democratic political process in British Guiana and later, Guyana

AS FOREIGN MINISTER UNDER JAGDEO

The remainder of the PPP/C's five-year term was completed with Bharat Jagdeo as President while I continued as Minister of Foreign Affairs. Those remaining two years were characterized by emphasis on border matters, multilateral and bilateral affairs with a discernible shift to economic, financial and foreign trade matters.

THE SURINAMESE ATTACK

It was during this period, that on June 3, 2000 to be exact, a Surinamese gunboat expelled a CGX, Canadian-owned petroleum exploration vessel from territorial waters within Guyana's maritime boundaries.

Suriname claimed that the vessel was operating within its EEZ. The forced expulsion of the exploration vessel resulted in heightened tension between the two neighboring countries.

In 1998, Guyana had exercised its sovereign right by granting to CGX Resources Incorporated, a licence to conduct offshore petroleum exploration in an area within its maritime boundaries – as stipulated in the 1977 Maritime Boundary act of Guyana.

The Government of Guyana deemed Suriname's action as an act of aggression against a fellow Caricom country and began to press for a resolution within a CARICOM multilateral setting.

Suriname on the other hand, wanted the dispute to be treated with as a bilateral matter. We rejected their proposal but later, after a flurry of exchanges of diplomatic notes, summoning the Surinamese Ambassador to the Foreign Ministry followed by consultations between the Guyanese and Surinamese Presidents, we agreed to engage Suriname in bilateral discussions within the ambit of CARICOM. Our bottom-line was to find a peaceful resolution of the dispute while at the same time, holding steadfastly to the protection of Guyana's territorial integrity and national sovereignty.

Guyana's relations with Suriname has been plagued by issues from licencing of Guyanese fishermen to ply and to fish in the Corentyne river, to crime fighting, determining the maritime boundaries between the two countries and the source of the Corentyne River as well as the land boundaries between the two countries. These were some of the controversial matters that surfaced in the ensuing bilateral discussions between the two sides.

Based on an exchange of diplomatic notes between the Foreign Ministries of Guyana and Suriname and later, conversations between Presidents Jagdeo and

Wijdenbosch it was agreed that high level representatives led by the Foreign Ministers would engage in negotiations with a view to arriving at recommendations for submission to their respective presidents.

In a note verbal despatched to the Surinamese Foreign Ministry on June 2, 2000 the Government of Guyana stated that it remained favourably disposed to engage in dialogue either at the bilateral or multilateral levels with a view to addressing any misunderstandings that may exist on the Surinamese side concerning the common maritime boundary between Guyana and Suriname. The Government of Guyana extended an invitation for the Government of Suriname to send a high-level delegation to Georgetown within twenty-four hours to commence dialogue '…. on these and other related matters.'

On June 3, 2000, President Jagdeo despatched a letter to Denzil Douglas, Prime Minister of St. Kitts-Nevis and the then Chairman of CARICOM, bringing to his attention the situation which had arisen between Guyana and Suriname.

In his letter, Jagdeo reminded Douglas, that following the decision by CARICOM Heads at their 6th Intersessional meeting held in February 1995 in Belize, which approved Suriname's application to join the Caribbean Community and Common Market, a commitment was made "To make every effort towards the resolution of the Suriname-Guyana border controversy as well other outstanding difficulties which impede the development of relations between the two countries"

The Guyanese President called on the Chairman of CARICOM to "Use his Good Office to take what ever action he deemed appropriate at the political and diplomatic levels consistent with the decisions of Heads".

The first round of discussions between the Foreign Ministers of Guyana and Suriname was held on June 6,2000 in Port-of-Spain, Trinidad and Tobago. The Surinamese delegation was led by its Foreign Minister, Errol Snijders while I led the Guyanese delegation. Both of us were accompanied by a number of high- level functionaries from several government agencies and departments in Georgetown and Paramaribo.

That meeting dealt with a number of houses keeping matters such as Guyana's proposal to establish a Joint Technical Committee to draft a Memorandum of

Understanding pertaining to the granting of petroleum licences by Guyana and Suriname within the area of the North Eastern and North Western seaward boundaries of Guyana and Suriname respectively.

The Port-of-Spain meeting also dealt with schedules for future meetings, venues for future meetings and recording the decisions of all meetings.

The elements of cordiality and acquaintances between the two delegations was shrouded by feelings of suspicion and skepticism on both sides.

The second round of discussions were held in Georgetown from 13 to 14 of June 2000. The venue was Herdmanston House in Queenstown. The Surinamese delegation was led by its Minister of Foreign Affairs, Errol Snijders and included; Errol Alibux, the Minister of Natural Resources as well as other high-ranking functionaries in the Surinamese administration.

These discussions did not get very far since the Surinamese delegation from all appearances, began to dig in their heels. Suriname proposed that Guyana revoke the licence that it had issued to CGX and that Suriname in turn would re-issue the licence. Guyana for its part proposed joint sharing of the resources and rejected the Surinamese proposal regarding the revocation of the licence to CGX.

The Georgetown meeting was inconclusive. Suriname was presented with a document entitled; "The Basic Elements of the Guyana Proposal" which in effect captured the basics of our proposal submitted to the Surinamese delegation at the Port-of-Spain meeting.

The third round of negotiations were held in Paramaribo, Suriname from 17 to18 June 2000.

With former Foreign Minister R. Jackson, Former Suriname Foreign Minister E. Snijders & the negiotiating team in Parimaribo.

The Surinamese delegation remained basically the same, but the Guyanese delegation was expanded to include; Rashleigh Jackson, Former Minister of Foreign Affairs, Dr. Barton Scotland, Attorney-at-law and consultant on the Convention on the Law of the Sea, Brian Sucre and Newell Dennison of the Guyana Geology and Mines Commission, Ambassadors Elisabeth Harper, Donald

Abrams and Rudy Collins of the Ministry of Foreign Affairs, Commander Gary Best and Col. Chabilall Ramsaroop of the Guyana Defence Force, and Mr. R. Jaggarnauth, technical expert on boundary affairs from our Department of Lands and Surveys.

Our delegation put forward additional proposals which included designating the area in dispute as a 'Special Area for the Sustainable Development of Guyana and Suriname' and the establishment of an 'Inter-governmental Guyana/Suriname Authority' which would manage the area pending a settlement of the maritime boundary between the two countries.

By this time, the hard liners in the Surinamese delegation desirous of playing to the national gallery attempted to gain the upper-hand. They became increasingly assertive in their demand that a totally new and unrelated question of the New River Triangle be included as an integral part of the negotiations.

Suriname's approach was not surprising since throughout the negotiations it was hinting at the so-called 'package approach.' The Guyana delegation wasted no time in rejecting Suriname's insertion of a totally unrelated matter into the negotiations.

Holding fast to its mandate which had evolved to the issue of joint exploration of resources and which it had placed on the table during the negotiations in Georgetown, the Guyanese delegation further advanced the concept of joint exploration and utilization of resources by suggesting that a management and administrative structure, composed of qualified experts and specialists from Guyana and Suriname have oversight of the joint project.

From all appearances, Suriname had no answer to Guyana's constructive proposals, backed into a corner therefore, the Surinamese resorted to the New River Triangle issue knowing that it would be a contentious nature hoping perhaps, that Guyana would fall into the trap of negotiating border problems rather than how to jointly explore and share in the petroleum resources. Moreover, there was some talk that the Surinamese consciously inserted that issue to bring an end to the negotiations.

The Guyanese delegation returned home empty-handed. The cabinet was briefed on the state of play up to that point in time. Our proposal on joint exploration and joint sharing of petroleum resources in the disputed area were approved by cabinet and instructions were given to pursue the proposal at any future engagement.

Before the next round of negotiations came around, the 21st Summit of CARICOM Heads of Government held their Meeting in of Conference in July 2000 in Canuan, St. Vincent and the Grenadines under the chairmanship of the then Prime Minister Sir James Mitchell.

Our delegation was led by President Jagdeo, myself as Foreign Minister, Elizabeth Harper and Keith George of the Ministry of Foreign Affairs, and Dr. Roger Luncheon, Head of the Presidential Secretariat.

The Surinamese delegation was led by President Wijdenbosch accompanied by his Foreign Minister and other officials.

President Jagdeo briefed Heads of CARICOM in Caucus about Guyana's position on the controversy. He thanked CARICOM for playing the role of Facilitator. He supported the negotiating process within the ambit of CARICOM and called on his Surinamese counterpart to demonstrate goodwill in the search for a resolution.

The Surinamese President for his part explained to his colleague his government's position on the matter and pledged his government's support to find an amicable solution to the controversy but would have preferred if the matter would have been dealt with at a bilateral level. Though he did not insist, he expressed gratitude to CARICOM for facilitating the talks.

Jamaica offered to host the next round of negotiations between the two delegations. The offer was made in the context of the bilateral engagements being done under the auspices of the Caribbean Community

The negotiations started out at the Half Moon Holiday Resort at Montego Bay; capital of the Parish of St. James situated at the Northwestern part of Jamaica. Presidents Jagdeo and Wijdenbosch were present led off the discussion. Clear and precise instructions were given to the two teams, one led by me and the other by my Surinamese counterpart

The two delegations left Montego Bay and flew to Kingston to continue the negotiations. We worked two full days and late into the evening of the last of the two days. On that evening, we met with Jamaican Prime Minister Patterson at his office for further advice on modalities. The Prime Minister spent a considerable amount of his time with both teams sharing with us his years of experience as an international negotiator. A fairly spacious conference room, courtesy of the PM was made available to the delegations with two smaller rooms available for individual delegation consultations.

The Surinamese delegation took full advantage of their room for internal consultations. They spent hours consulting among themselves at the end of which, they informed us that they could not reach a decision one way or another.

The Jamaican Prime Minister was duly informed. He expressed his disappointment and wished us well. The talks had collapsed with no results

On my return to Guyana, I took the opportunity first to brief the President and then Cabinet about what transpired in Jamaica and offered my view on options for the way the way forward. It was in the course of the ensuing discussion that I took the opportunity to mention a view that was passed to me by a Jamaican specialist on the United Nations Convention of the Law of the Sea (UNCLOS) and the functions of the International Tribunal of the Law of the Sea (ITLOS) and their relevance to the issue we were seeking to find a resolution with Suriname. I felt this was good advice, took note of it, and passed it on for what its worth.

In an effort to bring a successful closure to the controversy, the two leaders, with the agreement of CARICOM, agreed to move the discussion to a secondary level. In the circumstances, the two leaders agreed that two bodies that existed for years within the context of Guyana –Suriname bilateral relations should be reactivated. The two bodies were; the Guyana/Suriname Border Commission and the Guyana/Suriname Joint Commission on Economic and Technical Cooperation. Suffice it to say that just two years earlier, when President Janet Jagan paid an official visit to Suriname, it was precisely these two mechanisms the Guyanese and Surinamese Presidents had agreed to operationalize but, as was pointed out earlier, notwithstanding our painstaking efforts to move the process along, the Surinamese did not budge.

After two days of discussions, it became clear to us that no agreement would be reached at the level of the Border Commission, our side had anticipated this logjam due to the fact that the Surinamese had sought to reintroduce their earlier proposal that the land, river and sea borders be dealt with as a single issue. This was a clever way to bring the question of the New River Triangle into the negotiation.

Insofar as the Joint Commission was concerned, the only issue that attracted the attention of both sides was the use of the Corentyne River by Guyanese fishermen for purposes of traversing the river to go out to sea for fishing as an economic activity for their livelihood. But again, it was this very issue that Presidents Jagan and Widjdenbosch during the latter's visit to Suriname in 1999, had agreed would be negotiated with a view to reaching a fishing agreement between the two sides. One bilateral meeting took place in Paramaribo but to no avail.

It was not after years of quiet, methodical and careful preparations as well as with the recruitment of some technical specialists on the matter, that Guyana announced on February 24 2004 that it was taking the matter to ITLOS for a ruling on the dispute between Guyana and Suriname regarding the maritime boundaries at sea.

It was not until September 17, 2007 that a decision favourable to Guyana was handed down by the Tribunal.

The Tribunal fixed the boundary along a 10o North line beginning at a marker on the left bank of the Corentyne River laid down in 1936 and continuing for a distance of three miles thereafter. The Tribunal applied the principle of equidistance to the 200 miles limit of the EEZ claimed by Guyana and Suriname. As a result of its ruling, Guyana gained sovereignty over 12,837 sq. miles of the costal waters further to the north and west, while Suriname received 6,900 sq. miles to the south and east.

Suriname was surprised and disappointed with the ruling.

The ruling constituted a significant and historic political and diplomatic victory for Guyana, one that was never achieved by any previous administration. And notwithstanding, the ups and downs of the lengthy engagement we had with Suriname in search of a solution, long before, the dispute went before ITLOS, I felt proud to know that my colleagues who worked with me, made a modest contribution to this great achievement by our government and people.

THE THREAT FROM THE WEST

Hugo Chavez came to power in December 1998 and was installed in February 1999. Janet Jagan was in Caracas in July 1998 for talks with President Caldera, eight months later she was back in Caracas this time, to attend Chavez's inauguration. Chavez was re-elected to office in 2000, 2006 and 2012. During this entire period, the PPP/C was in office up May 2015 when it "lost" the elections.

I had the privilege of meeting with President Chavez once, on a one-on-one basis while representing the Government of Guyana at a consultative meeting of the Heads of State of the Rio Group held in Mexico City in 1998. Unfortunately, due to the unstable political situation at home President Janet Jagan could not attend.

During the lunch break, President Chavez invited me for a brief walk with him in a small garden just outside the Presidential library within the Presidential palace where the meeting was held.

Chavez asked about the political situation in Guyana. I gave him a brief overview. He then asked me to convey his personal greetings to President Jagan and wished her well during the difficult period she was experiencing at that time. He asked me to convey to her his assurances that Venezuela under his presidency would not stir up a legacy that the colonial powers had left behind and that he would do his level best to promote friendly and good neighbourly relations with Guyana, I thanked and assured him that I would convey his sentiments to President Jagan

In May 1999, Beal Aerospace Technologies Inc (BATI)., based in Dallas, Texas, approached the Government of Guyana with an expression of interest to establish a satellite launching site at a determined location at the Waini River.

The Waini River is located in the Barima-Waini Region of Guyana. It flows into the Atlantic Ocean. It is 11/2 kilometers or one-mile East of the international land boundary between Guyana and Venezuela.

BATI wanted eleven acres for the launching site, twenty-six acres for the primary site and seventy-five acres for the buffer zone, a total of 112 acres of land. The company was prepared to pay a total sum of US$50 million for all the lands which they claimed would create no less that five hundred jobs. The assurance was given that the facility would be a non-military facility, with no military troops on site and that it would be purely of an economic character.

As the Government of Guyana and BATI negotiations proceeded on the one hand, the Chavez administration on the other, raised its objections to the project. Rangel travelled to Washington where he met with senior officials of the State Department to whom he registered his government's objection of the project.

For his part, the Venezuelan President in August, 2000, stated; "It is not Venezuela's desire to have a conflict. Venezuela will not permit the establishment of the base. Venezuela will ask the United States not to permit the transfer of technology so that the project will not be implemented. Venezuela will not allow this base to be established."

At the domestic level, a number of local NGOs and the political opposition began to raise a hullaballoo over the project. In response to the Venezuelan protests, President Jagdeo accused the Chavez administration of scaring off investors from Guyana. And in June 1999, while I was attending a meeting of the OAS in Guatemala, Venezuelan Foreign Minister, Jose Vincent Rangel raised the issue with me. My response to him was that if he has any questions about the project, he should ask them and he would be provided with the answers.

Following a visit to Guyana by the Good Officer Jackman who had replaced McIntyre, I held a press conference on March 22, I told the press that "the Essequibo region is part of our national territory and that Guyana is indivisible". I rejected Venezuela's objection to the BATI investment and any interference to block it. I also made the point that "there is precedence for foreign investments in the Essequibo and that government's efforts to conclude an agreement with Beal Aerospace was nothing new."

Addressing the 51ˢᵗ Session of UNGA - 1996, Meeting with Kofi Annan & Miguel Burelli – 1997 & Meeting with UN Secretary General – 1998

Photos courtesy UN/DPI by Evan Schneider and Milton Grant

In May 2000, the Government of Guyana and BATI signed an agreement under which US$100 million instead of $50 million would be paid to the government. However, under mounting pressure at home and abroad particularly from Venezuela, the Jagdeo administration presented a copy of the BATI/GOG agreement to the Government of Venezuela. This move was deemed an act of appeasement by Stabroek News in its September 4ᵗʰ, 1999 edition. And in October 2000, BATI announced its withdrawal from the deal claiming 'competitive financial developments within the US space industry as well as uncertainty in the advice received from US State Department'.

It was around this time in June 2000, that a major Chinese company by the name of Jilin Forestry Industry Group Corporation of China through its subsidiary Jilin Industries (Guyana) Inc. was granted a forestry concession the size of 167,125 hectares in the Essequibo region. The lease was for a period of three years with an initial investment of US$1million, and in the second phase of US$11-15 million. However, in light of strong opposition once again by Venezuela to large scale investments in the Essequibo and concerns they had earlier expressed over environmental degradation, the Jilin company pulled out.

In light of Jilin's pull-out, I was called upon to meet with the Chinese Ambassador to remind him of Guyana's territorial integrity and national sovereignty and inform him of Guyana's displeasure and disappointment with Jilin's decision to pull-out from investing in what is legally and internationally recognized as Guyana's national territory. The ambassador could not offer a plausible explanation save and except to express regret over Jilin's decision and to reiterate his government's respect for Guyana's territorial integrity and national sovereignty. As an aside, and, in keeping with my instructions, I reminded the Ambassador about the overtures the Taiwanese had been making towards Guyana and the interest they had expressed in doing business with the Government of Guyana. As was to be expected, the Ambassador reminded me of his government's 'One China, Two Systems Policy' which was adopted by the United Nations. He nevertheless told me that while his government is not opposed to any private company in Guyana doing business with Taiwanese private companies, when it comes to diplomatic recognition and government to government relations his government is strongly opposed to any move in that direction.

In August 2000, during Good Officer Jackman's visit to Guyana, accompanied by officials from the Foreign Ministry, the military, the Police and the Lands and Mines Commission, I briefed Mr. Jackmanon latest developments as regards Guyana/Venezuela relations.

THE JAGDEO/CHAVEZ FIRST ENCOUNTER

Jagdeo and Chavez met for the first time at the South Summit held in April 2000 in Havana, Cuba. Later, in August of the same year, they met once again while attending a UNASUR Summit in Brazilia. The two Presidents met again during the 3rd Summit of the Americas held in Quebec, Canada in April 2001.

President Chavez paid an official State Visit to Guyana in February 2004. It was during his visit   at a public forum held at the Pegasus Hotel that Chavez, declared; "Through a process of positive dialogue and mutual understanding differences can be narrowed." Chavez announced the cancellation of US$12.5 million bilateral foreign debt Guyana owed to Venezuela.

Chavez visited Guyana again on November 26, 2010 to attend the 1V Regular Summit of the South American Community of Nations (UNASUR). The main objective of the meeting was the handing over of Pro-tempore Presidency to Guyana and to reaffirm the principles of the Group.

Reflecting on President Chavez's visit, the Kaieteur News one of Guyana's daily newspapers had this to say;

'The Chavez administration has in fact ushered in a new era of relations between Venezuela and Guyana. The Venezuelan government has not been aggressive towards Guyana, but it has been a friendly partner in developing closer hemispheric relations.'

During the period I served as Jagdeo's Foreign Minister up to 2001, meetings between me and Venezuelan Foreign Minister Rangel took place in Georgetown, New York and Caracas At the same time, meetings between technical officials were held to address issues such as the illegal drug trade, technical cooperation and cross border security and movement of persons across the borders.

Like previous meetings, the one held at the UN in October 1999 between me, Rangel and the Secretary General of the United Nations, was a good meeting in that, like previous meetings, they gave assurances to Guyanese at home and abroad that the border controversy was in the hands of the UN Secretary General and that the emissaries from Guyana and Venezuela were talking. Yet nothing of substance emerged from those encounters, save that from time to time, efforts would be made by senior staff functionaries at the SG's secretariat to egg us on to arrive at consensual positions that would show movement towards a practical solution to the controversy.

In August 2000, I travelled to Caracas to meet with Rangel. The need for us to meet was suggested and agreed upon during our meeting in October 1999 in New York with the UN Secretary General and the Facilitators. At our Caracas meeting, Rangel and I assessed the progress made by the High-Level Bilateral Commission's implementation of its work programme. We assessed the state of our bilateral relations in light of the border controversy and our recent meeting with the UN Secretary General. We explored possibilities for an understanding of Guyana's right to encourage foreign investments in any part of Guyana's national territory. We also discussed issues pertaining to environmental degradation. No agreement was reached on the latter matters. Two months later, following intense exchanges between our two governments, the BATI and Jilin pulled their investments from Guyana

A FRIEND NAMED BRAZIL

In contrast to our relations with Venezuela, our relations with Brazil, our southern neighbour, irrespective of whether it was during the Presidency of Itamar Franco, Fernando Henrique Cardoso, Luiz Ignacio Lula da Silva or Dilma Rouseff, has always been excellent and extremely productive based on mutual respect. Because of the visits by Presidents Cheddi Jagan, Janet Jagan and Bharat Jagdeo to Brazil, our bilateral relations with Brazil assumed a dynamic and a results-oriented character.

Brazil plays an important geostrategic role in respect to our border controversy with Venezuela, any aggressive power play by the Venezuelan authorities towards Guyana, can be easily countered by the Brazilians at the political/diplomatic level in the first instance. In that regard, Brazil is an important strategic ally for Guyana insofar as safeguarding our national sovereignty and territorial integrity is concerned.

I loved visiting Brazil. The contrasting nature of the country and its population was of great interest to me. There are some similarities between Guyana and Brazil especially in Belem in the state of Para, Manaus in the State of Amazonas and Boa Vista in the State of Roraima, all of which neighbour Guyana and Suriname.

Salvador in the State of Bahia in the Northeast of Brazil is also of great interest to me.

I visited Brazil on many occasions as Minister of Foreign Affairs and as Minister of Foreign Trade and International Cooperation. The Brazilians would always ensure that I paid a courtesy call on the sitting president. In this respect, I was privileged to have sit down conversations with Presidents Franco, Cardoso and Lula.

Franco was kind of an aloof President, whereas Cardoso was more of the intellectual economist who loved to talk about the developmental and structuralist economics of Raul Prebisch, an Argentine economist with whom he shared a common vision for the economic and social development of Latin America. Interestingly, President Cardoso once told me that he considered Cheddi Jagan a member of the pantheon of South American economic theorists and thinkers.

During one of my visits to Brazilia as Minister of Foreign Trade and International Cooperation I was granted the courtesy of having a one hour sit down conversation with President Cardoso.

In the course of my conversation with the Brazilian President, he enquired of me whether I liked working as Foreign Trade Minister or Foreign Minister. I responded saying that I enjoyed working at both ministries. He said he liked my answer because his Foreign Minister Celso Amorim functions in both capacities and that a Foreign Trade Minister is to some extent a Foreign Minister though the latter has wider responsibilities than the Foreign Trade Minister. President Cardoso then asked about the political situation in Guyana. I provided a comprehensive brief to him and he in turn briefed me about the latest developments in his country.

President Lula da Silva was clearly a man with a vision for Brazil. He reminded me a lot of Cheddi Jagan, they both had a visionary and a pro-poor, pro-people approach. Because of his busy schedule, I was never afforded a one-on-one sit-down conversation with President Lula, though I did meet with him together with his Foreign Minister and other officials to talk about Guyana Brazil bilateral relations.

Military and police cooperation between Guyana and Brazil as well as our bilateral cooperation in the field of agriculture, an active Joint Border Commission treating with Guyana/Brazil border markers, visa abolition agreements and above all, infrastructure cooperation proved to be mutually beneficial to both countries.

Infrastructure cooperation under the rubric of the 'Initiative for the Integration of Regional Infrastructure' as exemplified in the construction of the Bridge across the Takatu River linking Guyana and Brazil was realized thanks to the Brazilian Government. The construction of the bridge, resulted in the signing of three major agreements; First, was an International Road Transport Agreement (IRTA, Feb. 2003) to facilitate cross border free movement of goods and services by vehicles owned by Brazilians and Guyanese.

Second, was the signing of a Partial Scope Trade Agreement (June, 2001), 'to foster bilateral trade flows, by the exchange of tariff preferences between the parties, cooperation in trade matters and increased participation of the private sector.' Third, was the establishment of a Free Trade Zone (July, 2009) covering the States of Roraima and Amazonas on the Brazilian side and Lethem to Kurupukari on the Guyana side. The free trade, duty free arrangement excludes, alcohol, cigarettes, arms and ammunition and explosives.

In the course of these activities, I managed to develop an excellent working relationship with Brazilian Foreign Minister Celso Amorim. We became close friends during my first official visit to Brazilia in June 1994. At the end of my official visit, we travelled together by aircraft, to Belem in the State of Para in northern Brazil to participate in the Twenty-Fourth Regular Session of the OAS.

Celso opened many doors for Guyana at the hemispheric and global levels. He introduced me to many Latin American Foreign Ministers at the time and showed me the way to make Guyana become an associate member of Latin America Common Market (MERCOSUL), later, for Guyana to become a member of the RIO GROUP and subsequently a member of (UNASUR).Guyana subsequently became CARICOM's representative at the Rio Group

FOREIGN TRADE NEGOTIATOR

Two years after I had assumed the portfolio of Minister of Foreign Trade and International Cooperation (March 2001), at a CARICOM Heads of Government meeting in Barbados in February of 2002, I was handed the responsibility to be CARICOM's Ministerial Spokesperson on WTO matters and to Superintend the region's negotiations at the WTO. Later, I was assigned the additional responsibility as CARICOM's Ministerial Spokesperson on sugar at the on-going bilateral and international negotiating levels.

It was Celso who had recommended and facilitated my participation at meetings of the G20, a coalition of developing countries who once held differing, if not opposing negotiating positions on agriculture at the World Trade Organisation (WTO). A concrete example of this situation was to be found in the fact that Guyana and other agricultural producing countries in the African, Pacific and Caribbean (ACP) group of countries held positions that differed from those of the G20 particularly at the WTO negotiations on agriculture. However, with the creation of the G20 coalition and with Guyana's active participation at its meetings, we managed eventually, based on compromise to establish common positions within the Group thus providing CARICOM with a formidable negotiating platform at the WTO negotiations.

Two years before I was shifted to the newly-created Ministry of Foreign Trade and International Cooperation I was already deeply involved in external trade negotiations. But I was extremely pleased to hold the exclusive, new and challenging foreign trade portfolio after serving as Foreign Minister from 1992-2001.

AT FOREIGN AFFAIRS

As Minister of Foreign Affairs, I travelled extensively on government business. Looking back, it seems as though there is no part of the world my job did not take me. Of course, there were certain annual routine events I had to participate in including; CARICOM Foreign and Trade Ministers' meetings, Caricom Heads of Government meetings, ACP ministerial meetings, OAS General Assembly meetings as well as meetings of the United Nations General Assembly. I had the honour and privilege to address the 50th Session of the United Nations General Assembly on October 11, 1995; the 51st session on October 2, 1996; the 52nd session on September 25, 1997 and the 55th session on September 19th, 2000.

In my address to the 50th session on behalf of the Government of Guyana, I stressed Guyana's continued support for the restoration of democracy in Haiti; for the urgent need to address the growing divide between rich and poor countries; the challenges in addressing the problems of environment and development and the issues confronting small vulnerable economies at the WTO global trade negotiations.

At the 51st Session, I called for continued support for the concept of a New Global Human Order; for a global partnership between countries of the North and the South; for the peaceful resolution of conflicts and for recognition of the interconnection and interaction between peace and development.

In my address to the 52nd Session of the world body I placed emphasis on the Agenda for Development, and the World Social Summit; I called once more for a partnership between countries of the North and the South and I alerted the forum to the impending national election in Guyana.

At the 55th Session which marked my last address to the UNGA, the issue of globalization and the call for a level playing field was prominent in view of the growing gap between rich and poor countries and within countries as well.

I used every one of these meetings to learn and to educate myself as much as I could about topics being discussed at the meetings and to acquaint myself with the politics of the host country. But above all, what I enjoyed most of all was the conversations I had in the course of bilateral meetings with participants at the meetings.

TRANSITIONING FROM FOREIGN AFFAIRS TO FOREIGN TRADE

Prior to my appointment as Foreign Trade Minister, I met with President Jagdeo to discuss the specificities of the portfolio. I suggested to him that the portfolio responsibilities be enlarged to include International Cooperation. Jagdeo readily agreed and instructed Dr. Roger Luncheon, Head of the Presidential Secretariat to make the adjustment as I had suggested.

Swearing as Minister of Foreign Trade & International Cooperation - 2001

I was pleased with the expanded portfolio because as Foreign Minister, development and technical cooperation between developing countries and South-South Cooperation were areas I enjoyed working in because they helped forge functional cooperation among like- minded countries who shared common challenges in areas such as institutional strengthening and capacity building. In that regard, Joint Commissions between Guyana and a number of other developing countries in my view, play an important role in promoting functional cooperation and solidarity between developing countries especially those with limited human resources and weak institutional capacity.

Having served as Foreign Minister under four presidents, I had accumulated sufficient experience to serve in any other capacity that had to do with external relations. The Foreign Minister of Guyana is also responsible for Caricom affairs which imposes upon the Minister the responsibility to attend meetings of the

Council for Foreign and Community Relations (COFCOR) and the Council for Trade and Economic Development (COTED). The Foreign Minister would usually accompany the President to meetings of Conference of Heads of Government. In some instances, when the President is unavailable, the Foreign Minister would represent the President at international gatherings hosted by governments or inter-governmental organisation.

WHILE AT FOREIGN AFFAIRS

Nine years of exposure to the vagaries of international diplomacy put me in good stead to serve in a corresponding capacity. However, in retrospect, I must concede that had it not been for the persistent tutoring on international relations by Cheddi and Janet Jagan while I served as International Secretary of the Party, and the confidence reposed in me by appointing me Foreign Minister following the election victory of the party 1992 and 1997, my tenure in that exalted position would not have been successful. Suffice it to say that my own efforts through long hours of reading widely, listening to speeches and conversations, making notes on observations, in effect, my own self-education, not having benefitted from an established college/high school or university education was of great assistance to me along the way.

At the Ministry of Foreign Affairs

A Mission Statement of any government agency or department is of great importance and use if the political head is to be guided as per his or her role agency or department. It is for that reason that I made it my duty not only to become acquainted with the Mission Statement of the Ministry of Foreign Affairs but to study its components in great detail and to apply my practical knowledge and experience to the relevance of the ministry's mandate in light of President Jagan's vision that our foreign policy must complement and reinforce our domestic policies and seek to further our national goals. And though a small country with its attendant disadvantages, we, nonetheless, must be principled in the pursuits and forging of foreign relationships.

It is against this background that the following principles guided me throughout my tenure at the Ministry of Foreign Affairs. Adherence to world peace and for the Caribbean to be a Zone of Peace; expand our relations with all countries regardless of their socio-economic systems; promote good neighbourly and mutually beneficially relations with our neighbouring countries; support the all-round work by the United Nations; be actively involved in regional bodies mainly Caricom and others primarily of South America; ensure that our diplomatic missions are increasingly active in promoting our economic diplomacy efforts; actively participate in international multilateral bodies to bring medium and long term benefits to our country; fulfill our international treaty obligations; resist in a principled way, any and all attempts that will affect our economic development, impact adversely our democracy and undermine our territorial integrity and national sovereignty.

After settling in at the Ministry for a period of about one year, I set about restructuring of the ministry internally, to correspond with the exigencies of the foreign policy thrust of the new government. In this regard, in consultation with senior staff members of the ministry, I established a Department of the Americas and Asia, a Multilateral and Global Affairs Department, an Economic Affairs Department, a Protocol and Consular Affairs Department, a Public Affairs and Information Department, a library and a National Advisory Committee on External Negotiations.

Under multilateralism we pursued our political and economic interests at the United Nations, the G77 which we chaired in 1999, the Economic and Social Council (ECOSOC); faithfully holding our treaty obligations. In this regard, we set up an inter-agency committee to examine ways and means of honouring our treaty obligations. We were actively involved in the Law of the Sea negotiations; as far as the Non-Aligned Movement was concerned, I participated at Ministerial meetings of the Movement held in Colombia, South Africa, India and Egypt. At the level of the Commonwealth, apart from participating meetings, we pursued our interests through Technical Cooperation with Developing Countries (TCDC) within the Commonwealth, in the same way as we did with the UN through the United Nations Development Programme (UNDP).

A major platform that was of great help to us in pursuit of our economic interests in the areas of sugar, rice, bauxite and fisheries and infrastructural projects was our ACP/EU and CARIFORUM economic and financial cooperation programmes. My attendance at ministerial meetings of these two bodies in Brussels played a big role in helping understanding the vagaries and complexities of the EU's bureaucracy, its practice of multilateral diplomacy and its impact on the political, economic and social-well-being of the peoples of African, Caribbean and Pacific group of countries. My visits to many ACP member countries to participate in meetings and conferences bought home to me the stark socio-economic contradictions and living realities obtaining in those countries.

At the hemispheric level, we actively participated in the activities of the Organization of American States (OAS) especially in relation to the fight against the illicit trafficking of narcotic drugs and firearms as well as in the critical area of cyber crime and cyber security. The OAS like the Commonwealth, have ben extremely helpful to Guyana as regards our electoral process. The Amazon Cooperation Treaty (ACT), the Rio Group, the Summit of the Americas (SOA) and its follow-up activities as well as visits to Latin and Central America countries to promote and strengthen our bilateral relations was of great assistance to the ministry and the government as a whole. Consideration of candidatures for posts at various international organisations was a matter to which we paid a lot of attention especially as regards the quid pro quo inherent in support of one candidate or another. Diplomatic leverage utilized to advance the interest of one's country can play an important role in the question of candidatures.

At the regional level, emphasis during my tenure was on Caricom, the Association of Caribbean States (ACS), the Assembly of Caribbean Community Parliamentarians, promoting cooperation programmes with VSO and Peace Corps volunteers. While ensuring that we do not carry all our eggs in one basket, we broadened and deepened our bilateral functional cooperation programmes with as many countries as possible. This approach was reflected in the maintenance or establishment of Joint Commissions with many countries, the signing of Bilateral Investment Treaties with a number of countries, visa abolition and exemption agreements with many countries, establishing diplomatic relations with a number of countries and negotiating Intellectual Property Rights Agreements with the United States and engaging in cooperation agreements in a number of areas with many countries around the world.

On the domestic front, the Ministry launched its first ever Radio Programme called 'Foreign Policy Focus' The programme soon became a popular talk show programme. A TV programme called 'Towards the 21st Century' was also launched. The two weekly programmes opened up government's foreign policy initiatives to the public and helped to inform and involve the public in and about the Ministry's activities. And as though this was not enough, we printed and published a quarterly bulletin named 'Takuba News' whose objectives were the same as the TV and radio programmes though aimed at different audiences at home and abroad.

Apart from these information outlets, I held regular press conferences and issued press releases on all topical and news-worthy occurrences on the international level.

THE FOREIGN SERVICE INSTITUTE

Of major importance was the establishment of the Foreign Service Institute. This was a ground breaking initiative. At no time in the history of Guyana was such an institute ever conceived nor realized. The Institute was established with the specific aim of providing Guyana with a corps of professional diplomats whose skills will enable them to assist in maintaining Guyana's security and in advancing its social and economic development. Thanks to the tremendous assistance from the Commonwealth Secretariat and the Brazilian Foreign Service Institute at Rio Branco I was able to establish the Institute. The Institute was formally launched on December 7,1998. The keynote address was delivered by President Janet Jagan.

In her address, President Jagan pointed out that; "As we will never have more than a small diplomatic corps, a corps of generalists, it is therefore imperative that they should be broadly and deeply trained whether they work at the Foreign Ministry or at missions overseas."

President Jagan continued; "I wish to emphasize that diplomacy and the formulation and execution of a foreign policy is not a mechanism devised to provide trips or high living at foreign capitals. It is directly related to the bread and butter issues of maintaining markets and preserving and creating jobs. The diplomacy which as a small state we must pursue in cooperation with other small states and in particular our Caricom neighbours, must ensure that in the evolving global economy we are not squeezed out altogether."

President ended her address stating; "In the defence of our economic security, our diplomats are in the front line. The Foreign Service Institute will enable them to pursue their tasks more effectively and for the benefit of our peoples. The FSI will ensure that they are equipped with the necessary techniques and sensitivities to cope with the global realities which have so little regard for the plight of small states such as Guyana."

The objectives of the Institute were to; train new entrants to the diplomatic service of Guyana; Provide intensive refresher courses for diplomats in mid-career and orientation courses for Heads of Missions and other foreign service personnel on posting overseas; Conduct awareness and specialized courses for senior government officials, the media, private sector and other groups.

To administer the Institute a small permanent staff including a Director, a Programme Coordinator and an administrative officer were recruited. In addition, an Advisory Board with broad-based membership, which I chaired was established to give general direction and instructions to the Director and the permanent staff. Included on the Board were; Ambassador Rudy Collins, Komal Samaroo from the private sector, the Director General of the Ministry, Dr. Mark Kirton from the University of Guyana, Lloyd Searwar Director of the Institute and Imtiaz Mohammed the Programme Coordinator who performed the duties as Secretary of the Board.

The courses taught at the institute included; International relations, international law, international organisations and protocol, foreign policy analysis, international economic relations, promotion of trade, investment and tourism, negotiations and new areas of international relations. Practical skills taught included; financial administration, planning and organization of a conference, effective writing and public speaking, diplomacy and culture, preparing position papers, speeches, briefs and reports.

Courses were taught by guest lecturers, ministers of government, senior staff members at the Ministry, retired ambassadors and senior foreign service officers and senior lecturers from the University of Guyana and senior ranks of the GDF. Whenever a new non-resident diplomat was being accredited to Guyana or a visiting dignitary was paying a visit to the country, they would be invited to deliver a guest lecture on a topic either about their country or based on their curricula vitae. In addition, the VIP's would also be invited to deliver a public lecture which were well attended and highly successful.

The FSI through its Board successfully negotiated with the University of Guyana accreditation of the Institute. Graduates from the Institute were at the same time graduates from the University of Guyana.

Another step I took to enhance the capacity of the Ministry was to establish a full-fledged library for staff members of the ministry. To assist in the initiative, I sought and got the assistance from the UK-based Volunteer Overseas Services (VSO) who was kind enough to provide for a period of two years (1997-1999) Ms. Heather Sydney, a British professional librarian. The British government and other donors donated a number of books to the library. This initiative marked the establishment of a well-equipped and professionally administered library at the Ministry.

But the final stroke had to do with moving away from using desk-top computers as glorified type-writers and to transition to a modernized, comprehensive computerization and electronic data management system at the ministry along with the establishment of a wide-area network to facilitate inter-departmental internet connectivity at the ministry as well as with our overseas missions and the world at large. The whole idea was to facilitate networking amongst staff members at home and abroad, using desk-top computers to assist in the efficiency and labour productivity at the Ministry. The UNDP was generous enough to provide the

Ministry with a computer engineer and programmer to assist in setting up a small computer unit at the ministry to support and to maintain the effective functioning of all aspects of the Ministry's activities.

THE RE-MIGRATION UNIT

The establishment of the Re-migration Unit at the Ministry was challenging. With government agreeing to encourage overseas-based Guyanese to return home with their tools of trade to either take up residence and/or to invest in Guyana it meant that the institutional arrangements had to be put place to facilitate the remigrants. The Foreign Ministry was charged with the responsibility to assist with processing applications while the Ministry of Finance responsibility was to consider granting of duty-free concessions. The process worked well until it was subject to abuse by some unscrupulous persons who were bent on engaging in activities not permitted by the established rules. Thanks to the watchful and attentive eyes of Mrs.Lena Ramotar who was responsible for processing the applications at the Ministry of Foreign Affairs instances of abuse were uncovered and the culprits 'applications rejected.

STREET FAIRS

Another initiative I introduced while at the ministry was the hosting of the annual street fairs on the streets surrounding the ministry. The first street fair was held in September of 1996. The fairs allowed the foreign embassies, high commissions and international organisations based in Georgetown to mount and exhibit in specially provided booths, printed materials about their activities, country, their culture and people. Handicraft and memorabilia were exhibited and handouts provided to visitors to the various booths. The fairs were held every year until 2001 when I was shifted from the Ministry.

A HEADQUARTERS FOR CARICOM

In the meanwhile, during my bilateral meetings at home or abroad with representatives of foreign governments I sought to impress upon them the need to establish diplomatic missions at Georgetown having regard to the fact that Guyana was host to the headquarters of the Caricom Secretariat. However, on-going political instability in Guyana made accomplishment of this task even more difficult.

As Minister of Caricom Affairs, I was called upon to provide my Caricom ministerial counterparts with regular progress reports on the status of the construction of the headquarters of the Caricom Secretariat. There were occasions when they were not pleased with the reports, I provided but that was the most I could do at the time since many of the stages in the construction process were beyond my control.

The turning of the sod at the site for construction took place in February of 1998.The contract for construction of the building was signed in April 2001, but actual construction began in May of the same year. The building was completed and handed over in July 2005 to the then Secretary General, Edwin Carrington. The Secretariat commenced operating from the building in July 2006. Construction of the building was financed by a loan from the National Insurance Scheme with significant grant aid provided by the Governments of Japan and India. It pleased me knowing that I no longer had the responsibility to report to my colleagues about the progress being made on construction of the building.

ON THE CARICOM CIRCUIT

If there was one thing that pleased me with my participation at Caricom meetings was my visits to the various member states and my interest in becoming acquainted with their local politics as well as their foreign policy interests. Participating in debates at Caricom meetings is respect to the Single Market and Economy, the Free Movement of Skills, the establishment of the Caribbean Court of Justice which agreement I was pleased to sign on behalf of the government in February 2001in Barbados.

HIPPIC, CHAPTER 7 AND THE RDF

Of great interest to me was the discussions at COTED on trade and development policy matters. It is at COTED that real discussions take place that could be life and death matters for workers and the business community in members states. It was at COTED that I brought to the attention of my colleagues the harm that was being done to our agricultural exports to member states compounded by the fact that Guyana at that time was reeling under economic and financial blows as a Highly Indebted Poor Country.

I argued that it was grossly unfair for Guyana, under these conditions, to be part of a single market and economy when it was not benefitting from being in such an arrangement while other member states managed to get off scotch free with all kinds of trade barriers, applications for waivers/suspension of the Common External Tariffs as well as by providing subsidies their to local manufacturers. I further advanced the case for the establishment of a Regional Development Fund to assist countries like Guyana to overcome its developmental challenges.

I made a case stating that under existing economic and social conditions obtaining in Guyana, and in light of member states' positive GDP indicators compared to Guyana's negative, Guyana should be designated a Least Developed Country (LDC) with all the benefits that accrue to those member states since in the Caricom context, the More Developed Countries (MDC's) like Guyana, had become LDC's while the LDC's had become MDC's.

The discussion at COTED on the matter was extremely heated at times with the LDC's refusing to agree with my request. Several rounds of discussion took place on the matter with no compromise being agreed to by the LDC's. Eventually, the matter reached the Heads of Government who endorsed a proposal that the Treaty Establishing the Caribbean Community, be amended to include what became known as 'Protocol VII; Disadvantaged, Countries Regions and Sectors. The amendment stated that 'COTED shall to the extent necessary and for a period to be determined, apply the provisions of the Special Regime for the less developed countries to the Highly-Indebted Poor Countries.' The only Highly Indebted Poor Country in Caricom at that time was Guyana.

A further amendment favourable to Guyana was an amendment stating; 'Notwithstanding any provisions to the contrary in this Treaty, Guyana shall be allowed, for as long as it continues to benefit from wheat imports under PL 480

Agreements with the United states of America, to impose quantitative restrictions on the importation of wheat flour.'

The entire 'Chapter Seven-Disadvantaged Countries, Regions and Sectors' was favourable Guyana. The fact that it was agreed and inserted in the Revised Treaty to benefit of the LDC's and moreso, the fact that Guyana, within the meaning of an Highly Indebted Poor Country was, for the purposes of the CSME, considered an LDC, meant that Guyana would be a beneficiary from all the Chapter Seven provisions.

Mention must also be made of Article158 of the Revised Treaty which makes provision for the establishment of a Development Fund '...for the purpose of providing financial or technical assistance to disadvantaged, countries, regions and sectors.'

Guyana under President Jagan had pressed for the establishment a Regional Development Fund patterned after the Fund at the European Union. Caricom Heads of Government had agreed to the establishment of such a fund as reflected in Article 158 of the Treaty. In this regard, Guyana made submissions at COTED to the effect that because of the negative impact of the impending removal of the European Union's preferential treatment to its imports of Guyana's rice and sugar, compounded by the non-tariff barriers imposed by some Caricom member States particularly to its rice exports, both sectors should be considered disadvantaged.

Moreover, a case was made out that Guyana's bauxite industry had become a disadvantaged sector because financing under the EU's special financing facility known as Sysmin was no longer available and moreso, bauxite prices on the international market had declined significantly leaving the bauxite mining town of Linden depressed. In that regard, we argued that Guyana's Region Ten be considered a disadvantaged region because of the socio-economic impact caused by the failing bauxite industry in that particular region.

These are what should be considered stellar achievements while I served as Minister of Foreign/Caricom Affairs. It was these achievements amongst others that gave me a tremendous sense of satisfaction as I prepared to leave the Foreign Ministry to serve in another capacity.

FOREIGN TRADE …FULL STEAM AHEAD

Setting up a new ministry is no easy task, but my job was made easier due to the fact that the incubation of foreign trade matters within the bossom of the Ministry of Foreign Affairs began long before an actual Ministry of Foreign Trade came into existence. In fact, it began with the increasing awareness at the level of cabinet,  that the Ministry of Tourism, Industry and Commerce lacked the capacity and enthusiasm to actively pursue external trade negotiations be they for a Free Trade Area of the Americas (FTAA), Economic Partnerships (EPA's) with the European Union, a new Development Round at the World Trade Organization (WTO), or the Single Market and Economy at CARICOM's Council for Trade and Economic Development (COTED).

At a cabinet meeting with my colleagues - 2001

With the intellectual capacity and institutional memory of the key and critical issues on foreign trade, issues both domestic and foreign already available and at my disposal, my immediate task was to find competent and qualified human resources with the relevant intellectual skills to build human resource capacity for the new ministry. Cabinet agreed that to get the new ministry up and running, the members of staff at the Ministry of Foreign Affairs whose responsibility it was to address foreign trade matters would be shifted to my ministry along with those at the Ministry of Commerce who were involved with foreign trade matters and attended COTED meetings.

With the passage of time and with technical personnel provided through the Commonwealth Secretariat and UNDP the ministry emerged as a formidable force at the domestic and international levels. Due to the cordial and friendly relations I nurtured with Ambassador Richard Bernal, Chief Negotiator for the Regional Negotiating Machinery, Edwin Carrington, Caricom Secretary General; Peter Gonzalez, Henry Gill, Gail Mathurin, Irwin LaRoque, Kusha Haraksingh, David Hales, Nisa Surujbally, Neville Totaram, Patrick Antoine, Ian Mc Donald, all very knowledgeable men and women in foreign trade, WTO and external negotiations matters, I was so successful in fulfilling my foreign trade responsibilities.

With my small but competent, efficient and reliable staff working out of space provided at the Ministry of Foreign Affairs, we formulated the following Mission Statement of the new ministry.

'To formulate and advocate a coherent and effective trade policy that will advance Guyana's multilateral, regional and bilateral trading interests; identify opportunities for developing markets for existing goods and services and new exportable goods and services; combine conventional and other approaches to the critical issue of resource mobilization through technical cooperation with the developing countries and the donor community of the industrialized states, multilateral financial and development-oriented institutions.'

Before I was shifted from Foreign Affairs to Foreign Trade and International Co-operation, I was in effect serving as Minister of Foreign Affairs and at the same time, as Guyana's external trade negotiator.

CARICOM Heads of Government, in light of the impending plethora of external trade negotiations, decided to establish a Regional Negotiating Machinery (RNM) with Sir Shridath Ramphal as the Chief Negotiator. It was further recommended that in each member state, a National Advisory Committee on External Negotiations be established to serve as the focal point for interaction with the RNM.

In light of what appeared to be looming increased responsibilities, I found it necessary to establish while at the Foreign Ministry, the necessary goals-oriented mechanisms. The mechanism in my view, must have discernible elements of inclusivity peculiar to Guyana. My decision was based on the earlier decision adopted by CARICOM Heads of Government to the effect that:

'In order to have a cohesive regional approach for these complex and varied negotiations, some of which have already been initiated, there needs to be established a machinery which will maximize the region's chances of success in the negotiations by harnessing all talents to successfully undertake the process.'

On September 1st, 1997 while at the Foreign Ministry, we launched our National Advisory Committee on External Negotiations (NACEN). Key stakeholders on the committee included the Ministries of Agriculture and Commerce, the Guyana Agricultural and General Workers' Union, the Guyana Rice Producers' Association and the Guyana Rice Development Board, the Guyana Manufacturer's and Services Association, and the parliamentary opposition. They all served through their representatives on NACEN.

NACEN's main task, was to identify and coordinate issues of national concern that accord with Guyana's strategic trade and economic objectives; provide advice to and facilitate government's effective participation in the three theatres of external trade negotiations; and to serve as the designated National Focal Point for the RNM thereby ensuring that Guyana's trade and economic interests are mainstreamed in the RNM process.

Had it not been for the visionary leadership by CARICOM leaders at the time, especially Prime Minister PJ Patterson of Jamaica, who chaired the Prime Ministerial Sub-committee on External Trade Negotiations, but above all, the initiatives taken by our own Ministry of Foreign Affairs to establish the appropriate internal mechanisms and to hammer out our national positions with the help of NACEN, we would have been woefully lacking when we arrived at Seattle, in the USA for the Third Ministerial Conference of the WTO. CARICOM leaders at a Special Meeting held in Trinidad and Tobago in late October 1999, had endorsed the strategic approach we were to pursue at the Seattle meeting.

SEATTLE

I arrived in Seattle, on November 31st,1999, the day before the start of the Ministerial Session of the conference. Rather than head for my hotel, I proceeded with my luggage to the Washington State Convention and Trade Centre, the venue for the conference. Downtown Seattle was under siege by protestors who I learnt later from my colleagues were from local and international media houses based in the United states, Canada, Europe and Latin America. They were thousands of them. They were protesting against the WTO as a global governance body over which they had little of no influence but who, they claimed, took decisions that impacted their lives negatively. The protestors tried to block the entrance to the conference venue but thanks to the strong efforts by law enforcement, delegates to the conference were allowed to enter the building. Armed with my luggage and brief case, I managed to force my way to the venue.

Hundreds of delegates, from Governments and international organisations, support staff, WTO officials, media personnel from all over the world as well as US and conference centre security personnel were swarming all over the six floors of the convention centre. I managed to make contact with Sonny Ramphal, Ambassador Richard Bernal from Jamaica and Secretary General Carrington of the CARICOM Secretariat. With the help of the support staff of some Ministers present we managed to find a room allocated to the African delegation to have a debriefing/strategy session amongst ourselves. We decided that our immediate objective was to target our long-standing allies in the ACP, and since the African group was the largest represented the Seattle meeting it was incumbent upon us to 'break bread' as it were with our African brothers and sisters at Seattle.

The meeting with the Ministers from Organisation of African Unity, which I shall call the OAU group proved to be difficult at the beginning but with skillful negotiating, patient explaining and compromises we managed to accommodate each other and to go forward together in the ensuing negotiations. Contact was also established with Ministers from the Pacific group with whom we had favourable exchanges that took into consideration the special circumstances affecting the small island developing states. With the majority of the countries in these groupings being constituents of the Group of 77 and China it required further consultations on the broad issues with other governments in the G77 and China which turned out to be agreeable.

The key and critical issues that were of common concern to the developing countries were; implementation concerns, special and differential treatment, a new negotiating round and labour standards, but our bottom line was that the Seattle conference resolve that the entire WTO regime be reviewed, repaired and reformed. We were also committed to the position that development must be at the centre of the on-going negotiating process at the WTO.

For us the 'Implementation Concerns' had to do with the WTO being responsive and sensitive to the development needs of small economies and that the international trading system must serve and not demand more and more concessions from the developing countries. We also called for a review of the Uruguay Round Agreements.

Under Special and Differential Treatment, we brought to the attention of the conference the social and economic consequences of conditionalities imposed on developing countries due to structural adjustment programmes sponsored by the international financial institutions which preceded the WTO and Uruguay Round. It was in this context, that we demanded that in the ensuing negotiations special and differential treatment be based on specific developmental criteria and not be arbitrarily defined transition periods.

As regards a New Negotiating Round, we called for the rectification of the imbalances of the extant global trading system. In this regard, we called for better market access for our agricultural products. We also demanded the elimination of tariff peaks and tariff escalations and that further disciplines be introduced to prevent abuse measures including anti-dumping, countervailing measures, sanitary and phytosanitary regulations and technical barriers to trade.

Finally, in connection with core labour standards, a controversial issue that plagued the WTO throughout the conference deliberations, we advanced the position that barriers to trade should not be used to deprive workers of their right to belong to trade unions of their choice and that labour standards should not be used to institute barriers to trade.

On the surface, these issues appeared to be merely technical issues, but in the context of the WTO negotiations they assumed a political character because in effect, they were fundamental policy issues linked to the economic survival and social conditions of the people in the member countries of the WTO. Thus, it became important, if not necessary for us as ministers, to be acquainted with the issues because our counterparts and their officials from the developed industrialized countries came better equipped than we were as regards support staff, most of them being knowledgeable and old hands on the WTO circuit. In some cases, their teams included experts on each issue. In any event, it was precisely these issues that kept coming up in almost every discussion during the conference.

It was at Seattle that I experienced at first hand, the intrigues, and attempts by a few powerful countries who were attempting to manipulate the proceedings of the conference with a view to influencing the outcome.

A key internal mechanism used to out-manoeuvre the developing countries and to build consensus among the industrialized nations is the so-called Green Room which is actually the on-site conference room of the WTO Director General. The Green Room is used as a venue for meetings for representatives of the industrialized countries to hammer out common positions favourable to them. It was this exclusive and high-handed behaviour by the players in the Green Room that Ministers from developing countries found unacceptable. As the days dragged on with much confusion and with no emerging consensus in sight, attempts at arm-twisting and bullying intensified. The conference eventually degenerated into shouting matches and hurling of unfriendly remarks between some representatives of the developing countries and some of those from industrialized states. Consequently, the conference went into a tailspin, delegates became deeply divided around issues that they considered non-negotiable.

When it became clear to the movers and shakers in the Green Room that unless and until an accommodation was found with the developing countries, a last-minute attempt was finally made to include us in the Green Room process. But the 'too little too late' move was done to get us to buy-in to a WTO Secretariat draft on agriculture intended for inclusion in the conference's final declaration. We found the draft completely unacceptable and rejected it. As the process went on, it became obvious that the conference was headed for the rocks. Efforts by the organisers, the Green Room players and others, who were exerting every effort to bulldoze a fiddled declaration, became unrealizable and a total catastrophe. The Third Ministerial Conference of the WTO ended up as a colossal failure.

And as though this was not enough, there was much disagreement over the hosting of the fourth ministerial meeting. Chile and Qatar were the two contenders. Eventually, Chile pulled out leaving Qatar to run with the ball.

AT THE 54TH UNGA

Prior to my participation at the 3rd WTO Ministerial meeting, in my dual capacity as Foreign Minister and External Trade Negotiator, I accompanied President Jagdeo to the 54th Session of the United Nations General Assembly between September-October 1999. It was his first General Assembly. At that time Guyana chaired the Group of 77 and China.

In his address to the Assembly, Jagdeo said;

"...However, Mr. President to benefit from the international system, developing countries must receive significant debt relief and necessary ODA to boost the overall productive capability. Consequently, in the face of rampant globalization, it is imperative that the international community should come together to create a modern development vision and strategy aimed at bridging the dangerous division which now separates the prosperous from the poor nations. This new approach should be based on an international consensus on development and on the rights and obligations of the partners."

President Jagdeo went on to state;

"Speaking for Guyana, I wish to reaffirm our Government's intention to continue working for the creation of a New Global Human Order aimed at the eradication of poverty and the establishment of a just and more humane system of international relations. Conceived by our later President Cheddi Jagan whose entire life was dedicated to empowering the poor and the weak, not only in Guyana, but throughout the world, the outlines of this New Order have been presented at major international fora, including the World Summit on Social Development which was held in Copenhagen, Denmark. All fourteen Heads of Government of CARICOM, along with other world leaders and eminent personalities, have declared their full support of the proposal and their commitment to its widest promulgation. We will, therefore, seek at this Assembly, to advance it for further consideration."

Based on my personal experience as Foreign Minister, participation at General Assemblies of the United Nations tend to be extremely hectic with lots of prearranged bilateral meetings with carefully chosen delegations from other countries with whom we have special interests. The Assembly provides the opportunity for world leaders, accompanied with their Permanent Representative and in some cases their Foreign Ministers, to engage in one-on-one bilateral to discuss matters of mutual interest. It also provides for wider meetings of groupings such as the countries in the Rio Group, or the Africa Group or even the Asian group to meet with other groupings for exchange of views on issues of interest to them. CARICOM leaders take the opportunity to engage in such meetings during the Assembly.

Foreign Ministers have specific roles to play at meetings of the Assembly. In my case, I would   participate in meetings of Foreign Ministers to review matters discussed and agreed at the Economic and Social Council (ECOSOC) of the UN, the G77 and China or perhaps at the level of the Council of Foreign and Community Relations (COFCOR) of CARICOM.

A FRESH INITIATIVE

It was during the proceedings of this 54th Session of the Assembly, that I took the opportunity to meet with Foreign Ministers or their Representatives of Antigua and Barbuda, Bangla Desh, Belize, Canada, South Africa and the United Kingdom to follow up on the letter I had written to them concerning the proposal to establish a group of countries within the Commonwealth to monitor developments concerning the Guyana/Venezuela border controversy. The countries were well represented at the meeting. They were all supportive of the initiative and confirmed that their delegations attending the 16th Meeting of Commonwealth would be supportive. This was good news for me and Guyana.

The16th Meeting of the Commonwealth was held in Durban, South Africa in November 1999. Of the fifty-two member countries of the Commonwealth, forty-seven Heads of State and Government attended. As a matter of public record, the meeting was the largest and best attended. I took note of the fact that it was the first ever CHOGM to be held in the history of South Africa because of apartheid. Secondly, that the meeting was being held as a mark of solidarity with the government and people of South Africa, four years after apartheid had been dismantled and a democratic government established with Nelson Mandela as President. Five years after Mandela's retirement, Thabo Mbeki succeeded him as President of South Africa and acted as Chairman of the meeting of the 16th CHOGM.

I accompanied President Jagdeo at the meeting. In a caucus with leaders of the countries proposed to form the Commonwealth group to monitor developments in relation to the border controversy with Venezuela, President Jagdeo provided the background to the controversy as well as an outline of the rationale behind the proposal. From all appearances, apart from Antigua and Barbuda and Belize, whose leaders were well versed with the issue because of their participation at CARICOM Heads of Government meetings, and the UK historically, the leaders from Canada, South Africa and Bangla Desh appeared to have been fully briefed on the matter by their respective foreign ministries. The response of the leaders gathered in the reasonably-size conference room, courtesy of our South African hosts was one of unanimity and firm solidarity with Guyana. They would support the call by Guyana at the plenary or in caucus.

The Durban Communique issued at the conclusion of the meeting stated inter alia:

'Guyana'

26.The Heads of Government expressed their firm support for and solidarity with the Government and people of Guyana in the maintenance of their territorial integrity and sovereignty. They also commended the continued commitment to a peaceful settlement to the controversy between Guyana and Venezuela.

27.Heads of Government took note that the relations between the two countries had been conducted over recent years in an atmosphere of mutual understanding and respect and through the development of programmes of functional cooperation. They expressed the hope that both countries would resolve their differences on this matter peacefully and welcomed the good offices process of the United Nations Secretary-General.

28.Heads of government mandated the Commonwealth Secretary-General to establish a ministerial group on Guyana to monitor further developments in respect of the existing controversy.'

This was indeed a landmark achievement for me personally, the staff at the Foreign Ministry, and by extension, the entire Government of Guyana. Never before, even though the past Burnham/Hoyte administrations had participated in eleven previous CHOGM meetings beginning from 1971 to 1991, they never found it necessary to seek the support and solidarity of the Commonwealth, notwithstanding the fact that the border controversy with Venezuela existed more than one hundred and fifty years ago. It took just three CHOGM meetings for the PPP/C to recognize how inter-governmental fora and multilateral diplomacy are tools that can be utilized to advance the national interests of Guyana.

COMMONWEALTH ANTECEDENTS

For the first time, since the PPP/C's assumption to office in October 1992, the newly elected President of Guyana, Cheddi Jagan had participated in the thirteenth meeting of CHOGM held in late October 1993 in Limassol, Cyprus. The theme of the Cyprus CHOGM was 'The Emergence of a New Global Humanitarian Order' Coincidentally, the 47th Session of the United Nations General Assembly held the year before, had adopted a resolution entitled; 'New International Humanitarian Order.' Dr. Jagan was very much aware of these developments. Under his guidance, and in collaboration with the Ministry of Foreign Affairs, a paper entitled; 'Towards the Establishment of a New Global Humanitarian Order.' was drawn up for his consideration and for presentation at the Cyprus meeting. Dr. Jagan went to the Cyprus meeting prepared to fully participate.

At The Commonwealth Summit in Cyprus – 1993 & Meeting with Commonwealth Secretary General at State House - 1995

The Limassol summit was the first major international event in which Guyana's newly elected President participated. He was warmly welcomed by his colleagues from the other Commonwealth countries and I could see from his interactions with them that he was glowing with deep appreciation and gratitude for their support and bursting with energy as he went about participating in the business meetings and other social events of the event.

In the end, the results of his contribute shone through. At paragraph six of the communique issued at the end of the meeting, the Heads of Government stated:

411

' Having discussed the Special Theme of the meeting; 'The Emergence of a Global Humanitarian Order' and acknowledging its importance, Heads of Government requested the Commonwealth Secretary-General to constitute, in consultation with Commonwealth governments, a high-level intergovernmental group to examine the specific ways in which the Commonwealth could make the fullest possible contribution to the work of the international community on this theme. The report of the group would be for the consideration of governments.'

The communique made some specific references to sovereignty, security, governance and solidarity in respect to Mozambique, Belize, Haiti, the Cameroon, Bosnia Herzegovena, and Cyprus, Angola, the Meditteranea and the Middle East. I took note of this for future reference.

When President Jagan died in March 1997, the PPP/C-led government entered a period of transition. Prime Minister Sam Hinds was sworn in as President while Janet Jagan was sworn as Prime Minister. It was during that period, a mere six months in the run-up to the December 1997 elections, that I was asked to represent the Government at the 15th Meeting of Heads of Government of the Commonwealth held at Edinburgh in the UK in late October 1997.

It was the first time in my life and tenure as Minister of Foreign Affairs that I was afforded the opportunity to sit, and later, mix and mingle among Kings, Presidents, Prime Ministers and the Queen of England as well as colleague Foreign Ministers from thirty-three of the thirty-five members of the Commonwealth.

During a break in one of the sessions, I approached Prime Minister Mahathir of Malaysia and reminded him of my visit to his country in 1993 with President Jagan. His face lit up. He was pleased to be reminded of the visit and reminisced briefly about his admiration of Cheddi Jagan. He expressed regrets to learn of his passing. I reminded Prime Minister Mahathir about what he said after I sang Frank Sinatra's 'My Way' by karaoke. He had mentioned to me at that time that 'My Way' was his favourite song he enjoyed singing by karaoke. While conversing with him he said "There one part of that song I like remind people about, and that is, "I haven't decided to 'face the final curtain' as yet".

It was at Edinburgh that I saw Nelson Mandela for the first time. Naturally I could not avoid the opportunity to meet and greet him, shake his hand and convey greetings from the PPP and the Government of Guyana.

At the official reception hosted by Queen Elizabeth, I met Prince Charles and engaged him in a feisty discussion about Guyana's relations with the UK. I told the Prince that I was not pleased to know that he had never visited Guyana and that as soon as I returned to Guyana, I would meet with the British High Commissioner to arrange for an invitation be sent to him. The Prince expressed his satisfaction with the arrangement and assured me that he would take up the invitation to visit Guyana.

About a year later, the British High Commissioner Edward Glover (1998-2002) called saying he wished to meet with me. We met, and following the exchange of pleasantries the High Commissioner informed me that the Prince conveyed his gratitude for the invitation to visit and had indicated a period when the visit could take place. Prince Charles visited Guyana in February 2000.

At the conclusion of the Edinburg CHOGM, the usual Communique was issued. The communique made reference to issues pertaining to sovereignty, independence, territorial integrity and unity of Cyprus. In respect to Belize, the Heads of Government reaffirmed their strong support for the territorial integrity, security and sovereignty of Belize. Once again, I took note of this for future reference.

The CHOGM meeting in Durban presented the opportunity and the forum to translate what I had observed at two previous CHOGM meetings into a living reality. I had resolved that another CHOGM must not pass without the support and solidarity of the entire Commonwealth being extended to Guyana vis-à-vis the border controversy with Venezuela.

MOVING ON

With my Foreign Affairs footprints behind in 2001 for others to follow or not to follow, I was now fully engrossed in my new job as Minister of Foreign Trade and

International Cooperation knowing that I had under my belt, experiences accumulated while performing the functions of the de facto Foreign Trade Minister and in the capacity as the substantive Minister of Foreign Affairs.

FRUITS ON INTERNATIONAL COOPERATION

During period 1999 to 2001 the MOFTIC on the international cooperation side, sought to place emphasis on human, financial, in the form of grant aid and technical assistance mobilization through what was known then as Technical Cooperation among Developing Countries (TCDC).

Japan was of great assistance to Guyana with grant aid provided for the construction of a new public hospital at New Amsterdam; technical assistance and infrastructural works to facilitate potable water supply to villages in Region six where it was seriously lacking; Japan also provided much needed assistance to Guyana Power and Light; studies for the construction of a deep water harbour and a modern container terminal; infrastructural works for the fisheries sector and volunteers to work in the public sector. Japan also provided assistance for the construction of the new, modern headquarters of the CARICOM Secretariat.

China was also of great assistance to Guyana. The PRC facilitated significant debt write offs; the provision of two modern roll-on, roll-off passenger ferries; medical brigades; training courses; technical assistance for the agriculture sector; the construction of a modern conference centre and grant aid for small community-based projects.

Signing Agreement with representatives of the Chinese Government - 2002

India was very supportive through the granting of ITEC scholarships; the provision of photovoltaic powered water pumps, installation of traffic lights in the city of Georgetown, the provision of legal draughtsmen for the Attorney General's Chamber and the construction of a cricket stadium outside the city. India also committed to the provision of two modern sports facilities for Regions two and six as well as a modern ICT park.

Nigeria provided badly needed legal draughtsmen for the Ministry of Legal Affairs while the Commonwealth Secretariat provided technical assistance to the Ministry of Foreign Affairs and the Ministry of Foreign Trade.

Cuba provided assistance to the Ministry of Culture and to the Ministry of Health with a constant flow of medical doctors and specialists for the public health sector.

Meeting with Fidel Castro -2001

For a new ministry with an extraordinarily small staff, the MOFTIC did a fantastic job in fulfillment of its mandate for both foreign trade and international cooperation. What assisted in the fulfillment of the ministry's twin mandates was the favourable international climate existing at that time supported by the fact that the government of the day recognized South/South cooperation as the vehicle to assist in capacity building and institutional strengthening primarily in the public sector which had suffered tremendously during the previous PNC administration. Moreover, the convening of the first-ever South Summit in Havana, Cuba, the 3rd Conference of the Association of Caribbean States at Margarita, Venezuela as well as the United Nations, Conference on Financing for Development at Monterrey, Mexico were all held at a time when governments in developing countries, including Guyana were favourably disposed to engaging in functional cooperation through distinct mechanisms negotiated between their respective countries. In addition, the whole question of financing for development had emerged as a priority issue for the developing countries either by way of debt relief, international development assistance, lines of credit, grant aid or soft loans.

I thoroughly enjoyed working in these areas, because they brought a sense of genuine cooperation based on mutual understanding and interests between Guyana and like-minded countries. But more importantly, to me, it was the beneficiaries who mattered most of all, especially when it was people at the grassroots level who, as a result of the cooperation programmes either developed their skills, their collective or personal entrepreneurship which in the long run, resulted in the overall development of our country.

Having been assigned CARICOM's spokesperson for sugar and WTO matters at the external negotiations, we began preparations in earnest for some gruelling and protracted negotiations with the European Union, a number of other non-ACP sugar-producing countries as well as WTO member states who we considered flexible based on previous discussions with them.

Meeting with Barbados High Commission - 1997

My representing the Government of Guyana at the Seattle WTO Ministerial in 1999 was an important benchmark signaling my transitioning from Foreign Affairs to Foreign Trade. It also meant that the Ministry, at the level of NACEN, began in earnest its preparations for the 4th WTO Ministerial along with my CARICOM colleagues and the Regional Negotiating Machinery.

A HECTIC INTERNATIONAL AGENDA

Between the period December 1999 and November 2001, that is, between the 3rd WTO Ministerial and the 4th to be held in Qatar, there was a flurry of international engagements that required President Jagdeo's intervention at the domestic or participation at the international levels.

President Jagdeo with President Castro - 2000 & President Putin - 2007

First, there was the first ever South Summit scheduled for April in Havana, Cuba which was a must in terms of our participation in light of the fact that Guyana was chair of the G77 and China. Guyana was to co-host the Summit in collaboration with the Government of Cuba. Then there was the 21st Caricom Heads of Government Conference, scheduled to be held during the first week in July 2000 in Canouan, St. Vincent and the Grenadines. It was vitally important that the President and I be present at Canouan conference because at that time, Guyana and Suriname were locked in political, diplomatic and legal battles over disputed maritime boundaries, and by extension, access to a disputed area of the sea where large amounts of deposits of oil were said to be located.

On the domestic front, it was in October of that year that Beal Aerospace Inc. succumbed to pressure from the Venezuelan and US governments and decided to pullout from a large-scale investment project in the Essequibo, that had been negotiated with the Government of Guyana.

Most importantly, national and regional elections were due to be held in March 2001, the ruling PPP/C was seeking a third term in office with Bharrat Jagdeo as its Presidential Candidate. This meant that Jagdeo was required to be campaigning at home to ensure another victory for the PPP/C.

The PPP/C scored another stunning victory at the 2001 elections. Of the 396,516 total valid votes cast, the PPP/C won 210,013 or 52.96 % of the votes cast. Thus, with fresh mandate from the people, the newly elected Jagdeo administration recommenced its activities at the international level.

The first of the President's international engagements was in April 2001 at the 3rd Summit of the Americas in Quebec City, Quebec, Canada. I accompanied the President to the Summit. Apart from the usual acknowledging, reaffirming, recognizing and reiterating of goals, principles and commitments, the leaders at the Summit called for the formulation of a 'Democratic Charter to reinforce OAS instruments for the active defence of representative democracy'.

The main focus of the Summit was negotiations of an agreement that would result in the establishment of a Free Trade Area of the Americas (FTAA), one of the three theatres of external trade negotiations in which I was deeply involved together with my CARICOM colleagues at the Caribbean Regional Negotiating Machinery (CRNM). PJ Patterson of Jamaica who was at the Summit and who, cognizant of the result of the recent election at home, called out to me as a 'conquering hero' as he entered the Quebec City Convention Centre.

When CARICOM leaders met in Canouan, St. Vincent and the Grenadines in July 2000, earlier in the year, they discussed 'The strategy for the next stage of the FTAA negotiations and the unfolding negotiations in the WTO. They emphasized the need for sustained vigilance by the region in securing the implementation of beneficial agreements already negotiated and for more vigorous action by the regional private sector, both in this regard and generally.' It was obvious to me therefore, that CARICOM leaders went to the Quebec Summit armed with a clear strategy in mind.

The leaders at the Quebec Summit adopted a Plan of Action to; 'Strengthen representative democracy, promote good governance and protect human rights and fundamental freedoms.' Importantly, the leaders called for the conclusion of the FTAA negotiations by January 2005 and to seek its entry into force as early as possible thereafter. As regards the FTAA, the leaders stated that; 'The agreement should be balanced, comprehensive and consistent with WTO rules and disciplines and should constitute a single undertaking and that importance be attached to the differences in size and levels of development of participating economies.'

During the Summit, some 150,000 protestors made their presence and voices heard on the streets of Quebec City. The police (RCMP) had cordoned off the area where the Summit was held with high and strong fences. The high point of the protests was the convening of the 'Second People's Summit of the Americas' a gathering where speeches of a political, labour and ideological orientation dominated. A number of protestors, some peaceful, some violent were arrested. Rubber bullets and tear gas were fired directly at protestors causing injury to many. To me it seemed like a replay of what occurred on the streets of Seattle some two years ago.

Because the agenda was dominated by external trade negotiations matters, I accompanied the President to the Quebec meeting. About one month after the elections in May 2000, Samuel 'Rudy' Insanally succeeded me as Minister of Foreign Affairs. 'Rudy' had for years been our Permanent Representative to the United Nations in New York.

Following participation at the Quebec SOA, President Jagdeo and I headed for the Bahamas in July 2001 to participate in the 22nd Meeting of the Conference of CARICOM Heads. At that meeting, the Heads reviewed the progress of the FTAA negotiations and 'reiterated the need to increase efforts to have the region's interests and priorities included in the FTAA negotiations.'

In respect to the negotiations at the WTO, the Heads reaffirmed their commitment to a 'rules-based multilateral trading system which caters for the concerns and peculiarities of smaller economies such as the Caribbean Community.' But more importantly, the 'Heads recognized that the next phase of the negotiations at the

420

hemispheric. Bi-regional and multilateral levels will take place simultaneously and therefore to meet those demands, the Heads agreed on 'the urgency for strengthening the institutional arrangements for coordinating the Region's participation in external trade negotiations.'

Following on the heels of this decision, concrete steps were initiated to broadening the shoulders of the Regional Negotiating Machinery. While assigning specific theatres of the negotiations to those Foreign Trade Ministers who the Heads felt were sufficiently knowledgeable and capable to be a lead-person for the area assigned to them, the Machinery was kept technically intact to provide the necessary technical support to the ministers.

If there was a Foreign Affairs or Foreign Trade Minister who were involved at the time in all the meetings preparatory meetings of the three negotiating theatres and who felt that he or she were not fully equipped nor ready to rumble, then I have to disagree because neither the Prime Ministerial Sub-committee on External Negotiations nor the Regional Negotiating Machinery were to be found lacking in their responsibility to provide necessary policy guidance to their Foreign Trade Ministers and their technical support staff.

As for me, I felt well prepared and equipped to fire on all cylinders in the ensuing negotiations, which from all indications were going to proceed at one and the same time. My comfort was also premised on the fact that, apart from strong regional support, I had a strong technical back up at home technically and politically

9.11

On the morning of September 11, 2001, while preparing to leave home for my ministry, my daughter Rima, drew to my attention to a scene on the TV screen showing two aircraft flying head-on into the Twin Towers at the World Trade Centre in downtown New York city. It was an unbelievable sight to watch and to see people jumping to their death believing it was to safety while the towers were collapsing. Not only was the scene shocking it was unbelievable. Seconds later, we saw images of another plane attack on the Pentagon in Washington, DC. The mighty United States was under attack by terrorists who had not only chosen their targets but also their weapons to execute their barbarous acts of terrorism against the government and people of the United States. Of the 2,996 persons killed, 2,763 died at the World Trade Centre and the surrounding areas, 189 at the Pentagon, 265 on the four planes, and 19 hijackers. All told, more than 6,000 persons were injured.

The September 11 terrorist attacks on the Twin Towers and the Pentagon in the US became known world-wide as 'The 9/11 Attacks' The events sent shock-waves through out the entire world. There was no doubt in my mind that the event would impact profoundly, the security situation in the United States and by implication, the rest of the world.

Addressing the 56th Session of the United Nations General Assembly in November 2001, Insanally, Guyana's new Foreign Minister had this to say; "Although the embers from the towering inferno which resulted from the attacks on 11th September have not fully died, it may nevertheless be possible to analyse the impact which that horrific disaster has had on international relations and, more particularly, the political, economic and social consequences which it is likely to have for the world."

The eventful and sad occurrences in the United States notwithstanding, we at the Foreign Trade Ministry continued with our preparations for the Fourth WTO Ministerial Meeting at Qatar just a mere month away.

DOHA

The big question on everyone's mind at that time, was whether in light of the events in the United States, the meeting in Qatar would go on. We gleaned from international press reports that some members of the WTO had reservations about attending the Qatar meeting because of security concerns and that the meeting would not be well attended. Our position at NACEN and the CRNM was that we should continue with our preparations as though the Qatar meting will be held. And just before the end of September 2001, communications from the WTO secretariat in Geneva informed us that the meeting in Qatar go on as planned.

We arrived in Qatar well prepared. Our plan was basically the same and our allies during the interregnum was solidified through regular contact and informal meetings. Our Qatari hosts were much better organised and so were the arrangements for the conference at the huge Sheraton Doha Hotel and Resort venue for the conference.

We did not attend the WTO Mini-ministerial meeting in Singapore in view of the fact that national elections in Guyana was a mere four months away and we were all required to be at home for the elections campaign. However, as a region we were not completely absent because Jamaica represented the interests of the Caribbean region at that meeting at which only twenty-two countries were represented. From all appearances, the Singapore mini-ministerial had all the characteristics of a Green Room meeting. But we refrained from being too critical principally because of Jamaica's participation.

While official reports emanating from Singapore spoke about a positive outcome, on the ground reports indicated that not all the countries that were present shared that view. The 'Implementation Issues' remained contentious if not divisive, with developing countries still pressing for the Doha Ministerial be assigned a 'Development Round' rather than a new round based on a new set of issues known as the 'Singapore Issues'. 'The Singapore Issues' included; the Environment, Intellectual Property Rights, Trade Facilitation, Transparency in Government Procurement, Trade Related Intellectual Property Rights, (Trips), and Public Health. In the meanwhile, draft texts on these and on agriculture, non-agriculture market access and other outstanding issues in preparation for the Doha Ministerial remained unresolved.

My absence from the Singapore mini-ministerial did not hamper my full participation in any of the meetings at Doha since we in the CARICOM and ACP groups worked as a team. While the usual mundane speeches were being delivered at the plenary, and specialized meeting were in progress, we were busy in bilateral or wider alliance meetings trying to find acceptable language for a draft declaration prepared at Geneva and already in circulation.

The meeting dragged on for about three days without an acceptable draft in sight. Meanwhile it was clear from the beginning of the meeting that the key players were Pascal Lamy, representing the European Union, Robert and Zoellick the United States Trade Representative (USTR) and Mike Moore, the Director General of the WTO.

I recall late one evening Lamy, who had apparently heard about my assertive, pro-development interventions, invited me to meet with him at the suite he was occupying. Accompanied by a couple of my CARICOM colleagues we found the French man who engaged us in a discussion during which he tried to convince us about the pressure he was under by certain countries. According to him. those countries were exerting pressure on EU to make concessions particularly in respect to trade preferences in agricultural products granted by the EU to ACP countries. Apparently, he wanted to make some trade-offs with the countries he claimed were pressurizing him. The trade-offs were to be on some of the Singapore issues as a quid pro quo so that there could be a favourable or win-win outcome of the meeting. The whole idea was to get us to drop what we were pushing for in order to achieve the so-called 'bigger picture.' We weren't convinced, but it seemed as though we were in a dilemma like that of a reluctant bride.

Actually, we were in a complicated situation at Doha. While were fully engaged in the negotiations, at the same time, we were pressing the EU, through our negotiations at the ACP/EU level to maintain, for as long as possible, the preferential market access we were enjoying with Europe for our agricultural products. The trouble was that trade preferences or preferential market access was viewed by a large number of countries as discriminatory and as a trade distorting measure that had to be phased out, if not abandoned entirely. In this regard, our alliance with the EU, though necessary, was viewed with deep suspicion by the Cairns or G20 Group, some countries of Latin and Central America as well as the countries from South East Asia. Interestingly, while maintaining its association with the G20 group, Brazil struck up a relationship with India and, notwithstanding our differences with Brazil and India on preferences, on the basis of their support for Special and Differential Treatment for small vulnerable economies, and the need to reinforce the notion of a Development Round at Doha, we formed the G33.

Subsequently, four more negotiating alliances emerged at Doha; The 'Alliance for Strategic Products and a Special Safeguard Mechanism' or G33 which demanded specific measures to protect vulnerable sectors in developing countries; the Group of Ninety or G-90 which included the Least Developed Countries (LDC's); the African Union and the ACP group of countries as well as the 'Friends of Multifunctionality' or G-10 who supported new exceptions based on the concept of non-trade concerns.

While the Doha meeting saw the emergence of these numerically powerful groupings of developing countries who were committed to ensuring that the meeting end up as a truly development- oriented round of the negotiations, the final declaration that emerged was disappointing to say the least.

Throughout the days I spent at Doha, my position has always been that the Doha Round should not be allowed to conclude without a clear understanding and well-defined commitments to the development dimension of the negotiations. Moreover, having regard to the mandate given to us by CARICOM Heads, who had insisted, that the Round must have a 'Development Vision' there was absolutely no question nor doubts in the minds of the CARICOM team that the declaration fell woefully short of our expectations. While some claimed that progress was made others held the opposite view. The road to Hong Kong was now scattered with Ramjohn Holder's 'plimplas'.

Mike Moore was right in his letter welcoming to journalists to Doha when he said;

'…But I believe it is true that the trade focus will shift away from Geneva if we fall short at Doha. I've said it many times because I believe it: trade liberalization negotiations will take place next year, the only question is whether they are conducted, bilaterally, regionally or multilaterally.'

Looked at in today's context, it is clear that Moore's statement was somewhat prophetic in that most of the trade liberalization negotiations are currently taking place bilaterally, regionally since the WTO driven process has virtually ground to a standstill.

Moore went on to point out: 'Unless all members are fully engaged in the process of negotiating and feel confident that they comprehensively understand the issues, we run the risk of creating new implementation problems in the future. Any negotiations that are launched in Doha cannot be completed if some members feel marginalized from the process and the way to address this problem is through more and better targeted technical assistance.'

Here again, Moore was spot on. Nineteen years after, from Doha to Hong Kong and up to this day, developing countries do not feel otherwise about their involvement in the trade liberalization negotiating process. It was clear to me that the vagueness of the Doha Declaration was in effect, a reflection of the less that stellar achievements of what was championed as a 'Development Round' and that notwithstanding the shout of 'Hurrays!' from some countries, sharp differences still remained amongst the wider WTO membership.

The Doha Declaration called for, substantial improvements in markets access, reductions of, with a view to phasing out, all forms of export subsidies, and substantial reduction in trade distorting domestic support. Strong emphasis was given to Special and Differential Treatment(S&DT) for developing countries as an integral part of all the negotiations on agriculture.' In addition, the Doha Declaration set three important deadlines; modalities for further commitments by March 2003, a comprehensive draft schedules based on the modalities by September 2003 and completion of negotiations by January 2005 as part of the Doha Round single undertaking.

OPPORTUNITY KNOCKS

A tremendous boost for the foreign trade portfolio presented itself whilst travelling on an overseas trip with President Jagdeo sometime in September 2001, I came across an advertisement published by Harvard University in the Economist magazine. The advertisement had to do with a short course on 'The Practice of Trade Policy: Economics, Negotiations, and Rules' sponsored by the John F. Kennedy School of Government at Harvard University. The course was open to applicants from all over the world at a cost. I drew the advertisement to Jagdeo's attention and expressed my interest in enrolling for the course. To my pleasant surprise Jagdeo readily agreed.

On our return to Guyana, Jagdeo gave instructions to Cabinet Secretary, Dr. Luncheon to have the matter passed through Cabinet for consideration and approval.

I was deeply grateful for this opportunity, having assumed the important portfolio of foreign trade. Jagdeo and I knew the benefits that could be derived from participating in such a course since it was being offered at a time when international trade negotiation at the World Trade Organisation had assumed

426

international importance and attention. Further, we both knew that participation in the course would help Guyana be better equipped to understand the complexities of multilateral trade negotiations. Moreover, the outcome of the course if creatively applied would enable us to navigate our positions in the myriad of multilateral negotiations and to work along with like-minded members of the WTO who shared similar views and expectations.

I thoroughly enjoyed my stint at Harvard. It is the oldest university in the United States.

Certificate received from Harvard University

The City of Cambridge in Massachusetts, apart from being a university city with institutions of higher learning, is a beautiful city. Peaceful, quiet with large parks and sports facilities. A stroll across the Harvard Bridge which spans the Charles River provides a relaxing view of another side of the city which is also home to many libraries, museums, bookstores and restaurants.

It was first time in my life I had the privilege to study, albeit for just one month, at a prestigious university campus in the United States. My enjoyment had to do principally with the university atmosphere, the conditions and facilities provided for study, but above all, the distinguished lecturers on subjects that were both relevant and topical to global economic and trade conditions and their impact on the extant international trade negotiations.

I finally got the opportunity to pursue academically, subjects that were of interest to me and my portfolio responsibilities. In the years gone by, my political career took precedence over my deep and abiding interest to pursue, even for a short while, subjects that were of interest to me academically. While many of my Party Comrades had elected to go off to pursue their academic pursuits at the University of Guyana and further afield, I chose to remain at home and to dedicate myself to work at Party Headquarters, though I must confess that the opportunity did present itself earlier.

Following our participation in a number of activities at the United Nations in October 1995 to mark the organisation's fiftieth anniversary, I accompanied President Cheddi Jagan on a lecture tour to two top universities and one college in the United States. In preparation for the President's participation at the UN's 50th, and knowing his interest in always having a programme of activities in the country he may be visiting at the time, me and Ambassador Rudy Insanally, Guyana's Permanent Representative to the United Nations put together a draft programme that included the lecture tour which Dr. Jagan eventually approved.

President Cheddi Jagan's tour included Guest Lectures at the Medgar Evers College in Brooklyn, New York; at Columbia University in New York and at Princeton University in New Jersey. The topic of his lectures would be; "Towards a New Global Human Order."

All three lectures were well attended by academics, lecturers, students and staff members of the respective institutions and were highly successful. Numerous questions were asked and answers provided to the satisfaction of all those in attendance. But there was one particular visit that stood out. It was our visit to Princeton University. Protocol required that before delivering a lecture, visiting guest lecturers would meet privately with academic heads of the institution for a brief conversation. On this occasion, during the conversation, President Jagan enquired about the possibilities for the Government of Guyana being granted short-term scholarships in specific disciplines for individuals the government may wish to recommend. The answer was in the affirmative, but such a facility could only be granted based on certain criteria and conditionalities. President Jagan suggested me as an example. Again, the response was a positive one. And to back the offer a number supporting documents were provided for me to consider. I accepted the documents fully aware that my political and ministerial responsibilities would make it almost impossible to take up such an offer.

The missed opportunity at Princeton, had re-emerged six years later at Harvard's John F. Kennedy School of Governance. The course I pursued there in December of 2001, a mere eight months after being appointed Minister of Foreign Trade and International Cooperation proved to be of immense value to the Government of Guyana.

The efficacy of my studies at Harvard began to show through with my ability to apply and articulate what I had learnt plus lots of reading on the subject and knowledge of the local conditions at home. I believe it was my interventions at CARICOM and ACP meetings where these matters were discussed and, based on reports CARICOM Heads may have received from their representatives, that I was considered competent enough to represent their interests and demands at the WTO as well as the challenges to sugar and the need for strong representation at both the WTO in Geneva and the European Commission in Brussels.

My foreign trade agenda was extremely hectic. Even before I was handed the portfolio of Foreign Trade fully, my introduction to the vagaries of multilateral trade negotiations began while I served as Minister of Foreign Affairs and with my acceptance, on behalf of the Government of Guyana, the Chairmanship of the Group of 77 and China for the period September 1999 to September 2000.

MOROCCO

It was in my capacity as Chairman of the Group of 77 and China, I participated its Ninth Ministerial Meeting held in Marakesh, Morocco in September of 1999. In my address to the opening session of the meeting I made known Guyana's philosophical outlook and expectations of the on-going global trade negotiations when I said; "The international trading system is central to the on-going process and structures of globalisation and trade liberalization which affect all developing countries irrespective of their levels of development. The functioning of the World Trade Organization must, therefore, be responsive and sensitive to the development needs of all its developing member states. So, what does the developing world require from the multilateral trading system? First, the full implementation of existing liberalization commitments. In this regard, many developing countries suggest that the Third WTO Ministerial Meeting in Seattle, USA should be a time to initiate a process of 'review, repair and reform.'

Moreover, it was at the Morocco meeting that came into contact with a number of Foreign Affairs/ Trade Ministers and WTO officials who were deeply involved in the preparations for the WTO ministerial meeting at Seattle. Fortunately, for me a large number of Foreign Ministers had portfolio responsibility for foreign trade and so in my bilateral meetings with them I was able to glean some of the intricacies of the global negotiations.

Following my completion of the course at the Kennedy School of Government, the Ministry of Foreign Trade and International Cooperation (MOFTIC) was now 'firing on all cylinders 'as it were, in fulfillment of its Mission Statement and any additional or complimentary tasks assigned to it by cabinet.

MEXICO

In May 2002, I was invited in my capacity as Caricom Spokesperson on WTO matters to participate at a Ministerial Meeting of the Organisation for Economic Co-operation and Development (OECD) based in Paris, France. Peter Gonzalez, the RNM Representative in Geneva and Director of WTO matters accompanied me to the meeting. I always felt comfortable with Peter at my side, he was one of the most competent, open and meticulous technical advisers on WTO matters in particular, and trade matters in general I have ever worked with.

Like most international bodies in different parts of the world, there was growing interest in the on-going trade talks at the WTO and the OECD was no exception. Participating at a ministerial meeting of the OECD was a first for me as Trade Minister and as CARICOM's representative.

I like spending time in Paris if only for a few days. There is a 'hustle and bustle' about the city that reminds me of Manhattan in New York city. The multi-cultural aspects of the city can also be captivating though there was little time for exploring on this occasion.

PARIS

The OECD Ministerial meeting was held at its headquarters building, located on the Rue Andre Pascal. The exchange of views at the meeting was clearly biased in favour of the industrialized countries who were there in large numbers. To them, the Doha Development Agenda meant development favourable to them and at the expense of the poorer members of the WTO. Not surprisingly, while the communique issued at the end of the meeting stated that; 'Ministers welcomed the Doha Development Agenda and rejected the use of protectionism, at the same time, they 'Committed to building on the momentum from Doha and to making significant progress on all elements agreed at Doha in order to create the necessary conditions for a successful Fifth WTO Ministerial meeting to be held at Cancun Mexico.' This paragraph was clearly inserted to satisfy the industrialized countries. And as if to throw a palliative to the developing countries the statement; 'Called on all WTO members to address the concerns of the developing countries including market access, recognizing they have a particular interest in a number of areas including agriculture, textiles and clothing.'

BRAINSTORMING

Under the theme; 'Caribbean Region Pre-Cancun meeting,' Cariforum Trade Ministers met in Montego Bay in June 2003. At that meeting, we took stock of the progress at the Doha mandated global trade negotiations and formulated our own political guidelines on the way forward.

In our deliberations we noted that 'the achievements at Doha was very limited and the troubled talks were marked by missed deadlines in several key areas of the round'. During our four-day meeting also attended by officials and technical experts we discussed the controversial issues such as; agriculture, non-agriculture market access (NAMA), services, trade related aspects of intellectual property, (TRIPS) public health, geographical indicators, special and differential treatment, (S&DT) small economies and the Singapore issues, (Investment, competition policy, trade facilitation and transparency in government procurement) among others. Our goal was to enable the governments of the region to participate at Cancun with a clear understanding of the issues, their implications and where the interests of our countries lie, as well as the objectives of the other countries. At the end of our deliberations, we adopted a draft declaration reflecting our common positions to assist in the negotiations in the theatres of external negotiations in which we were engaged.

In preparation for the WTO Cancun meeting, I was invited by the WTO Director General to represent the Caribbean region at two WTO mini-ministerial meetings. The first was in June 2003 at Sharm el-Sheik, in Egypt while the second was in Montreal, Canada in July of the same year. In effect, these were expanded Green Room meetings. According to the newly elected Director General of the WTO, Supachai Panitchpakdi; `The meetings were organised to gather momentum and to mobilize stronger inputs to the Doha Round. `

SHARM EL-SHEIK

While there was wide-ranging discussion, and at times heated exchanges among the delegations at Sharm el-Sheik, the talks which were fundamentally informal, failed to reach any consensus on agriculture and non-agriculture market access. Agreement was reached to 'intensify' negotiations on the so-called 'Singapore Issues'. Greater clarification was made on the public health issues and on S&DT for developing countries as well as on the implementation issues. Since questions had arisen at the meeting about prospects of defaulting on the 2005 deadline, the Canadian delegation offered to host a follow-up informal mini-ministerial with hope of reaching some degree of consensus on all outstanding issues and in keeping with the thrust enunciated by Supachai.

MONTREAL

At the end of July 2003, I received another invitation letter from WTO Director General Supachai inviting me to a Mini-Ministerial meeting scheduled for

Montreal. It was to be the last in a series of Mini-Ministerial preparatory to the Cancun Ministerial. The Montreal meeting's agenda was restricted to; liberalization of trade in agriculture, non-agriculture market access, services, public health and S&DT. The movers and shakers at the WTO and the Canadians were of the view that were these four issues to be agreed consensually, a breakthrough was possible at Cancun. However, owing to pressure exterted by a number of countries, the Singapore issues found themselves on the agenda for the meeting.

MOBAY

Following our June meeting at Montego Bay, the Heads of Government of CARICOM met in early July 2003 at Montego Bay at their Twenty Fourth Meeting of Conference. In the communique issued at the end of their deliberations, the Heads 'Expressed deep concern at the failure of the WTO negotiations so far to effectively address the issues of critical importance to the region and other developing countries. The Heads endorsed the preparation of a Ministerial Declaration on the WTO process setting out the Region's aspirations and objectives in the WTO negotiations. The Heads endorsed the Region's strategy for the 5th Ministerial Conference including the convening of a meeting on small economies on the margins of the Cancun Conference'.

The communique issued by CARICOM Heads of Government was of great assistance in providing political guidance for our preparations for Cancun. Three months after our Montego Bay meeting, we met again in Georgetown in the first week of September 2003. This time, as trade Ministers at a specially convened meeting of the COTED. This was to be our final meeting prior to us meeting at Cancun.

At the Georgetown meeting, we adopted the 'Caribbean Ministerial Declaration on the Fifth WTO Ministerial Conference.' which was submitted to the WTO in response to the 'WTO's Draft Cancun Ministerial Text' slated for consideration at Cancun as 'a workable framework for action by Ministers at Cancun'

CANCUN

Our preparations for the 5th WTO Ministerial Meeting in Mexico scheduled for September 2003 actually began in May 2002. Our preparatory work at the ministerial level was made easier with the establishment of the Prime Ministerial Sub-committee on External Negotiations and the Regional Negotiating Machinery at the regional level plus our own National Advisory Committee. What was advantageous about these three bodies was the fact they reflected an excellent balance between the mature political and the excellent technical competencies of all those who participated. In this way, we were able to capture and be guided by both the political ramifications and the technical implications of whatever decision we made. Consequently, these excellent conditions enabled us to chart the appropriate tactical and strategic approaches to whatever the issue or issues might be on the negotiating table.

I arrived at Cancun on September 9th fully prepared and ready to work at the conference scheduled to last from 10 to 14th. After checking in at my hotel, I immediately set out for the Cancun Convention Centre, venue for the conference, where the Caribbean team had agreed we would meet for our first debriefing session in caucus.

Following our debriefing session, and while I was busy participating with my Caricom/RNM colleagues at a coalition meeting with another group to reaffirm areas of convergence and to settle our differences in the areas of divergence, I received a message from the Mexican Foreign Minister, Luis Ernesto Derbez, Chairman of conference inviting me to a meeting with him. On my arrival at the room where the meeting was being held, I encountered a number of ministers from other countries. The WTO Director General and some members of the Geneva-based directorate were also present.

We were welcomed and informed by the Mexican Foreign Minister that he was proposing the need for a group Facilitators, whose role would be to assist him with the negotiations at the conference by chairing open-ended working group sessions on various topics. We were to try to reach consensus on the topics assigned to us. This was to be done through a process of consultations with individual groups and delegations and to report back to the him on the outcome of our consultations. We were informed that we were invited to be Facilitators and were asked individually to indicate whether we found his offer acceptable, we all accepted. The topics assigned were as follows; Agriculture- Singapore, Non-agriculture market access-

Hong Kong, Development issues- Kenya, Singapore issues- Canada, Other Issues- Guyana. Other Issues, would include; TRIPS registry for Geographical Indicators for wines and spirits. TRIPS non-violation, trade and environment and other topics. No decisions only recommendations were to be taken at the working group level and be brought to meetings of Heads of delegations and the full membership of the WTO.

From the countries assigned, it was clear that an attempt was made by the chairman to adopt a more inclusive and transparent approach to the negotiations by involving countries that were supportive of issues of interest to small economies. However, this effort was off-set by including Canada, Hong Kong and Singapore who were supportive of the new issues being advanced by the more developed economies. I should point out however that the topics were of great interest to a number of delegations who participated in the consultations and who presented their views on the issues assigned.

On the second day of the conference, Facilitators were invited to a report-back meeting with the Chair. I reported that based on the presentations made by individual delegations and groups, there appeared to be general consensus where references on the specific topics appeared in the draft declaration save for a few amendments and a call that they be linked to the Doha Declaration. Further, I reported that some countries wanted the draft to include the relationship between intellectual property and the UN Convention on Bio-diversity, protection of traditional knowledge and eco-labeling. Another set of countries wanted the multilateral environmental agencies to participate as observers in the negotiations and that dedicated sessions on the subjects be held at Geneva the following year. In sum, I informed the chair and other participants, that from the contributions made during the deliberations at my working group, the paragraphs appeared to be generally agreeable and that the recommendations made were not controversial and could easily be negotiated.

Reports by Facilitators from the other working groups, indicated that serious differences had emerged between the Caribbean group and representatives of the developed countries on the interpretation of Special and Differential Treatment. On the one hand, latter wanted more specificities on S&DT before any reference to the topic could be included in the declaration. On the other hand, the Caribbean group wanted a broader understanding of the concept. The Chairman of conference while inclined to our position, nevertheless, saw it as a trade-off between our interest and the group that was pressing to have the Singapore issues be prioritized. That apart, based on reports from Facilitators, fundamental differences between members on agriculture, non-agriculture market access, services and the Singapore issues seemed intractable. As was mandated by Heads of CARICOM, we re-engaged countries in the G90 and found that with a few exceptions, negotiable areas with flexibilities were found thus making the Group favourably disposed to pressing the interests of small vulnerable economies.

As the meeting dragged on, mirroring a situation not dissimilar from what had occurred on day three of the Doha ministerial, warnings were made to the effect that we would only have ourselves to blame should no consensus be reached and the process were to fail. In the circumstances, a series of Green Room meetings were convened with a view to bridging, or at least to narrow the differences between those who held firmly to their positions and those who were prepared to advance the process on the basis of reciprocal flexibility.

From the outset, I had personally assessed the Mexican Chairman as a someone who was reasonable and who wanted a balanced outcome of the conference. Derbez, a politician and academic by profession, was appointed Foreign Minister of Mexico replacing Rosario Green, when Vincent Fox Quesada was elected President of Mexico in 2000. Fox's populist, National Action Party (PAN), defeated the powerful Institutional Revolutionary Party (PRI) that had ruled Mexico for seventy-one years. Fox's election campaign had focused on fight against corruption, improving education and human rights, ending poverty, and protecting the environment. Derbez could be viewed as the embodiment of these elements, were we to capture and roll all of them into one. We also took into consideration the fact that Mexico has a history of being an independent nation that has always pursued a progressive foreign policy notwithstanding its geo-political location.

Mexico, as an emerging economy, had many foreign policy disagreements with its more powerful neighbour, but at the same time, it managed to balance its independence as a sovereign nation with the promotion of good neighbourly relations with the United States as exemplified in the North American Free Trade Agreement (NAFTA), cross border and immigration issues. It was in the above-mentioned context that I felt it necessary to support Derbez's efforts at heavy lifting at the Cancun meeting.

Prior to the convening of the Green Room meetings in which I participated fully, but which did not yield the desired results, Derbez himself had warned; 'If Cancun fails, it may take along time for trade talks to recover.'

The negotiations were good examples of what can be described as the dialectical unity and struggle of the opposites. Here we had the EU represented by Pascal Lamy and the USTR, Robert Zoellick though united on the Singapore Issues were opposed to each other on the vexed question of agriculture and non-agriculture market access. At the same time, there was the G90 countries united to a large extent with the EU on issues of interest to small economies and agriculture but unsupportive of the EU's push for the Singapore Issues to be a part of the Development Round.

With no agreement in sight, eventually a six paragraph Ministerial Statement was circulated for approval. The statement instructed member governments to; 'Continue working on outstanding issues with a renewed sense of urgency and purpose and taking fully into account all the views we have expressed in the conference.' The statement called on the chairman of the General Council and the Director-General of the WTO; 'To coordinate the work and to convene a meeting of the General Council no later then December 15, 2003 to take necessary action.'

The Ministers reaffirmed their 'Doha declarations and decisions' and recommitted themselves to 'working to implement them fully and faithfully'. Thus, ended another failed attempt to realize a much-needed development oriented global trade agreement.

I was happy to have participated in the Cancun and other WTO Ministerial Meetings for many reasons. First of all, because it gave me and my CARICOM/RNM Ministerial and technical colleagues the opportunity to show case and put into effect our collective intellectual, profound political and technical awareness of the issues under discussion at the global trade negotiations. I believe that one of our greatest advantages was the fact that we had on our team a beautiful and harmonious combination of home-grown politicians like Billie Miller of Barbados, K.D. Knight and Anthony Hylton of Jamaica, Ken Valley and Ralph

Maraj of Trinidad and Tobago and Sam Condor of St.Kitts and Nevis as well as a team of competent technicians including Randy Isaacs, Byron Blake, Nigel Durrant and Fay Housty all from the CARICOM Secretariat.

Secondly, the negotiations gave us the opportunity to share experiences and to develop alliances with negotiators from like-minded countries with whom we were able to agree on common goals, based on agreed strategies and tactics within the ambit of the negotiations.

Thirdly, we were able to demonstrate on the world stage, that what mattered most, was not so much the numerical size of a country's delegation, but rather its all-round knowledge of the issues on the table, to be flexible in one`s positions and to keep one`s options open while maintaining certain principled positions.

Fourthly, for me personally, my participation at trade negotiations at the regional and international levels, allowed me to bond with my colleagues, to share in each other`s confidence, to gather as much knowledge as possible, to learn from the experiences of other countries and to be able to apply the knowledge accumulated to the local conditions obtaining on home ground. In this way, I was building capacity to effectively represent Guyana and the Caribbean since their respective governments, especially the Guyana Government had invested in ensuring that I was present at the international events. Above all, what I considered to be most important in the entire process was to keep the President and cabinet colleagues informed in order to have their backing at every stage of the negotiations.

With Cancun behind us and Hong Kong two years ahead of us we continued our routine Trade Ministers meetings at the national and regional levels. In this interregnum, I began to focus on the negotiations for a Free Trade Area of the Americas, one of the four theatres of external negotiations and the establishment of a Regional Integration Fund (RIF) which Guyana had advanced as a safe guard mechanism for the small and vulnerable economies in the hemisphere.

SUGAR LOBBY

Simultaneously, knowing that we were nearing the end of the significant benefits we had received over the years as a result of the preferential arrangements for sugar with Europe, we launched a series of targeted lobbying activities in Europe in support of compensatory measures. At that time Mauritius was Chairman of the ACP'S sugar producing group of countries, while Guyana was CARICOM'S spokesperson for sugar. In October 2004, together with Timothy Harris, Foreign Minister of St. Kitts Nevis, Arvin Boolell, Minister of Foreign Affairs of Mauritius and myself, we embarked on working visits to France, Denmark, Sweden, Portugal, Poland, Brussels, the European Parliament and the UK in support of the ACP Group's position. At each of our meetings with government representatives in the capitals of these countries, we made the point that the Sugar Protocol is an inter-governmental agreement with obligations to be met by all contracting parties.

On the EU side, the obligation was to respect the commitments enshrined in the Protocol in terms of the three guarantees; price, access and definition. We therefore called on the EU to ensure that in the process of its agricultural reform, the sugar regime should be appropriately structured to maintain the existing guarantees. For our part, we informed our interlocutors that CARICOM sugar producing countries, had undertaken programmes for the restructuring, adaptation and diversification of their respective sugar industries in anticipation of the impending changes in the EU's agricultural policy and trading arrangements.

Because Brazil was strongly against ACP/EU preferential trade arrangements, we undertook a special lobbying mission to Brazilia. At first talks did not go well but much later, as the negotiations at the WTO progressed, Brazil became much more sympathetic to our position, so much so that we were invited to join the G20 negotiating group making it the G33.

Our lobbying activities were buttressed by Heads of Government of the Caribbean Community who had called on the UK during its Presidency of the EU, to ensure that changes in the EU'S trade regime with CARICOM should be phased at a rate that would enable CARICOM countries to adjust. The leaders also made calls for price cuts less than the anticipated thirty-seven percent and a longer transition period. Peter Mandelson, the EU'S Trade Commissioner made a visit to Guyana in January 2005, during his visit he emphasized that funding from the EU "would anticipate rather than cushion change".

Our lobbying exercises were important in that they demonstrated to the Europeans, a conscious push back in favour our agenda. Further, these lobbying missions were important because they sent a strong signal to Guyanese in general and the sugar workers in particular about the seriousness the Government of Guyana attached to the sugar industry and the livelihoods of the workers.

To emphasize the importance, we attached to our sugar industry, I made statements to the National Assembly in August 2004 and June 2005 providing the nation with status reports regarding the negotiations with the EU. Also, on July 21st 2005, I laid and ensured passage of a resolution in the National Assembly calling on the European Union to; 1) Accept the ACP countries 'proposals to phase in the price cuts over a period of eight years commencing in 2008; 2) To cap the cut in the current prices between 16-20 percent; 3) That Government embrace private sector investment in the sugar industry; and 4) That the EU provide necessary funding in anticipation of any cuts in price, to assist in the adaption of the sugar industry resulting from the anticipated loss in revenue. Moreover, to put the sugar workers in the picture, I held regular briefing sessions with stakeholders including the sugar workers' union, Guyana Agricultural Workers' Union (GAWU) and the Guyana Sugar Corporation (GUYSUCO).

I wrote and had published a series of newspaper articles including, 'The Little you have will be taken away', 'Europe Friend of Foe?' 'Quo Vadis Europe?' Numerous TV and radio interviews were delivered on the subject at international fora around the world, as well as speeches and consultations with the European Commission, at CARIFORUM meetings in the Caribbean, the ACP Summit in Mozambique, the WTO in Geneva, and at ACP Sugar Ministers Meeting in Fiji, Kenya, Mauritius and Brussels. My speeches and articles have been published in a booklet entitled; "REFORM" OF THE EUROPEAN UNION SUGAR REGIME – ACP Sugar Industries Under Threat.' The booklet's title reflected the dilemma facing the European Union. On the one hand, they were under pressure from their beet sugar producers to scale down or stop the subsidies granted to ACP sugar imports and to increase the subsidies to local beet farmers. On the other hand, they were under pressure from the WTO to end their farm subsidies and to discontinue, what a large number of WTO member countries considered to be the EU'S discriminatory preferential arrangements with the ACP countries. At the same time, the EU was under pressure from the ACP countries to maintain the preferential arrangements. Small wonder why the EU kept 'dancing around' at Doha and Cancun while at the same time trying as hard as they could, under these pressures, to find a compromise with everyone which was well nigh impossible.

In retrospect, every one of these events were of critical importance to Guyana and the other ACP sugar producing countries. On each occasion, we used the opportunity to collectively assess where we were in relation to our negotiations with Europe, determine our strategy and tactics and make any adjustments we considered necessary.

At each of these meetings, I learnt more and more about the sugar industries in the countries I visited and the challenges any change in the sugar protocol would have for sugar workers and people in those countries. Suffice it to say, I also learnt a lot about the adjustment and transformational measures the governments of those countries planned to make by utilizing resources provided by the EU as the so-called 'accompanying measures.' Some governments even took steps to privatize their industries or to engage in public-private sector partnerships to save the industries and to prevent mass unemployment.

EPA AND SUGAR

By the end of 2005, following protracted negotiations with the European Commission it became clear that 'Economic Partnership Agreements' (EPA) would replace the Lome Convention. The EPA's were to be 'balkanized' in that, they would be framed on a regional basis so that there would be one EPA for the Caribbean, one for Africa and another for the Pacific region. At the end of the process, the EPA's would in effect be 'Regional Economic Partnership Agreements' or REPA's with Europe. A target date of January 1st was set as the target date for the REPA's to come into force.

Throughout the negotiations with the EU we, in the ACP group, held to the position that within the REPA's the benefits under the Sugar Protocol should be safeguarded. This proved to be untenable in a situation where Europe was under tremendous pressure at the WTO negotiations to abandon the preferential arrangements granted to the ACP.

In the end, what the Europeans proposed was that the preferential arrangements would not be renewed but that an additional 30,000 metric tonnes of sugar from Caricom countries would be extended under the Sugar Protocol up to September 2009, and that Guyana, Jamaica and Belize would share in providing the additional quantities. Moreover, the argument was advanced that should there be any shortfalls by CARICOM sugar producers, that shortfall would be distributed to the African and Pacific sugar producing countries.

By the end of 2005, Guyana had completed and submitted its Action Plan for the sugar industry in accordance with its request to the EU for 'Accompanying Measures' to be provided in light of the devastating social and economic impact the termination of preferential arrangement for sugar would have on Guyana's economy.

Following my departure from the Ministry of Foreign Trade and International Cooperation, the EU paid over US$5 million and US$44 million in two tranches as its commitment to and in support of Guyana's sugar industry under the EU's 'Accompanying Measures' package.

Today, many of those industries are a shadow of what they were before the Sugar Protocol came to an end. In the case of Trinidad and Tobago, its sugar industry at Caroni closed its doors in 2003. In St Kitts, the tourism and the light industries have replaced the once dominant sugar industry though enough sugar is produced mainly for domestic consumption. In Barbados, the number of sugar factories have been reduced from twenty-six to two. In Guyana, the previous APNU+AFC coalition administration closed a number of factories throwing thousands of workers on the breadline. While in opposition, the PPP/C pledged to re-open the closed estates and to put the industry back on its feet. Following its election to office in August 2020, the newly elected government took concrete steps in fulfillment of its promise.

FIGHTING FOR GUYANA AT COTED

On the home-front, I continued to press domestic producers, manufacturers and exporters to pay more attention to the implications of, and benefits that can be gained from the realization of the Caricom Single Market and Economy. I encouraged them to find the ways and means to take advantage of the CSME particularly as regards our exports within CARICOM. At the same time, I pressed at the level of COTED for the removal of non-trade barriers to Guyana exports to those CARICOM countries who persisted in maintaining such barriers against Treaty regulations.

To hammer home the point, I took the initiative to establish a Business and Labour Advisory Committee (BLAC) involving exporters and potential exporters. BLAC'S main task was to engage in information sharing amongst its members and to monitor decisions arrived at by COTED as well as the activities of CARICOM member states who were engaged in trade distorting measures and abuse of the Common External Tariff (CET). For example, Suriname prohibited the importation of logs and rice from Guyana, while St. Lucia refused to accept our rum. St. Vincent and the Grenadines imported Uncle Ben's rice from the United States and through a raft of non-tariff barriers prevented our rice from entering their domestic market.

But Guyana was no angel among the regional violators of the CET. With our local construction industry moving at a rapid pace, there arose a high and sustained demand for cement. Importers began looking for cement from outside CARICOM where it was cheaper and available all year round. Reliability and certainty of supplies were important factors to them. They wanted to move away from importing cement exclusively from Trinidad Cement Limited (TCL) and the ARAWAK Cement Company in Barbados.

In furtherance of their goal, our cement importers approached the Government with a request that they be allowed to import cement from extra-regional sources. We all knew that for this to happen, two steps were necessary; first, was to establish as a matter of fact, that TCL and ARAWAK were not in a position to supply the cement and secondly, that were this proven to be the case, then we would have to apply to COTED, the CARICOM body, charged with responsibility to grant or not to grant waivers of the CET in order for cement or any other product be imported from extra-regional sources. In the meanwhile, in flagrant violation of our treaty obligations, cement began flowing in from Venezuela, Colombia and the Dominican Republic.

As the Minister responsible for COTED matters I was put in a difficult position moreso, when Trade Ministers from Trinidad and Tobago, Barbados and Suriname raised the matter at several duly constituted meetings of COTED.

Prior to the COTED meetings, it had come to my attention that the Ministry of Finance in collaboration with the Guyana Revenue Authority had agreed to remove customs duty on building cement imported from outside CARICOM...with effect from 2, October 2006 and for a period of one (1) year. The CET was removed year after year up to the time when the matter eventually ended up three years later before the CCJ.

According to the Court's records, at the early stages of the hearings, Guyana conceded that it had breached the Revised Treaty of Chaguaramas (RTC) and that in its defence, it was not justifying the breach 'but advance this in explanation and mitigation of our breach.'

At the conclusion of its deliberations on the matter, the CCJ ruled that 'Guyana has since October 2006 been in breach of Article 82 of the RTC by failing to implement and maintain the CET. The Claimants are entitled to the benefit of having the CET maintained by Guyana subject to Guyana's right to make an application to COTED or the Secretary General pursuant to Article 83 of the RTC.'

The CCJ further ordered that Guyana within 28 days of the date of its order, implement and thereafter maintain the CET in respect to Cement from non-CARICOM sources without prejudice to its right to make an application to COTED or the Secretary General under article 83 of the RTC

Our rice exports faced two problems almost at the same time. In the first place, the European Union had closed off the shipment of rice to Europe via the Overseas Counties and Territories (OCT) route which, while in existence, proved to be a very profitable from a market access perspective for Guyanese millers. In the second place, some CARICOM countries claimed that Uncle Ben's rice from the US was much cheaper on their domestic markets so that market access for Guyanese rice was effectively blocked using price as a justification for doing so.

To address the twin problem, my ministry, together with a team from the Guyana Rice Producers Association (GRPA) and the Guyana Rice Development Board (GRDB) undertook a strong lobbying mission to Brussels to make representation on the matter. After careful consideration, the EU provided funds to assist in making the regional rice sector more competitive in respect to price. In addition, access for Guyana's rice to the EU was made 'Duty free, Quota free' from 2008 to 2010. This was for a transition period during which, access for 187,000 to 250,000 metric tones of rice would be allowed entry into Europe's domestic market. Back home, we called for the establishment of a CARICOM Regional Monitoring Mechanism (CRMM) for trade in rice among CARICOM countries.

Some countries resisted the establishment of the CRMM, they did not want to be policed as regards their imports of rice from extra-regional sources. The CRMM was nevertheless established and was effective while it existed.

With Trinidad and Tobago, the situation was even more scandalous. Trinidad refused to accept our rice using non-tariff barriers such as length of the grain and scent as disqualifying factors for its importation. The Trinidadian authorities also prohibited the importation of our beef and poultry meat on spurious sanitary and phyto-sanitary grounds.

In the case of the latter, following representation from poultry farmers and cattle rearers, I pressed CARICOM to establish a technical team whose task would be to visit the facilities where poultry and beef were processed for local and foreign consumption to determine the standards and sanitary conditions at the locations. The technical team was established. The team and paid two visits to Guyana. The submitted their report in which they approved the exportation our beef and poultry meat to Trinidad and Tobago.

I travelled to Port-of-Spain on two occasions for separate talks with the Trinidadian Ministers of Agriculture and my colleague Ken Valley, the then Minister of Foreign Trade. My conversation with the Minister of Agriculture was not helpful. He was defensive of the protectionist measures adopted by his government and gave me the distinct impression that he couldn't care less about his country's violations of Protocol IV of CARICOM'S Trade Policy.

My conversation with my friend Ken had to do with a proposal to the effect that his government or his country's private sector consider investing in the establishment of a sugar refinery in Trinidad or Guyana. In the case of the former, the proposal was that Trinidad accept Guyanese brown sugar and refine same in Trinidad instead of importing white sugar from outside the region.

The proposal arose because Trinidad and Tobago had been making applications repeatedly for waivers of the CET to import white sugar from extra-regional sources. Guyana on the other hand, kept making a case that sugar was available in

445

the region but what was needed was the establishment of either a CARICOM enterprise, a private sector or a public-private sector investment, that would, within the meaning of CARICOM'S Industrial Policy, to produce white sugar of common market origin to replace the white sugar that Trinidad and Tobago was importing from outside the region.

In the case of Trinidad investing in Guyana by setting up the proposed refinery, I pointed out that Guyana was prepared to facilitate such an investment and to supply the required amount of brown sugar necessary to keep the refinery going. Valley kept beating around the bush, making promises that he would consult with his government and the private sector and that he would get back to me. Ken never did. He eventually passed away and so did the proposal.

THE CSME

The Caricom Single Market and Economy CSME) was set to be established by 2005.Towards that end, the nine protocols had already been agreed by the Heads of Government and Guyana had been signed and ratified all nine protocols. A Prime Ministerial Sub-committee was established headed by Owen Arthur, the then Prime Minister of Barbados. Work was in initiated to harmonize existing legislation in the various CARICOM jurisdictions on intellectual property, government procurement, trade in goods from free zones, and free circulation.

There were many who had doubts about the CSME and the benefits that would accrue to Guyana. To address these lingering doubts, I traveled around the country with a technical team to explain and to answer questions people wanted to raise about the efficacy of the CSME and what it meant for their everyday lives. I made the point that our workers, farmers, public servants, businessmen, captains of industry, academics, intellectuals, members of the legal profession and our youths and students must have a good grasp and a first class understanding of the CSME protocols which would have a direct relationship with their everyday activities.

The hurdles notwithstanding, the Government of Guyana under the leadership of Cheddi Jagan at the 16th Meeting of Conference of Heads of Government held in Georgetown in July 1995 said;

"Regrettably, we have not made significant progress towards the realization of a Single Market and Economy. Here in Guyana there have been significant advances on this issue. I am pleased to announce that on July 1, Guyana joined other CARICOM countries in implementing full convertibility and repatriation of regional currencies, in a move to enhance our economic and trade relations with the rest of the Community."

Later, in July 1997, at the 18th Meeting of Conference of Heads of Government held at Montego Bay, Jamaica then President Samuel Hinds had this to say;

"Guyana is conscious that despite the distances separating us, we can find much benefit in a Singe Market and Economy. It would be for us to find arrangements which distribute the benefits widely, leaving no one out."

Then in July 1998 at the 25th Anniversary Summit of Heads of Government held in St. Lucia, former President Janet Jagan told her colleagues;

"Our efforts at a CARICOM Single Market and Economy are of primary importance if we are to make progress. An essential ingredient of this progress is the free movement of skills and people. Some work has been done in this direction, but more remains to be done. Of equal importance, is the strengthening of intra-regional trade; much more self-reliance is needed if we are to achieve goals set in the past."

In July 2000, at the Meeting of Conference of Heads of Government held at Canouan, St. Vincent and the Grenadines, then President Bharrat Jagdeo reaffirmed Guyana's commitment to the CSME when he declared;

"Guyana supports the early establishment of a single market and economy."

The activism of the Ministry continued with NACEN pushing at the national level for the completion of its priority areas for 'Trade Related Assistance or TRA. TRA had emerged in the process of our negotiations for a Free Trade Agreement of the Americas (FTAA). It was considered an integral part of the FTAA's, Hemispheric Cooperation Programme (HCP).

Canada was the first country to make a significant financial contribution to the TRA programme. The issue of assistance had arisen because at the negotiations, a number of governments had pointed out that in any free trade arrangement of the FTAA-type, small, vulnerable economies would not benefit in as much as the larger economies such as Argentina, Brazil, Colombia, Canada, the USA and Venezuela would.

And so, it was in the context of the decision to establish a HCP within the FTAA, that Guyana took the initiative to call for the establishment of a Regional Integration Fund (RIF) taking into consideration the European Union's integration experience where a similar RIF mechanism was established to help grow the weaker economies in Europe.

Senator Paul D. Coverdell, the then Chairman of the Western Hemisphere Subcommittee Foreign Relations Committee in a letter dated October 20, 1997 to our Washington Ambassador at that time wrote about the RIF saying inter alia; '…The proposal definitely merits our close attention. It is certainly an interesting proposal. Your efforts on behalf of the Government of Guyana, and all the smaller, developing countries in the Western Hemisphere, are appreciated.'

In the meanwhile, at the level of CARICOM, we were successful in negotiating free trade agreements with Venezuela, the Dominican Republic, Costa Rica and Cuba. At the national level we negotiated successfully a Guyana-Brazil, Partial Scope Agreement. Joint Business Councils were established with China, Cuba and India. And a framework for a national policy on GMO's was presented to cabinet for consideration.

INTELLECTUAL PROPERTY RIGHTS

Notwithstanding the paucity of staff at the Ministry, we did a considerable amount of work on the question of Intellectual Property Rights (IPR). A draft Copyright Bill of 1999 was formulated and submitted to cabinet for consideration. In the meantime, the US Embassy in Georgetown informed me that the relevant authorities in Washington had conveyed their interest in welcoming a delegation from Guyana to engage in negotiations on a bilateral IPR agreement. We welcomed the invitation. It was on that basis that I took a small delegation to Washington, USA to negotiate a bilateral IPR agreement with the US only to be told on competition of the negotiations that the US usually requires a Bilateral Investment and Protection Treaty as a companion agreement to the IPR agreement before there could be any further movement going forward. The process ended there.

PREPARING FOR HONG KONG

In 2005, two very important persons visited Guyana. The Director General of the WTO, Mr Supachai Panitchpakdi and John Tsang, Hong Kong's Minister of Commerce, Industry and Technology visited in May and November respectively. It was the first time ever that a Director General of the WTO and a Hong Kong Trade Minister would visit Guyana. The two distinguished visitors visited at a time when it was agreed that negotiations at the FTAA and ACP/EU would be on hold pending the outcome WTO negotiations. In effect this meant that the 'decks were cleared' for us to focus exclusively on the WTO Hong Kong Ministerial. The visits were a reflection of the significant inroads Guyana and the Caribbean were making at the global trade negotiations.

The Director General of the WTO visited because he wanted to have a first hand appreciation of the impact the loss by the Caribbean countries, of their preferential access for sugar and rice to Europe. He also wanted to talk about the chances of success for small and vulnerable economies and Special and Differential Treatment at the upcoming WTO ministerial meeting at Hong Kong.

As far as the visit of the Hong Kong Minister was concerned, his mission was more focused. He wanted me to play the role of a Facilitator at the Hong Kong meeting like I did at the Cancun Ministerial meeting. On this occasion, I would be Facilitator for 'Development Issues 'at the meeting. I agreed, knowing full well that the subject is a controversial, if not a complicated one. The Hong Kong minister took the opportunity to pay a courtesy call on President Jagdeo to brief him on the status of the negotiations since Cancun and the agenda for the Hong Kong meeting.

In the run up to the Hong Kong Ministerial, I received an invitation from Kamal Nath, the Minister of Commerce of India. I met Kamal, at previous ministerial meetings. His invite to me was to a G33 Trade Ministers' meeting in New Delhi. I gladly accepted the invitation to participate for two reasons; First, my participation would be consistent with the mandate of CARICOM Heads of Government and second; It was the first formal meeting of the group outside a WTO conference setting to which we were invited as an integral member of the Group with the potential of emerging once again as the Group of 90 at Hong Kong.

The G33 meeting proved to be extremely useful, in that it cemented the membership of the Group for the purpose of upholding common positions and direction on the key issues in readiness for the Hong Kong Ministerial. Further, it enhanced CARICOM'S presence and raised our profile as a valued member of the global trade negotiating process. It was in that context, as well as my role at previous WTO ministerial that the two distinguished visitors from Geneva and Hong Kong came to Guyana. The EU Trade Minister Peter Mandelson had visited earlier bringing the sad news about price cuts to the tune of US$37 million annually in respect to our export earning for sugar to Europe.

NATIONAL DISASTER INTERVENES

At the beginning of January (2005), a devastating flood due to heavy rainfall not experienced since 1888 hit Guyana affecting the lives and livelihoods of more than 300,000 persons. The areas affected were Regions three, four and five. Government declared the affected areas as 'National Disaster Areas' and immediately allocated millions for emergency relief.

Five committees treating with food, water, health care, infrastructure, shelter, donor support and information were established to assess the situation and to coordinate relief efforts. The parliamentary opposition was invited to name representatives to serve on each of the committees. State House was converted to an 'Operations Centre' and Ministers of Government were called out to visit affected areas and to deliver flood relief to affected households.

Soon after my return from Hong Kong, I joined with cabinet colleagues to visit areas on the East Coast affected and to deliver food hampers and water to families affected. I started out by visiting 'Babe Dam' a North Ruimveldt squatting area in Georgetown, to assess and to report back on the needs of squatters. On other occasions, I was asked to focus on East Coast villages where I joined Harry Persaud Nokta to deliver food hampers to residents at Betterverwagting. Henry Jeffery and I joined forces to deliver food hampers to families at Dazelle Housing Scheme at Paradise on the East Coast. And Odinga Lumumba and I delivered food hampers to residents at a number of villages on the East Coast including Vigilance, Friendship, Buxton, La Reconnaissance, Annandale, and Lusignan.

HONG KONG

I had arrived at the Hong Kong international airport on December 11, two days before the official start of the conference. I had planned it this way because of the twelve-hour time difference between Guyana and Hong Kong and the need to address the jet lag syndrome. In addition, I wanted to familiarize myself with the huge Hong Kong Convention and Exhibition Centre, the conference venue and to locate my CARICOM colleagues since we had agreed to meet in caucus to update ourselves with the agenda for the meeting and to fine tune our individual and collective responsibilities.

The usual routine followed, meeting with the chairman of conference to be assigned my responsibilities to assist with negotiations. The assignment of subjects this time around had a stronger developing country representation for both competence and image. We were to have informal meetings with the full membership and in smaller groups with a view to ensuring transparency and inclusivity and to ensure that all members are kept informed about the progress of the negotiations in the various areas. Our meetings with delegations were not meant to replace meetings of the Heads of Delegations process nor to detract from the decision-making rights of WTO members. On the contrary, we were tasked with the responsibility to help generate consensus that will be needed for the text of the declaration.

I started my open-ended meetings with delegations on the Development Issues following the official opening of the conference. The meeting room was already packed with Heads of delegations waiting to make their contributions based on a list system. I had competent technical RNM and Hong Kong trade officials with me throughout the entire process. For two full days, delegation after delegation made their contribution. I made my own notes while the technical officers fulfilled the roles assigned to them.

At the first meeting between the Facilitators and the Chairman, it became clear that differences had emerged on agriculture, non-agriculture market access and development issues. I reported that four issues dominated the discussion in my group, these included; preferences and preference erosion, cross cutting special and differential issues, aid for trade and duty free, quota free market access.

As the presentations in my group continued, it became clear that the LDC group tended to dominate the consultation using their overwhelming presence to push the duty-free quota free envelope. This did not go down well with other developing countries. As a consequence, some countries began to complain about the direction in which the consultation was heading, claiming that any attempt to prioritize the duty free, quota free issue at the expense of other development specific issues would not be a true reflection of the membership's position.

Some delegations argued that the duty free, quota-free market access question should not be just for one group of countries, it should be for all developing countries. At a certain point in the consultation, I intervened to make the point that were we to spend most of the remaining time on the duty free, quota free issue, aid for trade and commodities, we may end up with a disproportionate situation that leaves other developmental issues such as small economies and special and differential treatment unattended by not devoting some time for the membership to benefit from discussions on them.

But it was not only the LDC Group that was aggressively pursuing the duty free, quota free market access matter, the African Group, which included most of the LDC's was on the offensive on the cotton issue as well. Because the cotton issue was a big concern for the African group in particular and because of the large size of the Group at the conference a dedicated formal meeting was convened on the subject. One county described the cotton issue as "a bleeding wound on the conscience of the world". It was at that meeting that the African Group demanded a clear decision on the cotton issue from the conference.

On the second day of the conference, I held separate dedicated consultative sessions with the Central American and CARICOM delegations as well as a joint Japan, US and Canadian delegation. The major issue of concern to the Central Americans was the issue of preferences. They were not supportive unless it was considered a cross-cutting issue. As far as the CARICOM delegation was concerned, they wanted to put on record their contribution to the negotiations on the development issues. To them, there were specific issues in the text of the draft declaration that needed strengthening. Specific amendments were proposed. Further, the CARICOM Group submitted that development must be premised on assistance for small vulnerable economies including aid for trade which must be based on trade-related supply side assistance. As far the Japanese, Americans and Canadians, were concerned they raised a range of technical issues such as bindings on some or all agricultural products and whether product coverage should be one hundred per cent or less. The exchange of views clearly showed that there were fundamental differences between the three delegations. While the Canadian and Japanese positions coincided, the US had a completely different position.

By day three of the conference, I was in a position to inform the Heads of delegations that while the talks on the development issues had concentrated by and large on the duty free, quota free demand, the focus remained on reaching consensus on a 'development package' as a whole. I also informed the meeting that there appeared to be a marked willingness on the part of a number of countries to grant preferential market access to the LCD countries. The problem however was which countries should be the beneficiaries, the legalities involved, what products should benefit and the duration of the preferences. But there was another complication. A number of developing countries including the CARICOM Group made it clear that while they welcomed the granting of duty free, quota free market access to the LDC's they were not prepared to let specific development issues be diluted. They expressed a strong interest in having their interests reflected in the draft declaration.

By day five we moved to Green Room meetings to address amendments to the text of the draft declaration based on what had emerged up to that time from reports to Heads to Delegations from Facilitators.

The first Green Room meeting concentrated on an end date for the negotiations. The second meeting focused on the text of the draft declaration and what should be the main elements of a development package. The third and most crucial meeting, dealt with agriculture and non-agriculture market access, the phasing out of export subsidies and domestic support as well as the question of preferences. During the exchange of views. A number of technical issues arose but it was agreed that such issues would be better resolved preferably at Geneva and not a ministerial conference.

On the question of preferences, Brazil stated that while it was supportive of CARICOM's position on preferences, it would not wish to have such preferences utilized to perpetuate protection for big countries. India for its part expressed its unequivocal support for CARICOM on the question of preferences while the Jamaican delegation put up a strong fight in defence of preferences

Almost three hours were spent at the third Green Room meeting trying to hammer out the framework of a text on agriculture, non-agriculture market access, phasing out of export subsidies and domestic support, cotton, duty free, quota free market access and preferences. Complications arose at the meeting when the EU announced it will not to take any action on the matters raised. They argued that the 2010 deadline was not in syc with the reform of its Common Agricultural policy (CAP), that 'parallelism' (the equivalence between imports considered in the injury determination and those made subject to safeguard measures) and domestic politics were strong factors that influenced their position on the matters.

December 17th, broke with intense discussions on a draft ministerial text that would form the basis of a declaration. The draft made references to agriculture and non-agriculture market access, specific development issues, including duty free, quota free access for LDC's exports.

The draft Ministerial text was subjected to further revision in the Green Room. This time the main areas of focus were services, non-agriculture market access and development specific issues. The compromises struck were not really decisions per say but follow-up steps to be taken in Geneva in the wake of the Hong Kong meeting with hope of completing the round by 2006.

I had hoped that with the pleas and assurances by the chairman, Heads of delegations would have viewed the draft text as a 'workable' document, accepted it as a first step towards a final text and gone along with it. However, a number of delegations expressed dissatisfaction with various sections of the text, compelling the chairman to commit to meet with the complainants to iron out differences they had raised at the session.

On December 18th, one week before Christmas 2005, on our arrival at the conference centre on the morning of the last day of the conference, we were greeted with a final draft circulated for approval by the chairman of conference. Personally, I did not have any fundamental problem with text. I must concede however, that my general acceptance of the contents of the document had more to do with my deep involvement in the process and political awareness of the complexities of the various negotiated rather than as a representative of one of the 149 member countries who participated at the conference.

Meeting with my CARICOM colleagues to go over the text, I got a sense that though there was disappointment that the issues we came to press for were not reflected in the wording as we would have liked it to. For example, on the question of special and differential treatment the text reaffirmed that '…the provisions for special and differential (S&D) treatment are an integral part of the WTO Agreements. We renew our determination to fulfill the mandate contained in paragraph 44 of the Doha Ministerial Declaration … that all S&D treatment provisions be reviewed with a view to strengthening them and making them more precise, effective and operational.'

The text on S&DT was merely declaratory and a re-hash of what was agreed to at Doha. It was also a statement of intent rather than a clear-cut decision on the way forward. Further, in effect the text meant that the matter was sent back to Geneva for more technical work to be done on the subject. Therefore, from all indications, it seemed to me at the time, that the text on S&DT was the most digestible, given the prevailing circumstances. Any definitive text on the matter placed before the 149 country-representatives would have resulted, to my mind, in a contentious and divisive discussion that would have frustrated the efforts of the majority.

The section on small economies in the Ministerial Declaration was no less comforting. The text stated; 'We reaffirm our commitment to the work programme on small economies and urge members to adopt specific measures that would facilitate the fuller integration of small, vulnerable economies into the multilateral trading system'

The WTO General Council was instructed to "…continue the work on small economies in the Dedicated Session and to monitor the progress of the small economy proposals in the negotiating bodies …" Again, like S&DT, this matter which was critical to the interests of CARICOM, in particular, was left open-ended and thrown back into the Geneva negotiating court without any clear-cut decision being reflected in the final declaration.

Though not a happy ending, here was another example of a matter of great interest to the small, vulnerable member states of the WTO who had to satisfy themselves with the matter being designated, or rather diluted to the status of a cross-cutting issue rather than being elevated to a matter of high priority and reflected in the final declaration with definitive and explicit language. Would this have meant the unravelling of the entire final declaration? Possibly, and this was precisely what both developed and developing countries were afraid of. The compromise therefore was to settle for the language used in the final declaration.

WEIGHTY ROLE OF NGO'S

My friend Martin Khor, Director of Third World Network (TWN) a Malaysian-based independent, not-for-profit international research and advocacy organisation, in usual but profound analytical style was to write later about the outcome of the Hong Kong Ministerial Conference. Martin was an economist and journalist by profession.

I first met Martin at the Seattle Ministerial Conference where we struck up what turned out to be an extremely active, productive and lasting relationship. What I liked about Martin was his perceptiveness that had a strategic ring to it, the nimbleness of analytical skills, his biting sarcasm and his sharp witticism. Always with a smile, Martin was a good listener. He provided a balanced opinion on the issues under discussion, though his contributions unmistakably, were always people-centered and sympathetic to the cause of developing countries. It was these qualities that attracted me to Martin and TWN'S publications. But more fundamentally, it was the sharp differences in analysis of the outcomes of ministerial between the WTO and TWN that I found intriguing and as wake-up calls for critical analysis on my part and that of NACEN with a view to arriving at conclusions that were balanced, grounded in realpolitik and applicable to our own local conditions and peculiarities.

For example, as afar as TWN was concerned, the Hong Kong Ministerial Declaration was imbalanced against developing countries. In TWN's opinion, "The developing countries gave in on the key market access issues of services and NAMA. In return they did not receive any significant gain in cotton, market access for LDC's or aid for trade, the three main components of a so-called development package".

TWN went on to point out; "As far as the 2013 end-date for the elimination of agricultural export subsidies, the most publicized claim of benefit for Hong Kong, it was no victory – this was the greatest distorting subsidy of all and should have been eliminated many years ago and no price should have been asked for it". According to TWN, "The real prize the developed countries wanted out of Hong Kong was a change in the negotiating modalities in services, so that they would have new instruments to pressurize developing countries to open up their key services sub-sectors." Finally, TWN concluded; "Despite the massive opposition from a very large number of developing countries including the G90 for 5 days, the developed countries eventually got their way."

I bumped into Martin on my way out from the conference centre. We conversed as we left the building. Martin was clearly unhappy with the outcome of the conference. And though he didn't say it, I sensed he felt let down especially by the G90 for obvious reasons. But Martin was a tough guy. I knew he would use the tools at his disposal to tell the world about TWN" s assessment of global trade negotiations at Hong Kong and onwards. Martin moved on to become he Executive Director of the Geneva-based South Centre. My friend Martin passed away in April 2020.

GOING TO THE POLLS AGAIN

General election was held in Guyana on August 28th, 2006 with Bharrat Jagdeo as the PPP/C'S Presidential candidate and Sam Hinds as the Prime Ministerial candidate. The Opposition PNCR-One Guyana contested the election with Robert Corbin as its Presidential Candidate and Winston Murray as its Prime Ministerial candidate.

A newly constituted Election Commission (GECOM) was established, comprising M. McDoom, Dr. K. Mangal, and M. Shaw representing the PPP/C, and H. Parris,

L. Joseph and R. Williams representing the PNC with Steve Surujbally as the new Chairman, replacing Joe Singh, a former Chief of Staff of the Guyana defence Force (GDF).

Eleven other parties contested the election. The PPP/C won the election with 54.6 per cent of the valid votes cast gaining 36 seats in the National Assembly while the PNCR/R-One Guyana won 34% gaining 22 seats. The results of the elections demonstrated convincingly once again, the superiority of the PPP's electoral machinery.

The election was characterized by three firsts for the PPP in its recent electoral history. First, it was the first time that the Party contested an election without a Jagan heading its list of candidates. Second, it was the first time that the Party was able to surmount the challenges of holding an election in the wake of an unprecedented crime wave in the country and fear that people would not come out to vote. By dint of hard work, the Party was able to create the conditions necessary for the holding of free and fair elections under peaceful conditions unlike those held in 1997, 1997 and 2001 which were characterized by violence and street protests. The third first for the PPP/C was that for the first time the Party won seats on the Regional Democratic Councils (RDC's) in all ten regions.

MOFTIC'S ACHIEVEMENTS

I knew that the Ministry of Foreign Trade and International Cooperation would not last when cabinet portfolios were to be assigned. But I was proud and satisfied that the Ministry had accomplished many stellar achievements while it lasted. Never in the history of global trade negotiations was Guyana ever the lead-spokesperson at ACP/EU negotiations on sugar and the WTO negotiations on behalf of CARICOM. Nor did our international standing at global trade negotiations ever reach such international recognition and stature that we were admitted to the coveted Green Room proceedings during the negotiations.

Our first Trade Policy Review, formulated with technical assistance from Craig Van Grasstek who I met while at Harvard, was presented at the WTO in October of 2003. This was a great achievement for the government of Guyana not forgetting the many contributions at the level of CARICOM which resulted in the creation of the Regional Development Fund, the brainchild of Cheddi Jagan.

And irrespective of what the critics and the cynics might say to disparage my humble class background and my performance while I served first, as Minister of Foreign Affairs and later, as Minister of Foreign Trade and International Cooperation, save for the political hyperbole, the records at the two ministries and the Hansard at Parliament are there for anyone to fact check and ascertain the many unmatched and stellar achievements accomplished at the two high profile ministries. 'My story and my song' up to this stage of my contribution to public service can be likened to the expression "A prophet is not without honour save in his own country." Events in future would prove that it would be no different in years to come.

AT HOME AFFAIRS

In the distribution of cabinet portfolios following our victory at the 2006 elections, I was handed the critical and high-profile Ministry of Home Affairs at a time when the public security situation was characterized by an escalation of violent crimes, execution-style murders and the marauding gang led by Rondell Rawlings a/k 'Fineman.' A mere four months before the elections, on 22 April, 2006 to be exact, our colleague Minister of Agriculture, Sash Sawh had been brutally murdered along with his two siblings and a security guard.

Following the swearing ceremony of cabinet ministers on September 9, 2006, at State House, someone mentioned to me that 'I was given a basket to fetch water.' I paid no heed to what was mentioned, in fact I couldn't because within a few hours of my swearing in, news came that a building was on fire at the headquarters of Guyana Elections Commission. GECOM's headquarters is located at High and Cowan Streets in Kingston less than ten minutes away from State House where the swearing ceremony took place. In my new capacity as Minister of Home Affairs, I immediately took off on foot for the site of the fire.

Coming in the midst of a series of fires that destroyed or seriously damaged a number of government buildings, and more particularly, on the heels of the recent elections, the fire at the GECOM headquarters naturally attracted a lot of attention by the media, elections and opposition watchers. Suspicion was rife, and while investigations by the Guyana Fire Service suggested arson, no one was ever arrested, charged and placed before the court.

While at the site watching the firefighters hard at work someone mentioned to me that the scene represented my 'Baptism of fire'. Strangely enough, there seemed to be a rather uncanny co-incidence of the elements of water and fire in what was told to me about 'carrying a basket to fetch water' and my 'Baptism of fire'. I thus began to wonder how earth and wind; two of the five remaining natural elements would manifest themselves in my journey as Minister of Home Affairs.

On arrival at the ministry and having settled down to acquaint myself with the Mission Statement, staff establishment and internal structure of the ministry, I found that the previous administration had degutted the ministry and deprived it of any real teeth, save and except to write reports and fulfill a plethora of meaningless functions totally unhelpful insofar as the policy direction of, and manifesto promises made by the PPP/C during the just concluded elections campaign was concerned. More importantly, after careful consideration, I found that the ministry lacked the competent and experienced human resources necessary to effectively fulfill its mandate namely; 'To ensure the maintenance of public order and safety throughout Guyana by formulating appropriate security policies that are responsive to the changing environment; overseeing the effective implementation of these policies by related agencies and guaranteeing their execution as a result of appropriate resource allocation that include an emphasis on competent human capital as well as modern technology.' There was no way such a Mission Statement could be effectively realized by the Permanent Secretary and the Minister alone, their herculean efforts notwithstanding.

With fourteen years of experience at two ministries under my belt, I set about re-organizing the ministry internally. Those who were on contract and were performing sinecure duties were served notice, paid their entitlements and sent home. Some chose to resign for reasons known only to them while others whose qualifications and competencies were needed at other government agencies and departments were re-assigned accordingly. A Ministerial Secretariat and a Research Department was established with new recruits hired through the Public Service Ministry. A Senior rank of the Guyana Police Force was seconded to my office to act as a liaison between my office and the Guyana Police Force. Within a matter of six (6) years, the ministry's staffing compliment increased from twelve (12) to one hundred and twenty-seven (127). The new staffing compliment reflected an ethnic mix and a gender and next generation balance.

One morning, I was invited to State House where upon arrival, I was introduced to Bernard Kerik, a former Commissioner of the New York Police Department (NYPD) and told that Kerik would be assisting the Ministry and the GPF in the execution of their respective mandates. Kerik and I had a brief stand-up conversation after which I returned to the Ministry. A few months later, a scandal broke involving Kerik. He was under investigation for tax fraud and making false statements. He was found guilty and sentenced to a term of four years in a federal prison and three years' supervised release (probation). As was to be expected, local press 'went to town' on the matter. We decided to move on.

One of the first social issues that confronted me as I began to settle-in at the Ministry was the issue of noise nuisance. The issue had become a national one so much so that the mainstream media gave extensive coverage to the matter in their letter columns and editorials. I became aware of the extent of the problem and the way it was being handled by the police when I received a phone call from the parents of a couple whose son and daughter were in the midst of their traditional Hindu Guyanese wedding proceedings. The 'Kangan' was taking place at the time I received the call complaining that the police had turned up and demanded that the music be turned off. The family and the invitees were very upset and complained bitterly to me about what happened.

I called the Commissioner of Police and spoke to him on the matter, He promised to have the matter investigated. The Commissioner called to inform me that the police acted based on complaints from a neighbour. We discussed the matter. It turned out that the complaint was a vexatious one and even though the family of the house where the wedding was held had gone around the neighbourhood informing and extending invitations to all and sundry. Further, I asked whether the police had consulted with their superiors before intervening in a long held cultural practice much to the annoyance of the attendees at the 'kangan.' Eventually, I understand the police withdrew and the music at the 'kangan' resumed.

Weeks later, I took it upon myself to do the research on the matter because the complains were coming in 'fast and furious' from all over the country. It was turning out to be a very messy situation on the ground. Our research at the Ministry showed that persons seeking permission to play loud, repetitive and continuous music at a public cultural or entertainment event, were compelled to visit the nearest police station in their community for permission to do so. The permit granted by the police was called a 'pass.' The 'pass' had to be paid for with the understanding that the music would begin and end at a certain time. Those who didn't follow the practice would have the music turned off, their equipment seized and would be charged and placed before the court.

Our further investigation into the matter revealed that legally, not only was the police going about the matter in the wrong way, they had set up their own procedures as a money-making exercise. The law stipulated that persons wishing to play loud, repetitive and continuous music must first apply to the District Magistrate for permission to do so. The District Magistrate having granted permission under strict guidelines and hours during which the music should be played, the applicant would then take a copy of the magisterial permit to the nearest police station and lodge a copy there as a courtesy. The same would apply, were the event to be held at a location controlled by an NDC say, for example, a community Centre ground. There was therefore no need for a 'police pass' nor a fee be paid to the police for the said 'pass'. However, were complaints made by persons the loud, repetitive and continuous music was annoying to them, the police were required to act but not in the manner they did previously.

The results of our investigation were forwarded to Doodnauth Singh, the then Attorney General and Minister of Legal Affairs as well the Chambers of the Director of Public Prosecutions for a legal opinion on the matter. Both offices confirmed our findings. Copies of their correspondence to me on the matter along with a covering letter from me was sent to the Commissioner of Police with a request that its contents be circulated to all Divisional Commanders for their attention.

But complaints of noise nuisance were not only because of loud, repetitive and continuous music, complaints also came from persons living next to or not far from mechanical workshops using electric devices at bottom house mechanic shops, wood-working enterprises and car washing locations. This was different type of noise nuisance that required the cooperation and intervention of the Environmental Protection Agency (EPA). The EPA used a Sound level Meter (SLM) or the Integrated Sound Level Meter (ISLM) and Noise Dosimeter to measure the level of noise in decibels. However, because the EPA did not have an enforcement arm nothing was done to prosecute violators. Meetings between the MOHA and the EPA proved fruitless in respect to cooperation with the police to assist with enforcement. The EPA regulations did not allow for the EPA to call on the police for assistance nor was the EPA prepared to amend their regulations to allow for it either. The matter ended there. The EPA preferred to rely on 'moral suasion' to deal with violators.

THE NATIONAL COMMISSION FOR LAW AND ORDER

Of great assistance to me were the members of the National Commission on Law and Order (NCLO). This body was established in Guyana in 2005 based on a recommendation from Caricom Heads of Government. The NCLO is a unique body, in the sense that it brings together under one roof, the Commissioner of Police, the Director of Prisons, representatives from the Guyana Defence Force, the Attorney General's Chambers, the Ministries of Local Government and Public Works, the private sector, faith-based, women's' and youth organisations. Its terms of reference included inter-alia; 'To review the situation in the country as it relates to law and order and to make recommendations as it deems fit for the maintenance of peace and good order in Guyana'.

The Commission was also tasked with the responsibility to consider reports and consultations on crime with a view to examining their status and relevance to the extant crime situation. As well as to review and identify problems and weaknesses in the legislative, organisational and administration of law and order and to propose creative and sustainable interventions to remedy the situation.

The NCLO met one per month. In order to give members a greater role in the work of the Commission, I recommended, and it was agreed, that the Commission's work be farmed out through the establishment of five sub-committees on; Order, Decency and Culture, Crime and Violence, Public Confidence and Support, Legislative and Justice Issues and Out-reach Programmes.

Its members engaged in very useful exchanges of views on topical and concrete issues pertaining to anti-social behaviour, infractions of the law and challenges for law enforcement, issues related to traffic, domestic violence, noise nuisance and any issue a commission member wished to raise. Meetings of the Commission gave its members and their organisations a tremendous sense of inclusivity and in belonging to an organization in which they were making a contribution to the maintenance of peace and good order in Guyanese society.

I made every effort to avoid the Commission becoming a police-bashing and complaining forum as well as one to air personal grievances. While some of this was allowed, I made sure that the commission was not over burdened with those issues but that it focussed on the issues at hand with a view to coming up with positive policy recommendations to resolve, as far as possible, public safety and security challenges that confronted us from time to time. The NCLO proved a formidable forum for government/stakeholder partnership for the benefit of the citizenry. We held community out-reach meetings in every administrative region of the country. Former members including; Ramesh Sugrim, Taajnauth Jadunauth, Roshan Khan, Fitzpatrick Alert, Sydney James, Navin Chandarpal, Abiola Wong-Inniss, Godfrey Adams, Norman McLean, Omesh Satyanand, Sheila Veerasammy, Deborah Backer, Ameena Ali, Gerald Gouveia, Anil Nandlall, Welton Trotz, Henry Greene, Leroy Brummel, Robeson Benn, Mark Constantine, Dale Erskine and Mark Bender, all served well and made extremely useful contributions to enhance the activities of the Commission.

CITIZEN SECURITY

Already being executed at the Ministry was a US$19 million, an Inter-American Development Bank (IDB) –funded Citizens Security Programme (CSP) which I inherited from my predecessors. However, at a meeting at the Office of the President (OP) at which the Head of the Project Implementation Unit (PIU) was present and to which I was invited, I was made aware of OP's dissatisfaction with the emphasis the PIU was placing on intangible rather than tangible projects. The OP wanted greater sums of the IDB's funds to be spent on tangible projects and not hiring of consultants who were involved in useless and time-consuming back-room work. Following that meeting at OP, the contracts of some consultants were terminated. It was now my responsibility to exercise direct supervision as regards implementation of the project and to ensure the new direction.

In early 2006, the Government and the IDB had signed a contract aimed at enhancing citizens' security and to reduce the levels of crime, violence and insecurity in Guyana. The specific objectives of what became known as CSP (1) were to: a) Identify and counteract the risk factors and increase and promote protective factors in communities, families and individuals; b) Strengthen social cohesion within the community and their preventive capacity; c) Strengthen the capabilities of the Ministry of Home Affairs and the Guyana Police Force to implement crime prevention and crime fighting programmes at the national level.

In August 2007, after months of negotiating, an Interim Memorandum was signed between the Government of Guyana and the British Government to the tune of US$4.7M to finance a Security Sector Reform Action Plan (SSRAP) In November 2007, the government tabled the SSRAP in the National Assembly. The plan called for 'Adopting a holistic approach based on a comprehensive threat assessment'. It also called for 'bringing together existing sectoral strategies in the areas of drugs and disaster management to enhance coordination and rational resource utilization/mobilization and strengthening strategic planning and implementation capabilities within both government and the security institutions.'

Outwardly, everything seemed to be proceeding according to plan, but internally the chief negotiator for the government reported to us at the level of cabinet and the Defence Board that a back and forth discussion was taking place on the question of ownership that was negatively impacting the pace of implementation. The Brits were of the view that Guyana lacked the human resource capacity to implement the plan. They wanted British consultants be recruited and flown in

465

from the UK to occupy line positions at key institutions in the security sector. It would be those individuals who would be responsible for executing the plan. The implication was that not only would the US$4.7 million be spent on British consultants but ultimately, they would determine on who, and on what the resources would be spent.

Efforts to resolve this matter lasted for about four months at the end of which it became clear that the differences between the government and the Brits were irreconcilable. Eventually, talks broke down because the Brits refused to accept the Guyana government's position that since the SSRAP, will form part and parcel of Guyana's security strategy and policies, it followed that Guyana must have ownership and control over the execution of the SSRAP. This internationally recognized position had been settled and agreed four months earlier in Georgetown between Guyanese and British negotiators and communicated to the authorities in the UK. Subsequently, the Guyana withdrew from any further negotiations on the matter and announced that it would finance the SSRAP from its own budgetary resources.

It was against this backdrop, that I took on, as one of my immediate tasks, tackling the reforms envisaged at the Ministry of Home Affairs, the Guyana Police Force, the Guyana Prison Service and the Guyana Fire Service. To do so, meant that each department must have a five-year strategic and implementation plan and to have those plans costed. Fortunately, we already had in place the GOG/IDB CSP with funds available for its implementation. In order for the CSP to compliment the SSRAP we had to enter into negotiations with the IDB and our Minister of Finance. Our task was to convince the IDB about the complimentary role we envisaged the CSP playing in the new scenario that had unfolded in the security sector in light of the fall out with the Brits vis-à-vis the SSRAP.

In pursuit of reforms at and modernization of the Guyana Police Force financed by the CSP, I considered it necessary to engage in a meeting of minds between myself and the then Commissioner of Police Henry Green. I invited Green for a discussion of the matter. I proposed a change in the composition of the police Change Team. Green would be the Change Agent at the GPF while Crime Chief, Seelall Persaud would be the technical head of the Police Change Team. Correspondingly, a Strategic Management Department (SMD) would be established. Green agreed.

Cabinet had decided that the SMD would be composed primarily of suitably qualified and experienced civilians.

Enlightened as he was, Green offered no resistance and pledged his support. A panel of distinguished Guyanese was established to interview and to recommend successful applicants for ten (10) positions in the SMD. The SMD was to be responsible for overseeing implementation of the Force's G$23M (pa) Strategic Plan which was drawn up by a team of British consultants from the firm Capita Symmonds, while an Implementation Plan was drawn up by the US-based, Julian Laite Consultancy. Both plans were approved by cabinet.

POLICE REFORM

The Symmonds Group was later contracted to focus on four specific areas of the GPG's strategic plan; administration, succession planning, integrity/probity (professionalization) and public relations/communications. The cost for implementing the first phase of the four areas was to come from a GOG/CSP bridging financial arrangement.

That a civilian composed team of ten professionals would be responsible for overseeing implementation of the force's strategic plan did not go down well with some at the senior management level of the GPF. The few complainers were not bashful in stating their disagreement and displaying passive resistance to a civilian/police modus vivendi. When the complainants were reminded that it was a cabinet decision to have civilians serve on the SMD and the role of the Minister of Home Affairs according to Section II:6 (1) Ch:160:1 of the Police Act, they backed off but did not resile from making snide remarks from time to time about the arrangement.

In the meanwhile, training courses for ranks belonging to different branches of the GPF conducted by specialists from overseas proceeded apace. Many were selected to be trained locally while some were sent abroad. At the same time, cabinet had approved a 'Policy on Study Leave' enabling ranks from the disciplined services to pursue academic studies at the University of Guyana.

One of the major challenges I had with the GPF was corruption within the organization from top to bottom. Regardless of my public and internal exhortations, the cries and exposes from the citizenry and persistent references to the issue in the mainstream media the problem appeared to be cancerous. From one generation of recruits to another and from one generation of senior officers to another, institutional corruption could not be exorcised. However, this did not mean that there were no decent and incorruptible ranks with the organization. It was like searching for needles in a haystack to find them. I had suggested to the consultants from Capita-Symmonds that 'Integrity/Probity (professionalization)' one of the four specific areas identified in the strategic plan of the GPF be prioritized because I wanted them to address speedily issues such as ethics and professionalism, character and incorruptibility within the context of police reform.

While having oversight responsibility of the GPF for a number of years, I had caught the sight of the weaknesses of the GPF's Office of Professional Responsibility (OPR). Ultimately, I was convinced that what was needed was a more professionalised and transformed OPR somewhat along the lines of the NYPD's Internal Affairs Department. The consultants took note of my observation and my wish but insisted that by beginning with 'Administration' followed by 'Succession Planning' and ending with 'Integrity/Probity (Professionalization)' my objectives would be achieved. I had my doubts, but eventually conceded relying on the consultant's international experience on police reform and their explanation given as regards the logical sequencing of the topics.

INTRODUCING POLYGRAPHING

But all was not lost. Sometime back in 2006, at the level of Central Intelligence Committee, Dr. Luncheon, no doubt with the approval of President Jagdeo, had initiated a discussion on polygraphing law enforcement operatives. The aim was to tackle corruption in the law enforcement from a scientific angle. The exercise known as integrity testing was to target operatives belonging to the Guyana Police Force, Security Personnel at the Cheddi Jagan International Airport, the Customs Anti-narcotic Unit (CANU) the Guyana Defence Force (GDF) and the Guyana Energy Authority. Polygraph screening exams was being introduced for the first time in Guyana.

The screening process was to be carried out by Arno Horvath, a certified polygraphist and Director of the Academy of Polygraph Science Latin America, Inc. based in the United states. In discussion between Mr. Horvath, me and Dr.

Luncheon, Horvath informed us that one of the techniques utilized for the screening process was the 'Air Force Modified General Question Technique – Version one.' However, Horvath was careful to point out that that technique is usually utilized by all law enforcement departments for pre-employment screening known as 'Law Enforcement Pre-employment Testing' (LEPET) which has proven to be of great success and certainty in its results. Nevertheless, since in our case we wanted ranks already employed to be tested, Horvath recommended we do the 'Screening and Fidelity Maintenance 'multi-issue' Exams'. We were further advised that though the exams would be conducted on the 'Fidelity Maintenance multi-issue' basis, the LEPET technique could be used in its Phase Two application which would give results as 'SR' (significant response or deception indicated) 'NSR' (no significant response or no deception indicated) and 'NO'(no opinion or inconclusive). We agreed.

Between the Jagdeo and Ramotar administrations (2006 and 2012) approximately three hundred ranks belonging to the afore-mentioned organizations were polygraphed. However, more than sixty percent of all those screened failed the tests. By mid-2014 the matter was brought before the Defence Board for consideration. A report concluded that the results were not encouraging. In the meantime, employees at the Guyana Energy Authority and the International Airport sought the intervention of their Trade Unions to prevent termination of their employment. And the political opposition wasted not time jumping in to take political advantage of the issue.

The matter became more complicated at the level of the Joint Services. Ranks belonging to the Police and army could not be dismissed because they failed a polygraph test. In the case of Police, I was informed by the then Commissioner Brummel, that the dismissal of Police ranks is determined by the Police Act Chapter16:01. Further, he advised that no rank has been charged under the Police (Discipline) Act Chapter 17:01. The Commissioner went on to point out that if a rank is to be dismissed for failing a polygraph test, it should occur at the time when he /she is enrolling in the organization.

In his communication to me the Commissioner emphasized that he is unaware of what ranks are to be disciplined or charged for because they failed a polygraph test, he therefore recommended that those ranks who failed the polygraph test be transferred to another section since they did not commit any breach.

Views on the way forward varied, but in the end, we agreed that dismissal for failure at a polygraph test is eminently challengeable in a Court of Law. Further, we agreed that should polygraph tests be continued it must be done at the time of employment. In any event, the consensual view was that consideration should be given to amending certain sections of the Police Act and the Police (Discipline) Act as well as the Evidence Act to give effect to a new law or regulation that would be promulgated.

Interestingly, during the Ramotar Administration the question of polygraphing surfaced once again. The competent authorities of the US approached me with a request that, in the context of our cooperation in the fight against drug trafficking, they wanted to have their polygraph experts polygraph our law enforcement operatives for the purpose of information sharing, confidentiality and to avoid even the perception of corruption.

In considering the request, I concluded that from a realpolitik perspective, the request was a step in the right direction. The request was therefore granted with one caveat. If granting the request was to be based on my acceptance of the DEA's dedication to honesty and professionalism, and that there was no appearance nor perception of corruption on their part, then surely, it would not be unreasonable to request reciprocity in the spirit of service from the Guyanese side. Further, if I were to place the Americans implied perception of corruption of our law enforcement operatives above everything else and not call for reciprocity, then I would be failing in my responsibility to represent the interest of Guyanese law enforcement officers.

Co-incidentally, a meeting of CARICOM Public Security Ministers was due to take place around the same time. I attended the meeting and in my contribution to the discussions I called for a Standard CARICOM Policy on Polygraphing and for all member states to hold to one position on the question of polygraphing.

In the midst of all that was going on, I moved to take on the challenge of modernizing the Ministry of Home Affairs under the CSP. Local consultants were hired to draw up a strategic and implementation plan for the ministry. The plan was estimated to cost G$1.8bln over a five-year period, was submitted to and approved by cabinet. In accordance with the plan, a Strategic Management

Department (SMD) comprising of six suitably qualified persons was established to ensure implementation of the ministry's strategic plan.

Because a Change Team established at the Ministry, along with members of the SMD held seminars and communicated regularly with the staff at the ministry there was no resistance to the strategic plan nor its implementation. Internal personnel and organisational adjustments were made to the organogram of the ministry consistent with its strategic plan. In this regard, a Research and Documentation Unit, a Treaty and Legislation Unit, a Community Police Unit, an Immigration Services Unit, and an International and Regional Affairs Unit were established. And in view of the burgeoning cyber crime threats, a Cyber Security Unit was established as the harbinger for a National Computer Incident Response Team (NCIRT). The team was eventually established comprising of five technically qualified and competent persons who performed well as regards institutional strengthening as well as in tracking and exposing attempts at cyber crime.

The steady and reliable hands of Mrs. Greta McDonald, Registrar at the General Register Office (GRO) was of great assistance in facilitating the modernization of the functions of the GRO. Of top priority was the digitization of the GRO's birth, death and marriage records as well as the production and availability of E-birth certificates with a view to ensuring that each citizen as a birth certificate The de-centralization of the services provided by the GRO proved to be of great help to both citizens economically and the GRO as per its administrative efficiency.

Mrs. McDonald did a great job in stamping out corruption at the GRO with respect to the sale of birth, death and marriage certificates to shady individuals. Not only did this illegal practice become a thing of the past while she served as Head of that Department but applicants for documents from the GRO faced less hassles and did have to pay a bribe to get what they had applied for.

And the staff at the Ministry's Immigration Services Department, ably led at one-time by Narima Mohamed now Nazeem worked hard to ensure that the department was efficiently and effectively administered to provide a professional service to the public.

Based on lengthy consultations with senior management of the Guyana Fire Service (GFS) and the Guyana Prison Service (GPS), we agreed that since the

471

Ministry and the GPF were undergoing reforms aimed at modernizing their respective institutions it was not only logical, but vitally necessary that the GFS and the GPS proceed in a similar direction. To achieve that goal retreats were held with ranks of the two institutions.

PRISON REFORM

Again, as was done in the case of the Ministry, local consultants were hired to draw-up a five-year strategic plan for the GPS. It was my view at that time, that the GPS was required to play a critical role in the Criminal Justice System and thus the need to ensure that the GPS was modernized and transformed to meet the evolving challenges confronting a correctional institution such as the GPS.

A point I wish to emphasize is that on examining the situation at the five prison locations, I found that there was almost total neglect of the correctional and rehabilitative functions at each prison. No top position at any of the locations was held by a qualified and experienced civilian specialist in correctional and rehabilitative matters. Greater emphasis at all the prisons locations was placed on custodial duties.

While I had no difficulty with attention being paid to the custodial functions, but I was not satisfied with the significant imbalance with the custodial and rehabilitative functions. Nor was I satisfied with the qualifications of the persons in charge responsible for those functions.

After lengthy consultations with the senior management of the GPS I managed to convinced them about the need to rectify the imbalance. In the circumstances, I directed that suitably qualified and professional civilians with the necessary experience, be recruited to head the rehabilitative and correctional aspects of prison life and that more budgetary resources be made allocated to facilitate greater emphasis on the correctional and rehabilitation functions, equipping the trade shops and for training courses at each prison location. To facilitate the transformational process, civilian school teachers, medical doctors, trade instructors were hired to fill the positions held previously by Prison Officers.

The end result of these transformative initiatives saw a marked re-balancing of the custodial and the correctional and rehabilitative functions of the GPS. Peace and

472

good order prevailed at all prison locations save and except that on few occasions there were outbreaks by some prisoners who were bent on their criminal ways.

Following cabinet's approval of the GPS's G$831mln Strategic and Implementation Plan, a Strategic Management Department (SMD) comprising of four (4) civilian professionals was established at the headquarters of the GPS. Their main task was to implement and have general oversight of the GPS's strategic plan. The priorities areas identified to be pursued were to: modernize and make secure, the existing prison structure, enhance human resource management and financial administration, strengthen inter-agency collaboration, promote successful offender re-integration into society and modernize penal legislation. Based on a cabinet decision, I took steps to transform the Prison at Lusignan into a model prison only for first offenders and those inmates who were imprisoned for short sentences. The idea was to prevent the first offenders from being contaminated by the hard-core criminals and recidivists.

With a view to buttressing the work of the GPS's SMD, I took the initiative to establish a Recruitment and Training Board, a Sentence Management Board, and an Agricultural Development Board. A number of outstanding Guyanese were assigned responsibility to head these Boards including; Roylance Patricia David, Yojna Hernandez, Fay Clarke, Gerry Gouveia and Beni Sankar.

The Recruitment and Training Board, headed by Ms. Patricia David and assisted by Ms. Fay Clarke were responsible for ensuring that applicants for employment as Prison Officers were properly screened, and suitably qualified to be recruited to fulfill custodial duties. The Board was also required to draw up training programmes for officers performing custodial duties as well as for inmates at their differing levels of primary and or secondary education.

The Sentence Management Board headed by Gerry Gouveia, assisted by Yojna Hernandez, was responsible drawing up, updating and assisting the prison authorities to manage a register of inmates, the date they were incarcerated, their biographic data, duration of their sentence, their educational levels, their skill sets, levels of discipline, their contribution to the maintenance peace and good order at the prison, remission and parole entitlements and expected date of release from prison.

The Agricultural Board headed by Beni Sankar, assisted by the Prisons' Agricultural Officer were responsible for fostering agricultural development at the various prison locations where vegetables and 'greens' were cultivated on a sustainable basis, poultry, cattle and small ruminants were reared and fish farms introduced with a view to making the prisons self sufficient in food supplied from the prison farms.

On the intellectual front, I retained former Director of Prisons Cecil Kilkenny to review, formulate and produce the first ever printed and bound edition of the Standing Orders of the GPS. Mr. Kilkenny completed his assignment with flying colours before his passing much to my grief and sadness. Apart from the task he undertook, he was of great assistance to me during my tenure as Minister responsible for our five prison locations. The first ever Training School for Prison Officers built in Guyana under the PPP/C administration was named 'The Cecil Kilkenny Training Institute' in homage to a man who had given yeoman service to his country and people.

The Prisons' Visiting Committees (PVC's) for the five prison locations were reconstituted and given renewed mandates. The PVC's were dominated by civilians from all walks of life mainly from the community where the prison was located. The preponderance of civilians in the PVC's was in keeping with my conviction that greater civilian inclusiveness at all levels of the security sector would bring greater transparency and accountability in the functions of the country's law enforcement agencies. I also saw to it that the chairmen and secretaries of all five VC's together with the Director of Prisons and the Officers-in-Charge at each prison location would meet at what I called a Central PVC on an annual basis to exchange experiences and to make recommendations on how to improve the welfare of the inmates in particular and the conditions at the work-place for the Prison Officers and staff at the prisons in general. The men and women who functioned as members of these bodies gave yeoman service to the sector in particular and to their country in general.

INVOLVING CIVIL SOCIETY

President Cheddi Jagan's instructions to his 1992-1997 cabinet ministers, was that they establish at their respective ministries, Advisory Committees comprising of persons in good standing from civil society. Though some of my colleague ministers quietly balked at the decision, during my tenure as a minister of a government, I found the decision to be a very wise and efficacious one. It served me well at the Ministry of Foreign Affairs at my National Advisory Committee on Borders (NACOB). At the Ministry of Foreign Trade and International Cooperation, at my National Advisory Committee on External Negotiations (NACEN) and the Ministry of Home Affairs at my National Commission on Law and Order (NCLO). For all these bodies, and many others like the Prisons Visiting Committees, the Crime and Social Observatory, the Cheddi Jagan and Ogle International Airports Security Committees, the Task Forces on Smuggling and Contraband and Illegal Firearms and Drugs, the National Security Committee and the National Executive Committee of the Community Police Organization of Guyana, I made it my duty, in keeping with government's declared policy of inclusivity, to bring on board civilians from all walks of life with the appropriate skill sets, experience and willingness to serve.

These individuals did a great job in the areas where they served. It was this experience that convinced me, that inclusion of civil society representatives in governance of the security sector was a step in the right direction. It brought a tremendous amount of goodwill towards government's management of the sector and generated a greater sense of inclusivity on the part of stakeholders. Moreover, the knowledge I gained from interventions at meetings I hosted with these individuals proved to be extremely useful for policy formulation and policy guidance. This is an important lesson that policy makers should take into account, provided they are prepared to be good listeners, endure constructive criticism for mistakes made and short-comings overlooked and more importantly, to take unconventional ideas and suggestions on board where and when necessary.

MODERNIZATION OF THE FIRE SERVICE

In respect to reforms and modernization of the Guyana Fire Service (GFS), we adopted an approach not dissimilar to the one we took with the Ministry, the GPF and the GPS. Following extensive consultations between ranks of the GFS and the Ministry, a five-year Strategic and Implementation Plan costing G$276 mln. was drawn up and subsequently submitted to and approved by cabinet. As was the case with the Ministry, the GPF and the GPS, a Strategic Management Department, comprising four suitably qualified professionals and a Change Team at the GFS were established

A revised Mission Statement for the GFS consistent with the changed role for fire fighters at national and international levels read as follows: 'The Guyana Fire Service is committed to the protection of life and property from destruction by fire through employment of best practices for Fire Prevention, Fire Prevention and Public Education; attending to other disaster-related emergencies, effecting rescues and the rendering of humanitarian services in collaboration with other relevant agencies.'

The GFS identified seven goals as the pillars of its strategic plan. These included: 'accentuating and reinforcing human resource management, fostering high performance through realignment to support change, strengthening internal and external communication protocols and processes, building strong stakeholder/community partnerships, re-engineering infrastructural landscape, harnessing technology to propel institutional advancement in day-to-day work process and modernizing and harmonizing all fire administration-related administration'. According to the GFS, the bottom line of its strategic plan was to 'provide a blue-print for the transformation of the Service.'

In fulfillment of its objectives, a brand-new training school for fire fighters was established at Leonora on the West Coast of Demerara. After an absence of more than three decades I initiated the re-establishment and re-launch of the Auxiliary Branch of the Guyana Fire Service. The Branch was launched with some sixty-four (64) trained auxiliaries who were placed at fire stations in the communities where they lived. And for the first time in its history, a Welfare Department headed by a trained civilian Welfare Officer was established at the headquarters of the GFS. Moreover, from three closed and a handful of poorly equipped fire stations, nine new and three renovated and fully equipped fire stations were commissioned at various parts of the country. Moreover, a Hinterland Fire Protection plan was implemented to serve hinterland communities where such services never existed. The plan was implemented with the procurement of appropriate fire-fighting equipment suitable for interior conditions. And to address the shortage of staffing requirements, I sought and got cabinet's approval to increase the fixed establishment of the GFS from three hundred and sixty-eight (368) to five hundred and eleven (511) to facilitate the badly needed recruitment of fire fighters.

The establishment of four Strategic Management Departments at Home Affairs, Police, Prisons and Fire departments created the conditions for sectorial linkages and greater coherence for policy coordination amongst the constituent agencies vis-à-vis their respective strategic plans. In this regard, after extensive consultation and careful consideration, I found it necessary to create a Strategic Management Coordination Committee (SMCC) which brought together the Heads of the SMD's and Change Teams of each constituent agency. In reality, this was a body of eight persons, two persons each from the four constituent agencies plus myself and the Permanent Secretary at my Ministry.

This move on my part, insofar as implementation of plans was concerned, allowed for cross fertilization, exchange of experiences, and the avoidance and/or making of mistakes made at one agency at another.

IDB/GOG PARTNERSHIP WITH FLEXIBILITIES

In the midst of all these transformative activities, lengthy and somewhat tortuous negotiations with the IDB took place with a view to affecting some adjustments to the GOG/IDB contract. Negotiations with the IDB was successful in the sense that the contract was amended to include, the construction and outfitting of a modern state-of-the-art forensic laboratory, remodelling and enhancing of eighteen out of twenty-two police stations around the country, establishment of a crime fighting unit of the Guyana Police Force (GPF), establishment of a SWAT team, and a modern training facility for senior ranks of the GPF. In the meanwhile, the Ministry of Finance through its 2008 budget, made provision for $13.7 billion to the public safety agencies, marking a 10% increase to the capital and a 13% increase to the current budgetary allocations to the Ministry of Home Affairs. A significant step taken around this time was the decision to delink 'E' and 'F' divisions of the GPF. This resulted in the creation of two additional divisions, bringing the total number of police divisions to seven.

YOUTH INVOLVEMENT

Under the CSP, a number of training programmes in twenty-four (24) skills were initiated for over one thousand (1000 plus) at risk youths residing at ten coastland communities. The two-year programme also provided skills for employment and entrepreneurship, training in violence prevention, mentoring and suppression of anti-social behaviour. A Community Action Component of the CSP aimed at building social cohesion and the creation of safe neighbourhoods was initiated in a number of communities.

To further advance the building of social cohesion, a number of Rapid Impact Projects aimed at bringing together ethnically differentiated but bordering communities in the field of sports and multi-cultural activities were initiated.

HOUSES OF JUSTICE

In addition, under the CSP, a novel concept known as 'Houses of Justice' was introduced for the first time in Guyana. This multi-agency service centre was designed to improve the peoples' access to public services. Its genesis was derived from the Colombian experience where, in the Guyanese context, representatives of government agencies and departments such as the General Register Office, the National Insurance Scheme, Guyana Water Authority, Guyana Power and Light, the Ministry of Human Services, and the Guyana Police Force were brought together under one roof to unblock and eliminate the bureaucratic hurdles and the "royal run-around" resulting in frustrations citizens were experiencing because of lack of access to the relevant public officers who were responsible for ensuring the provision of public services to citizens on the ground. Frustration over lack of access to basic human and public services can lead to illegal practices to access those very services. To facilitate these services, ten (10) Houses of Justice were established in Regions two and three. Depending on the available of human and financial resources, similar initiatives were to be realized at other regions.

CRIME AND SOCIAL OBSERVATORY

Under the CSP a Crime and Social Observatory was established at the Ministry of Home Affairs. The Observatory was tasked with the responsibility of collecting reliable data and engaging in depth analysis of crime, violence-related incidents and anti-social behaviour in the country. The results of the analysis were to be used to track and prevent crime, violence-related behaviour and anti-social activities with the help of law enforcement and civilian bodies engaged in rule of law initiatives

INTEGRATED CRIME INFORMATION SYSTEM.

Most importantly, an Integrated Crime Information System (ICIS) was introduced to generate and to share with the Guyana Police Force (GPF) accurate digital and comprehensive crime data on a day-by-day basis with the aim of enhancing the analytical capacity of policy analysts and security personnel. Eighty-five (85) data entry clerks were recruited and placed at forty-eight law enforcement locations to input data for the ICIS. The stations were linked through a wide-area network with Force HQ. A civilian/professional policy analyst was recruited by the Ministry and placed at Force Headquarters to assist the GPF in analysing the data generated by the ICIS.

Not satisfied with the limited scope and output of the ICIS and its restriction solely to the GPF, I insisted that those responsible for designing the software take steps to modify and expand the ICIS by designing additional modules in the following areas; Ministry of Home Affairs/ Guyana Revenue Authority information sharing, management of Firearm licences, traffic ticket accounting, seizure of illegal narcotics and firearms, treatment and monitoring of deportees, monitoring of payrolees, creation of an E-occurrence book for Station Sargeants at police stations, monitoring of persons of interest and management of inmates at the five prison locations. I set May 6, 2015, four days before elections scheduled to be held on May 11, 2015, as the deadline for the completion of all modules. Regrettably, only thirteen of the seventeen modules were delivered and, in some cases, a few of those delivered had to be tested to ensure the reliability and efficacy of the data generated.

FROM CSP1 TO CSP2.

Save for an investigation conducted by the IDB's Office of Institutional Integrity into an allegation of fraud committed by the then Programme Coordinator and the subsequent administrative actions taken against him, CSP (1) was so successfully implemented that the IDB officially recognized its success by offering to the Government of Guyana a successor CSP (2) for consideration.

Afterall, over a seven-year period, the forensic lab, the police officers' training centre, the re-modeled police stations, the Rapid Impact Projects, the ICIS, the Houses of Justice, the skills training programmes for youths, the Crime and Social Observatory and the police training centre were all realized. Yet there remained a strong and compelling demand at the grass-roots level for an extension of the programme.

Taking into account the success of CSP (1) the Donald Ramotar administration which succeeded the Jagdeo administration readily agreed to the need for a CSP (2) and a contract to the tune of US$15 million, supporting CSP (2) was signed in December 2014. Five months later, in May 2015 elections were held in Guyana, the ruling PPP/C lost the elections and the incoming government assumed responsibility for implementing CSP (2).

COMMUNITY POLICING

Community Policing emerged way back in 1976 as an organized form of community partnering with the Guyana Police Force (GPF) to assist in preventing localized crime and/or community-based anti-social activities, to assist in investigating crime and in combatting the fear of crime.

Because of the people-centered policies of the PPP/C at the political, economic and social levels, it occurred to me that Community Policing fell in the latter category and must therefore be given the attention and priority it deserves within the meaning of the Mission Statement of the Ministry of Home Affairs. It from this backdrop that I saw the need to develop and expand Community Policing throughout the length and breadth of Guyana. In this regard, greater emphasis was placed on the quality of recruits, discipline, cohesion, the organisational structure, regularity of meetings at the group, divisional and ministerial levels as well as the annual general meetings and the social responsibilities of the CPG's in their respective communities.

In addition to the CPG's, the Ministry had the authority to appoint persons known as Liaison Officers who received a stipend. The Liaison Officers fulfilled the role of an intermediary between the Ministry and the CPG's. Among their several tasks, the Liaison Officers were required to work in close collaboration with an Administrator, a paid functionary at the Ministry whose task was to assist in the formation of new CPG's, ensure the proper functioning of the Groups and their relationship with the GPF, attend their statutory meetings of Groups in their assigned districts as well as the Annual General Meetings and to ensure that the groups were resourced with the necessary tools for their effective and efficient functioning.

Addressing Community Policing Issues

As with any organisation with mass membership, there are bound to be problems with respect to discipline, abuse of property belonging to the organisation, vexatious issues between residents and individual members of the organisation, breakdown in relations with Police Divisional Commanders and submission of misleading reports to the ministry. In any such occurrence, the Ministry would intervene and give guidance or read the riot act to the recalcitrant in order to ensure that the rotten apples do not spoil the entire barrel.

Following the Agricola massacre (Feb. 2006), the assassination of Sash Sawh (Apr.2006) and my swearing-in (Sept. 9, 2006), Guyana experienced another round of brutal murders; the Lusignan massacre (Jan. 2008), the murders at Bartica (Feb.2008) and the Lindo Creek murders in (June 2008). These occurrences were part and parcel of a crime spree unleashed by a criminal gang who broke out from the Georgetown Prisons in February 2002.

INVOLVING PARLIAMENTARIANS

In order to address the growing concerns over the crime situation and the mounting fears by the populace, community meetings were held in various parts of the country but more particularly in the areas affected. President Jagdeo hosted a series of meetings between February19 to March 12, 2008 to discuss the way forward with stakeholders, cabinet members and the Leader of the parliamentary opposition at his office. A dedicated meeting was held with divisional representatives of the CPG's. The outcome of these engagements was productive and positive. A political declaration unanimously agreed and signed by 51 organizations belonging to a 'Joint Stakeholders Forum' was issued denouncing violence, the atrocities committed by criminal elements. The stakeholders called for the peaceful resolution of conflicts. In addition, it was unanimously agreed between government, opposition and the stakeholders, that a bipartisan Parliamentary Oversight Committee of the Security Sector would be established.

The Community Policing Organisation of Guyana (CPOG) was given a 'shot in the arm' when it was announced by the President that government would allocate more resources to my Ministry for the procurement of land and water transport, firearms, communications equipment, accoutrements and uniforms for the organization. This announcement bolstered the morale and enthusiasm of members of the organization in particular and of the public in general. In fact, the news brought about a rapid growth and expansion of the membership of Community Policing Groups throughout the country.

To consolidate the re-renewed official recognition and stature of the CPOG, throughout my entire tenure as Minister of Home Affairs, I dedicated a lot of my attention and effort to the building and consolidation of the organisation. I travelled around the country visiting and holding community meetings with groups providing guidance and leadership to members. I encouraged communities where there was no CPG to band themselves together to form a group. The mobility and improvement of communications between Groups while on patrol with the police was greatly enhanced. And the social responsibilities of the organization were expanded to bring about improved all-round relations with residents in those communities served by the groups. Members of CPG's were encouraged to attend funerals of the deceased in their respective communities, to help fight fires with 'bucket brigades' where there was no fire station and to assist in community development projects as well. Regular audits were conducted to ensure that monies raised by groups at official CPG fund raising activities were accounted. And assets provided by government were beneficially used and maintained by the groups. At the end of the day, community policing made a tremendous contribution to ensuring safer communities through their routine foot, bicycle, vehicular and boat patrols and collaboration with the GPF.

Up to the time we left government in 2015, I was proud of the fact that I left behind a CPOG with approximately two hundred and seventy (270) CPG's with a total membership of over four thousand (4,000 plus) well organized, effective groups as popular force in service to the Guyanese people. Incidentally, it is apposite to note that at that time, the fixed establishment of the GPF was three thousand, five hundred and seventy (3,570) ranks.

NEIGHBOURHOOD POLICE

Another organisation which I paid a lot of attention to was the Neighbourhood Police. This was a standing body of persons, sworn as rural constables to serve in designated neighbourhoods on a permanent basis. Guyana is divided up into ten administrative regions, the ten regions are sub-divided into numerous localities known as Municipalities and Neighbourhood Democratic Councils (NDC's). There are approximately seventy (70) NDC's across the country. Their main whose task is to address the concerns of residents and to facilitate the maintenance, provision and improvement of basic social services and physical infrastructure in their respective neighbourhoods for the benefit of residents.

The Neighbourhood Police (NP) were recruited from within their respective neighbourhoods where they resided since they knew the people and the neighbourhood 'like the back of their hands.' The Neighbourhood Police were paid to patrol the neighbourhood and to report matters to the police. Ranks of the NP were vested with powers of arrest. I remain convinced that, if allowed to function professionally, NP can play a positive role in creating safeholds neighbourhoods. However, with the passage of time, due to the shortage of police ranks at some police stations in some police station districts, but moreso, because the

Neighbourhood Police was very effective in executing their duties and, in effect, exposed the weaknesses of the GPF in many neighbourhoods, ranks belonging to the Neighbourhood Police were removed from their regular patrols and placed at police stations to carry out station duties when in reality such duties are the responsibility of the GPF.

Such actions by the GPF were totally uncalled for. It smacked of laziness on the part of those in the GPF who, rather than rising to the challenges, chose to use the Neighbourhood Police as a means to prevent exposure of their laid-back approach to policing the neighbourhoods in their respective station districts. Surprise unannounced visits in my capacity of Minister of Home Affairs to a number of police stations made me aware of this deficiency and the need to correct it.

Knowing the police did not have the numbers to effectively manage some police stations and, as a consequence, sufficient ranks to routinely patrol the neighbourhoods effectively, I concluded, and so informed the then Commissioner of Police that the solution did not lie in digging a hole to fill a hole. We agreed that the solution lay on the one hand, in stepping up and flexing on the recruitment process into the GPF and training of the new recruits. On the other hand, that the Neighbourhood Police were to be released back into their regular patrols to help address issues such as domestic violence and other forms of anti-social behaviour that were regular occurrences in the various communities. At the end of the day our strategic objective was to create safe neighbourhoods.

Both the Community Policing Groups and the Neighbourhood Police ranks did a great job assisting the Ministry in its campaign to stamp out noise nuisance issues, based on legitimate complaints from citizens at various communities.

STATION MANAGEMENT COMMITTEES.

Another innovative institutional arrangement I took the opportunity to expand upon while at Home Affairs was the Station Management Committees (SMC's). Established long before I arrived at the ministry, I found the SMC's to be extremely useful to ranks at police stations. Because of insufficient funds allocated in the GPF's capital budget, many police stations were either badly in need of repairs or lacked certain basic amenities for daily use by police ranks at their respective stations or outposts. In the circumstances, through fund-raising activities organised by villagers, or based on the goodwill of members of the business community where the station or outpost is located, badly needed repairs or basic amenities were provided by members of the business community or public-spirited villagers. It was for these reasons that I encouraged and supported the growth and development of SMC's around the country.

DEALING WITH DOMESTIC VIOLENCE AND CHILD ABUSE

The challenge we faced up to mid-2014, a mere ten months before we left government, was that there were 1,743 cases of domestic violence across the country with 83.04 per cent of the victims being females and 16.96 per cent being males. There were also cases of primary, secondary and tertiary levels of crime and violence, as well as child maltreatment and molestation, attempted rape, intimate partner violence, drug trafficking, penetration of drugs in schools and drunken and abusive behaviour in neighbourhoods.

It was my considered opinion that ranks of Neighbourhood Police, once trained in social work can, along with teams of professional social workers, could be of great assistance in defusing tensions within and among families in particular and the neighbourhoods in general because they, as Neighbourhood police, were familiar with whatever festering problems there might be in the neighbourhoods where they functioned.

I held the view that a new pro-active approach should be introduced to prevent, as far as possible, domestic violence and child abuse. In the circumstances, I advanced the view that an expanded physical presence in the neighbourhood for the purpose of intelligence gathering and enforcement of preventative measures, would go a far way in reducing violent occurrences.

I therefore suggested a two-pronged approach. The first step would be, to recruit a number of trained social workers and to have them stationed at appropriate locations at each/magisterial district or NDC office. The second would be, to increase the number of Neighbourhood Police and their patrols in the neighbourhoods principally by day since, on the one hand, the police do not have the numbers to patrol each village on foot day and night, while on the other hand, members of Community Policing Groups are active usually at night. The idea was to have a coordinated approach aimed at ensuring maximum coverage of the neighbourhood.

I took a proposal to cabinet requesting an increase of one hundred (100) Neighbourhood Police ranks. Cabinet approved my request. As regards my request for the employment of seventy trained social workers, meaning, one per police station, I was advised to work closely with the Ministry of Human Services and Social Protection since that is the subject Ministry treating with social workers and, in any event, it was that Ministry that was responsible for recruiting and deploying that category of worker in the public sector. The problem however, I was running out of time because elections was looming on the horizon. As a consequence, my proposal was overtaken by events leading up to the 2011 elections.

FIGHTING TRAFFICKING IN PERSONS

Fortunately for me during my tenure under the Jagdeo administration, I received the support not only from the President's office but also that of the Head of the Presidential Secretariat who chaired meetings of the Central Intelligence Committee (CIC) while the President chaired meetings of the Defence Board. My participation in both bodies gave me deeper insight into the security sector. This collaborative and informed cooperation resulted in cabinet's approval, among other initiatives, of the establishment of a Ministerial Task Force on the Trafficking of Persons (MTFTIP) in February of 2007.

The Task Force comprised of; the Ministries of Home Affairs, Human Services and Social Security, Legal Affairs, Foreign Affairs, Amerindian Affairs, Help and Shelter and Food for the Poor. The latter organizations two being NGOs. I surmised that it was because of the pro-active nature of my ministry as well as the fact that it was the only ministry amongst those in the MTF that could issue general orders and directions to the Commissioner of Police to assist the TIP unit, and its operatives, to arrest and detain persons suspected of engaging in trafficking in persons. Sadly, the Task Force eventually devolved from a Ministerial to a Technical Task Force with the constituent ministries being represented by technical officials. I reciprocated accordingly. The devolution of responsibility notwithstanding, the technical staffers put their best foot forward in order to breathe life into the Task Force with a view fulfilling its mandate.

The Ministerial Task Force is government's primary body through which counter trafficking of persons programmes are coordinated and implemented. The MTFTIP arose from the Combatting Trafficking in Persons Act of 2005 which 'prohibits all forms of trafficking and prescribes sufficiently stringent penalties, ranging from three years to life imprisonment for offenders, forfeiture of property and full restitution of the victims.'

DEATH OF JANET JAGAN

Sometime in the evening of Saturday March 28, 2009 I received the news that Janet Jagan was hospitalized. I do not recall where I was at the time. Some of my colleagues, I was told, were at the opening of the ultra-modern New Thriving Chinese restaurant in the city. Regrettably, I do not recall why I was unable to leave what I was doing to go see her. Late in the night of the same Saturday, Barbara Jagan- Fries, Cheddi Jagan's sister called me at home to convey the sad news that she had died.

It seemed as if my political career had died with her passing. This was the woman who had brought me up in the Party from 18 years of age. She had kept a watchful eye on me, yet extended that steady but helping and guiding hand that allowed me to expanded my political, ideological and cultural horizons. Even though she had grown older and had passed away at the age of eighty-eight I could not imagine my world of politics without that stern yet pleasant look on her face. I remember the days when I used to smoke cigarettes and would be chatting with her in her office she would ask me occasionally for one of my cigarettes and we would continue chatting while she never inhaled but only puffed until she finished about half of the cigarette which she would snuff out in a rusty looking antique ash tray.

Though her husband and Party General Secretary was always present in my mind's eye, Janet Jagan was my lodestar, always shining, guiding and inspiring me to be in my own skin and not in someone else's. With Cheddi and Janet Jagan gone, we no longer had the two most senior and experienced leaders of the Party to tell us when we were going wrong politically and ideologically nor to call us together at any time of the night or day to consult on a matter of political importance. Somehow, I felt that Party life would never be the same, those of us in the leadership were now all equals and the competition and jockeying as to who would be the primus inter pares would soon rear its head. Whether it was Stuart Rendel's or Lloyd George's, I kept hearing the words "There is no friendship the top" in my head.

When I was called upon to prepare to read the eulogy for the late President at her State Funeral. I was pleasantly surprised although I was looking forward to be the one who would be called upon to do so. I was happy therefore that my colleagues had recognized that I would be the fit and proper person to do the job. Writing a eulogy for Janet Jagan was no easy task, so I chose to spend the rest of the week-end at home to work on the text. After completing an outline of what I wanted to say, I visited my friends Dale Bisnauth and Ian McDonald to get their thoughts about the style and content of a eulogy best suited for such a towering and feisty person and for the occasion as well. Dale and Ian had great command of the English language and had impressed me over the years with the style of their writings. But modesty having gotten the best of both men, both of them told me they had little to offer and that I must write as I knew her. I took their advice as a friendly compliment and as a comradely reprimand. It was like telling me 'Go do it your way and just write the way you feel about your Comrade while she was alive.'

On Tuesday March 31, three days after her passing, and with the nation griped in a state of mourning, thousands began flocking to parliament buildings, the official venue for the funeral service. Before proceeding to parliament, I went to the house of the Jagan's where there was a viewing for family, close relatives and friends.

As I walked pass the gate towards the casket in which she lay, memories rushed through my entire being of the political gatherings spent at that house at 65 Plantation BelAir. I spent a short while staring at the lifeless body of the woman many called, and justifiably so, 'my second mother'. I left after a short while and proceeded to my Ministry to go over once again the text of the eulogy which I had given the day before to Joycelyn, my hard-working Senior Confidential Secretary, the best I ever had, to type.

The Ministry of Home Affairs is about five minutes walk to Parliament Buildings. I chose to walk over. Thousands of ordinary Guyanese men and women were already gathered at the junction of the Northern, Eastern and Western sides of Brickdam and Avenue of the Republic. It was a bright Tuesday morning, with beautiful skies and appreciable sunshine.

On the courtyard and the balcony of the Parliament sat the dignitaries. President and former Presidents, Prime Minister and former Prime Ministers, Ministers of government, members of the Judiciary and the Magistracy, Members of Parliament, Government officials, diplomats, Representatives of the CARICOM, politicians, religious leaders' members of the business community, relatives, friends and many others. I watched as the cortege escorted by mounted police turned the corner westwards from Avenue of the Republic into Brickdam then Southwards leading to the entrance of the Parliament compound where her two children, Joey and Nadia, the in-laws grandchildren and closest relatives escorted the casket to rest under a large tent mounted in the courtyard.

The Master of Ceremony called on me to deliver the eulogy all eyes were upon me; they knew how close I was to Mrs. Jagan. I started out by stating that Mrs. Jagan was no doubt inspired by the famous and familiar words in the Declaration of Independence of the United States. I went on to add that her life 'was motivated by a strong, caring concern for people; the driving passion of her politics was the pursuit of their rights, particularly those of the poorer and marginalized classes'.

Overcome by emotion and with tears in my eyes, I did a tour d'horizon of her personal and political life. I pointed out how she brought a 'bustling energy to election campaigns that was matched by an easy grace and persuasive eloquence on her part'. She was imprisoned for six months because of her resistance to restrictions imposed by the colonial authorities. She was an internationalist well known for the contacts she established with fraternal parties, national liberation movements, peace and solidarity movements around the world.

She served as a member of Parliament for many years and as Ambassador to the United Nations. She became the first female President of Guyana after winning the1997 elections. I pointed out that "It was during her Presidency that the vilest and wickedest forms of protests, including public recourse to obeah, political manoeuvres and subterfuges were used in an effort dislodge her from office eventuating in the reduction of her term in office by two years. But she bore the indignity with dignity, the insults with courage and the gamut of indecency with resilience."

I ended the eulogy by saying: "Here was a woman, a humanist, simple and feisty as her editorials in the Mirror newspaper would indicate; industrious, committed and dedicated to the cause of the advancement of her people's welfare."

In accordance with her wishes, Janet Jagan was cremated later on the same day bringing an end to the Jagan era and opening up of another that would be characterized by us setting out to sail on uncharted waters. As for me, I was now on my own. And the question that kept turning over and over in my mind was; 'Am I prepared to deal with the challenges that lie ahead'.

ACTING AS PRESIDENT

In June 2010, I was sworn to act as President of the Republic in the absence of President Jagdeo who had departed the jurisdiction on travel duty. Prior to that acting appointment, during President Jagan's and Jagdeo's administrations I was called upon to act as Prime Minister on several occasions the first time being during the Presidency of Cheddi Jagan when I was called upon to act as Prime Minister. I considered these acting appointments to such high offices as a mark confidence in me and the esteem in which I was held by two sitting Presidents at the time.

To act as the President of a country is great honour even if it for a short while. What is important however is that the authority and power it vests in you does not go your head meaning that you do not display arrogance nor haughtiness while holding the position even if it for twenty-four hours. And though the experience can be exhilarating, at the same time, it allows for reflection and introspection of certain messages that may have caught your attention later-on in life but nevertheless, can remain with you for life. In this respect I recall the words of Barack Obama when he spoke in October 2020 at an elections rally at Detroit, Michigan; "The Presidency doesn't change who you are, it reveals who you are."

In early October 2011, at the Guyana Police Officers' Mess, I launched two books; 'Our Public Security Legislative Agenda' and another entitled 'Securing our Nation.' At the ceremony, I pointed to the significance of the power of the spoken word being translated to the written word which is manifested in the form of books containing knowledge to be shared. And though the contents of the publications may appear to be treating with the complexities of the security sector, it is nevertheless necessary to make the experiences available for public scrutiny. I added a personal touch to my presentation by stating that for a person who was involved and focused on international issues most of my political life, to find myself in 2006, in a totally different arena from Foreign Affairs to Home Affairs was completely new to me. But when consideration is given to the fact that foreign policy is an extension of domestic policy the challenges are easily understood. In any event, I have always stood by the belief expressed by the African-American Congressman Jim Clyburn who once said; "Work for what makes headway, not for what makes headlines" Most politicians however see work and headlines interconnected, they work for both.

ELECTION WITH A DIFFERENCE

General and regional elections were held in Guyana on November 2011. The PPP/C's Presidential Candidate this time around was Party General Secretary Donald Ramotar with Samuel Hinds as the Prime Ministerial Candidate. David Granger was the Presidential Candidate for the opposition A Partnership for National Unity (APNU) with the WPA's Rupert Roopnarine as the Prime Ministerial candidate. The Alliance for Change (AFC) led by Khemraj Ramjattan also contested the elections as his Party's Presidential Candidate.

Out of a total of 346,717 valid votes cast, the PPP/C won 166, 340 or 49.2 % of the votes cast, gaining thirty-two (32) seats in the National Assembly. The APNU won 139,678 or 40.8% with twenty-six seats (26) while the AFC won 35,333 or 10.3 % with (7) seven seats. The results showed clearly, that though the PPP/C had the majority of seats in the National Assembly, and would maintain control of the Executive, the combined opposition in effect had control of the parliament with a one seat majority.

The PPP/C's electoral fortunes had slipped by approximately 5,265 votes. Poll watchers and analysts claimed that the Party's poor performance had to do with a combination of arrogance displayed by some ministers of government, corrupt practices, the departure from the Party to the opposition by renegades Moses Nagamootoo and Khemraj Ramjattan and complacency on the part of Party structures.

During the election campaign, I was assigned to speak at public meetings Bath Settlement and at Cotton Tree, West Coast Berbice. The first meeting was scheduled to commence at 6:30pm however, up to 7:30 pm only six persons were present. I started the meeting at 7:30pm with about thirty persons scattered on the eastern side of the public road. After addressing the gathering for about one hour, I then proceeded to the next meeting where the attendance was just as sparce. At the conclusion of the meetings, I surmised that something was obviously wrong.

Having spoken before on numerous occasions, either alone or together with colleagues at these very locations known to be supportive of the PPP/C, I have witnessed much larger turn-outs. I reported my findings to Freedom House but was told not to worry the turn-outs will change for the better as the date of election drew nearer. Comparative results for the 2006 and 2011 elections show that the Party lost over 2000 votes in the Region Five Electoral District where Bath Settlement and Cotton Tree are located. It was a sign of things to come. The loss of support eventually showed up when the results of the General and Regional Elections were announced. The results were the closest results ever.

It was the first time in the history of Guyana's electoral politics that such a configuration would be found in our National Assembly with the PPP/C forming a minority government. But way back in the early1990's, prior to the 1992 election, Cheddi Jagan had opened up a debate with Party members and supporters and warned about the prospects for such an outcome in light of the impending '92, and future elections in Guyana.

Donald Ramotar was sworn in on December 3, 2011 as the new President replacing Jagdeo who had served for twelve years as President. President Ramotar's cabinet was sworn in on December 6. I retained the Home Affairs portfolio, expectedly, for another five years.

President Ramotar being sworn in as President of the Cooperative Republic by Chancellor of Judiciary (ag) Carl Singh

But as per normal in Guyanese electoral politics, when the major opposition political party lose an election their supporters would take to the streets with illegal marches and demonstrations. The first sign of what was to come when President-elect Ramotar received a call from David Granger proposing a meeting be held on the outcome of the election.

Granger proposed that the meeting between he and Ramotar be held at Parliament Buildings. Ramotar agreed and took me and a few other colleagues along with him to the meeting. It was about 9pm when we arrived at the entrance of parliament buildings. The place was pitch dark but we could feel the presence of hundreds of APNU supporters who had been mobilized and instructed to assemble in their numbers at parliament buildings. In one of the rooms sat Granger, Joe Harmon and Rupert Roopnarine of the WPA and others.

Granger began by expressing his concerns about the conduct and outcome of the elections. He claimed that the result laid the basis for inclusiveness and shared governance in accordance with the Constitution and that he was putting forward that for the PPP/C's consideration. Ramotar disagreed with Granger's assertion about the conduct and results of the election. He reaffirmed that the election was free and fair and that there was a clear winner. At that point, Roopnarine interrupted the dialogue. He pulled out from a satchel a handful of seals used to secure ballot boxes at polling stations saying that they were found some distance from a polling station implying that boxes were broken into and stuffed with ballots favourable to the PPP/C. No one took Roopnarine seriously, even Granger did not support what was intended to be a public relations stunt Roopnarine tried to pull at the meeting.

President Ramotar addressing the UNGA – 2011, Courtesy UN/DPI

PROTESTS AGAIN

The meeting ended without any agreement. On December 7, three days after Ramotar was sworn in the opposition applied to have a procession around the city but the route for the march posed some problems. Youth Coalition for Transformation (YCFT), an organisation associated with the main opposition party had applied for permission to have a procession through the streets populated by business places. The police refused the route applied for. The organisers were told to apply for another route. They refused and decided to challenge the police by proceeding with an illegal march on a different day protesting the results of the elections. The police again refused on the ground that they need forty-eight hours notice.

Despite warnings by the police, the marchers numbering about 300 persons led by Edward Collins, a retired army Chief-of-Staff and James Bond, the leader of the YCFT took to the streets. The police engaged the marchers at a certain point and warned them twice to end the illegal procession and to go home. The marchers ignored the police warnings and proceeded in a westerly direction towards the city centre. The police fired rubber bullets and tear gas at the marchers. The marchers split up and took off in two different directions. Several of the marchers, including Collins and Bond, the two ring-leaders, were injured by rubber bullets. They were arrested and later released. The police were accused of using of excessive force against the marchers.

President Ramotar meets Prime Minister Modi in India, President Ramotar greets President Carter at the Office of the President & President Ramotar and President Maduro arriving at International Conference Center.

ON TRIAL BECAUSE OF A BETRAYAL

In June 2014, the parliamentary opposition using their majority in the National Assembly passed a motion calling for the establishment of a Commission of Inquiry into the shooting of the protestors. The ruling PPP/C rejected the motion on the ground that the motion should have gone to the Parliamentary Oversight Committee on the Security Sector which was established as a mechanism for the resolution of security related issues but which the opposition had refused to establish since they had a majority in the House. Considering the embarrassment this caused to the opposition they eventually backed away from their call for a Commission of Inquiry.

But the political antics and provocations of the political opposition did not stop there, a second incident of greater proportion and of national significance occurred in July of 2012.

In preparation for presentation of budget 2012, government had invited the opposition for consultations on the question of a long standing, but burdensome subsidy for electricity at the bauxite town of Linden. The opposition had agreed they would support removal of the subsidies when the matter is brought to the National Assembly.

When Ashni Singh, the then Finance Minister in his budget presentation on March 30, 2012 stated that government will be moving to remove the subsidy for the supply of electricity to Linden, the opposition reneged on its prior agreement to support the measure. When news that the fifty- year old electricity subsidy for Lindeners amounting to $2.576bln was no longer tenable hit the Linden community, opposition party operatives on the ground at Linden wasted no time in stoking the fire. They demanded that government reverse its decision.

Protest demonstrations, marches, blocking the key and vital Wismar/Mckenzie bridge as well as acts of arson became the order of the day at the bauxite mining town. Blocking the bridge at both ends became a rallying point for confrontation between the protesters and the police. In the fracas that ensued the police were attacked. The police responded with the use of tear gas. Three persons were shot and killed and a number of government-owned buildings and vehicles were destroyed by fire.

At a meeting held at State House between President Ramotar and Opposition Leader David Granger at which I was present, Granger told the President that he was concerned not only with the incident at Linden but with the entire security situation obtaining in the country. President Ramotar opined that he preferred to focus on the incident at Linden to which Mr. Granger proposed that a Commission of Inquiry be established to enquire into the circumstances surrounding the shooting to death of the three persons. The President took the matter to cabinet for consideration. Cabinet concurred with the President's recommendation 'to have a Commission of Inquiry established to enquire into the shooting to death of the three named persons and the injuries of several other persons on the 18th of July, 2012 at the McKenzie-Wismar Bridge and to make recommendations.' The Terms of Reference of the Commission were also settled.

A five-person Commission of Inquiry comprising; Justice Lensley Wolfe, retired Chief Justice of Jamaica, Justice Cecil Kennard, former Chancellor of the Judiciary of Guyana, Justice Claudette Singh, former Justice of Appeal of Guyana, Senator K. D. Knight QC of Jamaica and Dana Seetahal SC of Trinidad and Tobago was established. Justice Wolfe was appointed Chairman of the Commission.

The Commission was set up in September 2012 and met for five months in Georgetown. I was summoned to testify before the Commission. I appeared before the Commission for two days. I was asked about instructions I gave to the police before, during and immediately after the events of July 18, 2011. I admitted that on the day of the 17th, I was told that the Police would be despatching half a unit of its Tactical Services Unit (TSU) to Linden, I gave general directions to the Commissioner of Police that he should take all lawful steps to maintain law and order.

In its report released in February 2013, the Commission found that '...insofar as instructions before July 18th are concerned, the evidence pointed only to the Minister giving a direction to the Commissioner on July 17th 2012 to take all lawful steps to maintain law and order at Linden'

The Commission also found that '...there is no evidence that the Minister gave instructions to anyone during the events of July 18th 2012. All that the Minister and the parties who testified on interaction with the Minister admitted that the Minister

497

was trying to obtain information as to what was happening in Linden on July 18th in his telephone conversation with the police during that day.'

In respect to my role after the events on July18th, at a meeting between President Ramotar and Opposition Leader Granger, the Opposition Leader called for the removal of Police Commander Hicken from Linden. The President assured that the request would be favourably considered. I was subsequently requested by the President to pass the relevant instructions to the Commissioner of Police who, acting on my instructions withdrew Hicken from Linden and posted him at Force Headquarters.

The Commission concluded the I had no place in relation to police operations but that I was in charge of policy. There was no evidence given at the hearings before the Commission to support the assertion that I gave 'instructions to the GPF in relation to the incident in Linden on July 18th other than testimony that I gave to the Commissioner that he should 'take all lawful steps to maintain law and order in Linden.'

Over seventy (70) witnesses appeared before the Commission. In its report, the Commission made fifty (50) recommendations among which included; training in relation to crowd control which it said 'needs to be revisited and that junior and senior officers need to be the beneficiaries of such training.' The Commission also recommended 'training in relation to crisis management'. It said that 'Things were allowed to happen rather than preventing things from happening. The Report called for 'better coordinated planning of operations of this nature.' Further, the Commission recommended 'a clear need for the urgent revision of the use of force policy in order to adopt international best practices.'

In its report, the Commission stated that 'the police must be held accountable for their behaviour and where abuses occur, these should be independently investigated in a professional way and thereafter appropriate action be taken whether through criminal, civil or disciplinary proceedings.'

But there was one particular observation by the Commission that attracted my attention. At paragraph 187 of their report the Commissioners said: 'We got the feeling that a significant number of persons who testified view the police cynically as agents of the government acting solely in the interest of the government and by extension, the political party forming the administration. There was no concrete evidence before us to substantiate that view but it is said that perception is nine-tenth of reality. This view can only be changed if there is insistence on the highest professional behaviour on the part of the police and the government demonstrates that politics and policing cannot be compatible bed-fellows'. The Report went on to state 'There is nothing more debilitating to proper policing than having political considerations or allegiance influencing the decisions and behaviour of the police to a particular segment of society which is known and perceived to be antagonistic to a political persuasion. All Guyanese regardless of their political persuasion are entitled to equal treatment under the Constitution and ordinary law of the country. Our observations are intended to deal with the perception and our urgings is that the perception be not ignored but that urgent steps be taken to deal with it as if it were a reality.'

I was happy that the Commission of Inquiry freed me of any direct involvement with the police in respect to the events at Linden. I knew I did nothing wrong and that experience from the protest demonstrations following the Lusignan massacre in 2008 had taught me as the Minister of Home Affairs how I should treat with such situations in future. Moreover, the long and chequered history of relations between the police and the PPP was absorbed in my psyche making me not rush to poor judgement but to be cautiously optimistic about police operations and crowd control.

REFLECTIONS

Being a Minister of Home Affairs puts you in situations that makes you defend the actions of law enforcement since, on the one hand, the minister is a representative of government. On the other hand, the police represent the coercive arm of the state which is the political organisation of the dominant class or classes in society.

The role of the police as an integral part of the coercive arm of the state is to safeguard the existing order and to suppress any resistance to that order. In other words, in a society based on private ownership of the means of production, distribution and exchange, the state is used as a tool of the ruling class or classes to suppress those who, through violent protest actions, seek to weaken, destabilize or overthrow the existing order.

In a Guyanese context, the democratically elected PPP/C has committed to the establishment of a national democracy. Cheddi Jagan in his 'The West on Trial' describes a national democracy as 'The partnership of all classes and social strata committed to a political democracy and social justice. It unites the workers, peasants/farmers, businessmen, professionals and intelligentsia in a broad alliance which allows for the satisfaction of the interests of these various groups. It prevents the dominance of any class or social strata and in turn protects each from being crushed.'

While stressing the need to uphold the tenants of a national democracy and the rule of law, the democratically elected government maintains the coercive apparatus or machinery of the state to ensure that laws or obligatory rules of behaviour are upheld. In the case of the events at Linden, the police, representing the coercive apparatus/machinery of the state was called upon to enforce the laws to safeguard the existing order or national democracy, the ethnic and political inspired overtones of the protests notwithstanding. In essence, no class or social strata was crushed at Linden as a result of police actions though operationally, their actions appeared to be militaristic and anachronistic. On the contrary, the police action quelled violent efforts by a small group of political activists belonging to the opposition political party. These activists, managed to manipulate a number of their supporters to become involved in violent protests to oppose government's decision to remove the subsidies on electricity, a concession that Guyanese in no other part of the country enjoyed.

CONFRONTATION IN PARLIAMENT

Long before the Commission of Inquiry started its work in September 2012, the Leader of the Opposition stood up in the National Assembly in July of the same year at the end of a twelve hour debate on a No Confidence Motion against me and publicly declared; "We will not wait for a Commission of Inquiry, we will ensure that there is justice tonight!" The no Confidence Motion, the first in the history of the Parliament, was brought against me by the parliamentary opposition after being prompted by the Speaker of the House to do so and after they refused to await a decision from the Privileges Committee to prevent me from speaking in the National Assembly without even indicating what privilege I breached!

Mr. Granger emphasized that he will continue to press to have me removed from the Ministry of Home Affairs. In the meantime, he encouraged his parliamentarians to create mayhem in the National Assembly to prevent me from speaking. On one occasion, he went as far as to prevent me from presenting the first reading of a Bill amending the Firearms Act making trafficking in Firearms and its components illegal in keeping with international treaties to which Guyana is party. The opposition was severely criticized by the media for opposing the Bill.

In July 2012, the parliamentary opposition used their combined one-seat majority in the National Assembly to move a Motion of No Confidence in me and calling on the Speaker to deny me the right to speak in the National Assembly.

In early November 2012, the Speaker ruled that he has 'no power to restrict or deny' me the right as a Member of Parliament 'from speaking or fulfilling' my 'ministerial duties and responsibilities in so far they relate to the House of Assembly.'

Speaking at a press conference following an opposition inspired fracas at a sitting of the National Assembly in November 2012, Attorney General and Minister of Justice Anil Nandlall pointed out that 'At the time when the opposition-sponsored No Confidence Motion was passed in the House' against me 'there was no basis under the rules of the Assembly or the Constitution for a no confidence motion to be brought against the minister.' Nandlall went on to stress that I was 'appointed by the President' and that I am 'an elected member of the National Assembly' and therefore sits there through my 'appointment by the President which is a Constitutional one' and my 'election to the National Assembly was done by the electorate.'

For my part, I made it my duty to stress how humbled I was 'by the support of my colleagues in the National Assembly', I also pointed out that 'any decision with respect to my future in parliament or my capacity as Minister of Home Affairs rests solely with President Ramotar.

In my address to the media, I made it clear that the leaders of the opposition are in no position to assess my performance as Minister; "They are not in cabinet and they are not in government, its only my colleagues who work and sit with me who are in the best position to judge and then at the end of every five years, it is the people who will judge". I reminded the House that I was "cleared to speak in the House and that I was very optimistic that when the report of the Commission of Inquiry is published, I will be cleared again".

In an effort to appear strong and combative Opposition Leader Granger declared "We will continue to act in the interest of the public, we will continue to ensure that Mr. Clement Rohee is not allowed to speak in this House as Minister of Home Affairs."

In January 2013, the then acting Chief Justice, Ian Chang ruled that I had the right to speak in the National Assembly as an elected member, with my ministerial portfolio being of no relevance. Justice Chang declared; "As a matter of pure law, he cannot be prevented from speaking and this is final." Justice Chang went on to state, 'While it is not usual for the courts to pronounce on rulings made in the National Assembly, when it involves the breaching of one's constitutional rights the court can intervene'.

The period 2011 to 2013 was an extremely trying if not testing period for me during my entire tenure as a minister of government. The experiences I accumulated during those years made me stronger not weaker. My determination to carry on serving the people and government of Guyana was strong. Save for my colleague and former Minister of Home Affairs, Ronald Gajraj, I do not recall any other Minister of the PPP/C government who experienced what I went through. Gajraj was relieved of his ministerial portfolio and was posted to India as High Commissioner. And Sash Sawh paid with his life for being one of the more forward-looking and results-oriented ministers during the PPP/C's 1996 to 2016 administration.

QUO VADIS HOME AFFAIRS?

 People tend to view the Ministry of Home Affairs (MOHA) in a narrow sense. They see the Ministry as a 'Police Ministry' - an extension of the GPF and vice versa. While this may be the popular perception, in reality this is clearly not the case. In any event, it would be inappropriate to view a civilian controlled ministry in that way.

The MOHA is a civilian controlled, policy formulation agency in the security sector. The Ministry has oversight responsibility for five departments that fall under the purview of the subject minister who is usually a civilian, a member of Cabinet and a member of Parliament. The five departments include: the Guyana Police Force, The Guyana Prison Service, The Guyana Fire Service, the General Register Office, the Police Complaints Authority and the Customs Anti-narcotics Unit.

The MOHA is a highly competent and modern institution that contributes to the maintenance of a secure, peaceful and prosperous Guyana through effective border management systems, and the adoption of internationally accepted best practices for public safety and security. The Ministry was established to ensure that the safety, rights, and dignity of all Guyanese are preserved.

In the same way that crime and violence are manifestations of inter-personal violence, so is the MOHA as part of a cluster of government agencies and departments who contribute to public safety and security, food security, economic and social security, environmental security and human security in general.

Under the Ramotar administration, we continued apace with the reforms of the security sector. More Data Entry Clerks were recruited and deployed to police stations around the country.

CHALLENGES WITH THE POLICE

And though the reforms were to the advantage of the GPF there were some at the senior level who did not look favourably on the reforms For example, by recruiting Data Entry Clerks to work at the ICIS at police stations, I was accused of 'inserting gestapo' into the Police Force, a most unhelpful assertion at a time when the police should have recognized the efforts government was making to improve data collection for the use of the Force which it was not capable of doing electronically.

Much can be achieved in the public safety and security sector provided there is a Commissioner and a senior management of the Force who are prepared to act professionally at all times and to get fully on board with the many dimensions of police reform with professional and suitably qualified civilians playing a supportive role. Police reform cannot be successfully implemented when the senior management of the Force plays the role of an unwilling bride. All the efforts by the Ministry of Home Affairs in general and the subject Minister in particular will come to nought were the senior management of the Force engage in passive resistance and maximum administrative delay.

The process of police reform in Guyana did make some baby steps. It was enhanced with the recruitment of a Policy Analyst whose task was to utilize the data generated by the ICIS in order to analyze spatial and temporal trends in crime, and to disaggregate the results as per police station and division by type of crime, victim and perpetrator and to recommend strategies to combat crime. This to my mind was a very valuable investment that contributed enormously to keeping the crime rate down were the police to utilize the intelligence data generated via the ICIS.

Moving around the country, I observed that the Police Force was badly in need of a modern Marine Branch. This important branch of the Force was neglected over the by the Force itself notwithstanding the fact that billions were allocated to the Force over the years for capital projects for every branch of the organization.

FOR A MODERN MARINE BRANCH

Guyana is a country with many rivers, creeks and canals. People live along the banks of the rivers and along the waterways. It is for these reasons we speak about the riverain areas. Crimes are committed in these areas, especially gun crimes, domestic abuse, praedial larceny, drugs, gun and fuel smuggling, trafficking in persons, physical clashes over ownership of land and of course piracy. The Guyana Police Force would be ineffective were it ill-equipped with vital water transport to enable its ranks to respond within reasonable time to any act of violence, anti-social behaviour or criminal activity perpetrated in riverain areas. It was these matters that raised my concern over the need for the Force to modernize its Marine Branch.

To realize this, I sought and got cabinet's approval to procure four aluminum boats and a 500HP sea worthy work boat to be used to train a new batch of police ranks recruited as coxwains solely for the Forces' marine wing. To this end, I contracted a retired ship captain with many years of experience to train a batch of new police recruits.

A senior rank of the GPF tried to sabotage the project by telling me that some of the just recruited ranks had lost interest in the project. He further added that the Force was short of ranks and could not afford to release so many to the Marine Branch. This I found not only surprising but self-defeating coming especially from a senior member of the GPF. In addition, I was told that the GDF had agreed to train those who had chosen to stay in the programme so that there was no need for the Ministry's training programme. I gathered from these excuses that for some strange reason some elements in the Force did not want a robust Marine branch of the GPF. To my mind, that was troubling. I asked that the matter be discussed at CIC and if needs be, at the Defence Board. With so many disagreements between me and the senior management of the GPF I felt it was necessary to have these matters discussed fully and openly. Cabinet and Defence Board supported my concerns.

FIGHTING ILLEGAL DRUGS

Another disagreement had to do with the performance of the Police sniffer dogs/canines. For quite sometime and for reasons unknown to us, the canines had proven to be ineffective at the international airport resulting in many occurrences of illegal drugs passing easily though the airport, on flights destined for JFK in the USA. The situation was becoming scandalous. I raised my concerns about the canines' ineffectiveness at our monthly airport security meetings where representatives of CANU and the Narcotics Branch of the GPF sat. I proposed that on-sight tests be carried out at the Ministry. James Singh, the Head of CANU put the necessary arrangements in place. To my surprise, the canines proved very effective.

The question therefore was, how come the canines were effective in one situation but ineffective in another? The answer had to do with the handlers. It turned out that there were some serious breaches there. Immediate remedial steps became necessary. But I had my doubts about the remedial measures proposed by the Police Narcotics Branch. I raised my concerns at a meeting of the Central Intelligence Committee (CIC) and got approval to make contact with the Global Training Academy Inc. at Somerset, Texas from whom we had procured the canines. I invited them to send a small team to Guyana to spend sometime with the canines whom they knew well.

In mid-October 2014, a two-man team of expert instructors arrived from the Global Training Academy. The instructors spent five working days with the canines at the end of which they submitted a report with a number of very useful and relevant observations and recommendations. I supported fully, the instructor's observations and recommendations. However, some in the police hierarchy tried to phoo-phoo the observations and recommendations. But I fought back and with the support of the Head of the Presidential Secretariat and got some of the more important recommendations implemented. There was a marked improvement in the performance of the dogs with new handlers at the airport. But it was like pulling teeth, more could have been done and much earlier had the Police cooperated in a more constructive and deliberate manner.

STEPS TOWARDS AN AREONAUTICAL BRANCH

The challenges notwithstanding, we at the Ministry continued to press ahead with institutional reforms at the GPF. Take for example the initiative to establish an Aeronautical Branch of the Guyana Police Force. This was something that was mooted for the longest while, long before I assumed responsibility as Minister of Home Affairs. The Force itself had recognized that they lacked the capacity to carry-out aerial surveillances and patrols of certain areas of the interior of our country. They went so far as to make public calls for the establishment of aeronautical branch. The Force had to depend on private aircraft owners from whom they would out-source aircraft at high costs for extended periods. This proved to be a very expensive excrcise and a heavy burden on their budget.

It so happened that while the prospects for the establishment of a GPF aeronautical branch was on-going, a number of unauthorized aircraft suspected of engaging in unlawful operations had illegally landed in the interior of the country and were seized by the security forces of Guyana. A case in point was an Ecuadorian registered Cessna aircraft. When the matter came up for discussion, I introduced the question of the aircraft's ownership being transferred by the civil aviation authorities and then to the GPF. I had in mind the realization of the long sought-after dream of the GPF having its own aircraft. The necessary legal procedures and paper work was left to be completed by the Civil Aviation Department. In the meanwhile, I held discussions with the then Commissioner of Police about the need to identify a number of ranks at the level of cadet officers who had expressed an interest in being trained as engineers or pilots for an aviation branch of the organization. We agreed to proceed in that direction.

I set up an Interviewing Panel comprising of experienced persons in the local aviation sector, and other related entities. Several ranks at the level of cadets with appropriate qualifications were identified by the Commissioner to pursue the two courses earlier mentioned. The most suitably academically qualified were selected by the panel and the names submitted for enrollment to be trained at the Art Williams and Harry Wendt Aeronautical Engineering School at Ogle and by the Guyana Defence Force (GDF) respectively.

The Police Cadets had originated from an initiative by President Jagdeo, who in 2008, had given the charge to the Police at their Annual Officers Conference to establish a Cadet Scheme in which fifty (50) recruits would undergo, with effect from 2009, a Basic Cadet Officer Training Programme. On graduation, a Cadet would be at the rank of an Inspector and after three years of service, would become illegible to be promoted to the rank of an Assistant Superintendent, assuming that there were no disciplinary charges against them. The objective of the Cadet Scheme was to strengthen and populate the officer corps of the GPF with young bright recruits who, in the context of succession planning would eventually move up the ranks of the GPF resulting in the emergence of a new breed of police ranks at the highest level of the organization.

My own enquiries told me that local and overseas training programmes for engineers and pilots would be very expensive but could not be avoided if success was to be achieved. I therefore adjusted the programme to address only the training of pilots at the local training school, since the GDF, which had its own aviation engineering corps, could take on the training of the engineers based on a Memorandum of Understanding between the GDF and the Ministry.

However, since we were a minority government following the 2011 elections and with the combined political opposition in control of the National Assembly, they wasted no time in using their majority to execute huge cuts in the estimates of expenditure for the fiscal years following the election. In the circumstances, central government was forced to be extremely prudent in the utilization of budgetary resources available to administer the affairs of the country. Sadly, the reforms initiated by the Ministry of Home Affairs at various departments under its purview were severely affected.

Notwithstanding the difficult circumstances obtaining in the country at the time, I continued to press ahead with a slew of new initiatives at my ministry. These difficult circumstances at the time, are to be laid at the doorsteps of the political opposition.

TRAFFIC CONTROL MEASURES

The introduction of Traffic Wardens to augment the ranks of Traffic Department of the Guyana Police Force in the capital city was one of such initiatives. That initiative had taken cognizance of the fact that the traffic situation especially in the city had become intolerable and grown to unmanageable proportions due to reckless driving and blatant disregard for traffic laws by motorists as well as failure by the police traffic department deal condignly with those who broke the law. Practical solutions became an urgent imperative.

In January 2014, a Bill was introduced to the National Assembly allowing persons issued with a traffic ticket to pay the prescribed penalty at any Magisterial District irrespective of where the traffic offence was committed. In the past, the fine had to be paid at the District where the offence was committed. In many cases, persons had to travel long distances to pay the fine. At that time, there were thirty-six (36) traffic offences for which tickets can be issued.

During the debate on the Bill, I made the point that while the Bill is intended to improve revenue collection, at the same time, it was aimed at ensuring that persons who commit offences would honor their obligations. The law when implemented, would also improve the efficiency of an electronic ticket accounting system I had put in place to track whether fines were paid or not. At the time of the debate more than 80% of the persons who were issued with tickets never paid the fines amounting to a loss of over $328mln. The Bill was passed with the unanimous support of the House.

But there was yet another off-spring of the problem. It had to do with traffic ranks handing down judgements on the road and soliciting favours while on duty from persons who violate traffic laws. This practice was becoming a huge problem resulting in persistent and numerous complaints by motorists. My branding the errant traffic ranks as 'Walking Magistrates' as well as my warnings to the ranks to desist from such behaviour and to their senior officers encouraging them to 'read the riot act' to their subordinates, seemed to fall on deaf airs. As a consequence, I decided to tackle the problem from another angle. I decided to publish in the mainstream print and social media and on TV an advisory to motorists advising that it is against the law to accede to a demand from police traffic ranks for a bribe in the form of meals, cash or anything not connected to the execution of their duties. In the Advisory I stressed that it was an offence to do so and encouraged persons who may have been asked to do so to inform the Ministry, the Police Complaints Authority, the Office of Professional Responsibility or any senior rank at the nearest police station.

During a business trip to Port-of-Spain, Trinidad and Tobago some time in late 2013, I was made aware of a Traffic Wardens programme that was established by the Ministry of National Security. Following a discussion with my good friend, Martin Joseph, the then Minister of National Security I was convinced that such a programme would be useful in a Guyanese context with some adjustments based on our local conditions.

On my return to Guyana I consulted with the then Commissioner of Police on the matter. The Commissioner appeared unconvinced but he went along reluctantly. I directed that he consults with the senior management of the Force and to let me know the result of his consultation. I took a proposal to cabinet for the recruitment of one hundred (100) Traffic Wardens. Cabinet approved my request. Following their training and being equipped with the necessary kits, the first eleven Traffic Wardens, belonging to the programme, was launched on July 2014 at a ceremony at the Stabroek Market Square.

I was very disappointed with the lethargic response by the Police Senior Management to this initiative. I could not see how or why only eleven of the one hundred Traffic Wardens could have been trained and graduated, especially when consideration is given to the fact that they would have received basically the same training that the police traffic ranks would normally receive. Nor did I see how in any way, the Wardens would pose a threat to the Police Force. Moreover, the Police had departed significantly from the design of the uniform for the warden which the Ministry had approved. To have the Warden bedecked in bow-ties under tropical conditions, was to my mind unconscionable and was probably done to frustrate the initiative. I did not hesitate to make my views known to the then Commissioner. I demanded that the uniform be replaced by the one the Ministry had submitted and that recruitment and training of the remainder of the hundred ranks be accelerated.

As to loose talk that was making the rounds within Police circles to the effect that the Traffic Wardens initiative was a step towards the civilianization of the Force, while this was indeed in the cards for quite a long time, but there was no way one hundred Traffic Wardens could out number the hundreds of Police traffic ranks scattered around the country. In any event, it was the police who recruited, screened and trained applicants desirous of joining the ranks of the Traffic Wardens. Sadly, the Traffic Wardens project was killed by the Guyana Police

Force. The records would show that the responsibility for its demise must be placed squarely at the doorstep of the GPF.

What amazed me even more was the fact that with so many new recruits to the Traffic Branch of the GPF and more so, with enhanced mobility with more cars and motor cycles yet the traffic situation continued to be unmanageable in the city. The installation of traffic lights at critical intersections of city streets and the mounting of CCTV cameras to spot violators and criminal activities did play a big role in regulating the flow of traffic yet the deficiencies persisted.

In February 2014, in collaboration with the Guyana National Road Safety Council and the Ministry of Public Works I convened a National Road Safety Conference. The aim of the conference was to examine and adopt road safety methodologies, create awareness and to formulate a Plan of Action from the National Strategy on Road Safety. I wanted to establish a platform for dialogue among national stakeholders.

In my address to the attendees I called for rigid enforcement of traffic laws and regulations. I pointed out that drunken-driving, speeding and inattentiveness were the leading causes for accidents and fatalities and that if they are be reduced action aimed at doing so should begin immediately.

I expressed my frustration with the court system whereby persons charged for causing death by dangerous driving and 'hit and run' are given pre-trial liberty much to the annoyance of the families of the deceased and the populace at large. I went on to add that with approximately 10,000 vehicles imported into the country annually and with the network of city roads remaining the same, challenges are bound to arise that would have to be addressed through infrastructural developments. I made reference to the new traffic laws that were passed in the National Assembly including the Evidence and Motor Vehicle and Road Traffic (Amendment) Act, the Pounds and Certain Other Enactments (Amendment) Bill, and the Motor Vehicles and Road Traffic (Amendment) Act.

The conference was a huge success. A number of recommendations were adopted with the Ministries of Home Affairs and Public Works, the Guyana Police Force, the National Road Safety Council and other stakeholders assigned responsibilities for implementation.

But just to be clear, we were not sitting on our hands plotting and planning such a conference 'while Rome was burning.' We at the ministry were always striving to address road safety challenges which were many and required the involvement of other stakeholders especially the public. One such issue that came up albeit three years later at the national road safety conference was the issue of stray animals on public highways, roads and streets in town and country. Connected to that road safety hazard was the absence of pounds at police stations to detain the stray animals when caught.

STRAY CATCHERS LAUNCHED

The solution to the problem required the setting up of an institutionalized and well-organized programme funded by government with a strong focus on road safety. We wasted no time in submitting what became known as a Stray Catcher Programme for inclusion in the Ministry's 2010 budget. Trucks had to be bought and persons known as 'Stray Catchers' had to be hired and trained on an on-going basis in accordance with the appropriate laws and specific guidelines drawn up to ensure the lawful and successful implementation of the programme.

In addition to the above, money was needed to either build or rehabilitate pounds at police stations where most of them were located.

We managed to get some of the funds we requested to kick-start the programme. We bought four trucks to be used to transport stray animals caught to pounds at the nearest police station. Twenty persons were hired and trained, and an administrator and drivers were employed. Units were established to work on a rotation basis in various parts of the country. The programme was launched in March 2011. But we made sure that before the launch, we had rehabilitated or constructed new pounds to hold animals until they were claimed by their rightful owners. But above all, before we launched, we mounted a sustained public relations programme to sensitize the populace about the serious nature of the programme.

And while the programme did have some teething problems at the beginning and did bring some financial hardships to poor farmers who owned just one or two cows or a small flock of sheep who they did not supervise because they were elsewhere working to eke out a living these were the issues that posed political challenges to me, the Stray Catchers and law enforcement challenges for the police. But the challenges notwithstanding, the stray catchers' programme achieved a considerable measure of success in that, since implementation of the programme there were no reports of fatal accident involving stray animals.

MY PARLIAMENTARY AGENDA

During my tenure as Minister of Home Affairs, I laid and had passed twenty-six (26) pieces of anti-crime legislations in the National Assembly including; The Summary Jurisdiction (Offences) (Amendment)Act (treating with the harboring and lodging of wanted persons); The Hijacking and Piracy Act; The Intercept of Communications Act; The Fugitive Offenders (Amendment) Act (extradition to third countries);The Private Security Services Act; The Intoxicating Liquor Licensing Act (for having persons under sixteen on licensed premises and for selling or supplying intoxicating liquor to young persons); The Gambling Prevention (Amendment) Act; The Juvenile Offenders (Amendment) Act; The Summary Jurisdiction (Offences) (Amendment) Act (to prohibit playing loud music in public transportation); The Prevention of Crimes (Amendment)Act (mandatory supervision after release from prison for crimes committed including domestic violence and sexual offences against children including paedophiles); The Criminal Law Procedures (Plea Bargaining and Plea Agreement (Amendment)Act; The Telecommunications (Amendment) Act (providers of SIM-cards and cellular phones to establish at their own expense, a system of recording and storing particulars of its SIM-card and mobile cellular phones and the customer utilizing them); The Immigration (Amendment) Act; The Criminal Law Procedures (Amendment) Act (paper committals of accused for High Court trials instead of awaiting the end of the preliminary inquiry); The Pounds and Certain Enactment (Amendment)Act; The Motor Vehicles and Road Traffic (Amendment) Act (definition of ATVs, use of a cell phone while driving, and false number plates); The Evidence (Amendment) Act (enabling the appearance of detainees before court for obtaining a hearing from the place of detention by audio visual link).

Some of the Bills treating with these matters were not supported by the parliamentary opposition. The Bills they opposed, they claimed, trespassed on the Constitutional Rights of citizens and were too draconian. For our part, we countered by stating that the crime situation in the country at the time required strong measures be taken to ensure the safety and protection of citizens and not those of criminal elements.

In Parliament with S.F Mohamed – 1997, with Reepu & Sam – 1998 & with my Parliamentary Colleagues - 2006

In my view, fighting crime should be seen as but one manifestation of our efforts to maintain public safety and security. It is but just one component of the bigger picture, that should be situated holistically in an economic, social and cultural framework. I am of the view, that once the crime fighting component is plucked, for whatever reason, from prevailing socio-economic conditions, we will end up with a distorted picture of the true state of affairs in respect to the public safety and security environment and the prospects for improvement. Therefore, any attempt to assess the effectiveness of government's fight against crime must be seen not from a narrow, but from a much broader perspective taking into consideration the economic, social, cultural and political conditions prevailing at a given time in the country.

TIME TO CHANGE NAMES

It was for these and other reasons, including generally accepted international best practices, that I took first to cabinet and then to the National Assembly recommendations for name changes to the Guyana Police Force (GPF), the Guyana Prison Service (GPS) and the Guyana Fire Service (GFS).

A s regards the GPF, I made the case that contextually, law enforcement agencies around the world are now under greater scrutiny by international human rights bodies who encourage them to engage in best practices in the execution of their duties. These developments have impacted governments and law enforcement agencies who are now seeking to strike a balance between law enforcement and human rights issues in relation to policing.

Similar arguments requesting the relevant modifications were made, in respect to the name changes for the Guyana Prison Service to the Guyana Prison and Correctional Service and from the Guyana Fire Service to the Guyana Fire and Rescue Service. Notwithstanding reservations expressed by some members of Cabinet, after some discussion, the name changes I recommended for the GPF, GPS and GFS were agreed with some amendments, and made to read as mentioned earlier.

In keeping with international standards, the GPF acknowledged that the rights of an individual must be accommodated in the execution of their duties. Consequently, the GPF began to place greater focus on police community interactions, with the formation of Station Management Committees, Community Policing, and a Traffic Advisory Board. These bodies allow the public to share experiences and ideas for a better managed Force.

Changing the name from Guyana Police Force to Guyana Police Service was meant to positively impact the delivery of services by the GPF to the public especially at the recruitment stage where entrants would be enlisted as representatives of a service organisation rather then one that relies primarily on the use force.

When the Bills for name changes for the GPF, the GPS and the GFS were laid in the National Assembly, I made the point that the name changes should not be seen as cosmetic. I reasoned that the name changes were of a fundamental nature in that, emphasis on the role of the GPF in particular, would be as a service provider rather than solely as an enforcer. And as for the GPS, much more emphasis would be on the correctional rather than exclusively on the custodial side. As far as the GFS was concerned, its role would be enhanced by the rescue and humanitarian dimension of the organization.

The Parliamentary opposition using their one-seat majority in the House voted against all three Bills on the ground that they were not disposed to support any Bills brought by me to the House. The rules of Parliament stipulate that the Bills not passed cannot be brought back to the House until another session following fresh elections.

In the meanwhile, the daily grind and disagreements with elements at the leadership level of the Police continued. These disagreements were not with the Force as a whole. On the contrary, the resistance came from certain senior ranks in Force who, in order to curry favour with the political opposition, kept grumbling about political interference in the Force when there was none. These very elements sought to disparage and undermine agreed initiatives connected with police reform initiated by the Ministry of Home Affairs.

MORE INITIATIVES

One such initiative was 'On-line Crime Reporting', a special designed social media platform that allowed any law-abiding citizen to report instantaneously, with the use of their smart phone, tablet or laptop, a crime they might have witnessed. The initiative was launched in October 2012 by the Ministry of Home Affairs much to the appreciation of the citizenry.

The initiative was designed to protect the identity of the person or persons sending the report either in the form of video clips, sound recordings, or text messages to a secure location at the Ops Room at Force HQ for onward transmission to the relevant police station for action. Reports included, domestic violence, damage to property, break and enter and larceny, accidents, robberies and trafficking in narcotics. Because the programme was widely publicized on TV, social media and the mainstream media, it was highly successful. Many Guyanese took advantage of the facility fundamentally, because it was based on the principle of anonymity.

But we did not stop here. We found another tool that we had been looking for a long time. We wanted a tool that could be used to determine trends in crime and violence, utilizing the large amount data harvested from the ICIS. One such tool we found was a Geographic Information System (GIS)-based on a crime mapping system. We were convinced that by utilizing that system we could integrate crime data in our possession with demographic and neighbourhood information so that spatial patterns of crime can be unlocked and areas where criminal occurrences persisted, identified. This system would introduce for the first time, crime mapping in Guyana. Moreover, the GIS system would help push law enforcement from a reactive to proactive posture in the fight against crime.

But this approach proved to be costly. Production of digitized crime maps required the procurement of satellite images of the capital city and the environs. We also contracted a consultant to help us frame the images captured in demographic and neighbourhood contexts.

The establishment in 2013 of a Computer Incident Response Unit (CIRU) at the Ministry was another step aimed at introducing and making operational, a modern platform aimed at improving government's cyber security capacity, preparedness and responsiveness through proactive security measures and information sharing mechanisms with E-government becoming increasingly prominent. To achieve this, a cyber security strategy was contemplated as yet another effective capability that would provide a specific service for government agencies and departments, the business community and private citizens.

And as though this was not enough, we created a Facebook page and website for the Ministry, so that citizens can access official posts containing data about the activities of the Ministry in particular and the security sector in general. To advance the public relations activities of the Ministry, we published a number of advisories in mainstream and social media such as; Playing of Loud Music in Mini-buses and Conditions of Road Service Licence for Minibuses; Community Policing; Traffic Offences For Which a Ticket May Be Issued; Payment of Inducements; Sale of Pornographic Materials; Responding to Vehicles with Siren; Setting of Fires in Public Places; Statements at Police Stations when making Reports about Crime; Tint for Owners of Motor Vehicles; Application For a new a Passport and Impounding of Animals. We also published a Security Guide for Citizens when Conducting Transactions at Commercial Banks.

SCIENCE TO HELP FIGHT CRIME

Thanks to resources provided by the IDB through the Citizen's Security Programme, we managed to complete in 2014 the first ever Forensic Laboratory in Guyana. At first, there were some disagreements with the Police about the establishment of the lab. The Police argued that rather than building another lab, the IDB resources should be used to refurbish completely the Police lab located at the compound at Force's headquarters. In retrospect, it seemed to me that the police's position was based on a recommendation contained in the Disciplined Forces Commission Report that called on government to 'acquire the means to conduct DNA testing and for the recruitment of scientific experts from society at large to serve the GPF scientific laboratory.'

I knew about the recommendation, but I nevertheless opposed the police's proposal on the ground that the popular perception is that the police is not trusted and is known to tamper with evidence from crime scenes. In any event, I pointed out that equipment purchased by government for the police's lab costing millions of dollars was never installed for use at the Police's lab and was left to deteriorate until they became useless.

My position was that the integrity of evidence stored at the lab must be safeguarded at all costs. In any event, speculative as it may seem, there were doubts about what could happen to evidence at a lab under the control of the police.

The risk of compromise and tampering of evidence at the Police lab was too great. International best practices had shown convincingly that labs of the type we were establish ought not to be under the control of the police, but should be at arms length from them. The services offered by the lab can be made available to the police on the same conditions as they should be to any civilian or organisation. Moreover, I proposed that suitably qualified persons be recruited from the civilian population for employment at the lab. To secure support for my proposals I made a submission to cabinet. My proposals were supported overwhelmingly. Consequently, I appointed a small team to enter into negotiations with the University of Guyana to lease to the Ministry of Home Affairs a portion of UG's property situated at the south/western part of the campus.

The Guyana Forensic Science Laboratory (GFSL) was finally completed in a building with two floors covering a total of 12,000 sq., ft. The lab was made up of four departments including; chemistry, toxicology, documentation and trace evidence with six laboratories as well as a library and a research section. The GFSL was commissioned in July 2014 by Dr. Roger Luncheon, Head of the Presidential Secretariat. Technically qualified staff suited for each department was recruited following the establishment of an interviewing panel. A 'land in exchange for training swap' was agreed between the University of Guyana and the Ministry of Home Affairs. In effect, the agreement meant that students from the appropriate faculties/departments at the University of Guyana would be allowed conditional access to the GFSL's facilities in order for the students to receive practical and advanced training as well as tutorials with the specialists at the GFSL.

The only regret I had about the GFSL at the time of its commissioning was that the lab did not have the capacity to do deoxyribonucleic acid (DNA) testing. But the IDB had made it clear to us from the inception that, were the limited funds budgeted for the construction and outfitting of the lab to be shifted from key components of the lab's construction and outfitting, in favour of DNA testing at the lab, then the lab would not be completed on time and cost over-runs would have to be borne by the government and not the bank.

I had made this fact known publicly, nevertheless sections of the media kept referring to the issue over and over again in an effort to sell a totally erroneous view that government made a conscious, unilateral decision to exclude DNA testing facilities in the laboratory's project formulation and execution.

Sometime later, based on advice I received from Guyanese legal luminaries, I took to Parliament a motion calling on the House to amend the Evidence Act in order to assign to the GFSL a legal persona allowing the results of its findings to be admitted as evidence in a court of law.

My own view was that the services provided by GFSL should be costed and sold to individuals and or private entities who wished to procure the services of the laboratory. In other words, the GFSL should provide a revenue stream for government. In this regard, I called on the Director of the lab to formulate a Strategic Plan as well as a Business Plan for the ministry's consideration.

A SWAT TEAM IS FORMED

In the midst of our efforts to modernize the security sector, a modern training centre for police officers was commissioned. Both local and overseas training was given top priority by the Ministry. In this connection, a significant step was taken with the establishment of a Special Weapons and Tactical Unit (SWAT).

With word out at home and abroad that the Government of Guyana had embarked on the process of modernizing its security sector, we received many offers from local and overseas security bodies who wanted to contribute to the process. One such offers came from The Emergence Group (TEG) in the United States who offered to set up a SWAT unit at the Guyana Police Force. I considered this project proposal timely and worthy of consideration. The IDB however, was not interested in funding such a project so we had to approach cabinet first to support the establishment of the unit and secondly, for money to fund the project. Fortunately, cabinet agreed.

After months of rigorous and new methods of training by specialized teams from the US, for the first time in the history of Guyana, the SWAT unit was launched in February 2014. Training of the unit's twenty-seven members was conducted in how to work as a team and to evaluate situations in a timely manner, saving lives as in hostage rescue operations, principles of close combat and how to dominate a small space. Actually, the trainers described the unit as 'an elite force to protect the people of Guyana'.

The political opposition had criticized the establishment of the unit deeming it a waste of time and resources and its irrelevance in the Guyana context. The Opposition Leader himself jumped into the discussion declaring that 'the experience of "special units in Guyana" has been very painful.' He went on to express fears about 'political interference and the tendency of the police administration to send low performing policemen to these units.' But I fired back stating that any new component of the Guyana Police Force that raises the effectiveness of force, and through that effectiveness, increases public confidence of the force should be welcomed. And the trainers expressed the view publicly that they were satisfied with the level of the ranks that had been chosen by the police to be members of the unit.

We who live and work in Guyana know full well that life is not as straight forward as some may want others to believe. A unit such as the SWAT which is not on beat patrol like regular police would be confronted with challenges. It was for this reason that the Granger administration, notwithstanding its admonishment of the unit while it was in opposition, found it necessary while in government, to despatch the unit to rural areas to engage in crime fighting, and not necessarily SWAT operations. Regrettably, the frailties of the human factor within the unit could not withstand the vagaries of a society infested with corrupt elements.

Three achievements considered stellar in our fight against crime was the establishment of several new police stations and outposts across the country. These included the establishment of the modern Police Officers' Training Centre, the state-of-the-art Forensic laboratory and the police outpost at Agricola Village on the East Bank. The Police Outpost at Agricola, commissioned in December 2012 meant that we now had 9 police stations and outposts in 'A' Division alone of the GPF.

FIGHTING CORRUPTION

Because of the high levels of bribery and corruption that permeated sections of the public service at the time, the Ministry considered it necessary to make a modest contribution to the fight against bribery and graft. In pursuit of its objective, an electronically-driven on-line platform titled 'I Paid a Bribe' was launched in May 2013.

Bribery and graft had become common place in certain areas of the private and public sectors public sector. Services which under normal circumstances were either free of cost or could only be obtained on a first come first serve basis or on the basis of an application made, were the most susceptible to corruption.

Since some preferred to pay a bribe and those rendering the service had no scruples in accepting or even soliciting a bribe, the scourge became widespread. Payment of bribes for a house lot, a birth certificate, a visa-on arrival, a work permit, an extension of stay, a passport, a firearm licence, a drivers' licence, to get a vehicle on a ferry, to get goods released from customs, to allow illegal items to enter the prison and even for a 'spot 'at the cemetery to bury the dead was the order of the day. Many poor people were forced to pay their last penny to a corrupt bureaucrat to have some paper work expedited.

The I paid a Bribe programme in Guyana, was modelled after similar programmes in Pakistan, Nigeria and India. The programme was aimed at serving as a deterrent and a forum for exposing wrong doing by unscrupulous individuals in the public sector. It provided another avenue for the citizenry to be involved in the fight against corruption by lodging complaints against bribe-taking individuals. While the site did not permit the victims to name the perpetrators they could however, name the department to where the bribe was paid, the date, the time and the amount of money that was paid.

In order to win country- wide support for the programme, the Ministry launched an aggressive public relations campaign to popularize the website. Reports received were forwarded to the Heads of the relevant government agency or department against which the complaint was made for whatever action they deemed fit. The Programme proved to be a tremendous success.

It was during this period that in keeping with its continuing efforts to modernize the security sector, government found it necessary to abandon the antiquated passport issuing system and to address regular reports about stolen passports and identity theft.

MRP'S FOR GUYANESE

To address this problem, government decided to introduce the Machine-Readable Passport Issuing System and Border Control System (MRPIS&BCS). The ministry was tasked with the responsibility to enter into negotiations with a Canadian company to produce the new passport and border issuing system. This was successfully accomplished a with effect from March 2015, issuance of the new passport with upgraded security features commenced.

PARTNERING TO FIGHT DRUGS

Illicit trafficking in narcotics in and out of Guyana proved to be, as it is universally, a major challenge for the ministry and by extension for law enforcement. The two law enforcement agencies responsible for prevention, interdiction and prosecution are the Customs Anti-Narcotics Unit (CANU) and the Narcotics Branch of the Guyana Police Force. Both fall under the responsibility of Home Affairs. The main challenge for us had to do with the continued branding of Guyana as a transhipment point for drugs from South America, to Guyana to the United States, Europe and Africa. This notion could hardly be disputed given the evidence and the facts. Our commitment to fulfilling our international obligations to fight the drug trade was not perceived by our international partners to be effective and strong enough to dismantle the innovative adaptations by the drug cartels and their local operatives who carry on with their illegal activities by shifting transit routes and the means of transporting the drugs.

Despite our participation at United Nations, OAS and CARICOM-sponsored activities aimed at heightening awareness, institutional strengthening and capacity building at the national level our responsiveness was not robust enough. The 'big fish' involved in the drug trade in Guyana were amassing great wealth, living the good life while and getting off scotch free. The long arm of corruption was reaching corrupt elements in law enforcement, the political and legal fraternity and eventually the courts.

Our airspace, water ways, the interior of the country and even some urban areas were used by the drug traffickers to carry on with their nefarious activities. With the use of self-propelled semi-submersible vessels, construction of illegal airstrips, use of fixed-wing one propeller aircraft, go-fast speed boats, drugs including cocaine and high quality 'super cannabis,' heroin and other synthetic drugs moved freely across our borders.

Steps had to be taken. I decided that we need to engage more constructively and aggressively with our bilateral and multilateral partners. At the multilateral level, we engaged more pro-actively with the United Nations Office on Drugs and Crime (UNODC), The Heads of National Drug Law Enforcement Agencies of Latin America and the Caribbean (HONLEA), the International Drug Enforcement Conference (IDEC) and the European Union/Latin American and Caribbean Working Group on Drugs.

At the bilateral level, we signed a number a drug-related agreement with Brazil, Colombia, Cuba, Suriname, UK and Venezuela. We entered into the multilateral and bilateral agreements in recognition of the fact that we cannot fight the drug scourge alone. In our view, the drug problem requires an integrated, balanced, and multidisciplinary response, and in order to provide this, there must be a common and shared sense of responsibility among all sectors and stakeholder agencies.

Apart from stepping up on our international obligations and despatching delegations to participate at both bilateral and multilateral fora, we took a number of steps at the national level to demonstrate how serious and committed we are to the fight against drug trafficking. We took steps to boost the capacity of law enforcement agencies. This meant providing them with additional resources to procure improved technological equipment and heightened surveillances capabilities at our airports, seaports and wharves.

A total revamp and restructuring of the Customs Anti-Narcotics Unit (CANU) was initiated with a change in the leadership of the organization. The Police Narcotics Branch made leadership changes as well. In an effort to find solutions, Cabinet decided to establish at my Ministry, a Task force on Narcotic Drugs and Illicit Weapons. The Task Force was established for the purpose of information and intelligence sharing to help in coordinating and advising on law enforcement operation as regards trafficking in narcotics.

The Task Force brought together five law enforcement agencies; the Guyana Police Force, the Guyana Defence Force, the Customs Anti-Narcotics Unit, the Guyana Revenue Authority and the Financial Intelligence Unit. The signing of a Memorandum of Understanding cemented the operational modalities for the five constituent bodies.

Later, because drug traffickers penetrated the wharves in Guyana and intensified the use of containers to ship drugs, we signed on to the Container Control Programme sponsored by the World Customs Union and the United Nations Organisation for Drug Control. Signing the agreement resulted in the establishment of a Joint Port Control Unit involving the Guyana Police Force, the Customs Anti-Narcotic Unit and the Drug Enforcement Unit of the Guyana Revenue Authority.

The next big project we had at the Ministry was to formulate a successor 2014-2018 National Drug Strategy Master Plan (NDSMP). The previous 2005-2009 plan, notwithstanding its limitations, was successfully implemented under its four broad areas; supply control, prevention, treatment and rehabilitation, and institutional and managerial framework.

Following a four-year lapse, and in light of the exigencies of the changing situation, the call was made to formulate a new drug strategy master plan. The donor community as well as our international partners and stakeholders involved were keen in having such a document in hand in order to determine where and how they can contribute to assist Guyana in the fight against illegal trafficking of drugs.

It seemed to me at the time, that we did not have the capacity at the ministry to do the job. In the circumstances, some suggested that we hire a consultant and assign the responsibility, but after much discussion at the level of the Task Force we agreed that we should pool our resources to draw up a first draft but by calling upon other related government agencies and departments to collaborate.

By the first quarter of 2014, we managed to complete the 2014-2018 Master Plan following extensive consultations throughout the country. The Plan inter alia, called for the establishment of new Ports of Entry at strategic riverain areas and where old ones exist, to reinforce the presence of law enforcement operatives. The plan also called for the development of national policies on the critical areas of demand reduction and supply reduction.

Of significance was a decision by government to re-establish the National Anti-Narcotic Commission (NANCOM) to oversee implementation of the Plan. As regards mobilizing resources to finance the various programmes of the plan, the Ministry of Finance was expected to provide budgetary resources and to assist in mobilizing donor funding

The cabinet decision however, did not envisage the establishment of a full-fledged NANCOM, on the contrary, its decision called for the establishment of a mere Steering Committee for NANCOM by 2014.

This was an interesting development. By not going the full Monty towards the re-establishment of a full fledged NANCOM meant going half-way in our effort at achieving a coordinated and full involvement of law enforcement together with the social sector as regards demand and supply reduction of illicit drugs in Guyana. My point is that the Force on smuggling of illicit drugs and firearms did not include the social sector and therefore NANCOM was the appropriate body for their incorporation.

I recall that sometime between 1995-1996, a full-fledged, functioning NANCOM did exist. That commission was chaired by the late President Cheddi Jagan. Fourteen years later, government found it necessary to re-establish NANCOM but not on a full-fledged basis. The body was re-established as a committee and not a commission, and this time around it was chaired by a minister which impacted negatively on its hitherto locus standi. The committee functioned for about one year during which its constituent members found their reporting responsibilities in the Task Force and NANCOM too onerous and indistinguishable. Lack of interest and absenteeism by key members at meetings of the committee became the order of the day.

But all was not lost at the institutional and capacity building level. What was extremely helpful to implementing the 2014-2018 National Drug Strategy Master Plan, was the legislative steps initiated by government between 2006 and 2008 based on the previous plan. The previous plan saw passage in the National Assembly of legislation treating with; Anti-Money Laundering and Countering the Financing of Terrorism, on Interception of Communications, on Telecommunications, on Money Transfer Agencies, on Criminal (Procedures) Plea Bargaining and Plea Agreement, an(Amendment) to the Evidence Act, on Mutual Legal Assistance in Criminal Matters, an (Amendment) to the Fugitive Act, and an amendment to the Firearms (Licensing) regulations.

Of great help to our fight against drug trafficking was the ministry's development and implementation of an integrated system to collect, analyse, maintain and disseminate drug related statistics. This mechanism established in mid- 2009 became known as the Drug Information Network (DIN). DIN'S membership comprised of the Narcotics Branch of the Guyana Police Force, the Customs Anti-Narcotics Unit, the Guyana Prison Service, the Ministry of Health, the Phoenix Recovery Project, the Salvation Army Men's Social Service, the Ministry of Youth, Sports and Culture and the Food and Drug Department.

The goal of DIN was to enhance the capacity of its constituent members to coordinate and collaborate in collating data generated independently by each constituent member, to analyse the data to assist in policy formulation and to design realistic responses and programmes.

DIN came at a time when the Crime and Social Observatory was up and running since 2007. The Crime and Social Observatory was expected to do what the DIN was expected to do, but it was not, it was collecting, compiling and analysing public safety indicators. DIN's establishment was therefore timely if not necessary. In light of what appeared to me to be superfluous in the reporting responsibilities of the two bodies, I recommended that reports on DIN's findings be presented to meetings of the full membership of the Crime and Social Observatory which I convened and chaired.

Information garnered from reports from the Crime and Social Observatory and DIN were released in Annual Drug Reports published every year by the Ministry. I considered it necessary to do so in order to provide the public with an appreciation of our efforts to combat the scourge of drug trafficking at national and international levels.

To assist in the fight against international crimes, a Treaty Section at the Ministry was established to address issues pertaining to Mutual Legal Assistance Treaty (MLAT) matters.

KICKING ASS

Notwithstanding criticisms from the political opposition and particular section of the media, which I knew had more to do with promoting a false perception as a means to an end, I considered it necessary to push back against falsehoods with help from the state-controlled media and our ministry's publications. From a political perspective, I enjoyed participating and leading the fight against drugs on behalf of Guyana at the national and international levels. It was challenging, troublesome and at times complicated especially since there were some who were identifiable but seemed protected by forces unknown to me at that time.

But there were times when my relationship with the police were not of the best. I recall on one occasion when at a meeting in April 2012 with representatives of the CPG National Executive Committee, the executive committees of the community policing groups from across the country and the ministry's Liaison Officers, I called on divisional commanders of the police force to abandon the administrative hostility towards community policing groups and to develop a more cooperative and constructive relationship with members of the groups.

The meeting was summoned in view of numerous complaints the ministry had received about the poor relationship between the police and the members of the CPG's. In some cases, the relationship had broken down and both sides were 'doing their own thing.' I considered the meeting necessary to heal CPG/Police relationships and to 'read the riot act' to both sides if necessary. As the meeting proceeded with both sides, airing their grievances, I discerned that certain police commanders assumed a rather hostile if not combative attitude, in the circumstances I warned that since poor police/CPG relationships impact negatively on communities and are taken advantage by criminal elements I intend to 'kick ass' in order to ensure that the safety and security of residents in the affected communities are maintained.

My 'kick ass' reference was recorded by someone who was present at the meeting and leaked to the press. The press went to town on the subject and twisted it with a view to driving a wedge between the ministry and the police. They didn't succeed. I responded to the matter by demonstrating the benefits of cooperation between the two crime fighting bodies.

But the contretemps between me and a few senior ranks of the Force became more personal and political. Just after the 2011 elections the opposition during a session of the National Assembly claimed that $90 million that should have gone to the police to off-set elections expenses for ranks kept in barracks. An allegation was made that a portion of the $90 million could not be accounted for at the Ministry of Home Affairs. As per the norm, the politician became fair game. The matter became personal when a police commander breached the Police Standing Orders and made a public statement accusing me as the person responsible for the 'disappearance' of the funds. The senior rank in a statement to the media declared that in view of the fact that he did not receive any funds from the ministry, he had to go around soliciting funds from private sources. He went on to show that all he managed to raise was $1.6 million which was insufficient to feed the ranks. The commander blamed the ministry for wilfully with holding the $90 million from the Police. The Auditor General was called in to investigate the matter and subsequently published his report. In his report, the Auditor General revealed that every cent of the $90 million was accounted for. The Auditor General also reported that a cheque amounting to $320,000 was cut from the $90 million and made out to the commander whose attempt to make public mischief was exposed when a copy of the cheque was made public.

I requested that the officer be disciplined for breach of the Police Discipline Act and the Police Standing Orders. The then Commissioner claimed that to do so would require at least two or three officers of similar rank to form a Board of Inquiry but this was not possible since officers of similar rank of were not available

THE WATER CANON ISSUE

As if this was not enough, I was confronted with another issue that had the potential of becoming mired in controversy. The issue at hand had to do with the operational capacity of the Guyana Police Force to address crowd control and street protest demonstrations. In a meeting with the then Commissioner of Police on the subject, the possibility of purchasing of a water canon surfaced. The Commissioner admitted that the Force was indeed in needed of additional operational capacity to address street demonstrations more effectively. After reviewing the use of a water canon over and over again and from different angles, the Commissioner supported the idea that a water canon should be procured.

At my weekly meetings with the Commissioner of Police such matters are discussed solely between me and the Commissioner. It is at those meetings where general directions are given and agreed to by the Commissioner. It is then for the Commissioner to pass down the general orders directions to the Heads of the relevant branch/es of his organization.

When news was leaked to the media about government's intention to procure a water canon for the GPF, a ton of criticisms surfaced from various NGOs as well as from the political opposition. Sections of the media known to be critical of the Ministry of Home Affairs jumped on the bandwagon.

My response was that no law-abiding citizen should feel threatened by the use of a water canon since, in defence of any modern democracy and the maintenance of public order, a modern police force, ought to have as part of its operational assets, a water canon as a non-lethal and not a life threatening asset.

In 2010 Cabinet granted its no objection for the purchase of a used water canon from a company in the People's Republic of China. Because a new water canon would cost approximately G$90 million and with only $20 million made available, the Ministry opted to procure a used water canon. However, before the vehicle was procured, due diligence investigations were conducted with assistance from our Embassy in China and the Chinese Embassy in Guyana concerning the vendor in China. Our fire service was also consulted as regards the specifications of the vehicle.

However, I have to concede that no on-site examination of the vehicle was done before its departure for Guyana. The water canon arrived in Guyana in November 2011.The following year, a successful trial run of the vehicle accompanied by TSU ranks was carried out at the National Park. All components were reported as being functional with one exception, there was no lachrymatory liquid dyes found in the vehicle.

Four years later, following the change of government in 2015, the water canon became an issue once again. Just one month after assuming office, the APNU+AFC coalition administration embarked on a witch-hunt and initiated a slew of forensic audits in an effort to find acts of corruption by former government ministers. One such audit in respect to the procurement of the water canon was conducted by Nizam Ali and Sons hired by the government.

Fifth columnists with a political agenda at the Police Force claimed that the GPF was not consulted as regards the purchase of the water canon. But it was interesting to find that the auditors were steered by the AFC minister Public Security to interview that particular police officer who the Minister knew would provide a totally biased and uninformed opinion about the procurement of the water canon.

For the Police Officer to claim that the GPF was not consulted was a blatant lie. And since the Commissioner did agree with the procurement of the water canon, I have to assume that he shared the information with his colleagues on a need to know basis. Obviously, the Commissioner, for reasons known only to him, did not consider it necessary to share the information with that particular officer.

According to the audit, the rank informed that 'no studies were done to justify the purchase of the vehicle' and that the vehicle was 'unsuitable' for use in police operations since it may be difficult to manoeuvre in the city due to the streets not being wide enough...'

The audit found that the entire procurement process for the vehicle was followed by the Ministries of Home Affairs, Finance and the Guyana Police Force. There were no breaches of the relevant laws and financial regulations. Long before the change of government and the audit, the Ministry had acknowledged that it should have been more assertive in respect to due diligence of the Chinese vendor and on-site inspection of the vehicle. We should have despatched a member of staff at our Embassy in Beijing to the location in China to conduct an on-site inspection of the vehicle. But costs to send someone, compounded by a shortage of qualified and experienced personnel to do the job was an inhibiting factor. In addition, the prohibitive costs for a new vehicle and the limited resources made available to purchase a used vehicle made it impossible for us to do so.

THE FIREARMS ISSUE

Another area of friction that arose between me and the usual suspects in the leadership of the Force had to do with the issuance of firearm licences. Long before my arrival at the Ministry, we had circumstantial and, in many cases, incontrovertible evidence that police ranks either among themselves within the organization or in collusion with employees at the Ministry of Home Affairs were involved in selling firearm licences in many instances, to undeserving persons who were prepared to pay a bribe.

To curb the malfeasance, I took advice contained in the Disciplined Forces Commission of Inquiry Report. Thee Report recommended that; 'Regulatory amendments to the Firearms Act should be introduced in order to bolster supervisory control over divisional commanders who grant firearm licences, in keeping with the general objective of the GPF Standing Order 91/64'. The Report went on to recommend; 'The Minister of Home Affairs should utilize his statutory powers to make standard and uniform regulations with regard to firearm licensing so as to guard against allegations of political interference.' The Report further recommended: 'The Commissioner of Police should continue to have strict supervision and control over divisional commanders with regard to the granting of firearm licences.'

To this end, in mid-2010, I tabled a motion in the National Assembly to amend the Firearms Act to facilitate implementation of these recommendations. The amendment was aimed at making the processing of applications for firearm licences transparent and free of political interference by inserting a mechanism between the police and the Ministry. That mechanism would be a Firearm Licencing Approval Board (FALAB).

In the past, it was the police in collaboration with the Minister of Home Affairs who were responsible for processing applications for firearm licences. The new arrangement took away the processing of applications from the police and the Minister and gave it to the FALAB.

The police were not too happy with the processing of applications being removed from them however, when confronted with the fact that the recommendations had their genesis in the Disciplined Forces Commission Report they backed off.

The Board was made up of four civilians including, Cecil Kilkenny, Dr. Peter DeGroot, Dr. Bhairo Harry, and Yojna Hernandez as Secretary. Later, following the departure of Dr. De Groot, Bertie Sukhai was appointed to the Board. The Board was tasked with the responsibility to process all applications received from the Commissioner of Police. The Board was required to submit the approved applications to the Minister for his no objections. During my tenure as Home Affairs Minister most of the approvals sent to me by the Board received my no objection.

Later, a Firearms Licensing Management System was established to allow for the monitoring of applications, processing, approval and or rejection of applications, payment of costs for processing and approval of licences by electronic means. The system was to be jointly shared between the Police, the Ministry and the Board with strict delineation or firewalling of responsibilities was built into the system. The long-established priority for granting firearm licences to farmers, Amerindians and businessmen remained in place.

EFFORTS AT DIGITIZING RECORDS

Records of my last internal minutes dated January 19 and March 10, 2015, the last being two months before the elections to Angela Johnson, the late Permanent Secretary at the ministry would show the issues that I was pressing to have settled before the elections campaign. These issues included; finalizing an electronic module for firearms regulations; introduction of E-number plates for motor vehicles; removal of deficiencies in the collection of fines resulting from the issuance of traffic tickets; introduction of E-visas for visitors; formulation of a new immigration policy; solutions for the 911 emergency system; recruitment of the first team of investigators to be attached to the Police Complaints Authority; increasing the establishment of the GPF at the level of constables; employment of welfare officers at the GPS; outfitting a floating base built for the GPF and submission of an evidence-based analyses of suicides and domestic violence in Guyana.

These were the matters I was spear-heading at the Ministry on the eve of the 2015 elections. It was my intention to have all of them completed before the elections. Regrettably, the electronic module for firearm regulations was not completed nor was the proposal to introduce E-number plates. The latter got caught up in bureaucratic process at the AG's Chamber and the Guyana Revenue Authority. And the electronic module for the firearm regulations was delayed, I believe intentionally, by the Brain street company that was contracted to complete the job. In the meantime, our search for a solution to collect unpaid fines from the issuance of traffic tickets was slowed down because of the lethargic approach by draftsmen at the AG's Chamber

E-VISAS, IMMIGRATION, TURF WARS, AND THE 911 SYSTEM.

The proposal to issue E-visas got caught up in an inter-agency turf war between Home Affairs and Foreign Affairs without any resolution and a draft New Immigration Policy formulated and circulated by my ministry for comments took an unacceptable amount of time to come back with comments for it to be finalized. And despite the progress made mainly though the heroic efforts of Mr. Radha Krishna Sharma, the then CEO at the Guyana Telephone and Telegraph Company (GT&T to assist in resolving the 911 Emergency System, the sloth by other members of a panel established to solve the problem left the matter unfinished. We managed to secure Cabinet's approval for the first team of investigators attached the Police Complaints Authority. The floating base for the GPF though completed, was not outfitted with the requisite equipment as required because the GDF who had volunteered to help with procurement, took an inordinate amount of time to procure the equipment for the base. And the evidence-based analyses in respect to suicides and domestic violence was not completed before I left the Ministry.

I was not happy with the status reports I received concerning these outstanding matters. And though I was conscious of the fact that, notwithstanding my best efforts to have these matters resolved before the elections, their resolution did not depend solely on me. Nevertheless, where applicable, I felt that my colleagues in the social sector could have been more supportive to resolve the challenges of the security sector. I remain convinced that public safety and security cannot be effectively and efficiently addressed without recognizing that there is a social dimension to the fight against crime and violence in particular, and for the maintenance of public safety and security in general

CONTINUING THE FIGHT.

It is for this reason that in late November 2013, days after my return home from hospitalization and medical treatment abroad, a major two-day 'National Conference for The Prevention of Inter-Personal Violence' was convened under the theme 'Working Together Against Inter-Personal Violence.'

We were preparing for this conference long before I fell ill. The technical staff at the ministry under the supervision of the Permanent Secretary did a great job putting the conference together while I was away.

We invited representatives from the social sector government agencies and departments, faith-based organisations, the business community, trade unions, women and youth organisations, the University of Guyana, the Police Force, the Prison Service, the Fire Service, members of the Task Force on Narcotic Drugs and Illicit and Weapons and the Task Force on Fuel Smuggling and Contraband, the Cheddi Jagan International Airport and Ogle airport security committees and the Community and Neighbourhood Police. The aim of the conference was 'lay the groundwork for practical partnerships in addressing crime and violence and for participants to gain a deeper understanding of the issues surrounding crime'.

Sections of the media that always bore a grudge against me at the helm of the Ministry made a song and dance about the significance and usefulness of the conference pointing to other bodies that, in their view, were established to do what the conference was expected to accomplish.

Addressing participants at the conference, President Ramotar said that the conference is aimed at; '...developing a framework that will see the creation of a national plan to counter violence in all its manifestations in Guyana". He added that the conference 'forms part of a broader on-going public engagement to address various aspects of public security in a comprehensive way though a participatory approach.' The President went on to say that, 'While the State has a general responsibility for the preservation of law and order and for the protection of its citizens, this issue can by no means be the exclusive preserve of government.'

Ramotar called for 'the rejection and condemnation of all forms of violence' He urged that; 'collectively, we must stand in solidarity with the victims of inter-personal violence and unite to fashion strategies to combat this threat.'

In my remarks to the conference, I urged participants to; '...ensure that the forum does not turn out to be just another conference or talk shop'. I stressed that 'law enforcement and the Ministry need the full support of social partners in order to address the scourge of inter-personal violence in a holistic and comprehensive way.'

The Representative of the Inter-American Bank (IDB) also addressed the conference. She spoke of the consequences of inter-personal violence, particularly to the social sector stating that 'inter-personal violence slows economic growth and impedes social progress.'

These were exactly the points I wanted to be emphasized throughout the conference. And that was precisely what took place during the break-out group sessions. I had encouraged the persons assigned to lead each group to ensure that notwithstanding the many opinions that would surface in the course of the discussion they should try their level best to ensure that the theme of the conference remains in focus.

Notwithstanding the efforts of the mainstream media to throw cold water on the conference it was a tremendous success. Being the first of its kind, it had attracted a broad cross section of Guyanese society including the key players in the security sector. Over one hundred recommendations emerged from the discussions. The recommendations were brought to the full plenary session of the conference for further refinement and approval which was given by acclamation.

My next step was to take to cabinet those recommendations whose implementation required inter-agency collaboration and, in some cases, direct financing through the Ministry of Finance. Cabinet advised that the recommendations that required financing, should secure the resources from the budget of the respective government agencies and departments. Those recommendations that required inter-agency collaboration would proceed accordingly. To get the process moving, I established a small body comprising members of civil society and the relevant ministries whose task was to oversee implementation of the recommendations.

As I continued my search for innovative ways to address the crime situation in Guyana, I paid a lot of attention to contributions from participants at meetings convened by the Ministry. One body from which ideas always came up was at meetings of the Crime and Social Observatory. I surmised this was because of the nature of the participants.

At one of the meetings of the Observatory which I chaired, Pastor Kwame Gilbert, a young man always full of ideas and very articulate, recommended the creation of a network he called the Cops and Faith Network. He was responding to a concern that I had expressed time and again on two matters. One was that too many juveniles were being picked up by the Police for committing petty crimes and misdemeanours such as loitering, wandering, petty theft, simple assault, disorderly behaviour, resisting arrest, indecent language and exposure. and other manifestations of anti-social behaviour in communities. The police response to my request for an alternative to their enforcement of the law was that they are not an organisation of social workers and that they had not alternative but to arrest and charge those who broke the law.

My second concern had to do with the involvement of parents and or guardians of the young persons arrested by the police. They would go to the police station to plead with ranks on duty not to charge the accused, but to release the youngster. The police as usual were unsupportive. I had asked why the faith-based organisations in general and particularly the local priest or pastor were not involved since they were always preaching the gospel and calling at the same time, for moral and ethical behaviour of their flock. I suggested a mechanism where the police, the parent or guardian and the priest, on the basis of a network created amongst themselves, would meet at police station to discuss the pros and cons of the incident involving the youngster and be required to arrive at a collective determination on the way forward short of police prosecution.

Pastor Gilbert drew to our attention an observation he made during visits to Los Angeles and Detroit in the United States where he witnessed a phenomenon called 'The COPS and Clergy Network' in action. According to Gilbert, the network was based in local communities and had as its goal problem solving for youths who came into conflict with the Law for minor offences in their communities.

We examined applying The COPS and Clergy Network to our own local conditions and peculiarities and found that its application was possible provided it was supported by the principal stakeholders. Following power-point presentations and bilateral consultations with the Police and a number of faith-based organisations, we received their overwhelming support for the project.

The Cops and Faith Community Network was launched in September of 2013. At a simple ceremony marking the launch of the network, I described the project as 'a beautiful and harmonious combination of law and moral enforcement aimed first and foremost at serving the people in their respective communities.'

CHALLENGES OF A DIFFERENT KIND

Working with President Ramotar as his Home Affairs Minister was not difficult for me. We had grown up in the Youth organisation and the Party together. Philosophically and ideologically we saw 'eye to eye' on many issues that came up at cabinet including foreign policy issues on which we held more positions of convergence rather than divergence.

Some how in the third year of the Ramotar presidency Lloyd George's warning that; 'There is no friendship at the top' began to shine through. It was during this period that cabinet memos in my name treating with security sector reform began to flow 'fast and furious' on to the agenda of cabinet meetings. Though Ramotar was generally supportive of the intent and purpose of my cabinet papers, I discerned a consistent push-back by a certain cabinet member who took it upon themselves to stonewall my security sector reform initiatives for reasons known only to them. At another political level, their approach would be subtle or aggressive depending on the issue under discussion. It was only years later that I realized what had happened.

These occurrences arose at a difficult time for the Party and government.

A big issue that arose early in the month of November 2014 was the threat of a No Confidence Motion which the parliamentary opposition had tabled in the National Assembly against the government prior to the parliamentary recess.

The casus belli for the No confidence motion was the postponement of local government elections which had been festering for a number of years notwithstanding the fact that the parliamentary opposition had agreed to postpone the elections on several occasions. However, now with its one-seat majority in the National Assembly it had latched on opportunistically to the issue for political reasons.

With parliament reconvened following the recess, the threat for passage of the no-confidence motion loomed larger and larger.

On November 4th, 2014 President Ramotar addressed the nation. In his address, Ramotar announced November 10th as the date for the first post-recess sitting of the National Assembly. He criticized the parliamentary opposition for passing a number of unconstitutional Bills and for blocking Bills treating with government business. Ramotar referred to Bills treating with Anti-Money Laundering and Countering the Financing of Terrorism, Telecommunications, Education, government procurement, financial papers as well as the timing for the holding of local government elections. President Ramotar warned that if the opposition chose to ignore those Bills and proceeded with their no-confidence motion 'I resolve to respond immediately by exercising my constitutional options to either prorogue or dissolve parliament paving the way for the holding of general elections.' In an effort to assuage the opposition, Ramotar announced his intention to hold local government elections in the second quarter of 2015.

Six Days later, with no political solution in sight, with a parliament stacked against the government and a Speaker prepared to allow the motion at a sitting of the House on November 10th, Ramotar responded immediately. In address to the nation, Ramotar announced that '…in accordance with powers conferred on me by Article 70(1) of the Constitution of the Republic of Guyana, I earlier today issued a Proclamation proroguing the 10th Parliament.'

Ramotar declared that had the sitting of the House proceeded, it would have led to confrontation whereas he preferred accommodation which, in his view, a prorogued parliament could facilitate. The President assured the nation that with prorogation 'the life of the Parliament is preserved up to six months as permitted by the Constitution.' He went on to add that 'It is my genuine desire to have the prorogation of the 10th Parliament ended sooner were my government and the opposition to reach an agreement for a return to normalcy.'

The Leader of the Parliamentary Opposition during the sitting of the House following the Proclamation proroguing the Parliament declared that Ramotar's proclamation to prorogue Parliament is a challenge to our people …' and that the 'opposition will not accept this denial of democracy…' He called for the 'earliest possible revocation of the obnoxious proclamation.'

In the meanwhile, the Clerk of the National Assembly in a circular dated November 13, 2014 to all Members of Parliament stated 'A prorogation does not end the life of Parliament. It terminates a session of Parliament and brings to a close all matters that were published on Notice papers and listed on the Order Paper for consideration of the National Assembly.' The Clerk went on to advise that all matters which were published on Notice Papers and listed on the Order Paper at the time of prorogation would have to be resubmitted in the next session, if they are to be further considered.'

Following the prorogation, the attacks came from several quarters; the political opposition, the media, the diplomatic community, trade unions, religious organisations and some entities in the business community. At a press conference held on the day of the prorogation, I debunked the view being peddled in certain quarters that the Party ran away from the no-confidence motion. In response, I stated; 'We in the PPP\C are not known for running from anything. We don't run from, we run with, meaning… we run with the people, we run to win elections'

In respect to the argument that we should have agreed to the sitting and used it as a forum to defend the government, I went on to say that for the PPP\C, there is no dependency on an NCM to defend itself. 'We've been defending our time in government every day…365 days per year including in a leap year we're out their defending government. We don't have to await the 'blessings' of an NCM to defend ourselves.'

One Caribbean newspaper, the Jamaica Observer, on November 12, 2014 joined the echo-chamber claiming That prorogation signalled that Guyana was 'headed for a dictatorship.' The newspaper described the prorogation as a move: 'To deliberately create a situation in which the executive is exercising power without a functioning parliament is a subversion of democracy…' And the Trinidad Express in an editorial published on November 14th, said: 'The Guyanese leaders must realise they are on a slippery slope, and they need to press a reset button for the conduct of their government and politics.'

In the meantime, the resident diplomatic community in Guyana joined in the fray. They requested a meeting with the opposition political parties who, according to a press statement issued after the meeting claimed that the diplomats, 'Seemed to favour an early end to the prorogation'. One diplomat was more forthright, he declared; 'The central message is absolutely clear: Parliament should re-sit in Guyana and get on with the business of taking the country forward.'

From their statements, it was obvious that the diplomatic community chose to ignore the fact that were the parliament to be re-convened, the opposition would have insisted on passage of their No-confidence Motion. That act by its very nature, would have resulted in the fall of the PPP/C government and the holding of fresh elections. The logical conclusion therefore was that the diplomatic community wanted the downfall of the Ramotar administration. The big question was, who else was part of that strategic objective?

In pursuit of their nefarious objective, the political opposition wasted no time in mobilizing their supporters and whipping up public opinion with hyperbole about a 'lack of parliamentary and local government democracy', the 'emergence of a dictatorship' and calls for 'sanctions by the international community'.

The APNU issued a statement stating; ... 'it will not accept the PPP\C's denial of democracy ... and its continued non-compliance with the Constitution, especially with regard to the compulsory conduct of local government elections.' The Party announced that it will 'launch a series of lawful and peaceful 'pro-democracy' protests to raise public awareness over the President's prorogation of Parliament...'

By November 14th,2014 Ramotar told a news conference that 'he will very soon be inviting the Opposition Leader to meet and discuss issues affecting the country'. 'I know they have been saying they will not want to speak... I would interpret that as their first position. Hopefully, when the emotions will be removed, good sense and maturity will prevail.'

In response to the opposition attacks, the PPP\C administration at various levels and by a variety of means went on a public relations offensive. It explained that prorogation was intended to allow for a period of compromise\ dialogue with the opposition that would lead to a return to parliamentary democracy. The government stressed that prorogation does not alter nor diminish the legality of Constitutional provisions and the financial statutes\rules and regulations. The statement added that 'the Minister of Finance remains obligated to report spending, to seek prior approval as required to spend, to spend appropriated sums from the

Consolidated Fund, and in in his own judgement, to spend from the Contingency Fund. In all cases cabinet's approval is required and the House has to be notified'

In reference to prorogation and the separation of powers and allegations of a dictatorship, the government pointed out that prorogation does not constitutionally provide the Executive with new or addition powers and that the functions of parliament are not and cannot be assumed by the President or cabinet. Finally, the government made it clear that there is a fundamental difference between the dissolution of parliament and the prorogation of parliament. As far as the government was concerned, dissolution ends the life of parliament whereas prorogation does not and cannot end the life of Parliament, on the contrary, it preserves the life of parliament for a period up to six months. In this instance, prorogation was used as a constitutional tool to put parliament on pause for two reasons; First, to deny passage of the no confidence motion that would have brought down the government resulting in the holding of general elections, and second, to give space for dialogue to take place between government and the parliamentary opposition on matters of mutual interest.

On November 18th, 2014 President Ramotar wrote Opposition Leader, David Granger proposing that '...we quickly commence a high-level engagement of two teams led by myself and yourself respectively, to agree on a post- Prorogation Parliamentary Agenda on which an Order Paper can be based. I stand prepared to meet at the shortest notice, to initiate steps. Alternatively, I am also prepared to have exploratory engagement on this subject delegated to identified persons nominated by both sides.'

Granger opted for the alternative proposal. In the circumstances, Dr. Roger Luncheon was identified to represent the government while Joe Harmon was designated to represent the Opposition Leader. Informal, extra-parliamentary meetings took place during which it became clear that while the government wanted the opposition to return to Parliament and Parliamentary normalcy with an agreed agenda. The opposition however, wanted 'systemic change' based on 'tangible concessions' before the high-level talks could begin.

The opposition did not clear the air about what they meant by 'systemic changes' nor clarify what were the 'tangible concessions' they were calling for before the high-level talks could begin, however, in an effort to move the informal talks forward, government indicated its willingness to accept certain amendments to the anti-money laundering Bill which the opposition had put forward but which the government had rejected.

Not surprisingly, the opposition made an about turn derecognizing their own amendments to the anti-money laundering Bill. Later, they sought to insert in the informal dialogue, demands for Presidential Assent to a number of 'unconstitutional' Bills they had passed in the National Assembly treating with Local Government Elections and the Public Procurement Commission. The bottom line of their position was the demand for a return to parliament knowing that were this demand to be granted their no confidence motion would be passed in the National Assembly. In the circumstances, the government found itself in a precarious position. Was it to accede to the opposition's demands, that the President assent to their Bills and re-convene Parliament without pinning down the opposition to a post-prorogation parliamentary agenda? In the circumstances, the opposition would still have its No-confidence Motion (NCM) to be used as a bargaining chip to eke out more concessions from government by using the NCM also like a sword of Damocles over the head of the government.

Despite the opposition's intransigence, the Office of the President disclosed that the President was not convinced that the doors to dialogue had been closed. In an interview with the press, Head of the Presidential Secretariat Dr. Roger Luncheon assured the public 'we are actively pursuing dialogue' And though we in the leadership of the Party knew the channels through which dialogue between the two parties was taking place, Luncheon did not disclose to the press the modus operandi by which dialogue was taking place; 'I am not allowed to divulge the practices of the political parties… I would not be able to speak of such interventions.'

At one time in the course of the informal talks, one particular issue appeared to be a deal breaker and that a solution was in sight but when the opposition side introduced the linkage between that one issue and others, it became evident that the opposition had dug in their heels in respect to the reconvening of parliament to facilitate passage of their no confidence motion. Faced with mounting international pressure, the President, on January 25th, 2015 announced a date for elections. By the end of February, Parliament was dissolved with the understanding that elections would be held in May 2015, within the three months statutory period.

During the prorogation period, Ashni Singh, the then Minister of Finance authorized the spending of GY$4.5bln, the opposition-controlled parliament disapproved spending of the money. Consequently, the opposition called for Singh to be taken before the Parliament's Privileges Committee on the ground that the money was spent 'illegally'.

Another challenge the government faced at the time was, because local government elections were not held for a number of years, many local government bodies were either not functioning or, if they were, were under severe criticism by residents. We were confronted with this situation during our cabinet out-reach meetings with the people. The problem was four-fold; local government bodies had become dysfunctional, delivery of basic goods and services was woefully lacking, complaints by the people were justified and the Party and government faced the risk of losing votes in many areas of traditional support.

Faced with the prospect of diminishing returns at on-coming elections, the government's response, through its Minister of Local Government, was to dissolve a number of local government bodies and to replace them with Interim Management Committees (IMC's) comprised of persons in good standing in those communities where the problem persisted. The reaction by political opposition was to condemn the government for not holding local government and for setting up bodies 'packed with its supporters. 'At the parliamentary level, the opposition-controlled parliament passed a Bill stripping the Minister of his powers to dissolve local government bodies and to vest them instead in a Local Government Commission. The President withheld his assent to the Bill.

UPSETTING THE APPLE-CART

At the political/diplomatic level, government came under heavy criticism when Priya Manickchand, speaking on behalf of the Government of Guyana at a twin function in July 2014, to mark the Ambassador's farewell as well as US Independence Day, delivered what was later described as a 'feral blast' criticizing the US government for interference in the internal affairs of Guyana. Sometime after, the UK High Commissioner to Guyana was subjected to similar treatment, this time by another high-level spokesperson for the Guyana Government. At the time, President Ramotar was overseas attending a summit of Caricom Heads in

Antigua and Barbuda From St. John's, he must have signalled his agreement to proceed with the political demarche on the US Ambassador.

Manickchand had criticized the US Ambassador, because according to the Head of the Presidential Secretariat, he had launched attacks against President Ramotar and me in my capacity as General Secretary of the Party and the Party itself in respect to the holding of local government elections. According to Luncheon, the Ambassador accused the President of duplicity of constitutional rectitude and belittled Rohee's intellect.'

Though it did not occur to me at the time, in retrospect, it seemed that the 'blast' was at variance with the political and ideological trajectory set by Cheddi Jagan before and after he assumed the presidency of Guyana. While lobbying in Washington to win support for free and fair elections, Dr. Jagan had set the tone for Guyana-US relations that both sides had expected was to be of a lasting nature with the PPP/C so long as the PPP/C was in government. For all intents and purposes, the feral blast temporarily interrupted that expectation, because in 2020 when international support for free and fair elections came around once again, it became politically expedient, if not pragmatic, to return to the path Cheddi Jagan had traversed prior to 1992. Again, it was to win support from the US for free and fair elections in Guyana. How true was Jean-Baptiste Alphonse Karr's words; 'The more things change, the more they remain the same.'

In the case of the US and UK governments, the prolonged absence of local government elections and the prorogation of Parliament were the bones of contention. In the case of the US in particular, an agreement between the two governments to 'put on hold' a US$1.2 million, 'Leadership and Democracy' USAID Project, first to re-design, and later to jettison it became a bone of contention for the US government. As far as the US was concerned, government's rejection of the programme negated the involvement of civil society in the parliamentary process as well as to strengthen women and youth involvement in the democratic process.

Government claimed that it was not consulted on the project and that the project was aimed at facilitating the growth and expansion of unfriendly organisations. In addition, based on a threat that the project would proceed notwithstanding government's objection, cabinet directed that my Ministry revoke the work permit of the head of the project.

CORRUPTION RETURNS TO HAUNT

Between 2013 and 2014 the print, electronic, social media and other newspaper columnists waged a tireless anti-corruption campaign against the PPP\C administration. The Kaieteur News, and to a lesser extent the Stabroek News, were the most aggressive the pursuit of the campaign.

In his weekly 'Conversation Tree' column published in Stabroek News in June 2013, Ralph Ramkarran wrote: 'It is now clear that the adamancy of the government and the PPP in refusing to acknowledge the level of corruption in the society, and to do something about it is linked to where the corruption is located.' Referring to instances of corruption, Ramkarran went on: 'And most important, none of them have come to light as a result of any action initiated by the government without prior exposure.' 'Corruption' Ramkarran wrote, '…has become so pervasive that it is no longer possible to keep the evidence away from the press and the police 'It is not known' he wrote, '…whether government spokespersons are still so blind about corruption that they are still asking, where is the evidence? Guyana will soon qualify as the Kleptocratic Republic of Guyana.' Ramkarran concluded. According, to Ramkarran.

It was on June 29, 2012 one year earlier, that Ramkarran at a stormy meeting of the Executive Committee of the Party, was accused of breaching the confidentiality of meetings in light of an article on corruption he had written and had published in the Mirror newspaper. Ramkarran became so incensed with the personal attacks and insinuations that he got up and left the meeting. The following day, June 30, 2012, Ramkarran resigned from the Party. In a brief statement issued by Ramkarran he stated; 'After being gratuitously and irreverently accused of being untrustworthy after forty years in the leadership of the PPP, such an accusation was about as much as I could bear.'

Ramkarran was a longstanding member of the Party. While studying law in the UK he joined the PPP UK Branch and developed close relationships with outstanding progressive political leaders residing in the UK. While overseas, he maintained contact with Cheddi and Janet Jagan. On his return to Guyana in 1973, Ramkarran joined the Party and in 1974, he was elected to the Central and Executive Committees of the PPP. He was called to the bar to practice law in and in 1996 he became Senior Counsel of Guyana's judiciary in 1996. He was the Party's point man on all legal matters including representing party activists who were harassed or arrested by the police. He served twice as the Party's representative on the Elections Commission. Later, he was elected Speaker of the National Assembly from 2001 to 2011. His departure from the PPP left a void at the leadership level of the Party for quite sometime.

The campaign against the perception of corruption continued throughout the period up to the 2015 elections. The Party and government did its best to push back against the barrage of propaganda but the problem with corruption in politics is that it is easy to stick especially when the mainstream media is on a rampage aggressively pushing to reinforce the perception as strongly as they can.

GEARING UP FOR THE FIGHT

In February 2015, a coalition of opposition political parties was launched having committed themselves to a document they described as the 'Cummingsburg Accord'. The coalition brought together six political parties including the Peoples National Congress\Reform (PNC\R), the Alliance for Change (AFC), the National Front Alliance (NFA), the Guyana Action Party (GAP), the Working People's Alliance (WPA) and the Justice for All Party (JFP). The grouping became known as the APNU+AFC Alliance. The Cummingsburg Accord was basically a declaration of general commitments and how the pie would be divided up among themselves were the alliance to win political power come the 2015 elections.

The emergence of the APNU+AFC electoral alliance marked a major development on the political landscape of Guyana. The APNU comprising five of the six political parties was the forerunner of the APNU+AFC alliance. The alliance was first established in July 2011 to contest the November 2011 elections. At those elections, the APNU won 26 seats while the AFC won 7 seats, combined they formed a majority of 33 seats in the National Assembly. It was that combination that was to initiate three years later, a No Confidence Motion against the ruling PPP\C with a minority of 32 seats in the 65 seat National Assembly.

MOSES NAGAMOOTOO

Moses Nagamootoo who always had his eye on the Presidency of Guyana was finally at the centre of his political universe not as a presidential candidate but as the prime ministerial candidate of the APNU+AFC electoral alliance.

On or around May 2005, Nagamootoo had resigned from the PPP after expressing some dissatisfaction with the leadership of the Party. However, in July 2006, he returned with the understanding that his concerns would be addressed after the 2006 elections. It took intense discussions internally before a decision was arrived at to enable his return to the leadership level of the Party as 'co-opted member' but without a vote neither at the Central nor Executive Committees. I was among a minority in the leadership who did not support his return to sit at the upper echelons of the Party. Knowing of Nagamootoo is one thing, but knowing him is a completely different matter. Save and except for Ramotar and Collymore two the longer-standing members of the current leadership of the Party, I believe I know the wiles of Nagamootoo quite well.

In my view, the decision to accept Nagamootoo back into the ranks of the party and more particularly at the leadership level, was a serious mistake. I knew Nagamootoo would not abandon his claim to fame nor to be the primus inter pares in the leadership of the party after the elections. We found ourselves in this situation because we dithered too long eventually accepting an explanation, he gave for pronouncements he made at home and abroad. Compounding the issue further was our failure to go to our members and supporters to expose Nagamootoo's anti-party positions as we did in the case of Ramjattan. Some feared that were we not to accept Nagamootoo back into our ranks our action would result in a split within the party as was the case in 1955.

Soon after the 2006 elections, Nagamootoo claimed that Janet Jagan had promised him a vice president position in the new government, when Janet Jagan denied ever making such a promise, he then claimed that Jagdeo had promised to appoint him a presidential advisor. He was quoted in the press as stating; 'I want to promote and perfect democracy, improve the system of governance and better manage the power of the president so that it can work for the betterment of the people.' And as a prelude to his 'declaration of intent' Nagamootoo had also expressed an interest in the Foreign Affairs portfolio and a senior position in Jagdeo's cabinet

For reasons known only to Jagdeo, Nagamootoo was never rewarded any position in government. Not too longer after, he accused the Party of not fulfilling its side of the agreement it had entered into with him prior to the elections. Eventually, he resorted to making public statements accusing the party of 'failing to address issues pertaining to national unity, governance and of being ineffective and non-responsive to the needs of its membership'. Nagamootoo went onto declare that if he cannot find a platform in the PPP to address his concerns, he will have to find another. With this in mind, he publicly expressed his support for a Third Force in Guyanese politics.

Nagamootoo left the PPP and joined Ramjattan in the AFC which entered into an electoral alliance with the APNU thus posing a major challenge to the PPP\C for the 2015 elections. The PPP\C was already in a minority government. The challenge facing the PPP/C was to return to power with a majority in the National Assembly and control of the executive.

The point I wish to make here is that we were approaching the 2015 elections in a bad way. In addition to the challenge posed by the newly formed APNU+AFC electoral alliance, the Ramotar administration was not able to do much due to it being legislatively hamstrung and starved of resources by an opposition-controlled National Assembly. At the same time, international pressure was mounting demanding local government elections, an end to prorogation and the re-convening of Parliament.

Unlike the Jagdeo administration, but more like the Sam Hinds, Janet Jagan administrations, the Donald Ramotar administrations, did not achieve much in relation to developmental initiatives. This was because they did have the time nor were the prevailing economic and social circumstances at the time favourable. This is not to say that the Jagdeo administration did not experience difficult circumstances for the twelve years while it lasted. The difference in my opinion was that, his administration was led by an enlightened economist who had a fairly good grasp of the prevailing local conditions, its constraints and possibilities and well as the international situation at the time. Jagdeo was able to take all those factors holistically and translate them into developmental projects and initiatives that moved the country forward in a positive way.

At a mass farewell reception in his honour held on September 16, 2011 at the National Stadium Jagdeo told the packed stadium; "Never allow foreign interests to become our agenda. We must fiercely defend our national interests while recognizing that we are part of a global village."As far as the Cheddi Jagan administration was concerned, even though his administration was short-lived like those who followed his, Jagan did achieve much as regards debt relief, rebalancing the economy, democratizing the society and shoring up the image of the country.

As I said in an interview with a local TV network just after we were voted out of office, I witnessed in each one of the Presidents I served, a totally different approach and style in the way they chose to govern the affairs of our country. But there was always that common thread that ran throughout their respective policies. They all ensured that there was heavy emphasis in the annual budgetary allocations for the social sector. Moreover, they all declared that people-centered development and national unity were the lynchpins for the economic and social development of the country.

RAMOTAR'S DILEMMA

As he prepared to run again as the Party's Presidential Candidate for fresh election slated for May 2015, Ramotar faced a peculiar situation. As a former Party General Secretary for almost sixteen (16) years he must have recognized the three poles of power that had emerged over the years. The first two of the three poles of power had emerged with the delinking of the post of General Secretary from the Presidency. Later, the third and last of the three poles of power emerged when former president Jagdeo made it clear that he was not going anywhere. These three poles of power manifested themselves in the presence of former President Jagdeo, who chose to stay in the game, me as General Secretary of the ruling Party and Ramotar as the sitting president. In the circumstances, it was critical for our members and the general public to see the triumvirate as a united and formidable group leading the political process.

As I saw it, my role while I served as General Secretary from 2013 to 2017, was to help promote   the foundation principles of the Party, comradeship, respect for one another and above all, to uphold the rules and provisions of the Party's Constitution. I must concede however, that at times this was easier said than done. It was in the context of these peculiar political circumstances that the Party unanimously endorsed Ramotar as its presidential candidate for the May 2015 election just as it did in April 2011 for the November elections of that same year.

THE MYSTERIOUS THIRD TERM CAMPAIGN

The emergence of peculiarities in the run-up to elections in Guyana is not unusual. Take for example the 2011 elections. Long before the run-up to those elections, and before Ramotar was endorsed as the Party's presidential candidate, somewhere around the last quarter of 2009, a mysterious campaign surfaced proposing a Third Term for Bharat Jagdeo. The sponsors of the campaign remained a mystery but the contradictory reality was that while the Party was yet to decide on its presidential candidate, a campaign promoting Jagdeo for a third term was in full swing in the public domain. What made the issue even more contentious, was the fact that the Third Term campaign in favour of Jagdeo continued long after Ramotar's nomination was made public.

In a press statement, the PPP rebuffed the parallel campaign by the shadowy group stating; 'Some mischievous elements have launched a pro-active campaign against the Party.' The Party added that '…it has noticed television advertisements and a billboard calling for a third term for President Jagdeo.' The statement emphasized that 'the persons behind the campaign are no friends of the Party.' One newspaper columnist wrote, 'An expensive campaign was put in place in 2010 which only fizzled out when General Secretary Donald Ramotar took a stand against a third term. Eventually it became known that a group calling itself the 'Guyanese Coalition for Jagdeo Third Term' was behind the campaign. By November 2010 the third term campaign was laid to rest… at least for the time being'.

In an interview in Stabroek News edition of January 2011, Mr. Jagdeo responding to questions about the ill-fated third term campaign was reported as saying; '… many persons from the PPP\C, the business community and even from some opposition parties lobbied me to go for a third term in office but my answer has always been no. I'm not interested in pursuing a third term.' Jagdeo went on to remind that it was he who signed the new constitution into effect that limits a president to two terms in office. 'I have to respect the constitution that I have put in place and so I have absolutely no interest in a third term.' declared Jagdeo.

Whether the 'third term' campaign had a negative impact on the 2011 elections results is a matter for analysis by others who are better equipped to do so and have the time, to cogitate, pontificate and articulate on such matters. However, with the third term side-show behind us, we proceeded, with our campaign for the 2011 elections. As I pointed out earlier, the results of that election put the PPP in a minority in the parliament but nevertheless, in control of the Executive with Ramotar as President.

Four years after the 2011 election and with the party still reeling from its devastating result, three key issues had to be settled, first was the Presidential Candidate for the upcoming election second was the Head of the list of candidates and third was, the Prime Ministerial candidate. We decided Ramotar will be the Presidential Candidate but that we not will go again with Samuel Hinds as our Prime Ministerial candidate.

By the time we came around to the actual campaign things were no better. Complacency, arrogance and a series of mis-steps by some ministers of government and members of parliament assumed prominence in the public domain. Perceptions of corruption, weak government, the disconnect between party and the popular masses especially a geographic swathe of its supporters were still with us.

Throughout the entire 2011 to 2015 period, the media, while ignoring the opposition's slashing of government budgets, and opposing funding for major developmental projects, kept up a vicious campaign targeting the party and government. And to sex up the debate on corruption they even threw in Jagdeo's house into the discussion. In the face of the barrage of negative and anti-government propaganda we established re-connect committees, adjusted our electoral strategy and tactics, ensured our party structures were functioning, did more political work among the Afro-Guyanese and Amerindian communities and refocused our public relations making it more targeted and community-specific demographics. The Party engaged the opposition on the burning question of corruption. This was done through a series of talk shows on television which proved to be highly successful while they lasted.

A FRESH ATTEMPT AT A THIRD TERM

But the 2015 election was not to be without its peculiarity. About one year before the election was due, a petition was filed at the High Court by an individual named Cedric Richardson who claimed his constitutional right was being denied to elect Bharat Jagdeo for a third term. This was the clearest indication ever that Jagdeo had his eye on the presidency.

The High Court ruled that the constitutional amendment which prevents a former president from running for a third term was unconstitutional. The state appealed the courts' decision. In February 2017, the Appeal Court upheld the decision of the High Court. The State then took the matter to the Caribbean Court of Justice (CCJ), Guyana's final court.

Four years after the matter was heard in Guyana's High Court, the CCJ in June of 2018, upheld that presidential term limits enshrined in the Constitution of Guyana, meaning that Jagdeo was ineligible for a third term. The CCJ effectively overturned judgements of two Guyanese lower courts.

The majority view of the CCJ was that Articles 1 and 9 of the Constitution of Guyana, did not confer on citizens an unlimited right to chose a Head of State. According to the CCJ, 'democratic governance allowed reasonable qualifications for eligibility to be a member of the National Assembly and hence to be President'. The CCJ further stated that 'new qualifications can be introduced by valid constitutional amendments and that the National Assembly had the power to amend the constitution by a vote of at least two thirds of all members of the Assembly, without holding a referendum.'

By the time the CCJ made its ruling public in June 2018, three important national events had taken place in Guyana.

First of all, general and regional elections were held in May 2015 resulting in a change of government. The May election result was devastating for the PPP\C. From a total of 570,708 votes cast, the PPP\C won a total of 202,565 or 49.19% of the votes giving it 32 seats in the National Assembly. For its part the APNU+AFC won a total of 207, 201 votes or 50.3% giving it 33 seats in the National Assembly. The PPP\C lost the elections by a mere 4,545 votes.

A BIG BLOW

The lost of government by the Party was a serious blow to all of us but particularly for Ramotar who should have called elections in 2016 but did so in 2015 to avoid passage of the opposition-sponsored No-confidence Motion as a consequence of the No Confidence Motion and all that flowed therefrom. In addition, early elections meant that Ramotar served as less than a one-term president. He was the only Presidential Candidate of the PPP to have been defeated at an election. And though he never conceded, the reality was that a new government had emerged from the election and the international community had declared the election to be free and fair. My own view, along with other party leaders at the time was that there were some sophisticated elements of rigging that gave the opposition coalition a razor thin majority over the PPP/C.

At a more personal level, I knew if Ramotar was re- elected he would have removed me from Home Affairs for reasons known only to him.

MISCALCULATING

After we had agreed that Ramotar would run again as our Presidential Candidate, we had two fundamental issues to settle; the Head of our list of candidates and the Prime Ministerial Candidate. At the time Ramotar was overseas. When the question of the Head of the list came up a proposal was made that the General Secretary be assigned that responsibility, I made the foolish mistake of accepting the recommendation. I was a miscalculation on my part.

On Ramotar's return the matter was revisited. I withdrew my acceptance to be Head of the list and in my place Ramotar's name was inserted. The arguments advanced in favour of Ramotar being head of the list were in my view logical and reasonable. Why I did not see it that way at the time was a mystery. Years later I understood what happened. I accepted the position of Deputy Head of the List. A proposal was made that should the party be victorious at the election, the positions for a Vice President and a Deputy Prime Minister be created but this was found to be unacceptable. Save for the Deputy Prime Minister position, there was precedent for the proposal to appoint a Vice President because following the 1997 elections and her swearing in as President, Janet Jagan appointed Repu Daman Persaud First Vice President.

Much later, following the Party's victory at the 2020 elections and the swearing in of Irfan Ali as President, Bharrat Jagdeo was sworn in as Vice President.

On the question of a Prime Ministerial Candidate after considering a number of possibilities, we eventually settled on Ambassador Elisabeth Harper, a career Foreign Service Officer, Director General at the Ministry of Foreign Affairs and Ambassador to Caricom. It was the first time that a woman was selected to be our Prime Ministerial Candidate.

ELECTING AN OPPOSITION LEADER

Following the return of the PPP to the opposition, the Party was called upon to fill the constitutional position of Leader of the Opposition to serve in the National Assembly. The debate centered around whether Ramotar, the former president, Jagdeo a former president or Rohee as the sitting General Secretary should fill the position.

As the beginning, I announced my non-interest in the position and withdrew from the contest. Initially, my position was that Ramotar should hold the position. With years of parliamentary experience, as the immediate past President and a former General Secretary of the Party, I advanced the view, along with others supportive of Ramotar, that given his stature, he would be a suitably qualified candidate for the job. In addition, there was precedent in that former President Desmond Hoyte had returned to parliament after serving for seven years as President to the post of Opposition Leader. Jagdeo's name was also supported by others.

As the discussion evolved, it became clear to me that there was a near tie between Jagdeo and Ramotar. In the end, an emissary was despatched to Ramotar, who was not at the meeting to enquire whether he had an interest in taking up the post. The emissary returned informing that Ramotar was not interested. With that information available all the Comrades present, including me as GS, who had supported Ramotar earlier, threw their support behind Jagdeo. Jagdeo was unanimously identified as the Party's nominee to hold the constitutional post of Leader of the Opposition in the 11th Parliament of Guyana.

JAGDEO AS OPPOSITION LEADER

Parliament had its first sitting in June 2015, about one month following the elections but it was not until August of the same year that the PPP/C MP's took up their seats in the National Assembly. Following their swearing-in, all thirty-two PPP/C MP's met in one of the committee rooms at Parliament Buildings for the purpose of determining one among their ranks to be the Leader of the Opposition. At that meeting, and in my capacity of General Secretary of the Party I nominated Jagdeo to be Leader of the Opposition, by acclamation Jagdeo was selected to fill the position. When the Assembly resumed the Speaker was informed about the results of our meeting.

In his acceptance speech to the National Assembly Jagdeo said; 'I am very much aware of the grave responsibility placed on our shoulders, although we are in opposition now, to ensure that our country continues to move forward.' He continued; 'We will work with the other side once they remain faithful to the promises, they made to the people of the country...'

CONGRESS MEETS

The third, event of national importance was the convening of the 31st Congress of the PPP held in December 2016 on the Essequibo coast. The congress was held against the backdrop of a devastating electoral defeat, compounded by the CCJ ruling. The PPP found itself in a precarious situation with just four years to extricate itself from challenging political circumstances and to gird its loins for the battle to return to power. The big question was, who would be the best presidential candidate to take the PPP\C to victory at the next election.

On the cusp of the congress, and as is normal in the run-up to our congresses, things began to heat up organisationally. With much experience in heading previous congress committees since the early 1990's I was unable to do so on that occasion because of the prevailing view that there was no precedent for the GS to chair a congress committee. The chairmanship of the committee was placed in the hands of the Executive Secretary and the congress committee was reconstituted.

A rumour making the round at the time, was that being one of the older and senior leaders of the Party, I was a defender of the status quo and opposed to change. Truth be told, I am a firm believer in the efficacy of Party structures beginning with the groups, the district and regional committees, as well as district and regional conferences, country conferences and congresses. It is through elections to the leadership of these bodies that new blood emerges and given the opportunity to grow and be assessed. I also hold to the view that if changes to what exists are to be made, then those changes must be of more advanced nature than what existed before.

Casting me in the role of a defender of the status quo was specious. The fact that I myself was a product of changes in the leadership of the youth organisation and the Party is testament to my acceptance of the inevitability of, and commitment to change. Moreover, the fact that the party had undergone changes in policy direction over the years which I helped shape, along with others, gave the lie to the claim about my resistance to change. Consequently, it was labelling me an opponent to change and as a defender of the status quo that led to me being cast in the role of an 'Old Guard' along with the use of invectives and disparaging remarks. The call to shift down didn't bother me since others before me shifted down to make place for others of my generation.

As we approached the date for the congress, it became obvious that this congress was going to be a congress with a difference. And that is precisely what happened. The results of the election to the new Central Committee reflected that difference.

The congress proceeded well save and except for heavy lobbying by candidates who were seeking election to the Central Committee. Over the years, we made great progress in minimising, by various innovative means, lobbying at congress by candidates seeking to be elected to the CC. However, because of a relaxed approach the practice arose once again.

CONTEST FOR A NEW GENERAL SECRETARY

I was happy the congress with all its inherent challenges was over, but I knew more challenges were yet to come. A date had to be set for the first meeting of the recently elected Central Committee at which the General Secretary and members of a new Executive Committee were to be elected. Members of the Secretariat would be identified by the newly elected General Secretary. Some wanted an early date while others preferred a later date around the second week in January of the new year. My task was to find a compromise date to accommodate the two options.

Long before the convening of the congress, I had indicated that I would not be seeking re-election to the post of General Secretary. Having experienced the most stressful last two of the four years in that position, I had made up my mind that I was not prepared to serve in that position once again. I was deeply grateful to all those who supported me while I served in that important position for the relatively short period of time.

Bharat Jagdeo and Frank Anthony had indicated their interest in the position. I had indicated my support for Frank on the ground that he came from a PPP family at Enmore, a traditional PPP stronghold. In addition, he was one of the first entrants in the pioneer organisation. Moreover, he was a family man, a young professional as a medical doctor and had come through the ranks. In sum, he was in my view, the ideal candidate for the position. Like everyone else, I knew Frank had some shortcoming and that some unfair and unsubstantiated criticisms had been levelled against him for being 'lazy' and that he had left some assignments unfulfilled. Those shortcomings notwithstanding, I still supported him because he had won the second highest number of votes at congress. I knew that were he or anyone else to be elected to the position of GS, they would need a support team around them to assist in fulfilling the wide range of responsibilities held by the General Secretary which was a full-time job.

With the field wide open for nominations to the post of General Secretary, it became clear to all thirty-five (35) members of the Central Committee that there were only two contestants for the post; Bharat Jagdeo and Frank Anthony. Long before the meeting, I had signalled to Jagdeo that I would be supporting Anthony and shared with him my reasons for doing so. My view was consistent with the Constitution of the Party which states that 'Every Party member in good standing has the right to be nominated and elected to all offices and committees as provided for by the Constitution...'

At the meeting, I nominated Frank Anthony while Luncheon nominated Bharat Jagdeo. Jagdeo won the majority votes cast by secret ballot. He immediately assumed the seat as Party General Secretary. In brief remarks to committee members I indicated that I would not be as active as I used to be in the past. I said so knowing that, having reached the pinnacle of the Party, and with a new General Secretary in place, it would not be proper for me to be seen as if I'm jockeying for space or relevance.

Further, I declined Jagdeo's offer to serve as International Secretary of the Party because I felt that having served for twelve years in that capacity and then as General Secretary, it would not be in the best interest of the Party for me to return to serve in a position where a younger member should be placed to gain experience and to build capacity for the future. I was quite satisfied being a member of the Executive and Central Committees.

WHILE TRANSITIONING...

In the process of transition from one GS to another, clarification about practices for which there are no antecedents will arise. The resolution of such issues is usually based on trust between the immediate past office holder and the newly elected office holder.

After the Central Committee meeting, save for meetings of the Central Committee and the Executive Committee, I chose not to return to Freedom House to occupy office space there, since, as far as I am aware, office space at Freedom House is reserved principally for paid functionaries where I once lived, worked and spent most of my political life. This was a very difficult decision in my personal and political life.

THE NO-CONFIDENCE MOTION

With the congress and the election of a new party leadership behind us, the focus of the Party in the months that followed was to prepare for the next elections. Following the resignation of Dr. Steve Surujbally, Chairman of the Guyana Elections Commission (GECOM) in November 2016, the Party embarked on a series of consultations with stakeholders to ascertain their views and recommendations on a suitably qualified person to fill the position

Between December 2016 and August 2017, the Opposition Leader, on three occasions, presented to President Granger, three separate lists with six names on each list 'not unacceptable' to the President. The expectation was that, based on the Carter Centre formula, the President would choose one of the names acceptable to him. In the end, Granger rejected all eighteen names and unilaterally and, unconstitutionally appointed a retired judge to the position on October 2017. The President took almost one year to act and when he did, he acted in violation of the Constitution.

The PPP challenged the President's appointment as unconstitutional. The matter wended its way through the court system in Guyana ending up at the Caribbean Court of Justice (CCJ), Guyana's final court.

In the meanwhile, political developments in Guyana took a turn for the unexpected. On the evening of December 21, 2018, in the National Assembly, the opposition PPP/C moved a Motion of No Confidence in the government. Brimming with confidence that the motion will not succeed, government MP's shouted "Bring it on! we are ready to defend our record!"

But lo and behold to their 'shock and awe' one of the thirty-three government MP's bolted and voted with the opposition PPP/C's thirty-two MP's giving the opposition a majority thus allowing passage of the motion. The government had fallen. It was like a political tsunami. After the vote, I saw Jagdeo walk across and speak to MP Joe Harmon, the President's 'right hand' man in Parliament. Later that night, government MP's led by Prime Minister Nagamootoo held a late-night press conference where they accepted the downfall of their government as a result of the successful passage of the No Confidence Motion.

At first, many could not believe what had happened. But it eventually soaked in and the following day, the nation woke up to a new political reality. But the push-back started. First, the ruling coalition made an about turn from the position it had taken earlier conceding it had lost government. They took the matter to the Parliament questioning the validity of the NCM. The Speaker reaffirmed that the motion was validly passed by a majority of 33 in favour of the opposition to 32 votes in favour of the government. Not satisfied with the response from the parliament, the government took the matter to the High Court.

On January 31, 2019, the Court ruled that thirty-three votes were needed for the NCM to be valid. The Court also ruled that persons holding dual citizenship cannot be seated in the National Assembly as a Member of Parliament. The government appealed the court's decision on the validity of the NCM. In March of the same year, the Appeal Court overturned the High Court's ruling. Using the 'half plus one rule', the court determined that thirty-two plus one half, not thirty-three was the greater number of sixty-five making Guyana the laughing stock for the rest of the world. In light of the Appeal Court's ruling, the opposition PPP/C wasted no time in taking up their legal cudgels by taking the matter to the CCJ.

In the meantime, on March 4th, Opposition Leader, Bharrat Jagdeo in response to a letter from President Granger inviting him to meet, despatched a letter to Granger detailing his conditions for a such a meeting.

In his letter to Granger, the Opposition Leader stressed; 'The proposed meeting can only and must only focus on ensuring that the Constitution is not violated, and, that general and regional elections are held in compliance with Article106(6) and 106(7) following the December 21, 2009 passage of the No-Confidence Motion.' Apart from agreeing to the meeting, a number of conditions were laid down including: i)The date of the general and regional elections to be held before the expiration of the present voters' list on April 30,2019; ii) No new contracts to be awarded by the State, including Regional Democratic Councils, and, State-owned corporations after March 21, 2019; iii) No new agreements, loans, grants, land leases, or any other such agreements or contracts after March 21, 2019, that bind Government; no abuse of State Resources for partisan activities/purposes; iv) Access to the State-owned media by all the contesting political parties.'

Meanwhile, the entire nation breathed a heavy sigh of relief when the CCJ, in June 2019 after hearing arguments since the beginning of May 2019, ruled that the NCM was successfully passed having acquired a majority of thirty-three votes from the sixty-five members in the National Assembly.

In determining that majority the court opined that "the half plus one rule is not applicable. When deciding the majority of the sixty-five members, such a majority is clear, 33 votes."

The Court referred to article 106(7) of the Constitution which states; 'Not withstanding its defeat, the Government shall remain in office and shall hold an election within three months , or such longer period as the National Assembly shall by resolution supported by not less than two-thirds of the votes of all the elected members of the National Assembly, and shall resign after the President takes the oath of office following the election.'

The CCJ also ruled that Patterson's appointment was unconstitutional and that the Leader of the Opposition and the President should get together to 'hammer out' the way forward with respect to the appointment of a Chairman for GECOM.

After twenty months, of 'feathering his nest' Patterson stepped down, but it took almost one month before the Leader of the Opposition and the President eventually settled on a new chairperson for GECOM. In the circumstances, in July 2019, Justice Claudette Singh was appointed chairperson of GECOM. Between December 2018 to December 2019 Guyana had entered a period of marking time during which legal, constitutional battles and political skirmishes were the order of the day.

SETTLING THE PRESIDENTIAL CANDIDATE

The next big question was who would be the Party's Presidential Candidate, Prime Ministerial Candidate and Head of the list of candidates.

On these matters, I shared with members of the Executive Committee, my documented views on the subject.

I felt confident that the arguments I had advanced had merit insofar as my interpretation of political and social developments in Guyana was concerned at that time.

Views began appearing in mainstream media listing what the attributes of the Presidential Candidate should be. Those attributes included; ability to deliver on promises, a visionary with the ability to bring people together, hard working, courageous and must possess management skills. I had no problem with those attributes but I added the following inter alia; a record for honesty and integrity and must carry no baggage, must speak out and commit publicly to the fight against corruption, must commit to constitutional reform within one year, must be a good listener to all sides and commit to consultative democracy, and must have a broad international perspective.

SPECULATIONS ABOUND

During the period 2018 to 2019 there was much speculation in the press about the PPP/C's Presidential Candidate for the 2020 elections. With Jagdeo disqualified from running for a third term, the press kept pressing for an answer to the question as to who would be the Party's Presidential Candidate. Public discussion on the subject was taking place at a time when the ruling APNU+AFC coalition administration had become very unpopular owing to their anti- working people and anti-business economic and social policies. corrupt practices, nepotism and favoritism were so rampant that the lives of hundreds of thousands were totally devastated especially the sugar workers who had suffered immensely because of the closure of a number of sugar estates.

The Amerindian people were no exception to the harsh policies of the coalition administration. Thousands who worked with the PPP/C administration had their services terminated and forced onto the breadline. And Afro-Guyanese who supported the APNU+AFC felt betrayed since the promises made to them by their leaders remained unfulfilled. The misguided economic and social policies of the Granger administration were compounded by their electoral shenanigans aimed at maintaining the regime in office by a hook or a crook. It was against this background that the PPP was engaged in the selection process of its Presidential Candidate for the 2020 elections. In the meanwhile, two issues surfaced that had the potential of upsetting the applecart. The Special Organized Unit (SOCU) had brought a number of charges against Ali in connection with the sale of state lands while he served as Minister of Housing and Water. At the same time, Ali's academic qualifications were challenged and became an issue for debate in the public domain. With respect to the former matter, several leaders of the party including me were summoned by SOCU to their headquarters to answer a number of questions with respect to the purchase of plots of land for housing purposes.

Notwithstanding the speculations swirling around during this period, most members of the Party's leadership had a fairly good idea who Jagdeo had in mind to be the Presidential Candidate. He didn't have to say it, we all new it. It was in this context that Central Committee members were canvassed in support for the two stronger candidates, Irfan Ali and Frank Anthony. And while Gail Teixeira, Vindhya Persaud and Anil Nandlall claimed they had support, that support was more public support rather than within the Central Committee.

On Saturday January 19, 2019 the date for the Central Committee, just before the elections were held Anthony announced he was withdrawing from the contest, so did Teixeira and Persaud. That left Nandlall and Ali in the race. Of the sixty-five members present twenty-four voted in favour of Ali while eleven including me voted for Nandlall.In both the General Secretary and Presidential Candidate contests, I exercised my democratic right to vote for the candidate of my choice. Others exercised their democratic as well within the meaning of inner party democracy and the exercise of their free will.

I continued to serve in the National Assembly. I enjoyed every moment of my twenty-seven years as a Member of Parliament. I found great joy doing the research in preparation for my speeches and presentations for debates on the various subjects that came up in the National Assembly. I also enjoyed listening to the presentations by my colleagues as well as from the opposition members of parliament. The across the floor banter and the heckling typical of a parliament was fun listening to and even participating in at times.

I took my parliamentary work seriously because I considered it a public service, and in my view, any job in service to the public that is recorded live on TV, radio and social media must be taken seriously because it is being viewed by the public and the quality of your is being judged by the viewers. Moreover, it is not so much the presenter as it is the party and government that is being judged. So, you have to be good or at least try to be at your level best when speaking on behalf of the party and government in the National Assembly.

The worst period for me in the National Assembly was when the then Opposition Leader, on July 2012 moved a Motion of No Confidence in me as Minister of Home Affairs to prevent me from speaking which made it impossible for me to present any Bills or move any motions on any subject in the National Assembly. The motion was moved at a time when the government had established a Commission of Inquiry into the shooting to death of protesters at the bauxite mining town of Linden. The Opposition Leader was determined to make political capital of the issue but as everyone recognized, his approach unmistakably had a racist ring to it.

In closing the debate on the subject which lasted for twelve hours Granger declared; "We will not wait for a Commission of Inquiry. We will ensure that there is justice tonight." Thus, with the majority in the House the opposition succeeded in having the motion was passed. It was the first time the National Assembly had taken such a step.

What pleased me immensely was the unswerving support I received from my parliamentary colleagues during the six months while the restrictions lasted. President Ramotar the sitting President at the time gave me his full support in fact he went so far to declare that he and his government lost support confidence in the then Speaker of the House Rafael Trotman. In the meanwhile, the matter was taken to the High Court and on January 2013, Ian Chang, Chief Justice (ag) in a thirty-four-page ruling declared that the motion preventing me from speaking in Parliament was flawed and that I can speak.

In his ruling the Judge said;

"If Mr. Rohee's name was on a successful list of candidates and his name was extracted from that list of candidates to hold a seat in the National Assembly on behalf of all members that supported that list but he was not assigned a ministerial portfolio, his right to or privilege to speak in the National Assembly would not have diminished one iota by his non- tenure of a ministerial portfolio. Therefore, the prohibition must necessarily relate to Mr. Rohee only as a Member of the National Assembly and not as a Minister of Home Affairs". Following the ruling of the Chief Justice Chang, The Speaker of the House lifted the gag order claiming it was a simple matter that was made complex."

I was happy with the outcome of the case and was deeply grateful to Anil Nandlall, the Attorney General and Minister of Justice who represented the matter in court. I was now able to carry out my parliamentary functions without any legal or parliamentary impediments.

While serving as a Parliamentarian, I participated in 24 budget debates as a minister of government and in four debates as an opposition MP. I tabled and had passed over 25 Bills and more than a dozen motions. Participating in Select Committees, Privilege Committees, providing answers to 'Questions without Notice' and presenting 'Statements as a Minister' were numerous. In effect, I had an extremely active parliamentary agenda which included a few overseas trips to participate at international parliamentary events.

At a press conference held in June 2018, Jagdeo was asked about suggestions that there is an attempt to divide the Party going into the 2020 elections and that there are no roles for Party stalwarts commonly referred to as 'Old Guard,' In response, Jagdeo was quoted as saying; "My ideal PPP is one where there is a place for everyone." Asked about his own role, Jagdeo had this to say; "I have to think about me too, I bought a lot of books and have them all stacked, I have not had time to read them. I just want to read them." Jagdeo went on to say; "I played no formal part in the 2011 to 2015 PPP administration. I intend to be a formal part of the next PPP government."

A NEW PPP/C GOVERNMENT

Parliament was dissolved by proclamation on December 30, 2019 and general and regional Elections were held on March 2, 2010. The PPP/C won by a narrow margin with Irfan Ali as President, Bharat Jagdeo as Vice President and Mark Philips as Prime Minister.

Irfaan Ali Swearing in as President Of Guyana - 2020

The road to the elections victory was not easy. It was dogged by a host of allegations and counter allegations by the political contestants. But it was the blatant attempt by the ruling coalition to steal the elections by manipulating the numbers on the Statements of Poll to favour the coalition and against the PPP/C that provoked a national and international outcry and condemnation of those efforts. The unity and solidarity of the opposition parties during those tumultuous days between March and August 2020 reminded me of past elections where that strong solidarity existed.

What was characteristic about that election was the deep involvement and assertive role of CARICOM electoral representatives including the US, Canadian, British and European Union diplomatic representatives. Their role was to press for free and fair elections and to utilize sanctions and the threat of sanctions on leading personalities in the coalition administration as a means of keeping up the pressure on the coalition to accept a comprehensive vote re-count and audit conducted by the Caricom team.

The wheel had turned a full circle. Ironically, it was the dawn of another era. But what my eyes have seen and my ears have heard during my almost half a century in politics have enriched me fully to the extent that no man can take it away from me. My only wish is to share the knowledge and experiences I have accumulated over those years with those with whom I would be favourably disposed to accept and to partake in what I have to share. This book is not about 'washing dirty linen in public' on the contrary, it is my way of sharing my past, glimpses of the present but absolutely nothing about the future.

They say, never judge a book by its cover. The book the reader now holds in their hands is a good example of a book that should not be judged by its cover because it has a title that is completely misleading. But the book can also represent a person who ought not to be prejudged for his or her worth. I had absolutely no difficulty nor problem finding the title of my book. It came naturally as if by 'divine inspiration'. Strange indeed for someone who was schooled in the materialist conception of history.

In closing, I sense that a large section of the Guyanese people is prepared, as they have always been, if needs be, to re-trace their footsteps in their struggle for free and fair elections. Guyanese are a resilient people. I have seen with my own eyes and on the basis of my personal experiences the hardships and deprivations they have endured over the years. Our country is on the cusp of great things provided the resources garnered are properly spent and transparently accounted for. The task ahead is to ensure that every Guyanese man, woman and child live a productive, secure, prosperous and happy life.

As for me, in and out of government I have made my views known and will continue to do so. I have no intention of disappearing or, as some may wish, to 'go out to pasture' nor to shelter in the dark-grey shades of irrelevance and obscurity. Everywhere I go, people recognise me and greet me in a most respectful way. This tells me that there is a body of Guyanese out there who recognize and value the contribution I have made to my country and people. For this, I remain deeply grateful.

I wish I could have done more in joining with others to bridge the deep ethnic and political divide that so menacingly, threatens to bust asunder the social fabric of our fragile democracy. But the age-old problem seems to be deeply embedded in the Guyanese national psyche, that is why it will take years of hard work before it shows signs of its beginning to gradually wither away. Perhaps it is the next generation to whom the responsibility will fall to heal the wounds and lift Guyana onwards, upwards!

With the sitting President Dr. Irfaan Ali at my daughter Rima and husband Paul's wedding ceremony – 2010

With my grand children Nikhail, Amira & Mariah

572

575

Moscow 64, 69, 105, 113, 114, 115, 116, 117, 118, 137, 138, 157, 159, 189, 190, 191, 249, 262, 279

Moses Nagamootoo   61, 86, 93, 120, 129, 159, 173, 266, 377, 415

Mother 5, 6, 10, 11, 12, 15, 16, 18, 19, 20, 27, 28, 29, 38, 84, 87, 88, 93, 113, 118, 119, 132, 146, 206, 207, 208, 234, 375

Moti Lall   74, 75, 142, 143

Movement Against Oppression (Mao)   67

My Roots   3

NACEN   318, 327, 331, 348, 354, 366

name changes   393, 394

NANCOM   255, 400, 401

National Assembly 63, 74, 99, 129, 139, 176, 178, 204, 233, 238, 240, 242, 252, 256, 262, 270, 271, 273, 274, 276, 277, 278, 292, 293, 342, 355, 360, 377, 378, 380, 383, 384, 389, 391, 392, 393, 394, 401, 402, 405, 409, 410, 412, 415, 416, 419, 420, 421, 423, 424, 426, 427

National Disaster   350

National Patriotic Front   167, 189

Navin Chandarpal   187, 234, 262, 263, 359

Nclo   359, 366

Neighbourhood Police   372

Nelson Mandela   208, 288, 322, 324

Nelson Rockefeller   63

New Global Human Order   223, 226, 231, 232, 233, 245, 285, 308, 321, 335

new government   124, 125, 204, 208, 215, 230, 234, 241, 242, 252, 310, 416, 419

New Guyana   97

New Jewel Movement   121, 166, 261

NGO's   193, 234, 242

Nicaragua   122, 123, 193, 194

Nichols   3, 12, 13, 14

No Confidence Motion   383, 384, 409, 415, 419, 424

Oliver Clarke   199

Organisation of American States (OAS)   179

Organization Of Islamic Conference   239

Overseas Volunteers   252

Owen Arthur   261, 274, 347

P.J. Patterson   198, 261

Paris   45, 336

Parliament2, 3, 41, 97, 139, 181, 184, 209, 225, 233, 260, 263, 274, 284, 342, 356, 375, 376, 378, 383, 384, 385, 393, 394, 396, 410, 411, 412, 413, 414, 416, 420, 421, 423, 424, 426, 427, 428

Patrice Lumumba   64, 116, 157

Patrick Manning   197, 205, 209, 222